Confessions of a Swinging Single Sea Turtle

Other Books by Jim Toomey

Sherman's Lagoon: Ate That, What's Next?

Poodle: The Other White Meat

An Illustrated Guide to Shark Etiquette

Another Day in Paradise

Greetings from Sherman's Lagoon

Surf's Up!

The Shark Diaries

Catch of the Day

A Day at the Beach

Surfer Safari

Planet of the Hairless Beach Apes

Yarns & Shanties (and Other Nautical Baloney)

Sharks Just Wanna Have Fun

Treasuries

Sherman's Lagoon 1991 to 2001: Greatest Hits and Near Misses

In Shark Years I'm Dead: Sherman's Lagoon Turns Fifteen

Confessions of a Swinging Single Sea Turtle

The Fourteenth *Sherman's Lagoon* Collection

by Jim Toomey

**Andrews McMeel
Publishing, LLC**

Kansas City • Sydney • London

Sherman's Lagoon is syndicated internationally by King Features Syndicate, Inc. For information, write King Features Syndicate, Inc., 300 West Fifty-seventh Street, New York, New York 10019.

Confessions of a Swinging Single Sea Turtle copyright © 2009 by Jim Toomey. All rights reserved. Printed in China. No part of this book may be used or reproduced in any manner whatsoever without written permission except in the case of reprints in the context of reviews. For information, write Andrews McMeel Publishing, LLC, an Andrews McMeel Universal company, 1130 Walnut Street, Kansas City, Missouri 64106.

09 10 11 12 13 TEN 10 9 8 7 6 5 4 3 2 1

ISBN-13: 978-0-7407-8551-1
ISBN-10: 0-7407-8551-6

Library of Congress Control Number: 2009921631

www.andrewsmcmeel.com

Sherman's Lagoon may be viewed on the Internet at
www.shermanslagoon.com.

ATTENTION: SCHOOLS AND BUSINESSES

Andrews McMeel books are available at quantity discounts with bulk purchase for educational, business, or sales promotional use. For information, please write to: Special Sales Department, Andrews McMeel Publishing, LLC, 1130 Walnut Street, Kansas City, Missouri 64106.

"Behold the turtle. He makes progress only when he sticks his neck out."
—James Bryant Conant

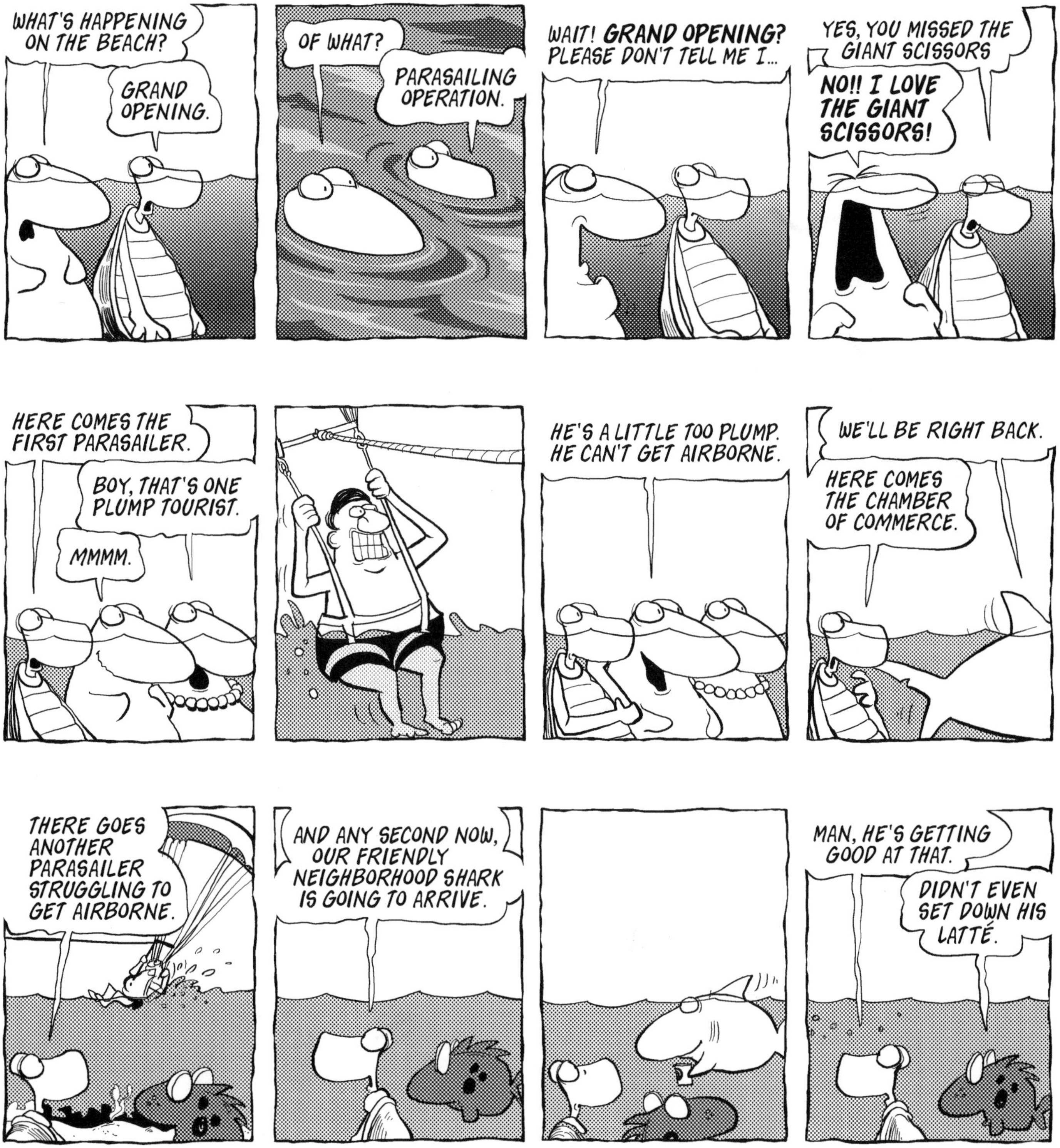
WHAT'S HAPPENING ON THE BEACH?
GRAND OPENING.
OF WHAT?
PARASAILING OPERATION.
WAIT! **GRAND OPENING?** PLEASE DON'T TELL ME I...
YES, YOU MISSED THE GIANT SCISSORS
NO!! I LOVE THE GIANT SCISSORS!
HERE COMES THE FIRST PARASAILER.
BOY, THAT'S ONE PLUMP TOURIST.
MMMM.
HE'S A LITTLE TOO PLUMP. HE CAN'T GET AIRBORNE.
WE'LL BE RIGHT BACK.
HERE COMES THE CHAMBER OF COMMERCE.
THERE GOES ANOTHER PARASAILER STRUGGLING TO GET AIRBORNE.
AND ANY SECOND NOW, OUR FRIENDLY NEIGHBORHOOD SHARK IS GOING TO ARRIVE.
MAN, HE'S GETTING GOOD AT THAT.
DIDN'T EVEN SET DOWN HIS LATTÉ.

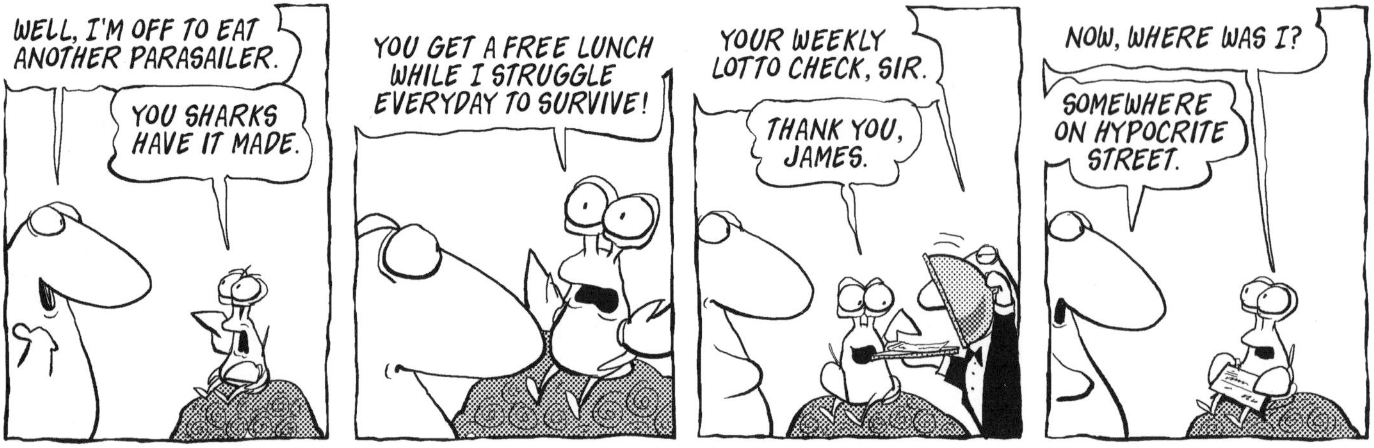
WELL, I'M OFF TO EAT ANOTHER PARASAILER.
YOU SHARKS HAVE IT MADE.
YOU GET A FREE LUNCH WHILE I STRUGGLE EVERYDAY TO SURVIVE!
YOUR WEEKLY LOTTO CHECK, SIR.
THANK YOU, JAMES.
NOW, WHERE WAS I?
SOMEWHERE ON HYPOCRITE STREET.

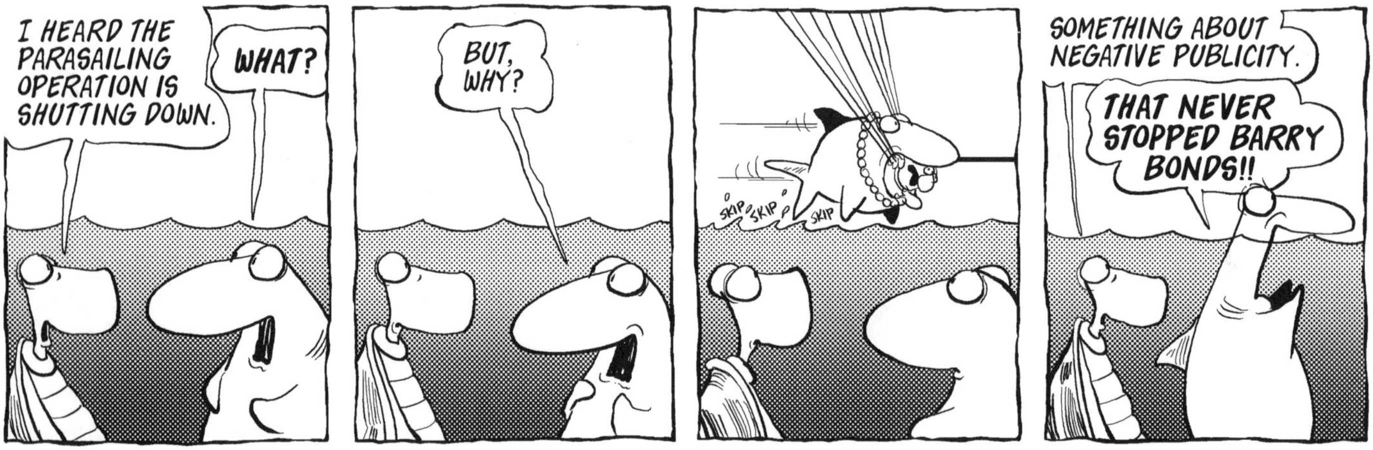
I HEARD THE PARASAILING OPERATION IS SHUTTING DOWN.
WHAT?
BUT, WHY?
SKIP SKIP SKIP
SOMETHING ABOUT NEGATIVE PUBLICITY.
THAT NEVER STOPPED BARRY BONDS!!

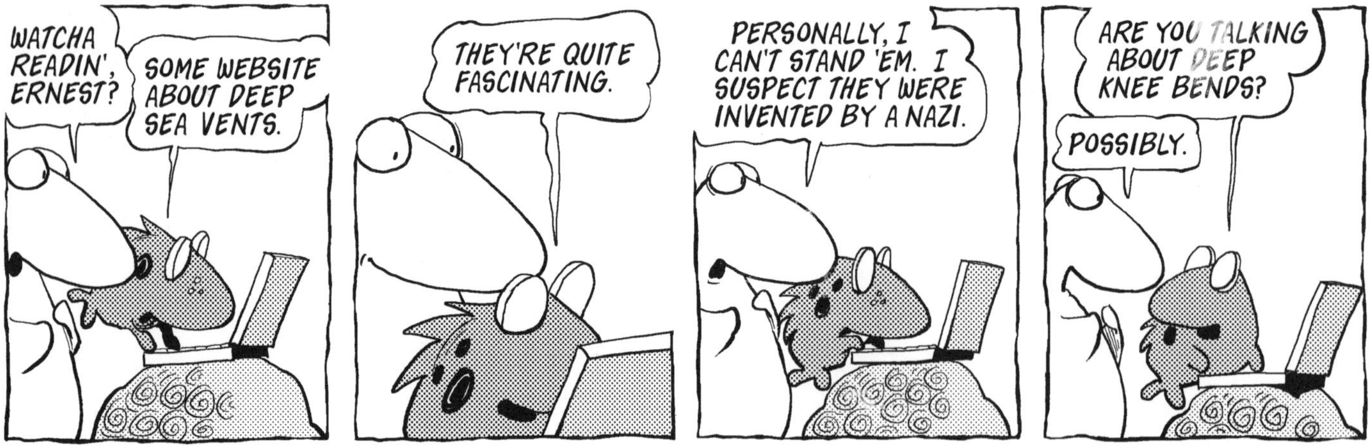
WATCHA READIN', ERNEST?
SOME WEBSITE ABOUT DEEP SEA VENTS.
THEY'RE QUITE FASCINATING.
PERSONALLY, I CAN'T STAND 'EM. I SUSPECT THEY WERE INVENTED BY A NAZI.
ARE YOU TALKING ABOUT DEEP KNEE BENDS?
POSSIBLY.

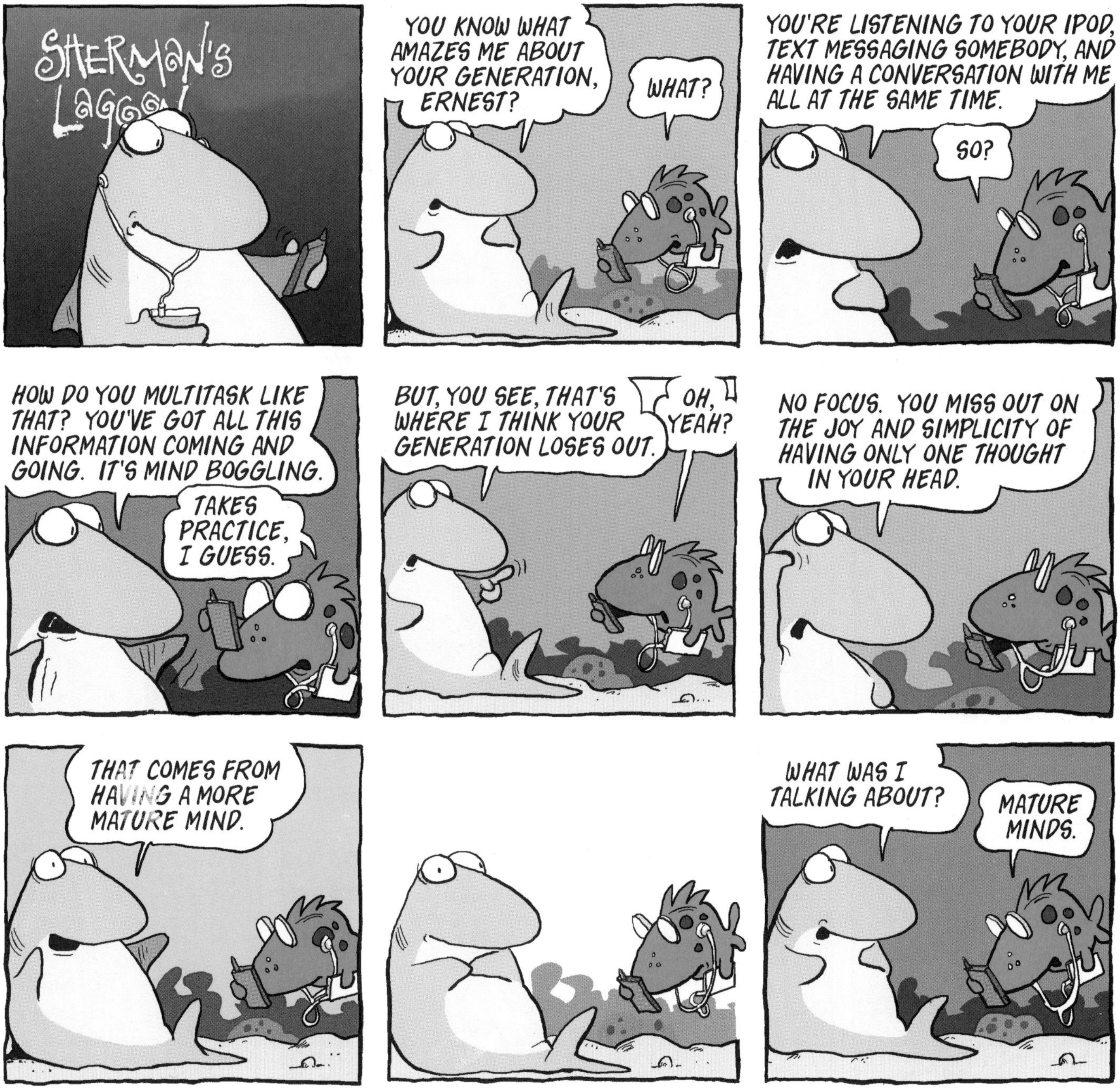
SHERMAN'S LAGOON
YOU KNOW WHAT AMAZES ME ABOUT YOUR GENERATION, ERNEST?
WHAT?
YOU'RE LISTENING TO YOUR IPOD, TEXT MESSAGING SOMEBODY, AND HAVING A CONVERSATION WITH ME ALL AT THE SAME TIME.
SO?
HOW DO YOU MULTITASK LIKE THAT? YOU'VE GOT ALL THIS INFORMATION COMING AND GOING. IT'S MIND BOGGLING.
TAKES PRACTICE, I GUESS.
BUT, YOU SEE, THAT'S WHERE I THINK YOUR GENERATION LOSES OUT.
OH, YEAH?
NO FOCUS. YOU MISS OUT ON THE JOY AND SIMPLICITY OF HAVING ONLY ONE THOUGHT IN YOUR HEAD.
THAT COMES FROM HAVING A MORE MATURE MIND.
WHAT WAS I TALKING ABOUT?
MATURE MINDS.

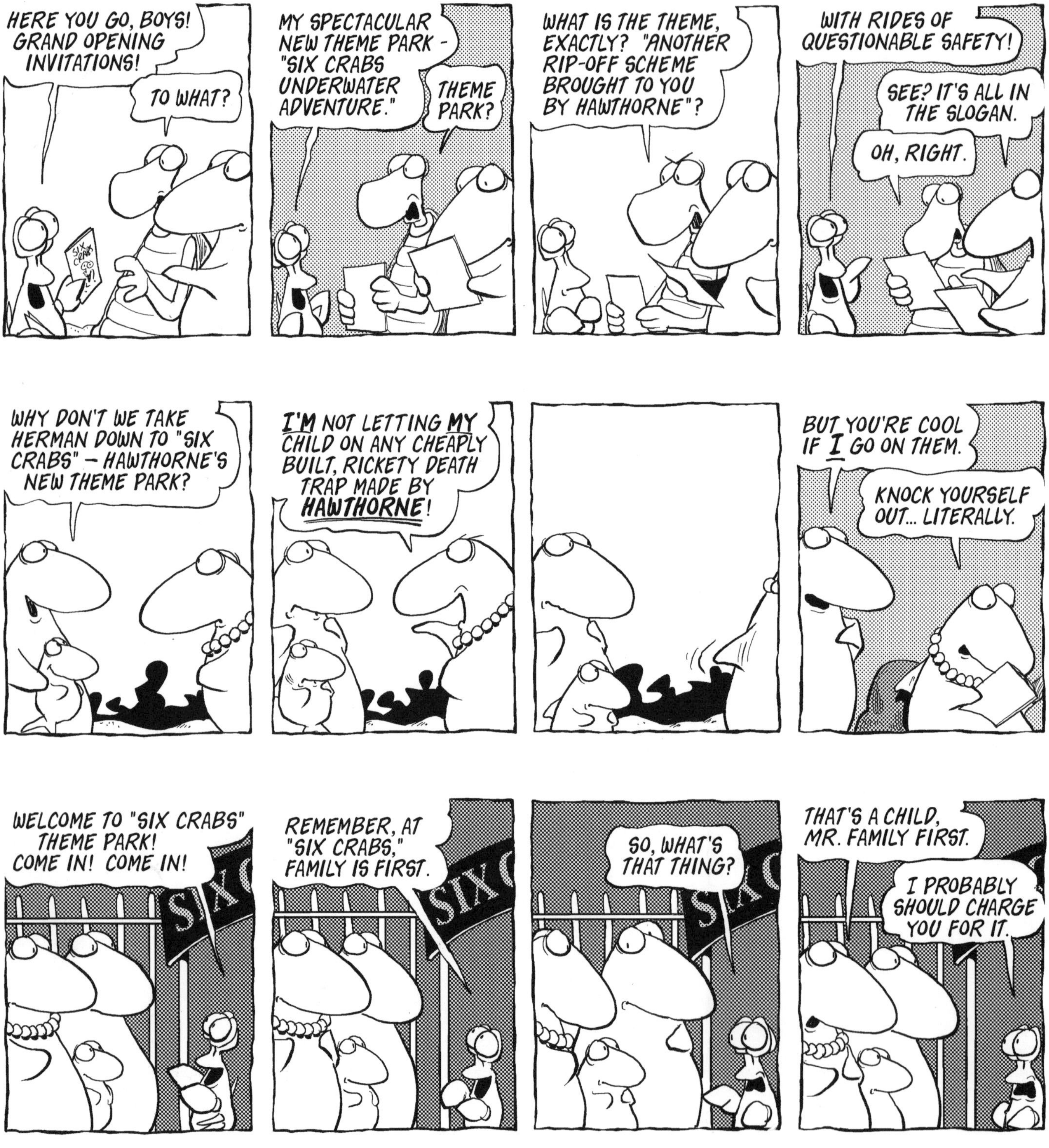
HERE YOU GO, BOYS! GRAND OPENING INVITATIONS!
TO WHAT?
SIX CRABS
MY SPECTACULAR NEW THEME PARK - "SIX CRABS UNDERWATER ADVENTURE."
THEME PARK?
WHAT IS THE THEME, EXACTLY? "ANOTHER RIP-OFF SCHEME BROUGHT TO YOU BY HAWTHORNE"?
WITH RIDES OF QUESTIONABLE SAFETY!
SEE? IT'S ALL IN THE SLOGAN.
OH, RIGHT.
WHY DON'T WE TAKE HERMAN DOWN TO "SIX CRABS" – HAWTHORNE'S NEW THEME PARK?
I'M NOT LETTING MY CHILD ON ANY CHEAPLY BUILT, RICKETY DEATH TRAP MADE BY HAWTHORNE!
BUT YOU'RE COOL IF I GO ON THEM.
KNOCK YOURSELF OUT... LITERALLY.
WELCOME TO "SIX CRABS" THEME PARK! COME IN! COME IN!
SIX
REMEMBER, AT "SIX CRABS," FAMILY IS FIRST.
SO, WHAT'S THAT THING?
THAT'S A CHILD, MR. FAMILY FIRST.
I PROBABLY SHOULD CHARGE YOU FOR IT.

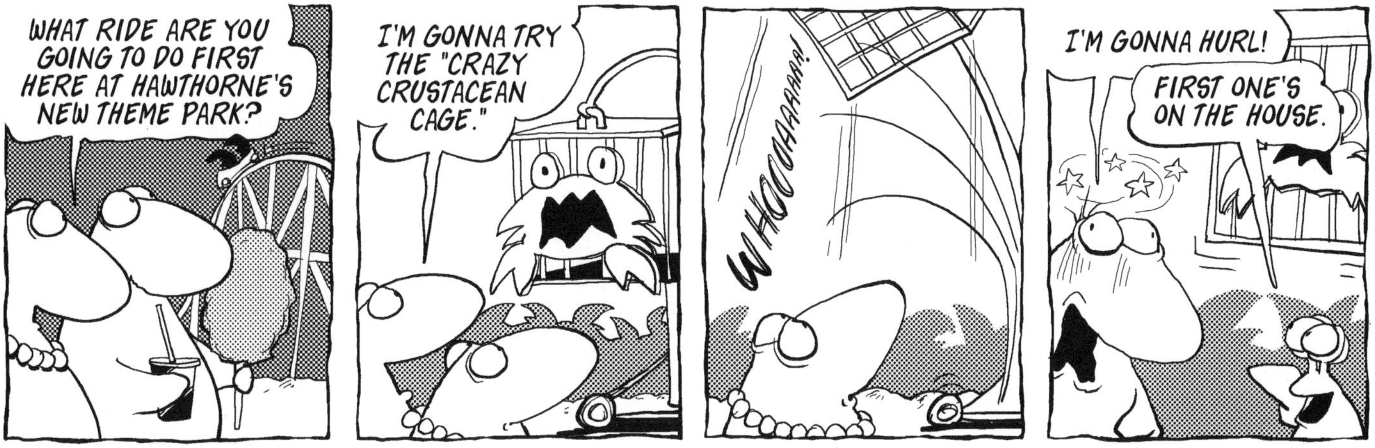
WHAT RIDE ARE YOU GOING TO DO FIRST HERE AT HAWTHORNE'S NEW THEME PARK?
I'M GONNA TRY THE "CRAZY CRUSTACEAN CAGE."
WHOOAAAAAAAA!
I'M GONNA HURL!
FIRST ONE'S ON THE HOUSE.

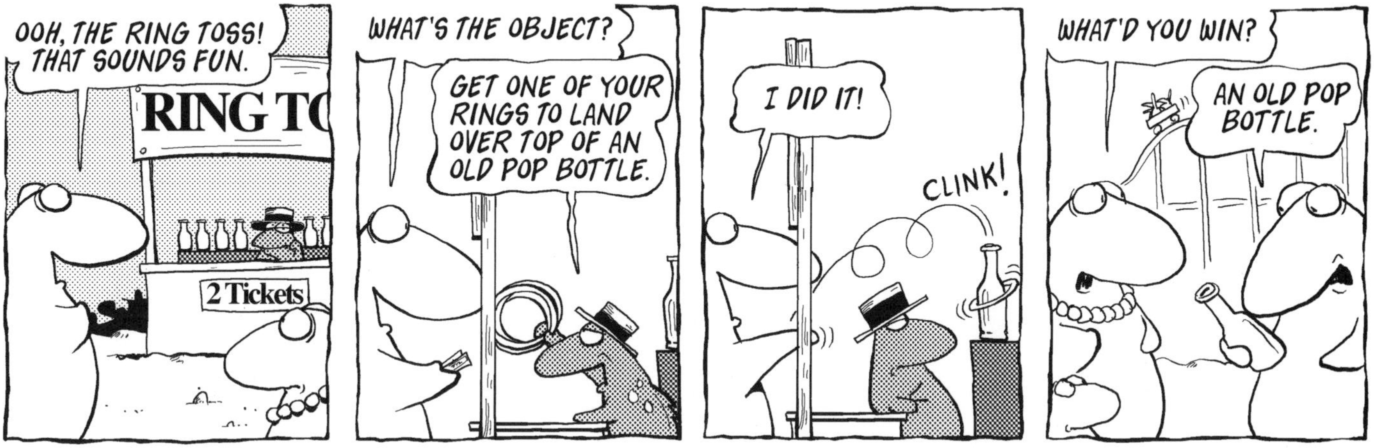
OOH, THE RING TOSS! THAT SOUNDS FUN.
RING TO
2 Tickets
WHAT'S THE OBJECT?
GET ONE OF YOUR RINGS TO LAND OVER TOP OF AN OLD POP BOTTLE.
I DID IT!
CLINK!
WHAT'D YOU WIN?
AN OLD POP BOTTLE.

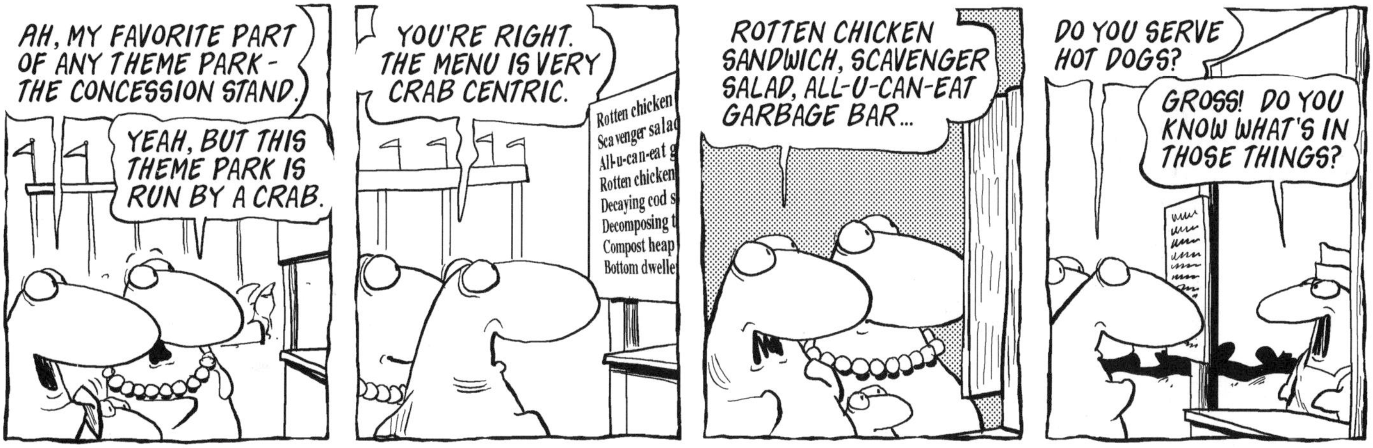
AH, MY FAVORITE PART OF ANY THEME PARK - THE CONCESSION STAND.
YEAH, BUT THIS THEME PARK IS RUN BY A CRAB.
YOU'RE RIGHT. THE MENU IS VERY CRAB CENTRIC.
Rotten chicken
Compost heap
ROTTEN CHICKEN SANDWICH, SCAVENGER SALAD, ALL-U-CAN-EAT GARBAGE BAR...
DO YOU SERVE HOT DOGS?
GROSS! DO YOU KNOW WHAT'S IN THOSE THINGS?

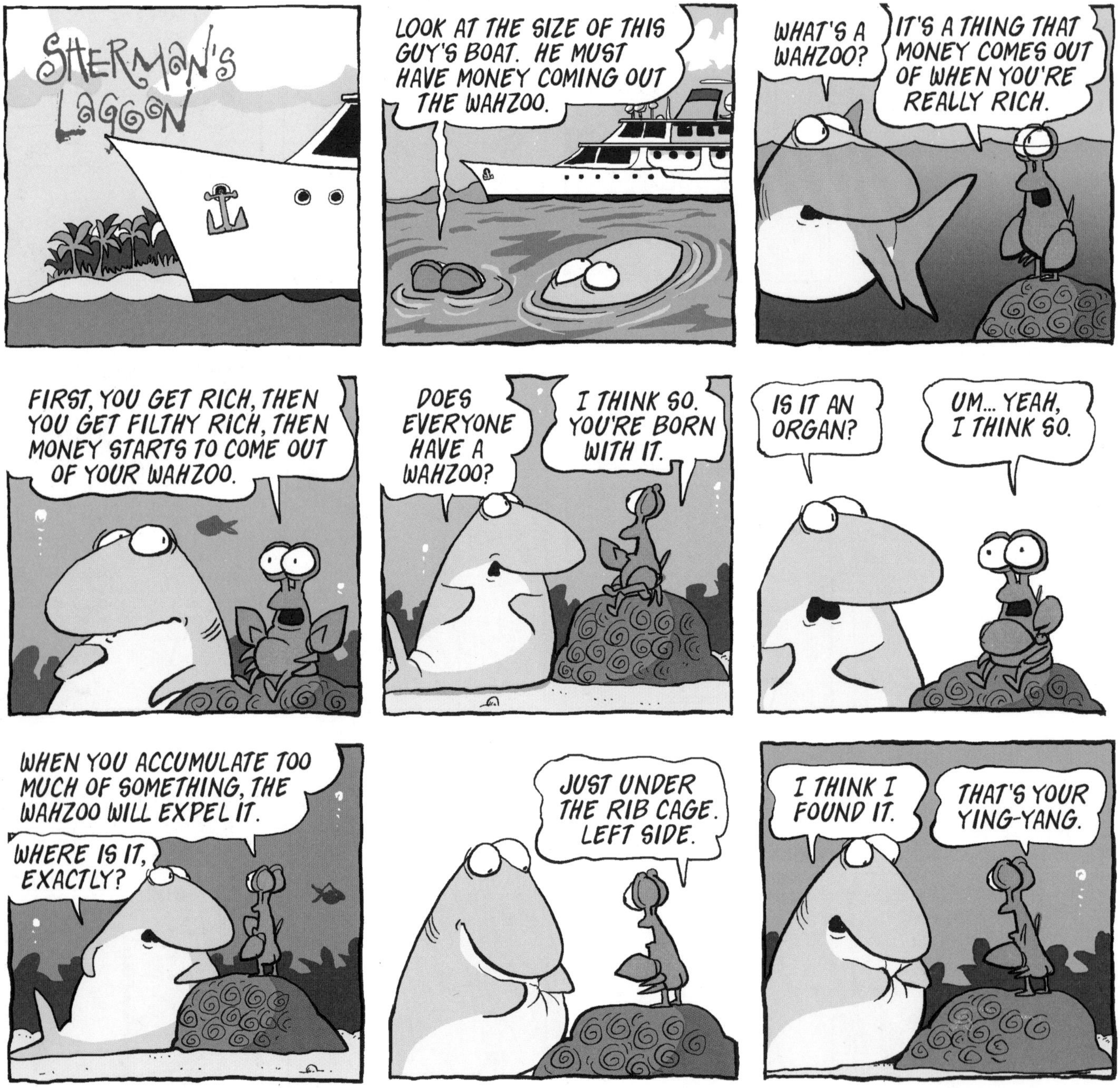
SHERMAN'S LAGOON
LOOK AT THE SIZE OF THIS GUY'S BOAT. HE MUST HAVE MONEY COMING OUT THE WAHZOO.
WHAT'S A WAHZOO?
IT'S A THING THAT MONEY COMES OUT OF WHEN YOU'RE REALLY RICH.
FIRST, YOU GET RICH, THEN YOU GET FILTHY RICH, THEN MONEY STARTS TO COME OUT OF YOUR WAHZOO.
DOES EVERYONE HAVE A WAHZOO?
I THINK SO. YOU'RE BORN WITH IT.
IS IT AN ORGAN?
UM... YEAH, I THINK SO.
WHEN YOU ACCUMULATE TOO MUCH OF SOMETHING, THE WAHZOO WILL EXPEL IT.
WHERE IS IT, EXACTLY?
JUST UNDER THE RIB CAGE. LEFT SIDE.
I THINK I FOUND IT.
THAT'S YOUR YING-YANG.

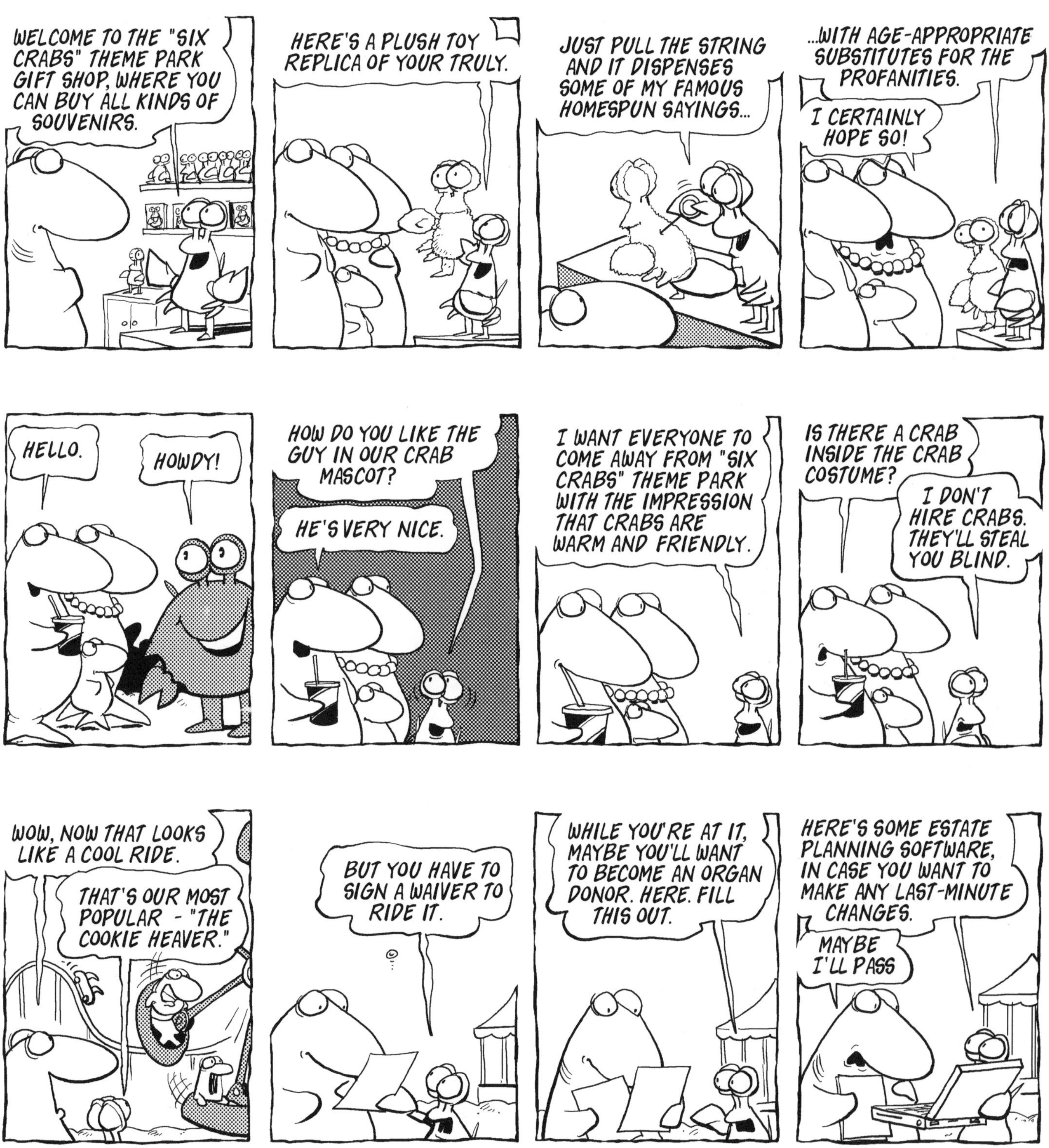
WELCOME TO THE "SIX CRABS" THEME PARK GIFT SHOP, WHERE YOU CAN BUY ALL KINDS OF SOUVENIRS.
HERE'S A PLUSH TOY REPLICA OF YOUR TRULY.
JUST PULL THE STRING AND IT DISPENSES SOME OF MY FAMOUS HOMESPUN SAYINGS...
...WITH AGE-APPROPRIATE SUBSTITUTES FOR THE PROFANITIES.
I CERTAINLY HOPE SO!
HELLO.
HOWDY!
HOW DO YOU LIKE THE GUY IN OUR CRAB MASCOT?
HE'S VERY NICE.
I WANT EVERYONE TO COME AWAY FROM "SIX CRABS" THEME PARK WITH THE IMPRESSION THAT CRABS ARE WARM AND FRIENDLY.
IS THERE A CRAB INSIDE THE CRAB COSTUME?
I DON'T HIRE CRABS. THEY'LL STEAL YOU BLIND.
WOW, NOW THAT LOOKS LIKE A COOL RIDE.
THAT'S OUR MOST POPULAR - "THE COOKIE HEAVER."
BUT YOU HAVE TO SIGN A WAIVER TO RIDE IT.
WHILE YOU'RE AT IT, MAYBE YOU'LL WANT TO BECOME AN ORGAN DONOR. HERE. FILL THIS OUT.
HERE'S SOME ESTATE PLANNING SOFTWARE, IN CASE YOU WANT TO MAKE ANY LAST-MINUTE CHANGES.
MAYBE I'LL PASS

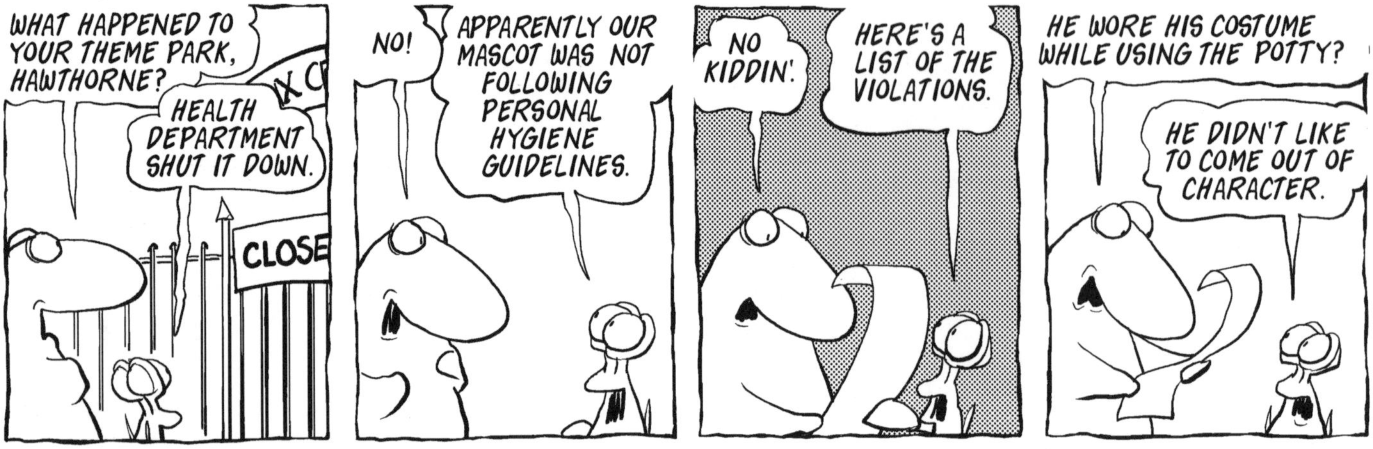
WHAT HAPPENED TO YOUR THEME PARK, HAWTHORNE?
HEALTH DEPARTMENT SHUT IT DOWN.
CLOSE
NO!
APPARENTLY OUR MASCOT WAS NOT FOLLOWING PERSONAL HYGIENE GUIDELINES.
NO KIDDIN'.
HERE'S A LIST OF THE VIOLATIONS.
HE WORE HIS COSTUME WHILE USING THE POTTY?
HE DIDN'T LIKE TO COME OUT OF CHARACTER.

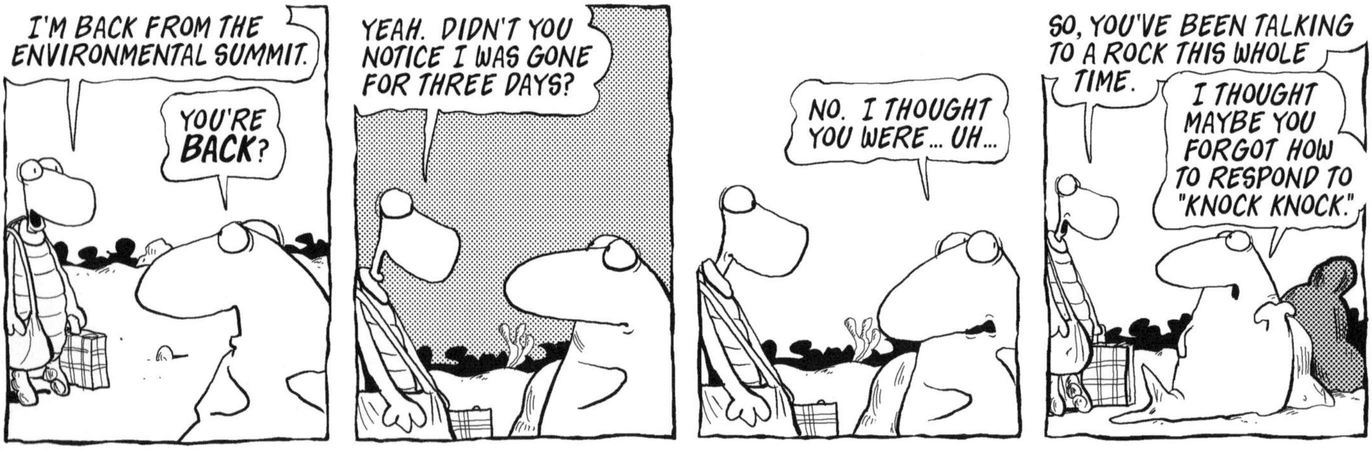
I'M BACK FROM THE ENVIRONMENTAL SUMMIT.
YOU'RE BACK?
YEAH. DIDN'T YOU NOTICE I WAS GONE FOR THREE DAYS?
NO. I THOUGHT YOU WERE... UH...
SO, YOU'VE BEEN TALKING TO A ROCK THIS WHOLE TIME.
I THOUGHT MAYBE YOU FORGOT HOW TO RESPOND TO "KNOCK KNOCK."

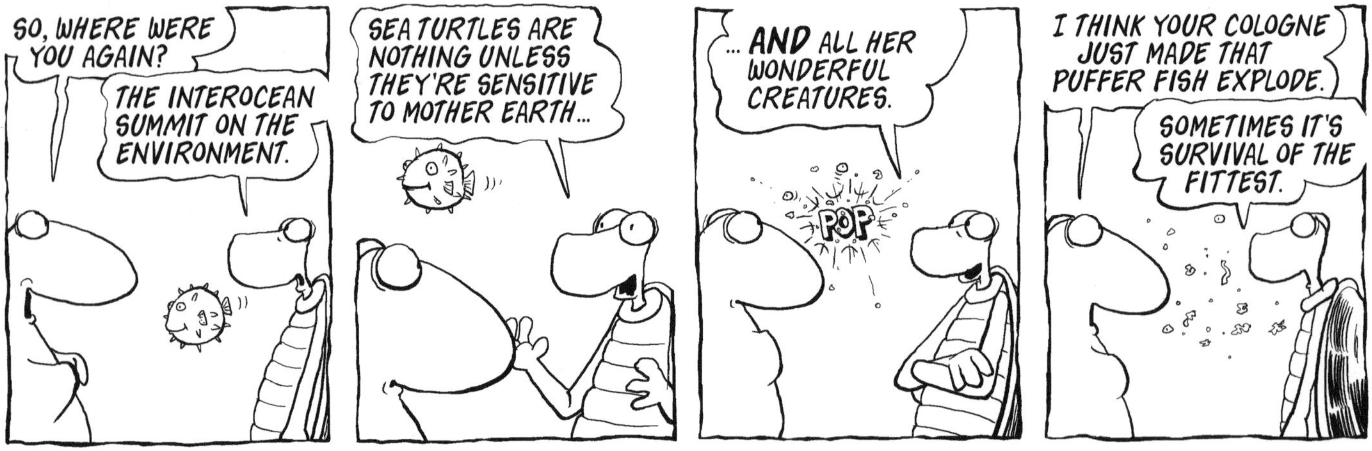
SO, WHERE WERE YOU AGAIN?
THE INTEROCEAN SUMMIT ON THE ENVIRONMENT.
SEA TURTLES ARE NOTHING UNLESS THEY'RE SENSITIVE TO MOTHER EARTH...
...AND ALL HER WONDERFUL CREATURES.
POP
I THINK YOUR COLOGNE JUST MADE THAT PUFFER FISH EXPLODE.
SOMETIMES IT'S SURVIVAL OF THE FITTEST.

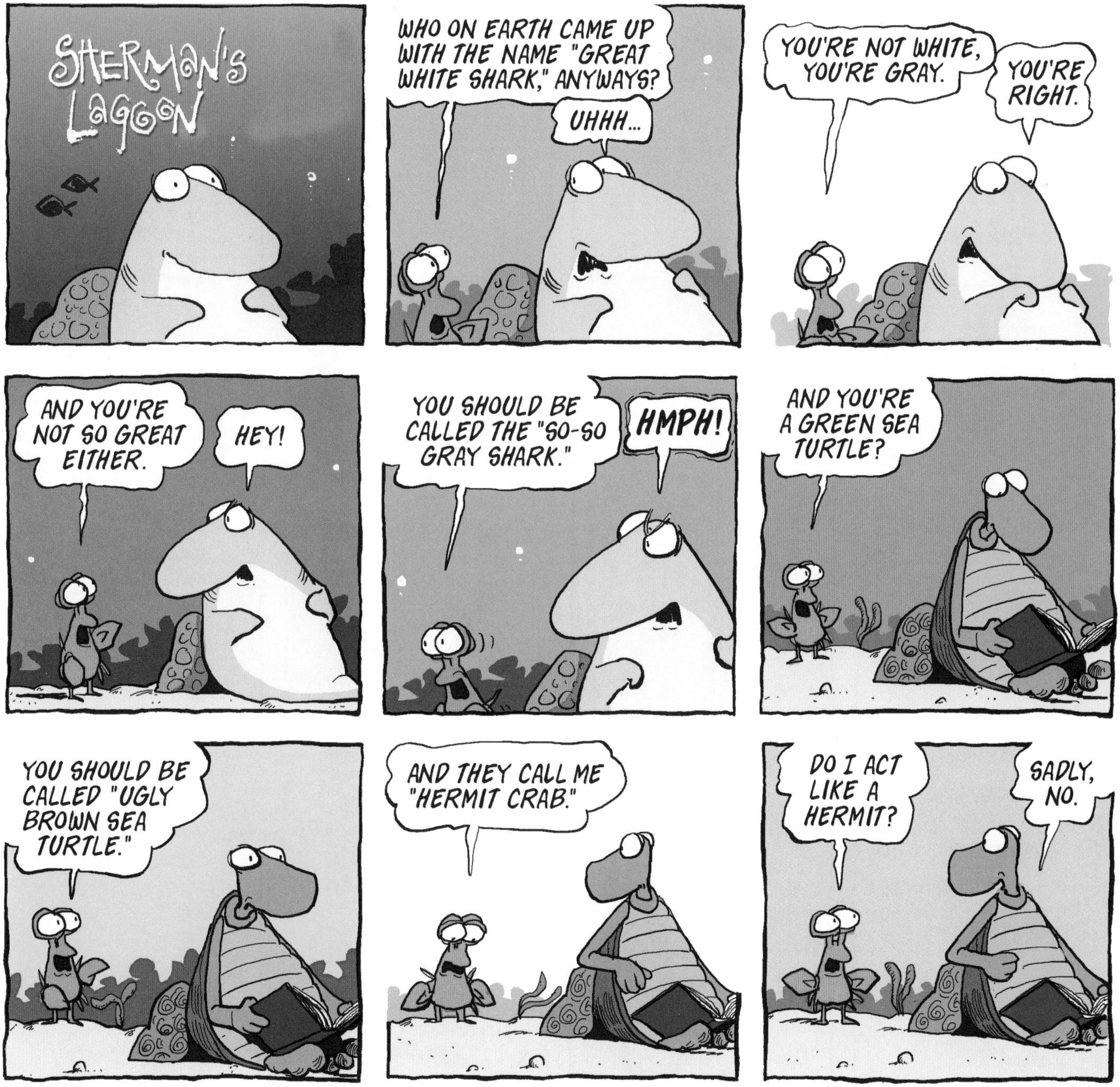
SHERMAN'S LAGOON
WHO ON EARTH CAME UP WITH THE NAME "GREAT WHITE SHARK," ANYWAYS?
UHHH...
YOU'RE NOT WHITE, YOU'RE GRAY.
YOU'RE RIGHT.
AND YOU'RE NOT SO GREAT EITHER.
HEY!
YOU SHOULD BE CALLED THE "SO-SO GRAY SHARK."
HMPH!
AND YOU'RE A GREEN SEA TURTLE?
YOU SHOULD BE CALLED "UGLY BROWN SEA TURTLE."
AND THEY CALL ME "HERMIT CRAB."
DO I ACT LIKE A HERMIT?
SADLY, NO.

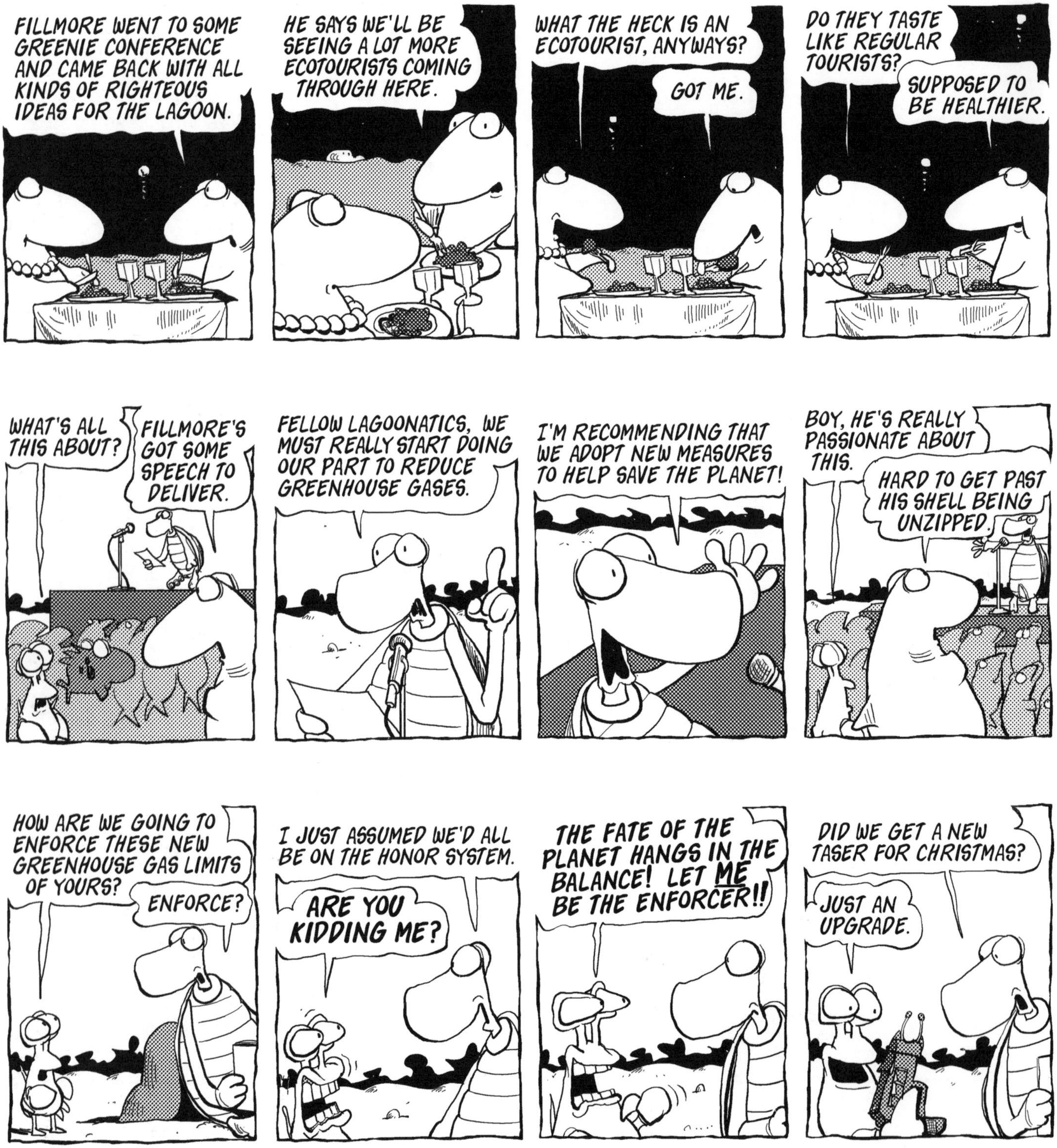

FILLMORE WENT TO SOME GREENIE CONFERENCE AND CAME BACK WITH ALL KINDS OF RIGHTEOUS IDEAS FOR THE LAGOON.
HE SAYS WE'LL BE SEEING A LOT MORE ECOTOURISTS COMING THROUGH HERE.
WHAT THE HECK IS AN ECOTOURIST, ANYWAYS?
GOT ME.
DO THEY TASTE LIKE REGULAR TOURISTS?
SUPPOSED TO BE HEALTHIER.
WHAT'S ALL THIS ABOUT?
FILLMORE'S GOT SOME SPEECH TO DELIVER.
FELLOW LAGOONATICS, WE MUST REALLY START DOING OUR PART TO REDUCE GREENHOUSE GASES.
I'M RECOMMENDING THAT WE ADOPT NEW MEASURES TO HELP SAVE THE PLANET!
BOY, HE'S REALLY PASSIONATE ABOUT THIS.
HARD TO GET PAST HIS SHELL BEING UNZIPPED.
HOW ARE WE GOING TO ENFORCE THESE NEW GREENHOUSE GAS LIMITS OF YOURS?
ENFORCE?
I JUST ASSUMED WE'D ALL BE ON THE HONOR SYSTEM.
ARE YOU KIDDING ME?
THE FATE OF THE PLANET HANGS IN THE BALANCE! LET ME BE THE ENFORCER!!
DID WE GET A NEW TASER FOR CHRISTMAS?
JUST AN UPGRADE.

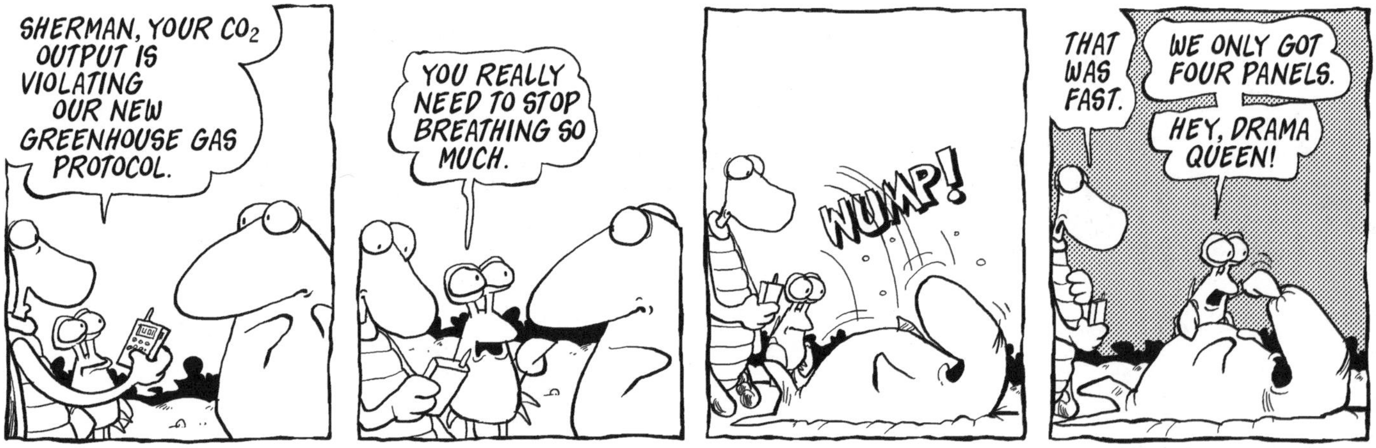
SHERMAN, YOUR CO_2 OUTPUT IS VIOLATING OUR NEW GREENHOUSE GAS PROTOCOL.
YOU REALLY NEED TO STOP BREATHING SO MUCH.
WUMP!
THAT WAS FAST.
WE ONLY GOT FOUR PANELS.
HEY, DRAMA QUEEN!

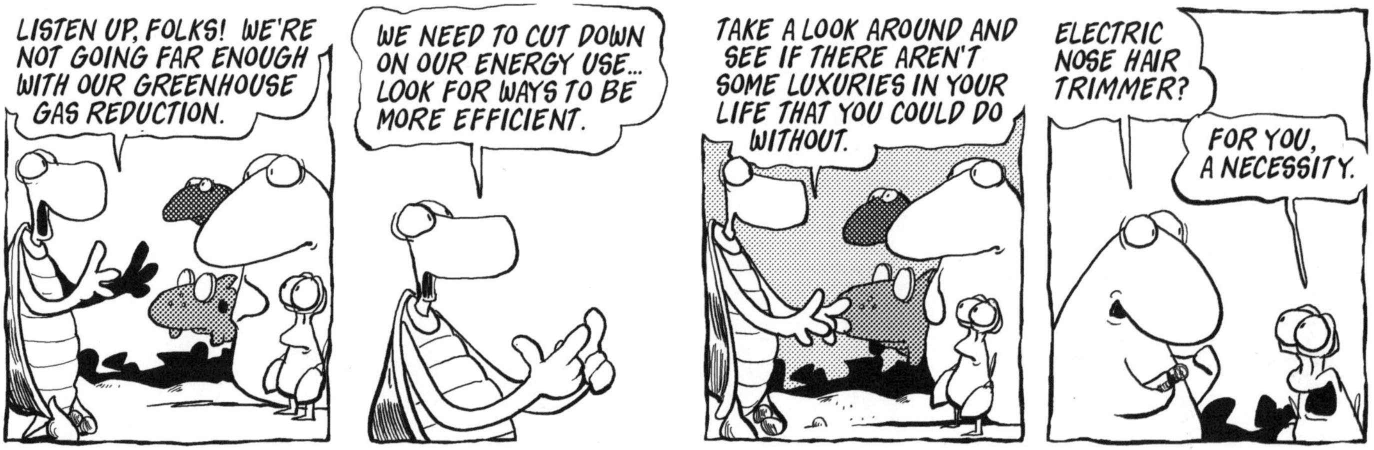
LISTEN UP, FOLKS! WE'RE NOT GOING FAR ENOUGH WITH OUR GREENHOUSE GAS REDUCTION.
WE NEED TO CUT DOWN ON OUR ENERGY USE... LOOK FOR WAYS TO BE MORE EFFICIENT.
TAKE A LOOK AROUND AND SEE IF THERE AREN'T SOME LUXURIES IN YOUR LIFE THAT YOU COULD DO WITHOUT.
ELECTRIC NOSE HAIR TRIMMER?
FOR YOU, A NECESSITY.

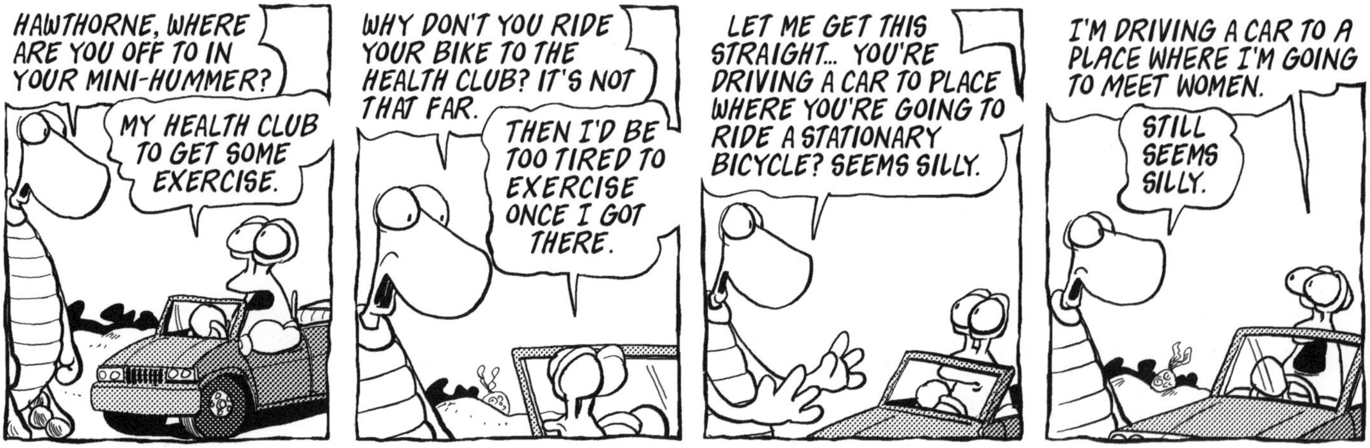
HAWTHORNE, WHERE ARE YOU OFF TO IN YOUR MINI-HUMMER?
MY HEALTH CLUB TO GET SOME EXERCISE.
WHY DON'T YOU RIDE YOUR BIKE TO THE HEALTH CLUB? IT'S NOT THAT FAR.
THEN I'D BE TOO TIRED TO EXERCISE ONCE I GOT THERE.
LET ME GET THIS STRAIGHT... YOU'RE DRIVING A CAR TO PLACE WHERE YOU'RE GOING TO RIDE A STATIONARY BICYCLE? SEEMS SILLY.
I'M DRIVING A CAR TO A PLACE WHERE I'M GOING TO MEET WOMEN.
STILL SEEMS SILLY.

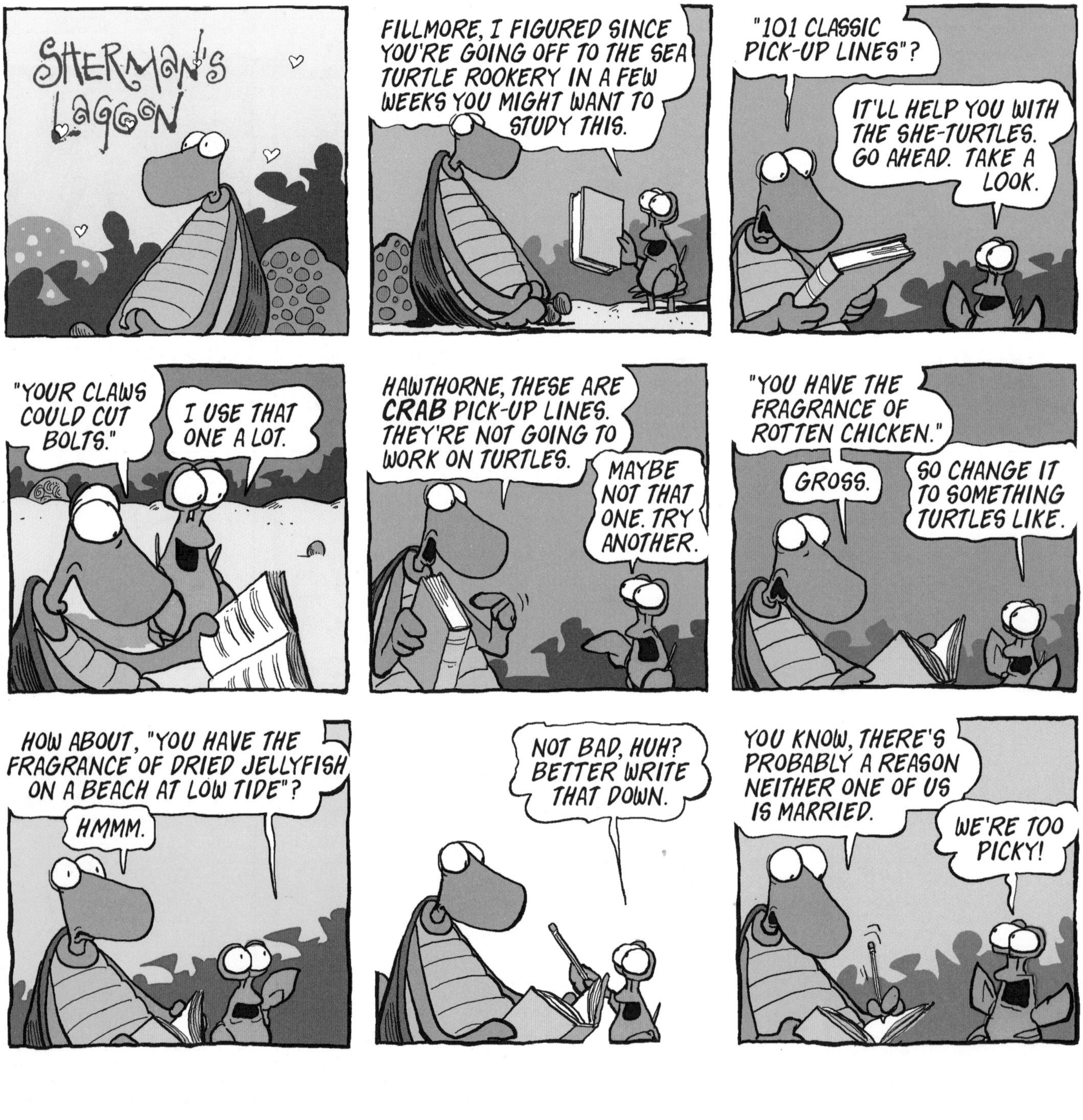
SHERMAN'S LAGOON
FILLMORE, I FIGURED SINCE YOU'RE GOING OFF TO THE SEA TURTLE ROOKERY IN A FEW WEEKS YOU MIGHT WANT TO STUDY THIS.
"101 CLASSIC PICK-UP LINES"?
IT'LL HELP YOU WITH THE SHE-TURTLES. GO AHEAD. TAKE A LOOK.
"YOUR CLAWS COULD CUT BOLTS."
I USE THAT ONE A LOT.
HAWTHORNE, THESE ARE CRAB PICK-UP LINES. THEY'RE NOT GOING TO WORK ON TURTLES.
MAYBE NOT THAT ONE. TRY ANOTHER.
"YOU HAVE THE FRAGRANCE OF ROTTEN CHICKEN."
GROSS.
SO CHANGE IT TO SOMETHING TURTLES LIKE.
HOW ABOUT, "YOU HAVE THE FRAGRANCE OF DRIED JELLYFISH ON A BEACH AT LOW TIDE"?
HMMM.
NOT BAD, HUH? BETTER WRITE THAT DOWN.
YOU KNOW, THERE'S PROBABLY A REASON NEITHER ONE OF US IS MARRIED.
WE'RE TOO PICKY!

WHY ARE YOU USING A GAS-POWERED LEAF BLOWER? WHY NOT USE A RAKE AND HELP THE PLANET?

RAKES ARE FOR WIMPS. WHEN I STRAP THIS BABY ON, I FEEL LIKE RAMBO.

VRRROOOOMM!

ALL THE CITIZENS OF LEAF-VILLE FLEE IN TERROR WHEN THEY HEAR THE ROAR OF THIS BIG BAD MACHINE.

VRRROOOOMM

THAT'S WHAT HAPPENS WHEN YOU PUT A CHILD'S MIND IN A SHARK'S BODY.

THEN ASK IT TO DO YARD WORK.

A TANNING SALON? THAT'S THE ULTIMATE WASTE OF ENERGY!

Tanning Salon

Grand Opening!

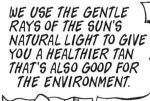
THIS ISN'T JUST ANY TANNING SALON. IT'S A **GREEN** TANNING SALON. WE'RE SOLAR POWERED.

WE USE THE GENTLE RAYS OF THE SUN'S NATURAL LIGHT TO GIVE YOU A HEALTHIER TAN THAT'S ALSO GOOD FOR THE ENVIRONMENT.

WE'RE GIVING OUT FREE SAMPLES TODAY.

GEE, THANKS.

Salo

I THINK I'VE COME UP WITH SOMETHING THAT WILL SAVE THE ENVIRONMENT.

NO.

REALLY. THE WAY I SEE IT, MY INVENTION IS GOING TO CHANGE THE WORLD.

FOR THOSE OF US WHO THINK DARK DAYS ARE AHEAD I BRING YOU THIS.

A WIND-POWERED BLENDER?

PAVING THE ROAD TO SUSTAINABLE SMOOTHIES.

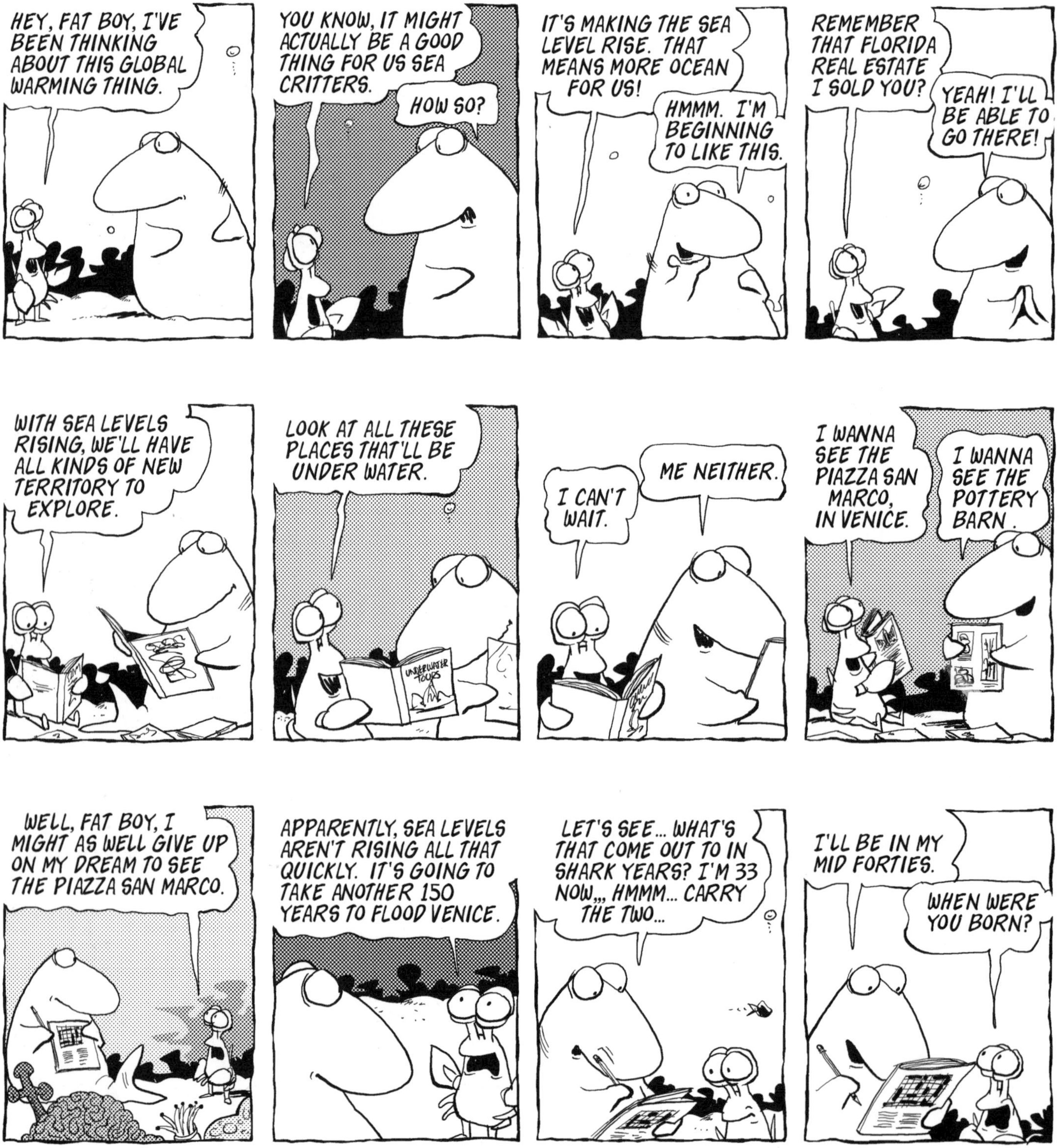
HEY, FAT BOY, I'VE BEEN THINKING ABOUT THIS GLOBAL WARMING THING.
YOU KNOW, IT MIGHT ACTUALLY BE A GOOD THING FOR US SEA CRITTERS.
HOW SO?
IT'S MAKING THE SEA LEVEL RISE. THAT MEANS MORE OCEAN FOR US!
HMMM. I'M BEGINNING TO LIKE THIS.
REMEMBER THAT FLORIDA REAL ESTATE I SOLD YOU?
YEAH! I'LL BE ABLE TO GO THERE!
WITH SEA LEVELS RISING, WE'LL HAVE ALL KINDS OF NEW TERRITORY TO EXPLORE.
LOOK AT ALL THESE PLACES THAT'LL BE UNDER WATER.
UNDERWATER TOURS
I CAN'T WAIT.
ME NEITHER.
I WANNA SEE THE PIAZZA SAN MARCO, IN VENICE.
I WANNA SEE THE POTTERY BARN.
WELL, FAT BOY, I MIGHT AS WELL GIVE UP ON MY DREAM TO SEE THE PIAZZA SAN MARCO.
APPARENTLY, SEA LEVELS AREN'T RISING ALL THAT QUICKLY. IT'S GOING TO TAKE ANOTHER 150 YEARS TO FLOOD VENICE.
LET'S SEE... WHAT'S THAT COME OUT TO IN SHARK YEARS? I'M 33 NOW,,, HMMM... CARRY THE TWO...
I'LL BE IN MY MID FORTIES.
WHEN WERE YOU BORN?

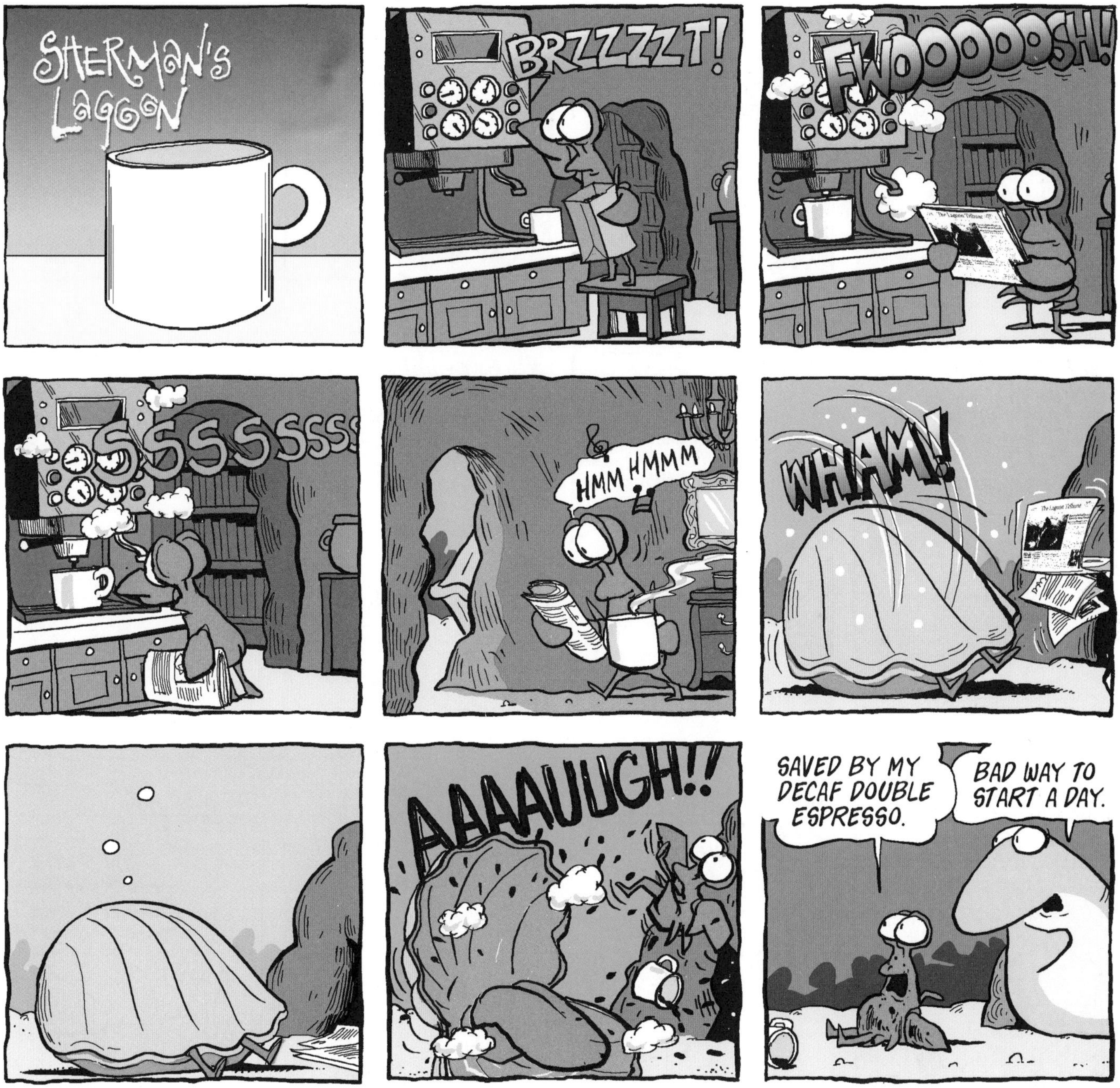
SHERMAN'S LAGOON
BRZZZZZT!
FWOOOOOOSH!
SSSSSSSSS
HMM HMMM
WHAM!
AAAAUUGH!!
SAVED BY MY DECAF DOUBLE ESPRESSO.
BAD WAY TO START A DAY.

Panel 1: BY MY ESTIMATES, WE'VE ACHIEVED OUR GOALS. OUR LAGOON HAS REACHED A STATE OF SUSTAINABILITY.

WHAT'S THAT MEAN?

Panel 2: THAT MEANS WE'RE KEEPING EVERYTHING ROUGHLY THE SAME FOR FUTURE GENERATIONS.

Panel 3: EVERYTHING THAT COMES IN HAS TO EQUAL EVERYTHING THAT GOES OUT.

Panel 4: SO, IF I MOVED AWAY, YOU'D HAVE TO FIND A NEW ME?

FOR YOU, WE'D MAKE AN EXCEPTION.

Panel 5: HEY, I RECOGNIZE THE GUY ON THAT YACHT... I'VE SEEN HIS PICTURE IN THE NEWSPAPER... HE'S THE PRESIDENT OF CUBALIBRÉ.

Panel 6: CUBALIBRÉ?

A SMALL ISLAND NATION NOT FAR FROM HERE.

Panel 7: HAVEN'T YOU EVER BEEN TO A CUBALIBREAN RESTAURANT? WHEN THEY BRING YOUR FOOD OUT THEY SET IT ON FIRE.

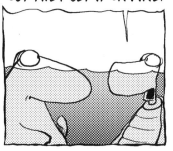

Panel 8: NO. SOUNDS LIKE FUN.

DON'T ORDER A SALAD.

Panel 9: SHERMAN! YOU *ATE* THE PRESIDENT OF CUBALIBRÉ?

SO?

Panel 10: SO? YOU CAN'T GO AROUND EATING THE LEADERS OF COUNTRIES!

Panel 11: IT JUST SHOWS THAT I FIGHT FOR EQUALITY. I STAND WITH THE COMMON FOLKS.

Panel 12: YOU ALSO ATE HIS BUTLER.

I STAND WITH THE REMAINING COMMON FOLKS!

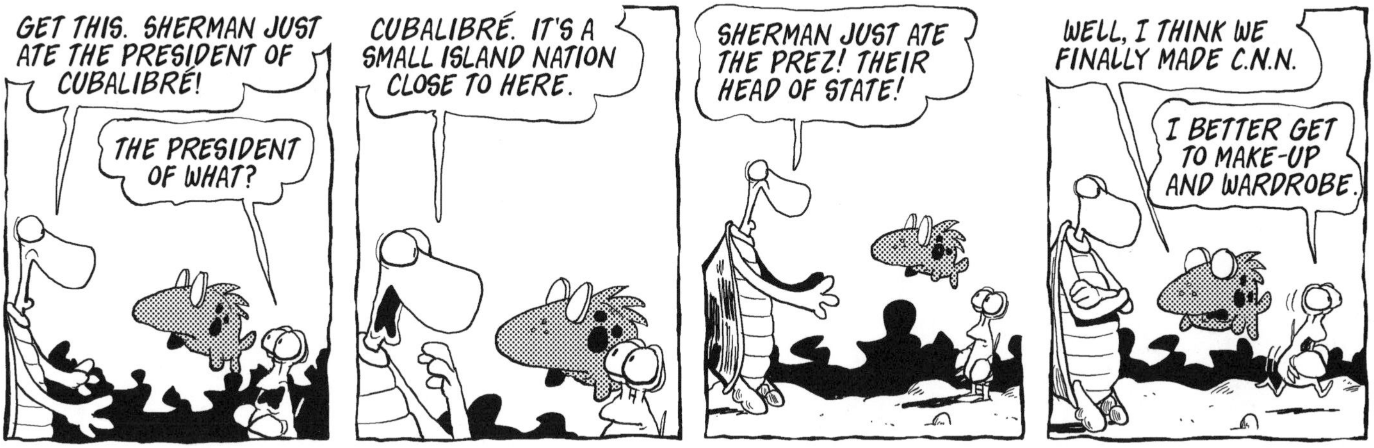
GET THIS. SHERMAN JUST ATE THE PRESIDENT OF CUBALIBRÉ!
THE PRESIDENT OF WHAT?
CUBALIBRÉ. IT'S A SMALL ISLAND NATION CLOSE TO HERE.
SHERMAN JUST ATE THE PREZ! THEIR HEAD OF STATE!
WELL, I THINK WE FINALLY MADE C.N.N.
I BETTER GET TO MAKE-UP AND WARDROBE.

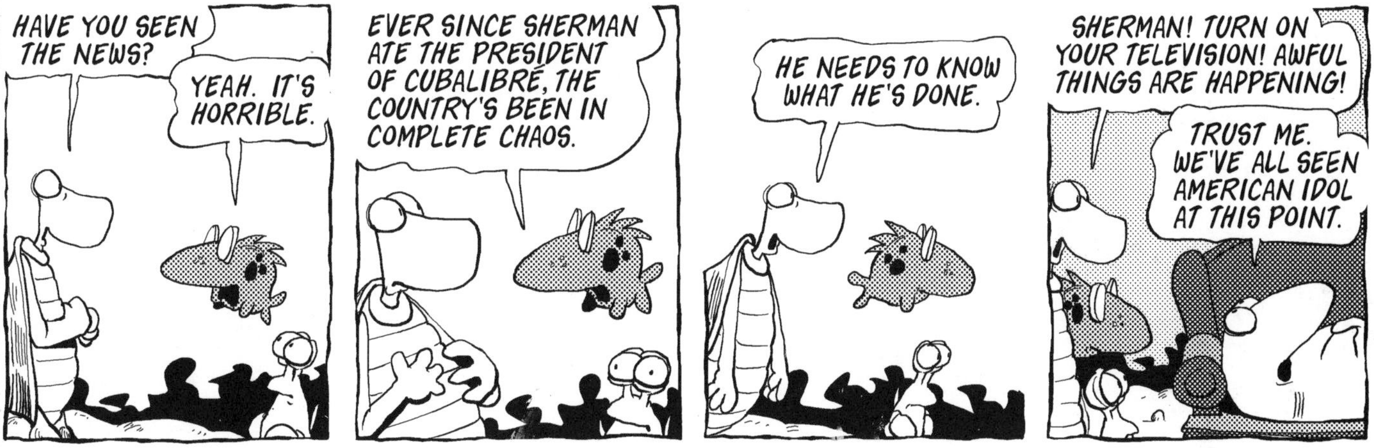
HAVE YOU SEEN THE NEWS?
YEAH. IT'S HORRIBLE.
EVER SINCE SHERMAN ATE THE PRESIDENT OF CUBALIBRÉ, THE COUNTRY'S BEEN IN COMPLETE CHAOS.
HE NEEDS TO KNOW WHAT HE'S DONE.
SHERMAN! TURN ON YOUR TELEVISION! AWFUL THINGS ARE HAPPENING!
TRUST ME. WE'VE ALL SEEN AMERICAN IDOL AT THIS POINT.

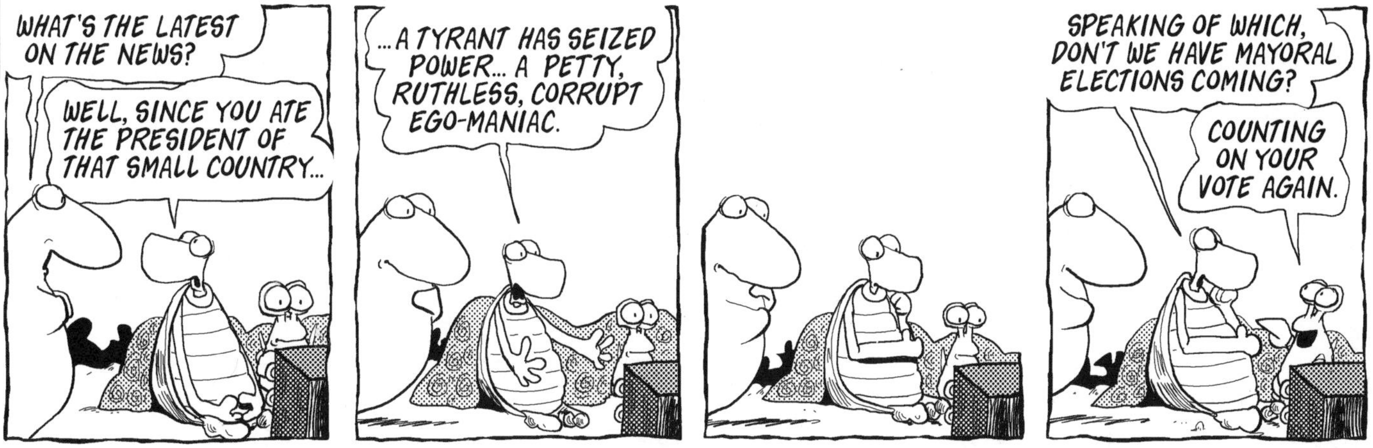
WHAT'S THE LATEST ON THE NEWS?
WELL, SINCE YOU ATE THE PRESIDENT OF THAT SMALL COUNTRY...
...A TYRANT HAS SEIZED POWER... A PETTY, RUTHLESS, CORRUPT EGO-MANIAC.
SPEAKING OF WHICH, DON'T WE HAVE MAYORAL ELECTIONS COMING?
COUNTING ON YOUR VOTE AGAIN.

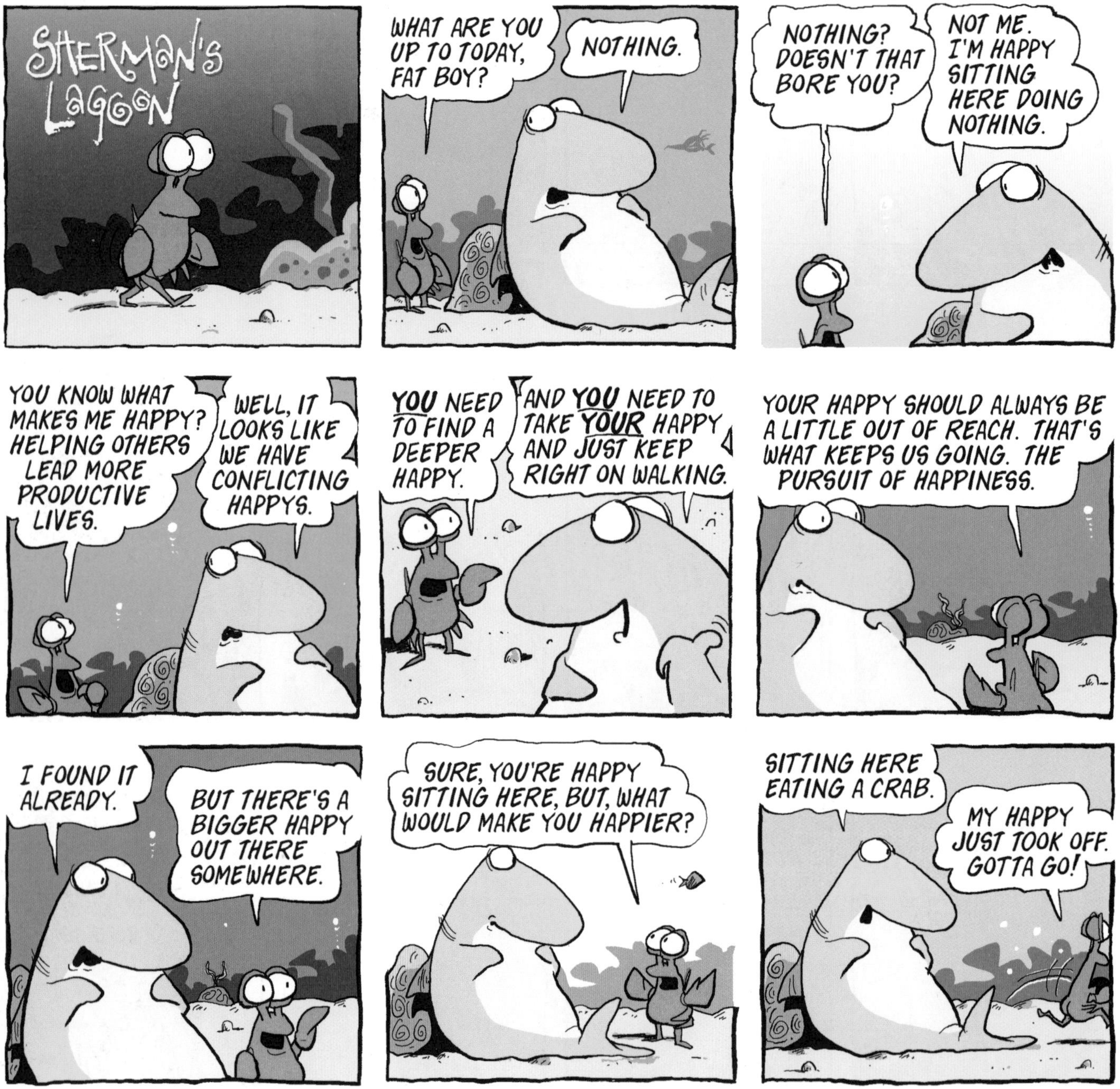
SHERMAN'S LAGOON
WHAT ARE YOU UP TO TODAY, FAT BOY?
NOTHING.
NOTHING? DOESN'T THAT BORE YOU?
NOT ME. I'M HAPPY SITTING HERE DOING NOTHING.
YOU KNOW WHAT MAKES ME HAPPY? HELPING OTHERS LEAD MORE PRODUCTIVE LIVES.
WELL, IT LOOKS LIKE WE HAVE CONFLICTING HAPPYS.
YOU NEED TO FIND A DEEPER HAPPY.
AND YOU NEED TO TAKE YOUR HAPPY AND JUST KEEP RIGHT ON WALKING.
YOUR HAPPY SHOULD ALWAYS BE A LITTLE OUT OF REACH. THAT'S WHAT KEEPS US GOING. THE PURSUIT OF HAPPINESS.
I FOUND IT ALREADY.
BUT THERE'S A BIGGER HAPPY OUT THERE SOMEWHERE.
SURE, YOU'RE HAPPY SITTING HERE, BUT, WHAT WOULD MAKE YOU HAPPIER?
SITTING HERE EATING A CRAB.
MY HAPPY JUST TOOK OFF. GOTTA GO!

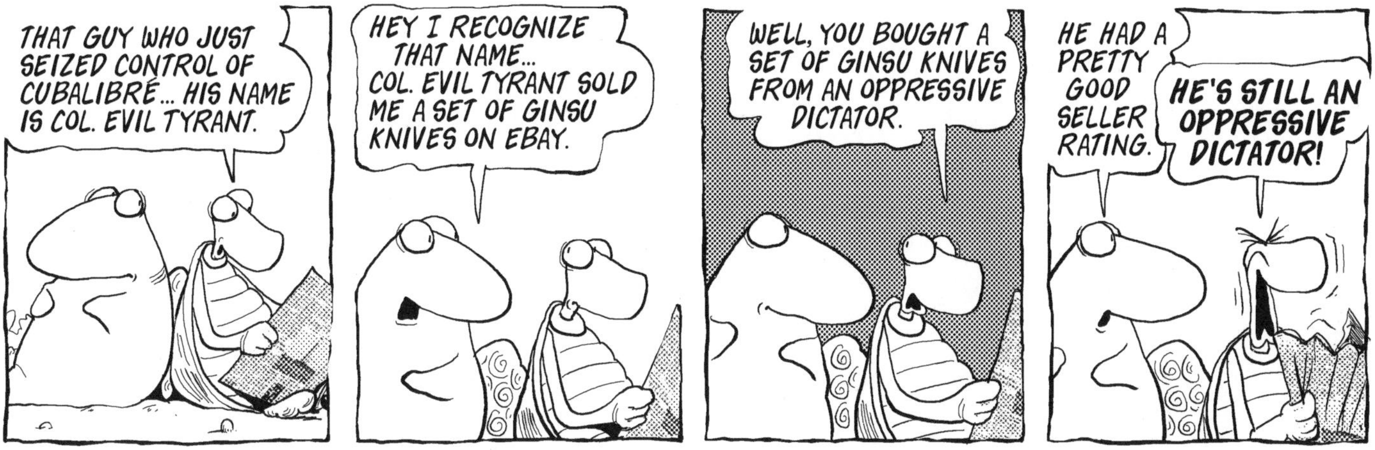
THAT GUY WHO JUST SEIZED CONTROL OF CUBALIBRÉ... HIS NAME IS COL. EVIL TYRANT.
HEY I RECOGNIZE THAT NAME... COL. EVIL TYRANT SOLD ME A SET OF GINSU KNIVES ON EBAY.
WELL, YOU BOUGHT A SET OF GINSU KNIVES FROM AN OPPRESSIVE DICTATOR.
HE HAD A PRETTY GOOD SELLER RATING.
HE'S STILL AN OPPRESSIVE DICTATOR!

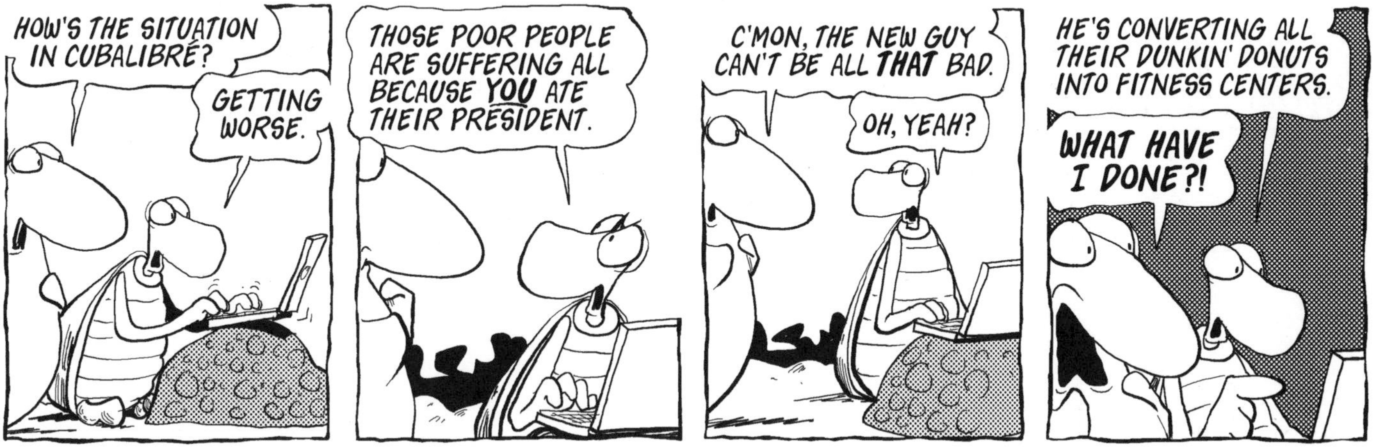
HOW'S THE SITUATION IN CUBALIBRÉ?
GETTING WORSE.
THOSE POOR PEOPLE ARE SUFFERING ALL BECAUSE YOU ATE THEIR PRESIDENT.
C'MON, THE NEW GUY CAN'T BE ALL THAT BAD.
OH, YEAH?
HE'S CONVERTING ALL THEIR DUNKIN' DONUTS INTO FITNESS CENTERS.
WHAT HAVE I DONE?!

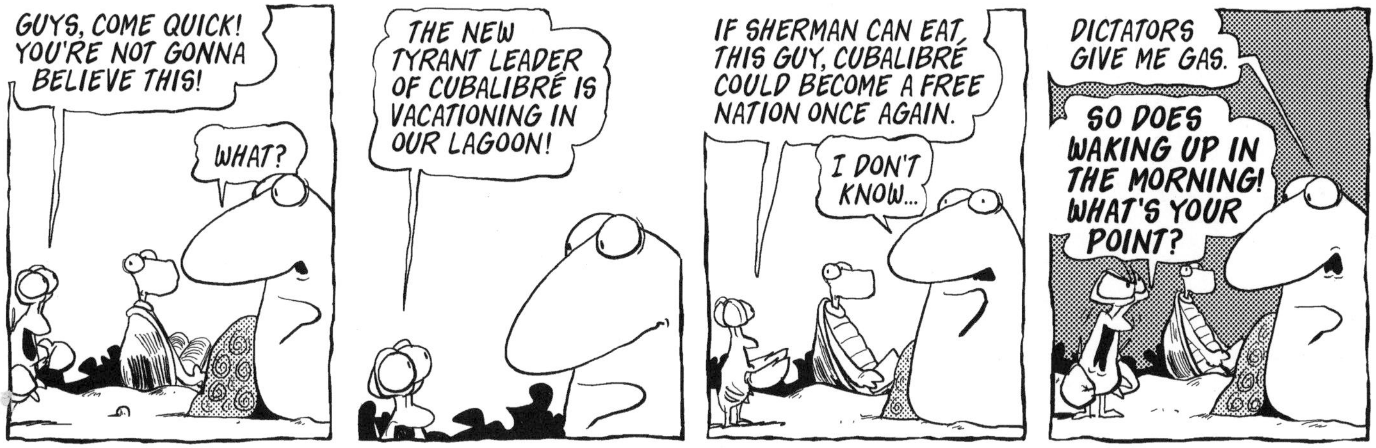
GUYS, COME QUICK! YOU'RE NOT GONNA BELIEVE THIS!
WHAT?
THE NEW TYRANT LEADER OF CUBALIBRÉ IS VACATIONING IN OUR LAGOON!
IF SHERMAN CAN EAT THIS GUY, CUBALIBRÉ COULD BECOME A FREE NATION ONCE AGAIN.
I DON'T KNOW...
DICTATORS GIVE ME GAS.
SO DOES WAKING UP IN THE MORNING! WHAT'S YOUR POINT?

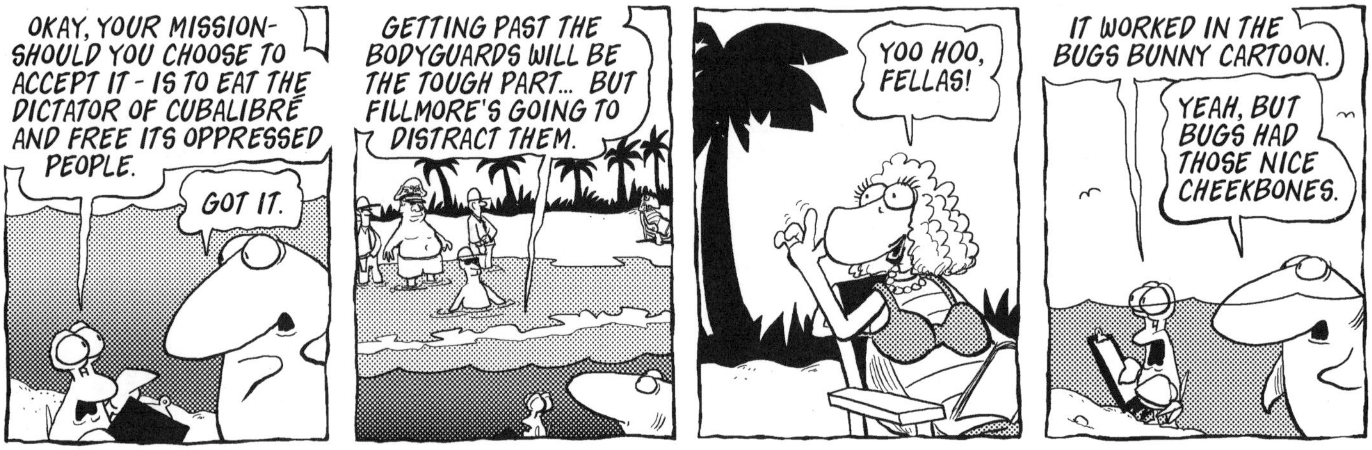
OKAY, YOUR MISSION- SHOULD YOU CHOOSE TO ACCEPT IT - IS TO EAT THE DICTATOR OF CUBALIBRÉ AND FREE ITS OPPRESSED PEOPLE.
GOT IT.
GETTING PAST THE BODYGUARDS WILL BE THE TOUGH PART... BUT FILLMORE'S GOING TO DISTRACT THEM.
YOO HOO, FELLAS!
IT WORKED IN THE BUGS BUNNY CARTOON.
YEAH, BUT BUGS HAD THOSE NICE CHEEKBONES.

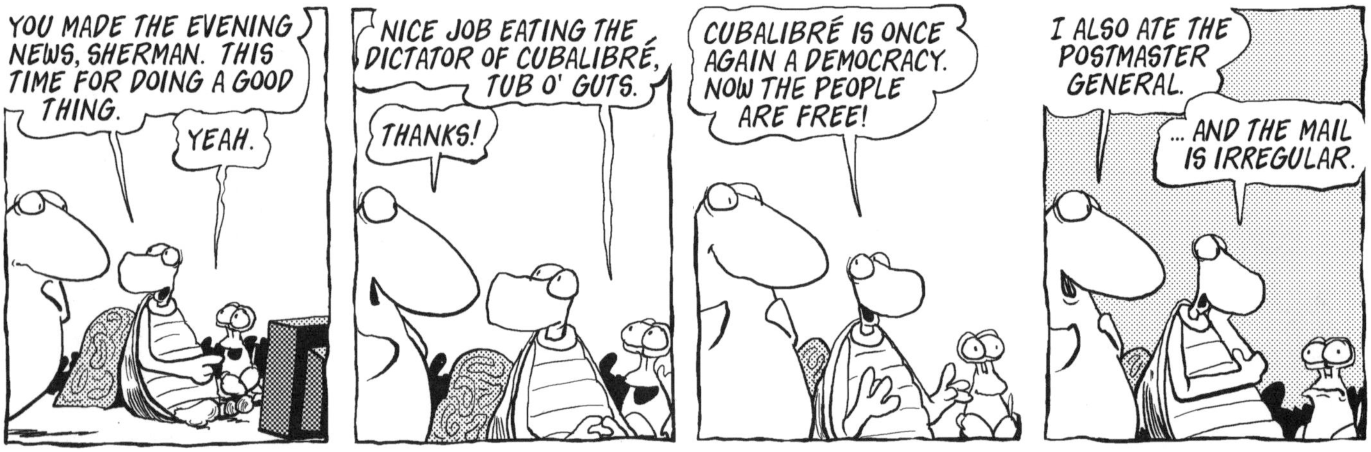
YOU MADE THE EVENING NEWS, SHERMAN. THIS TIME FOR DOING A GOOD THING.
YEAH.
NICE JOB EATING THE DICTATOR OF CUBALIBRÉ, TUB O' GUTS.
THANKS!
CUBALIBRÉ IS ONCE AGAIN A DEMOCRACY. NOW THE PEOPLE ARE FREE!
I ALSO ATE THE POSTMASTER GENERAL.
... AND THE MAIL IS IRREGULAR.

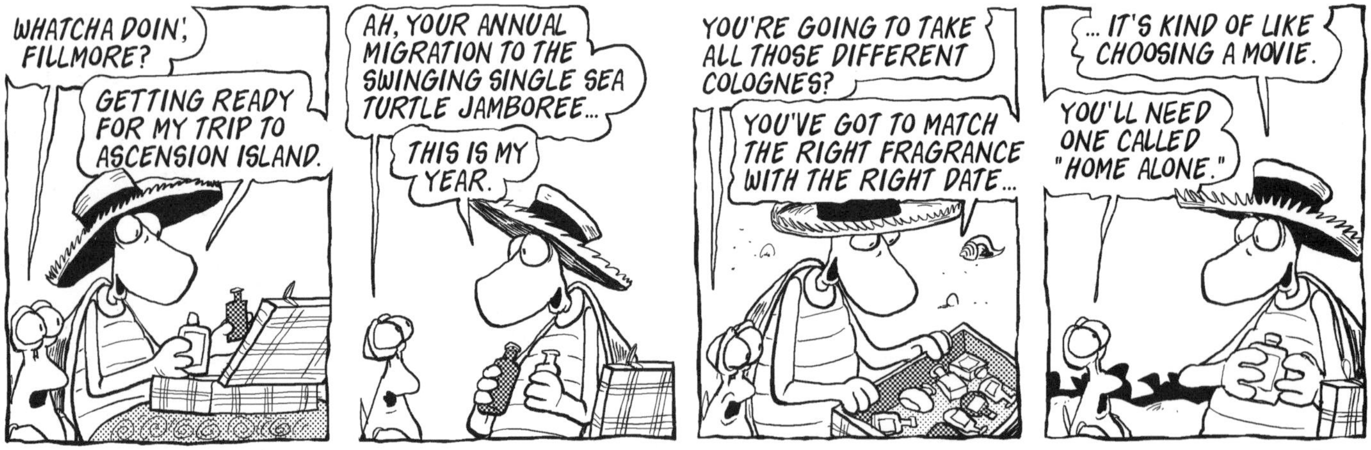
WHATCHA DOIN', FILLMORE?
GETTING READY FOR MY TRIP TO ASCENSION ISLAND.
AH, YOUR ANNUAL MIGRATION TO THE SWINGING SINGLE SEA TURTLE JAMBOREE...
THIS IS MY YEAR.
YOU'RE GOING TO TAKE ALL THOSE DIFFERENT COLOGNES?
YOU'VE GOT TO MATCH THE RIGHT FRAGRANCE WITH THE RIGHT DATE...
... IT'S KIND OF LIKE CHOOSING A MOVIE.
YOU'LL NEED ONE CALLED "HOME ALONE."

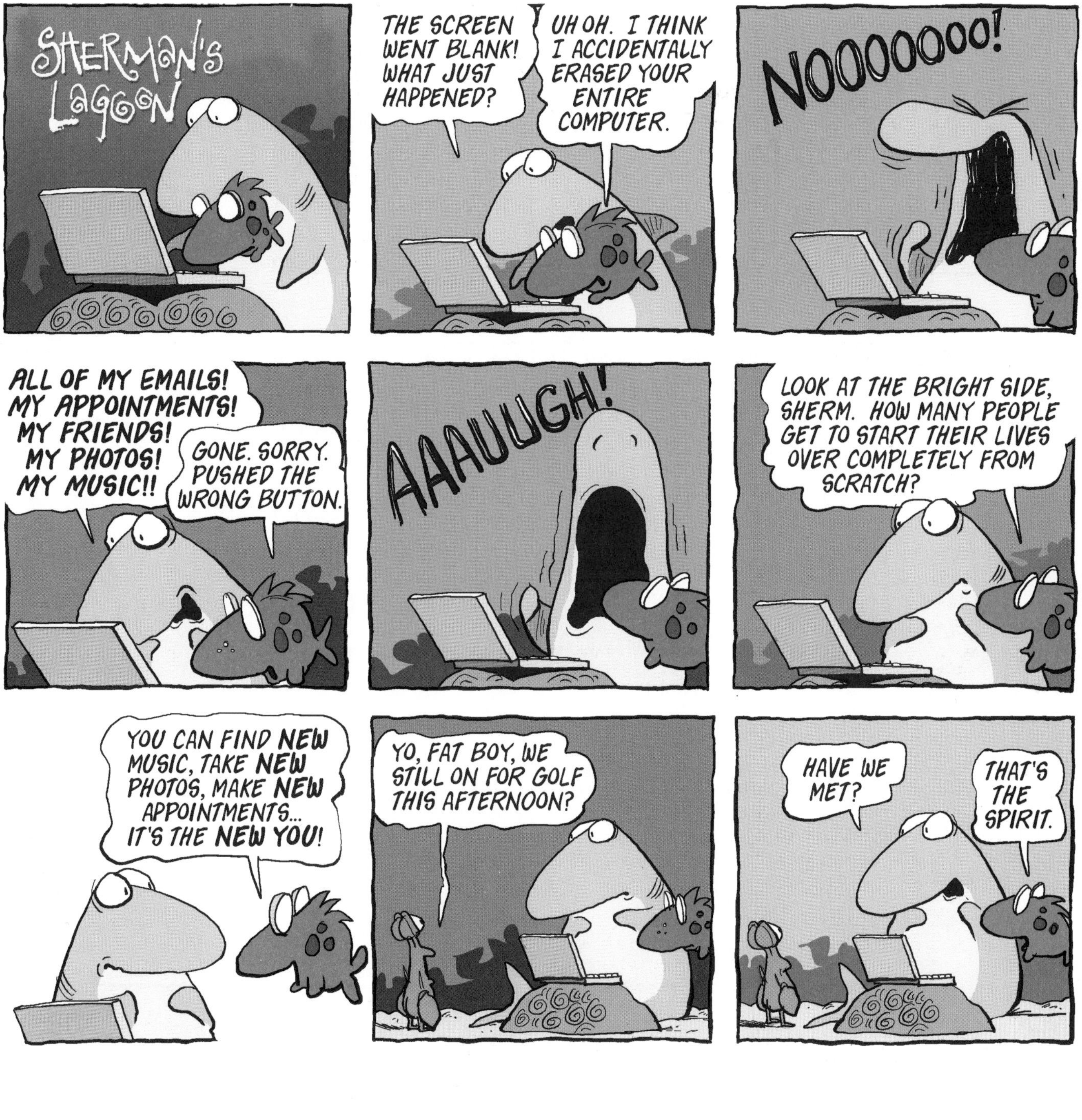
SHERMAN'S LAGOON
THE SCREEN WENT BLANK! WHAT JUST HAPPENED?
UH OH. I THINK I ACCIDENTALLY ERASED YOUR ENTIRE COMPUTER.
NOOOOOOO!
ALL OF MY EMAILS! MY APPOINTMENTS! MY FRIENDS! MY PHOTOS! MY MUSIC!!
GONE. SORRY. PUSHED THE WRONG BUTTON.
AAAUUGH!
LOOK AT THE BRIGHT SIDE, SHERM. HOW MANY PEOPLE GET TO START THEIR LIVES OVER COMPLETELY FROM SCRATCH?
YOU CAN FIND NEW MUSIC, TAKE NEW PHOTOS, MAKE NEW APPOINTMENTS... IT'S THE NEW YOU!
YO, FAT BOY, WE STILL ON FOR GOLF THIS AFTERNOON?
HAVE WE MET?
THAT'S THE SPIRIT.

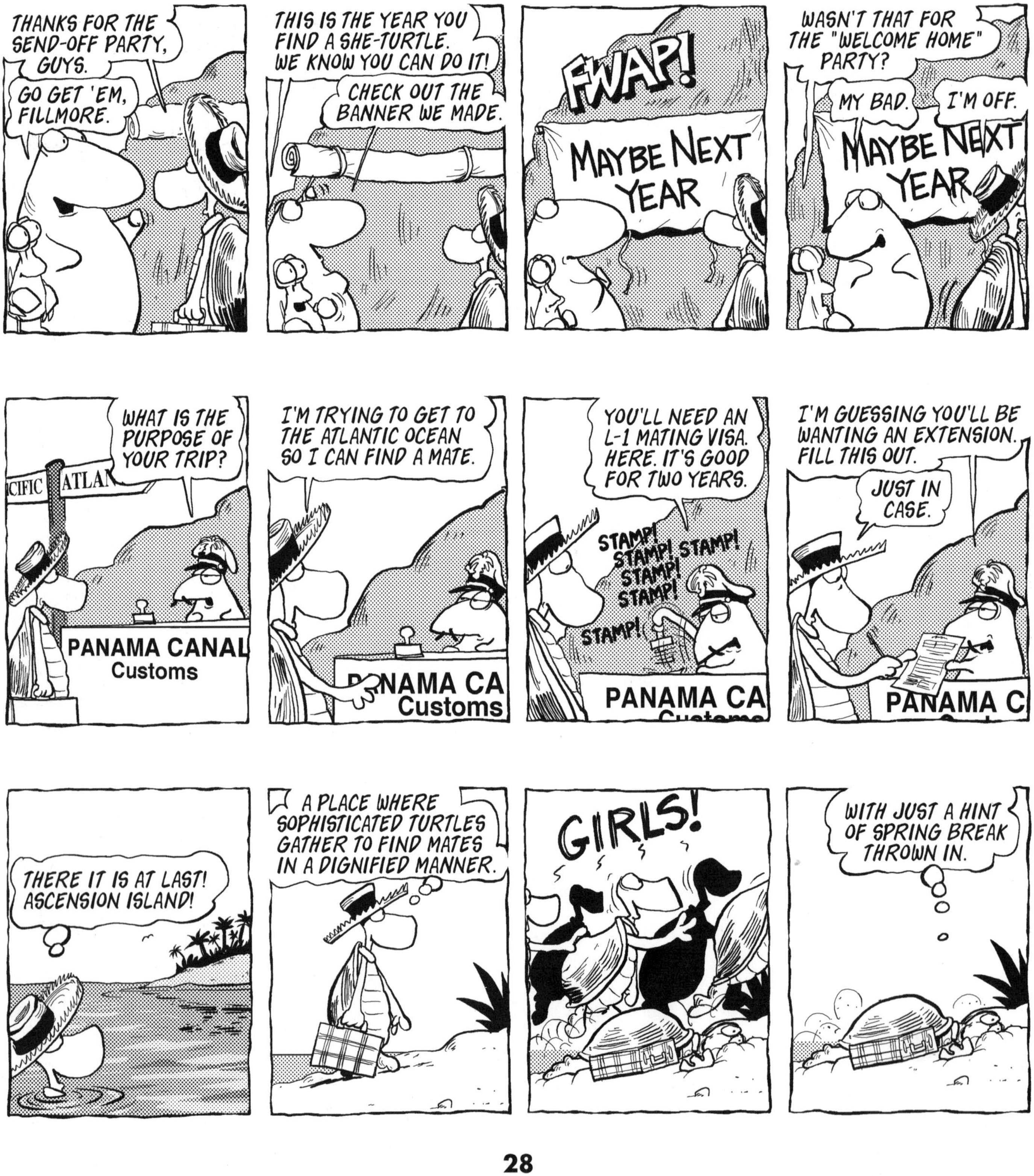
THANKS FOR THE SEND-OFF PARTY, GUYS.
GO GET 'EM, FILLMORE.
THIS IS THE YEAR YOU FIND A SHE-TURTLE. WE KNOW YOU CAN DO IT!
CHECK OUT THE BANNER WE MADE.
FWAP!
MAYBE NEXT YEAR
WASN'T THAT FOR THE "WELCOME HOME" PARTY?
MY BAD.
I'M OFF.
MAYBE NEXT YEAR
CIFIC
ATLAN
WHAT IS THE PURPOSE OF YOUR TRIP?
PANAMA CANAL
Customs
I'M TRYING TO GET TO THE ATLANTIC OCEAN SO I CAN FIND A MATE.
NAMA CA
Customs
YOU'LL NEED AN L-1 MATING VISA. HERE. IT'S GOOD FOR TWO YEARS.
STAMP! STAMP! STAMP! STAMP! STAMP! STAMP!
PANAMA CA
I'M GUESSING YOU'LL BE WANTING AN EXTENSION. FILL THIS OUT.
JUST IN CASE.
PANAMA C
THERE IT IS AT LAST! ASCENSION ISLAND!
A PLACE WHERE SOPHISTICATED TURTLES GATHER TO FIND MATES IN A DIGNIFIED MANNER.
GIRLS!
WITH JUST A HINT OF SPRING BREAK THROWN IN.

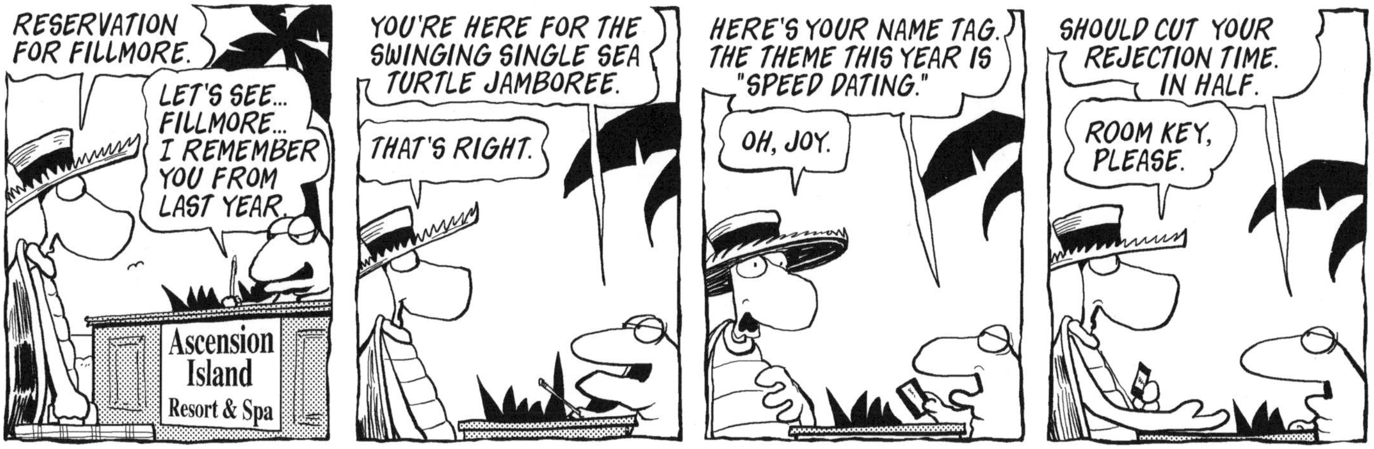
RESERVATION FOR FILLMORE.
LET'S SEE... FILLMORE... I REMEMBER YOU FROM LAST YEAR.
Ascension Island Resort & Spa
YOU'RE HERE FOR THE SWINGING SINGLE SEA TURTLE JAMBOREE.
THAT'S RIGHT.
HERE'S YOUR NAME TAG. THE THEME THIS YEAR IS "SPEED DATING."
OH, JOY.
SHOULD CUT YOUR REJECTION TIME. IN HALF.
ROOM KEY, PLEASE.

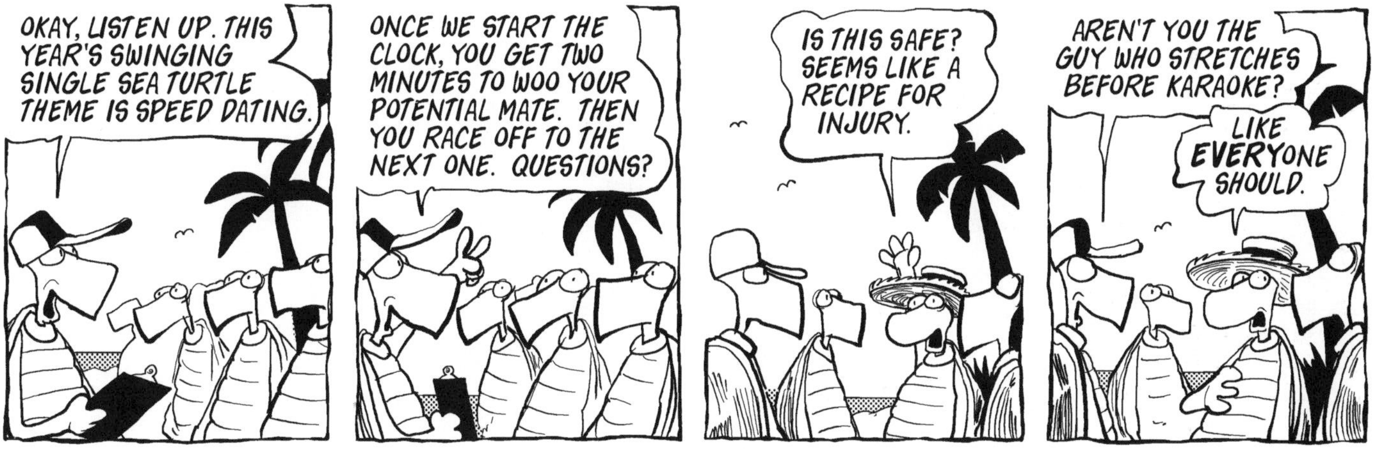
OKAY, LISTEN UP. THIS YEAR'S SWINGING SINGLE SEA TURTLE THEME IS SPEED DATING.
ONCE WE START THE CLOCK, YOU GET TWO MINUTES TO WOO YOUR POTENTIAL MATE. THEN YOU RACE OFF TO THE NEXT ONE. QUESTIONS?
IS THIS SAFE? SEEMS LIKE A RECIPE FOR INJURY.
AREN'T YOU THE GUY WHO STRETCHES BEFORE KARAOKE?
LIKE EVERYONE SHOULD.

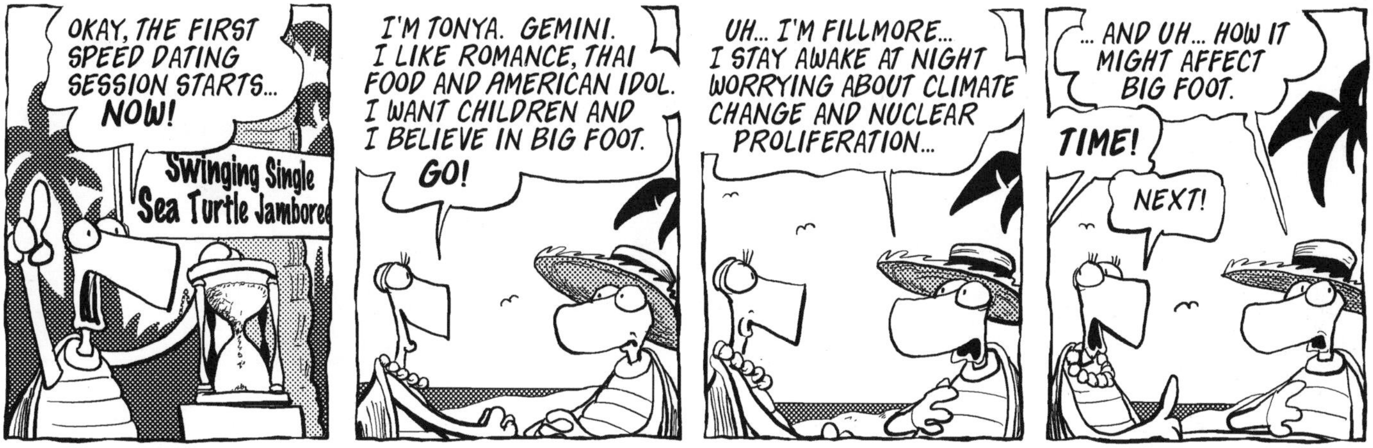
OKAY, THE FIRST SPEED DATING SESSION STARTS... NOW!
Swinging Single Sea Turtle Jamboree
I'M TONYA. GEMINI. I LIKE ROMANCE, THAI FOOD AND AMERICAN IDOL. I WANT CHILDREN AND I BELIEVE IN BIG FOOT.
GO!
UH... I'M FILLMORE... I STAY AWAKE AT NIGHT WORRYING ABOUT CLIMATE CHANGE AND NUCLEAR PROLIFERATION...
... AND UH... HOW IT MIGHT AFFECT BIG FOOT.
TIME!
NEXT!

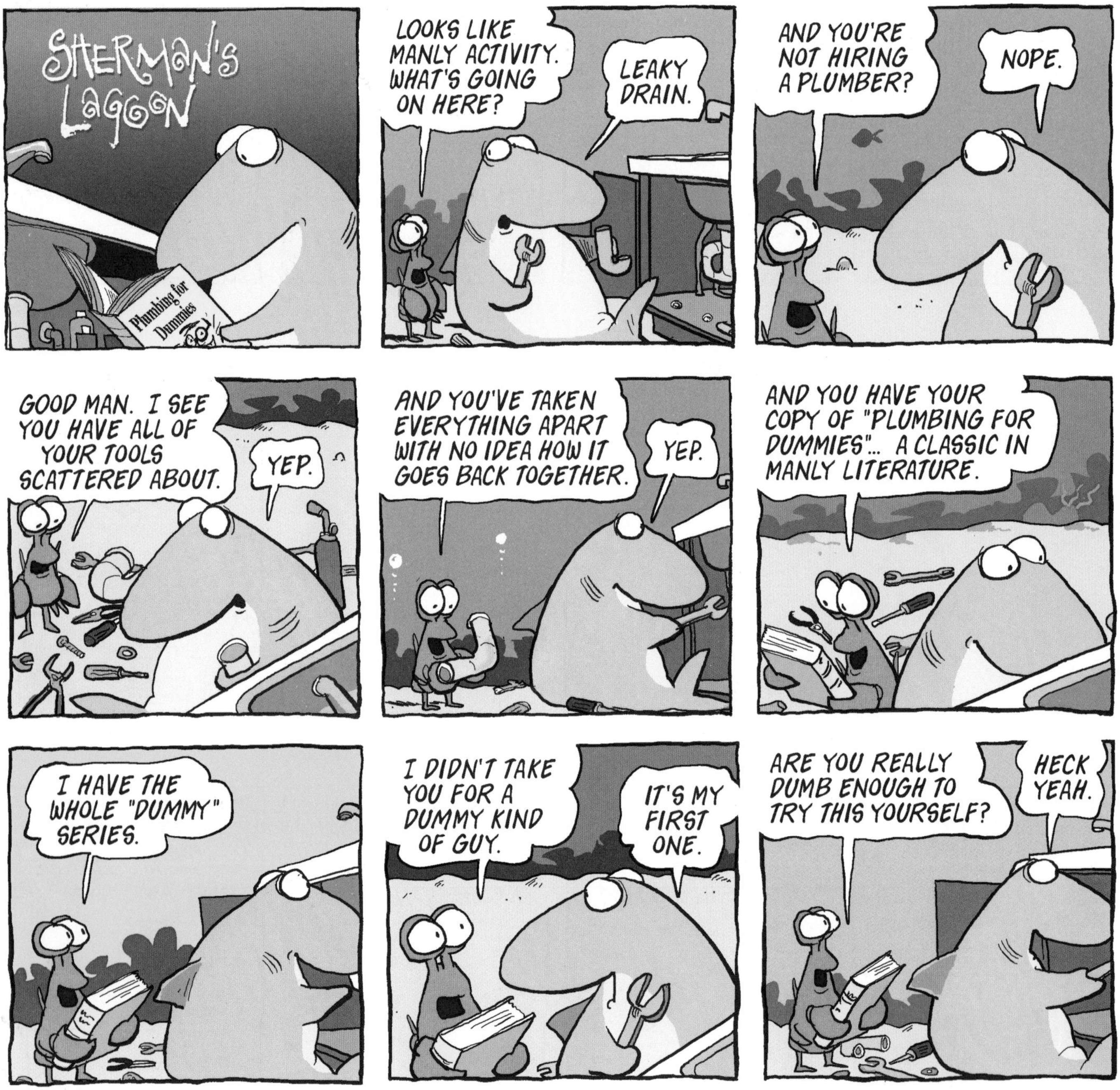
SHERMAN'S LAGOON
Plumbing for Dummies
LOOKS LIKE MANLY ACTIVITY. WHAT'S GOING ON HERE?
LEAKY DRAIN.
AND YOU'RE NOT HIRING A PLUMBER?
NOPE.
GOOD MAN. I SEE YOU HAVE ALL OF YOUR TOOLS SCATTERED ABOUT.
YEP.
AND YOU'VE TAKEN EVERYTHING APART WITH NO IDEA HOW IT GOES BACK TOGETHER.
YEP.
AND YOU HAVE YOUR COPY OF "PLUMBING FOR DUMMIES"... A CLASSIC IN MANLY LITERATURE.
I HAVE THE WHOLE "DUMMY" SERIES.
I DIDN'T TAKE YOU FOR A DUMMY KIND OF GUY.
IT'S MY FIRST ONE.
ARE YOU REALLY DUMB ENOUGH TO TRY THIS YOURSELF?
HECK YEAH.

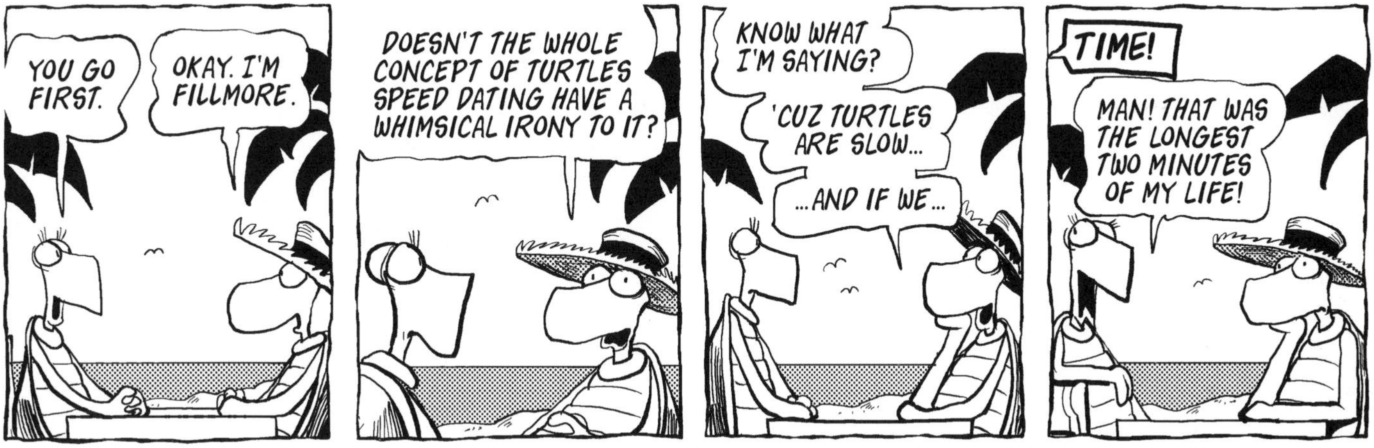
YOU GO FIRST.
OKAY. I'M FILLMORE.
DOESN'T THE WHOLE CONCEPT OF TURTLES SPEED DATING HAVE A WHIMSICAL IRONY TO IT?
KNOW WHAT I'M SAYING?
'CUZ TURTLES ARE SLOW...
...AND IF WE...
TIME!
MAN! THAT WAS THE LONGEST TWO MINUTES OF MY LIFE!

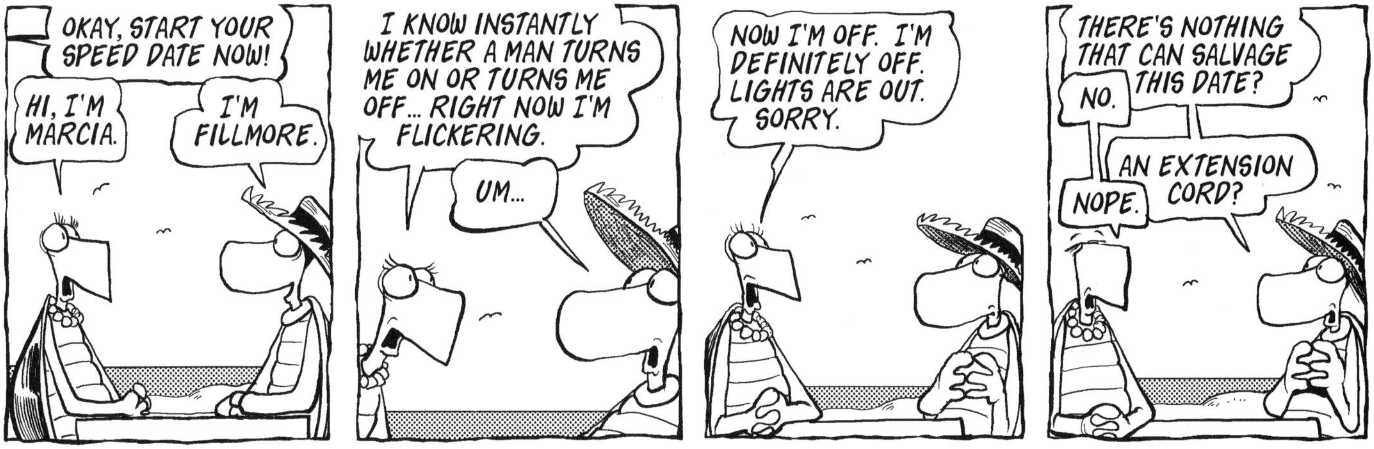
OKAY, START YOUR SPEED DATE NOW!
HI, I'M MARCIA.
I'M FILLMORE.
I KNOW INSTANTLY WHETHER A MAN TURNS ME ON OR TURNS ME OFF... RIGHT NOW I'M FLICKERING.
UM...
NOW I'M OFF. I'M DEFINITELY OFF. LIGHTS ARE OUT. SORRY.
THERE'S NOTHING THAT CAN SALVAGE THIS DATE?
NO.
AN EXTENSION CORD?
NOPE.

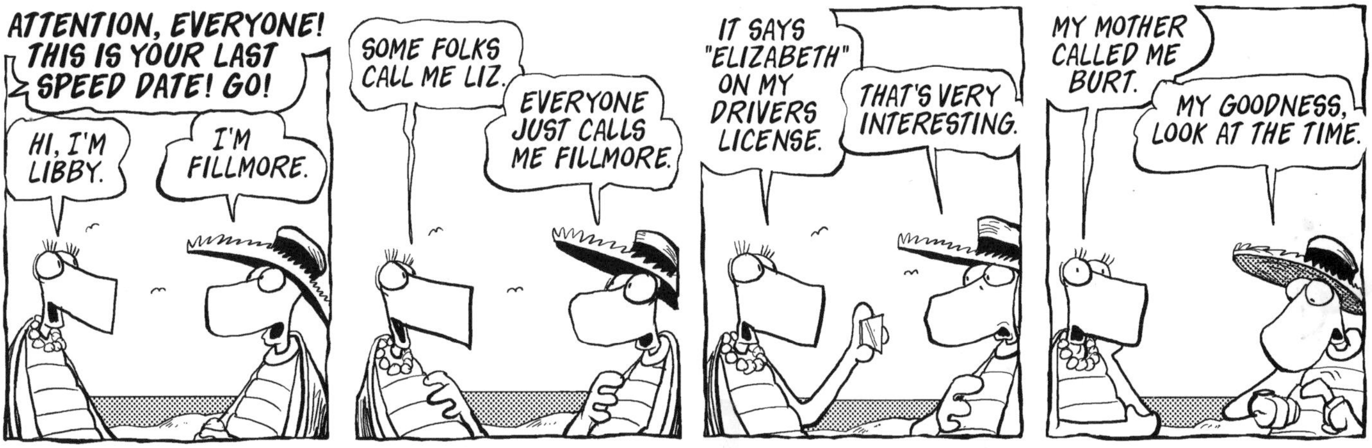
ATTENTION, EVERYONE! THIS IS YOUR LAST SPEED DATE! GO!
HI, I'M LIBBY.
I'M FILLMORE.
SOME FOLKS CALL ME LIZ.
EVERYONE JUST CALLS ME FILLMORE.
IT SAYS "ELIZABETH" ON MY DRIVERS LICENSE.
THAT'S VERY INTERESTING.
MY MOTHER CALLED ME BURT.
MY GOODNESS, LOOK AT THE TIME.

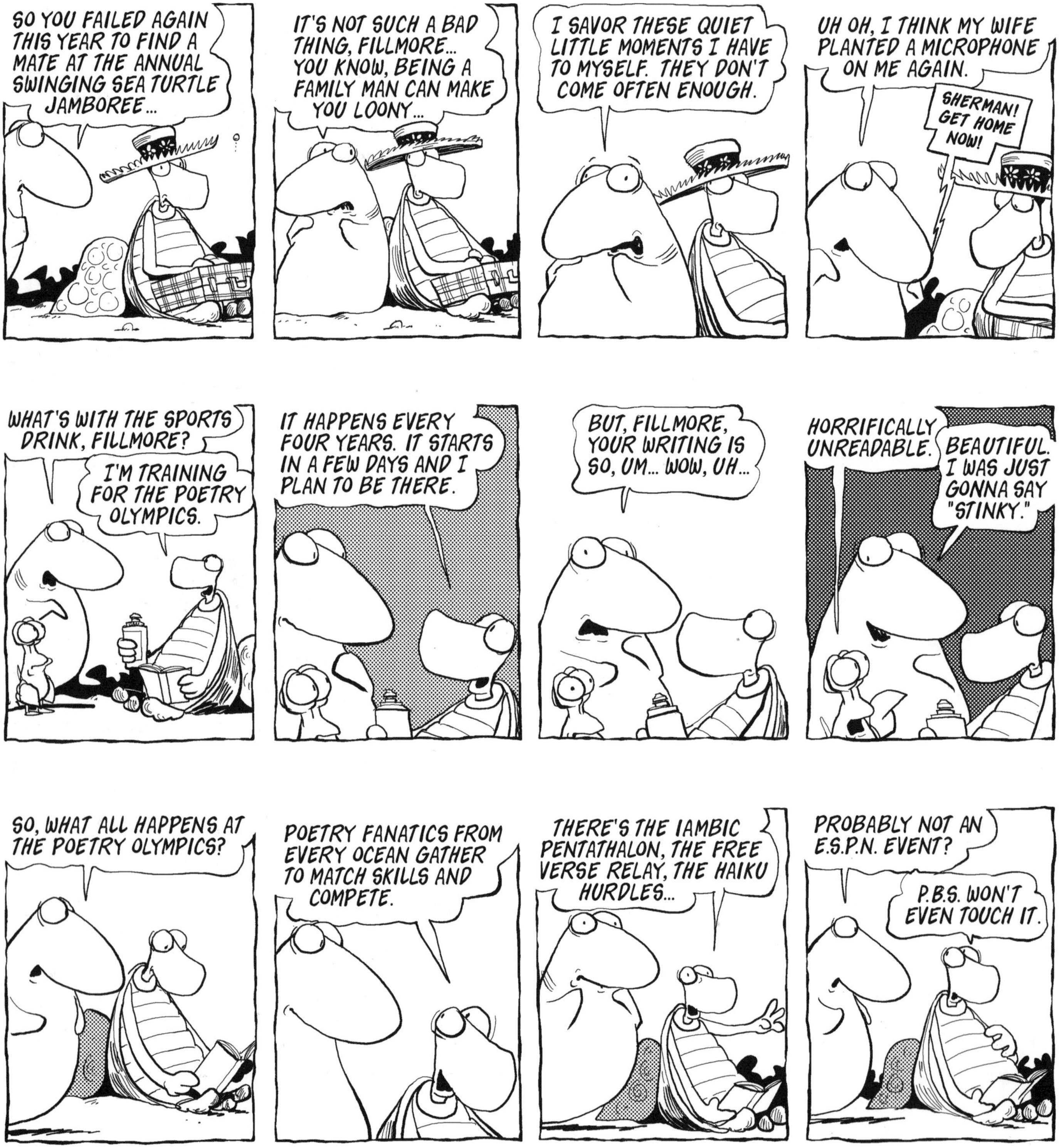
SO YOU FAILED AGAIN THIS YEAR TO FIND A MATE AT THE ANNUAL SWINGING SEA TURTLE JAMBOREE...
IT'S NOT SUCH A BAD THING, FILLMORE... YOU KNOW, BEING A FAMILY MAN CAN MAKE YOU LOONY...
I SAVOR THESE QUIET LITTLE MOMENTS I HAVE TO MYSELF. THEY DON'T COME OFTEN ENOUGH.
UH OH, I THINK MY WIFE PLANTED A MICROPHONE ON ME AGAIN.
SHERMAN! GET HOME NOW!
WHAT'S WITH THE SPORTS DRINK, FILLMORE?
I'M TRAINING FOR THE POETRY OLYMPICS.
IT HAPPENS EVERY FOUR YEARS. IT STARTS IN A FEW DAYS AND I PLAN TO BE THERE.
BUT, FILLMORE, YOUR WRITING IS SO, UM... WOW, UH...
HORRIFICALLY UNREADABLE.
BEAUTIFUL. I WAS JUST GONNA SAY "STINKY."
SO, WHAT ALL HAPPENS AT THE POETRY OLYMPICS?
POETRY FANATICS FROM EVERY OCEAN GATHER TO MATCH SKILLS AND COMPETE.
THERE'S THE IAMBIC PENTATHALON, THE FREE VERSE RELAY, THE HAIKU HURDLES...
PROBABLY NOT AN E.S.P.N. EVENT?
P.B.S. WON'T EVEN TOUCH IT.

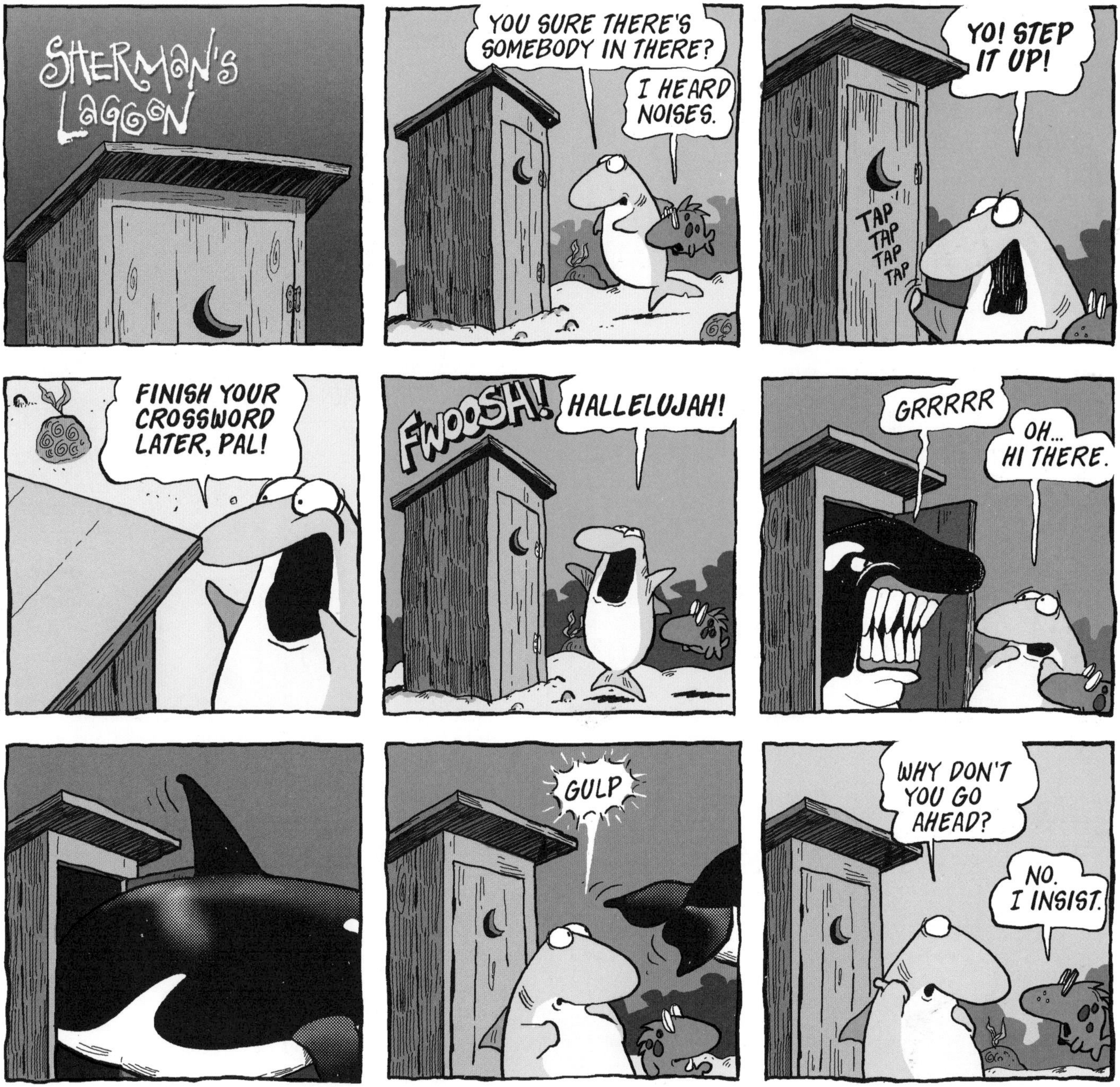
SHERMAN'S LAGOON
YOU SURE THERE'S SOMEBODY IN THERE?
I HEARD NOISES.
TAP TAP TAP TAP
YO! STEP IT UP!
FINISH YOUR CROSSWORD LATER, PAL!
FWOOSH!
HALLELUJAH!
GRRRRR
OH... HI THERE.
GULP
WHY DON'T YOU GO AHEAD?
NO. I INSIST.

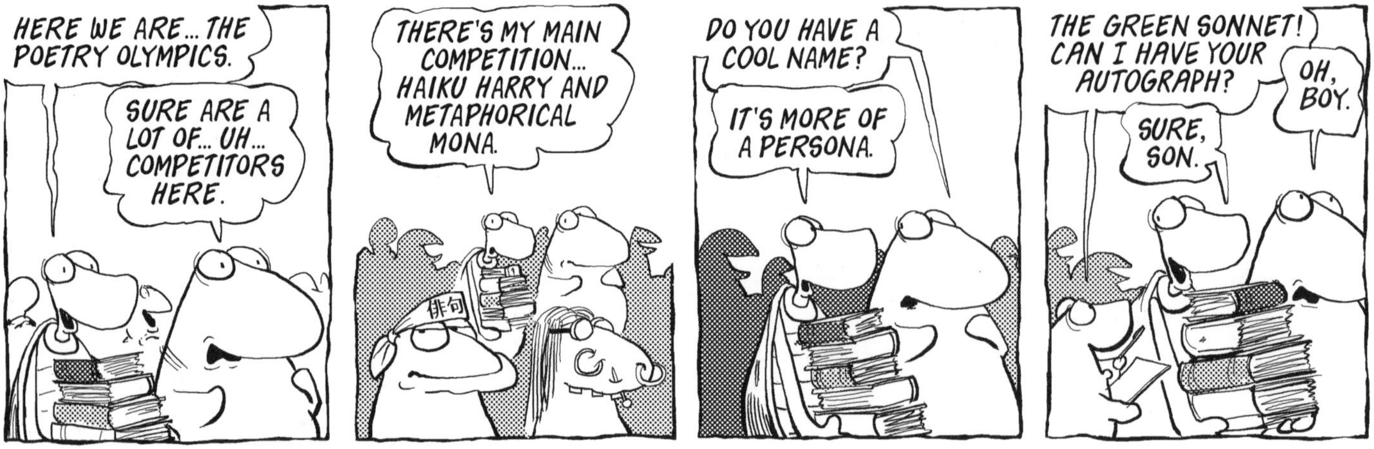
HERE WE ARE... THE POETRY OLYMPICS.
SURE ARE A LOT OF... UH... COMPETITORS HERE.
THERE'S MY MAIN COMPETITION... HAIKU HARRY AND METAPHORICAL MONA.
俳句
DO YOU HAVE A COOL NAME?
IT'S MORE OF A PERSONA.
THE GREEN SONNET! CAN I HAVE YOUR AUTOGRAPH?
SURE, SON.
OH, BOY.

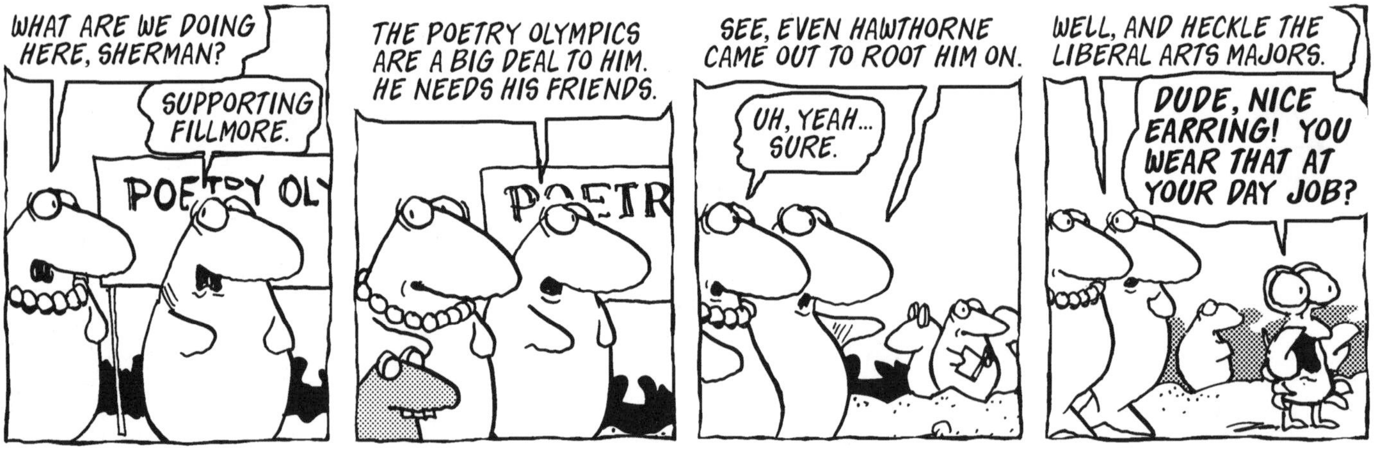
WHAT ARE WE DOING HERE, SHERMAN?
SUPPORTING FILLMORE.
THE POETRY OLYMPICS ARE A BIG DEAL TO HIM. HE NEEDS HIS FRIENDS.
SEE, EVEN HAWTHORNE CAME OUT TO ROOT HIM ON.
UH, YEAH... SURE.
WELL, AND HECKLE THE LIBERAL ARTS MAJORS.
DUDE, NICE EARRING! YOU WEAR THAT AT YOUR DAY JOB?

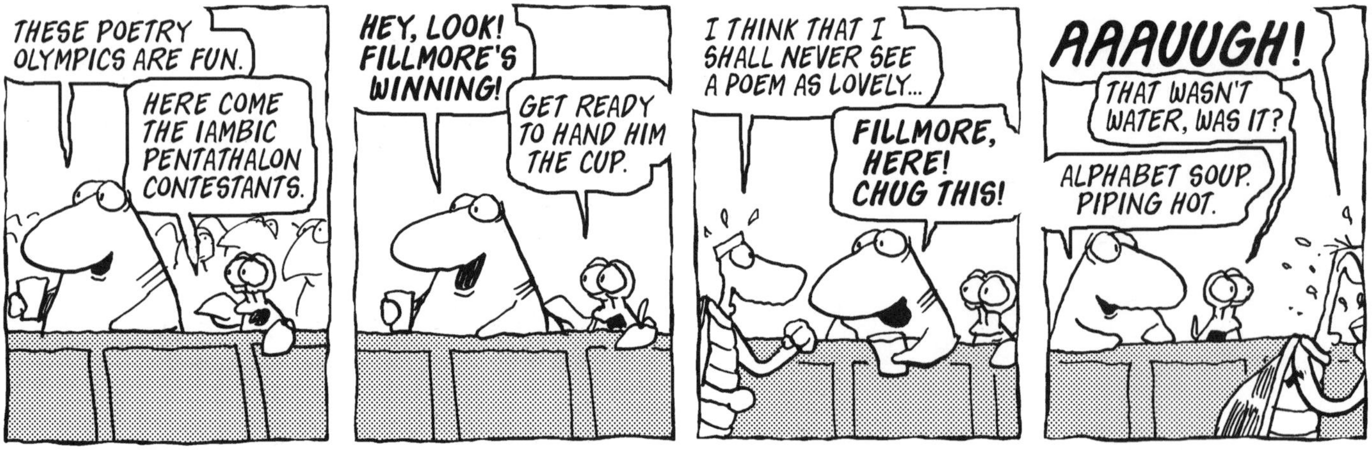
THESE POETRY OLYMPICS ARE FUN.
HERE COME THE IAMBIC PENTATHALON CONTESTANTS.
HEY, LOOK! FILLMORE'S WINNING!
GET READY TO HAND HIM THE CUP.
I THINK THAT I SHALL NEVER SEE A POEM AS LOVELY...
FILLMORE, HERE! CHUG THIS!
AAAUUGH!
THAT WASN'T WATER, WAS IT?
ALPHABET SOUP. PIPING HOT.

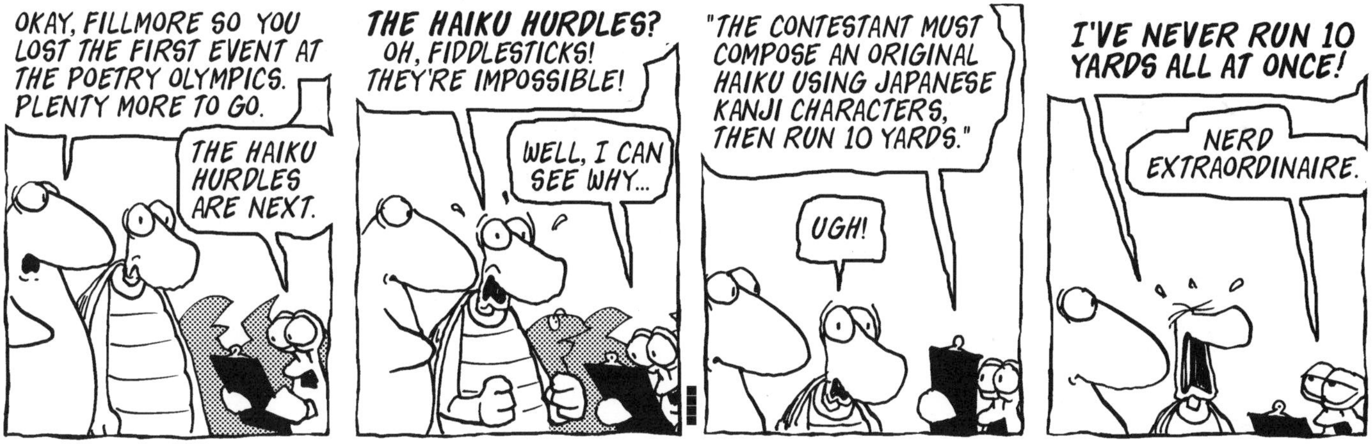
OKAY, FILLMORE SO YOU LOST THE FIRST EVENT AT THE POETRY OLYMPICS. PLENTY MORE TO GO.
THE HAIKU HURDLES ARE NEXT.
THE HAIKU HURDLES? OH, FIDDLESTICKS! THEY'RE IMPOSSIBLE!
WELL, I CAN SEE WHY...
"THE CONTESTANT MUST COMPOSE AN ORIGINAL HAIKU USING JAPANESE KANJI CHARACTERS, THEN RUN 10 YARDS."
UGH!
I'VE NEVER RUN 10 YARDS ALL AT ONCE!
NERD EXTRAORDINAIRE.

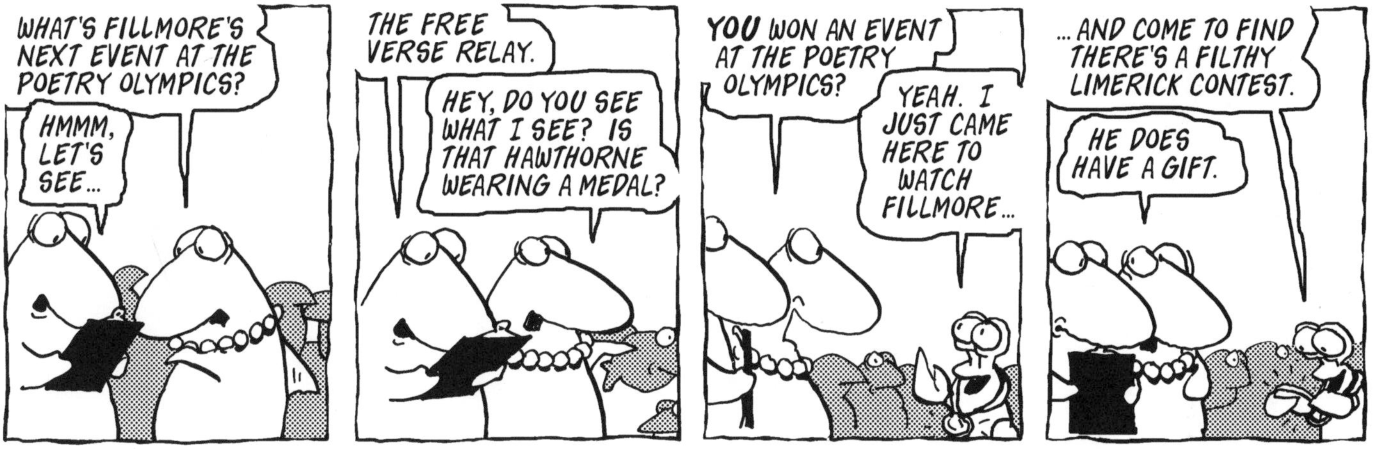
WHAT'S FILLMORE'S NEXT EVENT AT THE POETRY OLYMPICS?
HMMM, LET'S SEE...
THE FREE VERSE RELAY.
HEY, DO YOU SEE WHAT I SEE? IS THAT HAWTHORNE WEARING A MEDAL?
YOU WON AN EVENT AT THE POETRY OLYMPICS?
YEAH. I JUST CAME HERE TO WATCH FILLMORE...
...AND COME TO FIND THERE'S A FILTHY LIMERICK CONTEST.
HE DOES HAVE A GIFT.

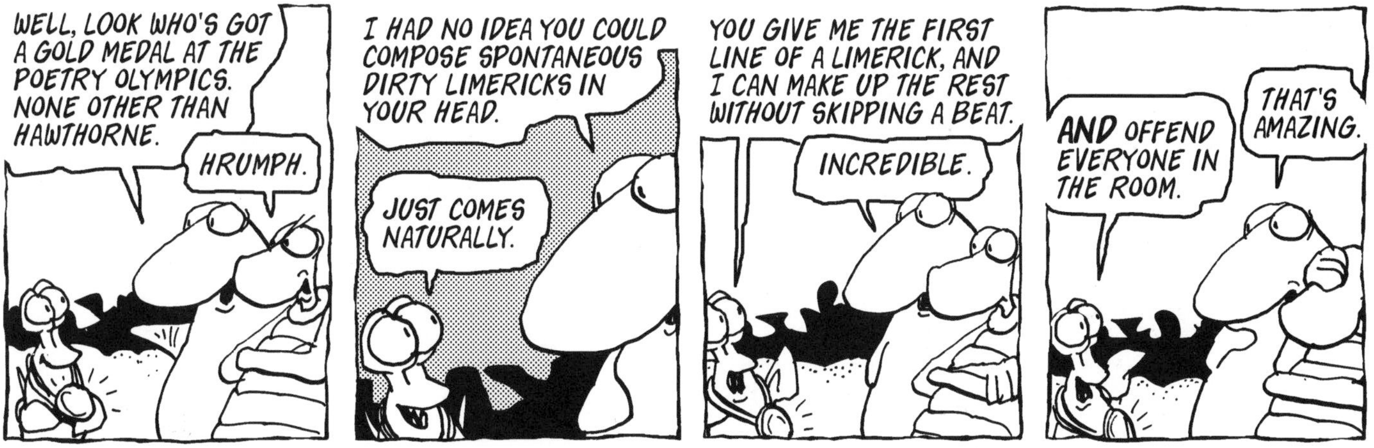
WELL, LOOK WHO'S GOT A GOLD MEDAL AT THE POETRY OLYMPICS. NONE OTHER THAN HAWTHORNE.
HRUMPH.
I HAD NO IDEA YOU COULD COMPOSE SPONTANEOUS DIRTY LIMERICKS IN YOUR HEAD.
JUST COMES NATURALLY.
YOU GIVE ME THE FIRST LINE OF A LIMERICK, AND I CAN MAKE UP THE REST WITHOUT SKIPPING A BEAT.
INCREDIBLE.
AND OFFEND EVERYONE IN THE ROOM.
THAT'S AMAZING.

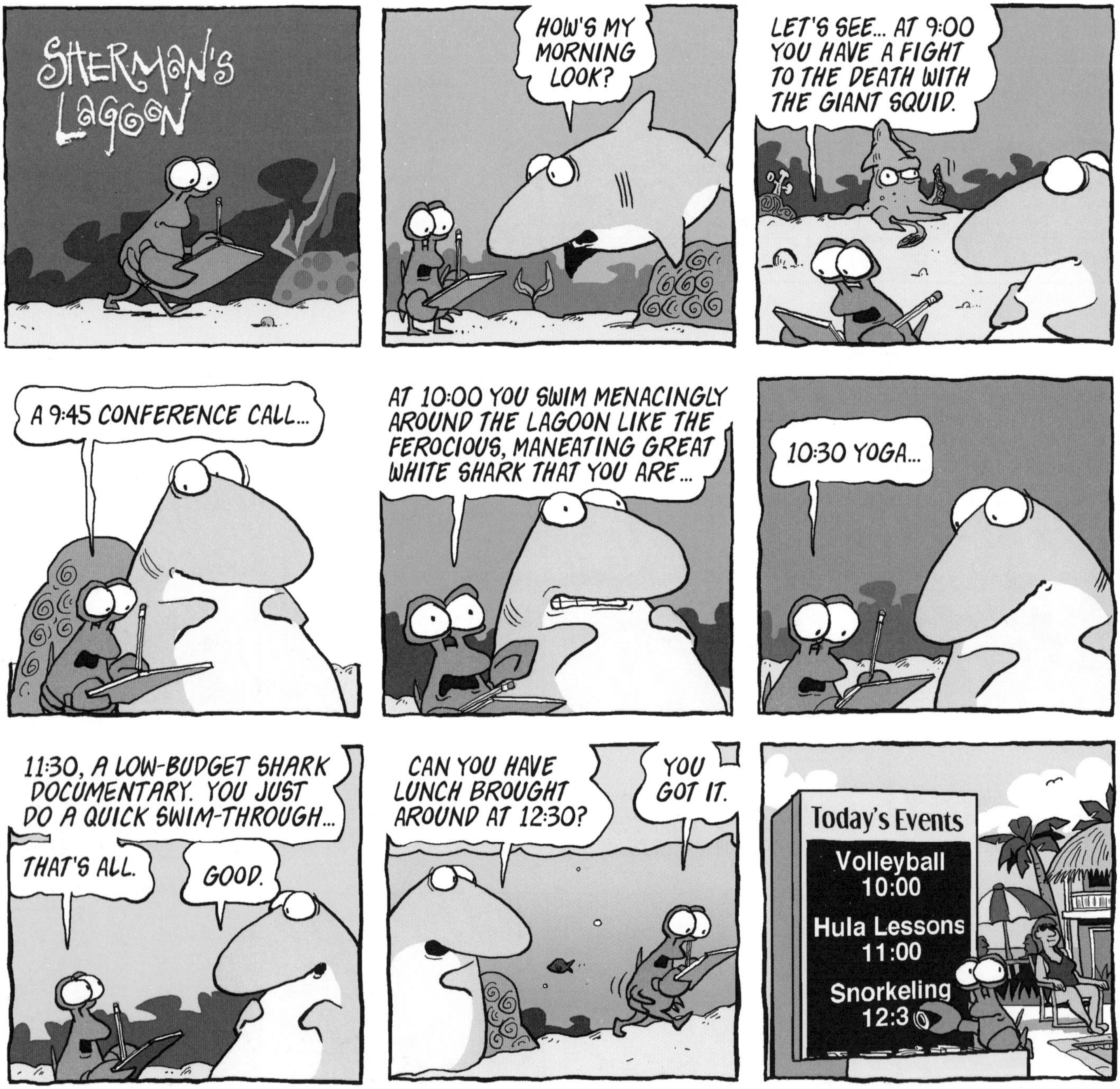
SHERMAN'S LAGOON
HOW'S MY MORNING LOOK?
LET'S SEE... AT 9:00 YOU HAVE A FIGHT TO THE DEATH WITH THE GIANT SQUID.
A 9:45 CONFERENCE CALL...
AT 10:00 YOU SWIM MENACINGLY AROUND THE LAGOON LIKE THE FEROCIOUS, MANEATING GREAT WHITE SHARK THAT YOU ARE...
10:30 YOGA...
11:30, A LOW-BUDGET SHARK DOCUMENTARY. YOU JUST DO A QUICK SWIM-THROUGH...
THAT'S ALL.
GOOD.
CAN YOU HAVE LUNCH BROUGHT AROUND AT 12:30?
YOU GOT IT.
Today's Events
Volleyball
10:00
Hula Lessons
11:00
Snorkeling
12:3

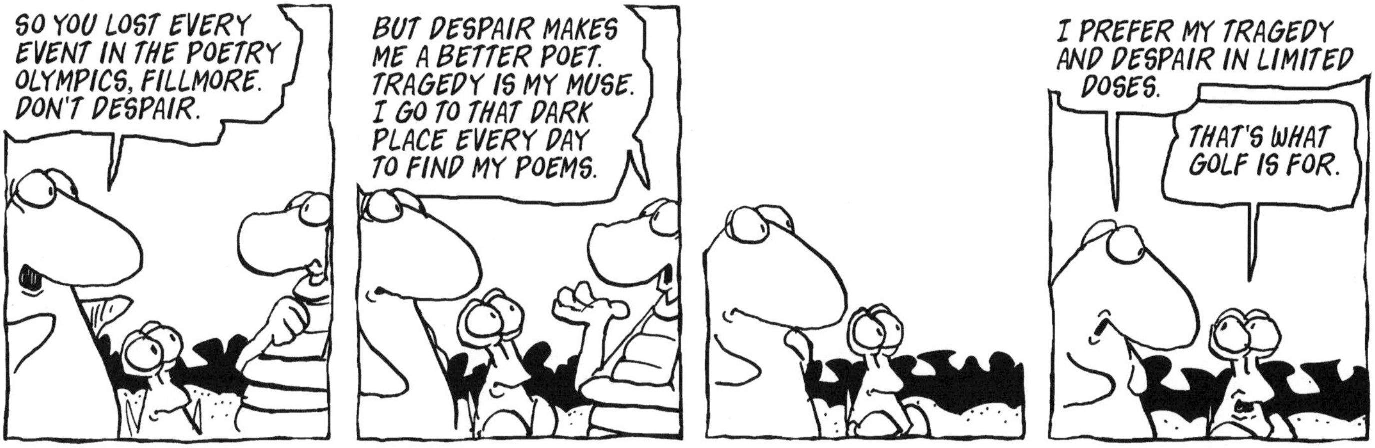
SO YOU LOST EVERY EVENT IN THE POETRY OLYMPICS, FILLMORE. DON'T DESPAIR.
BUT DESPAIR MAKES ME A BETTER POET. TRAGEDY IS MY MUSE. I GO TO THAT DARK PLACE EVERY DAY TO FIND MY POEMS.
I PREFER MY TRAGEDY AND DESPAIR IN LIMITED DOSES.
THAT'S WHAT GOLF IS FOR.

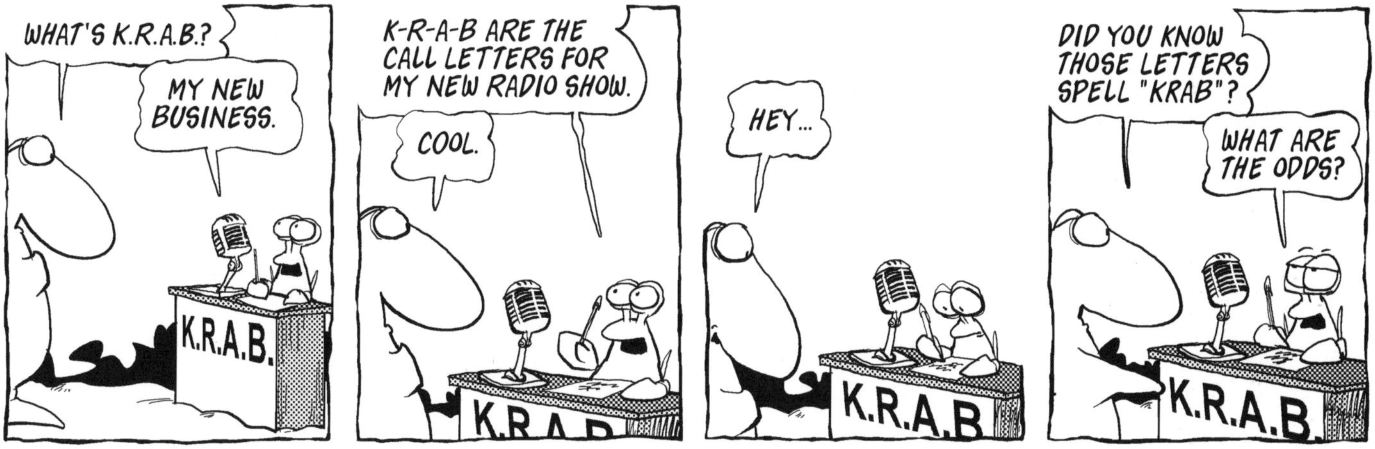
WHAT'S K.R.A.B.?
MY NEW BUSINESS.
K.R.A.B.
K-R-A-B ARE THE CALL LETTERS FOR MY NEW RADIO SHOW.
COOL.
HEY...
K.R.A.B
DID YOU KNOW THOSE LETTERS SPELL "KRAB"?
WHAT ARE THE ODDS?
K.R.A.B.

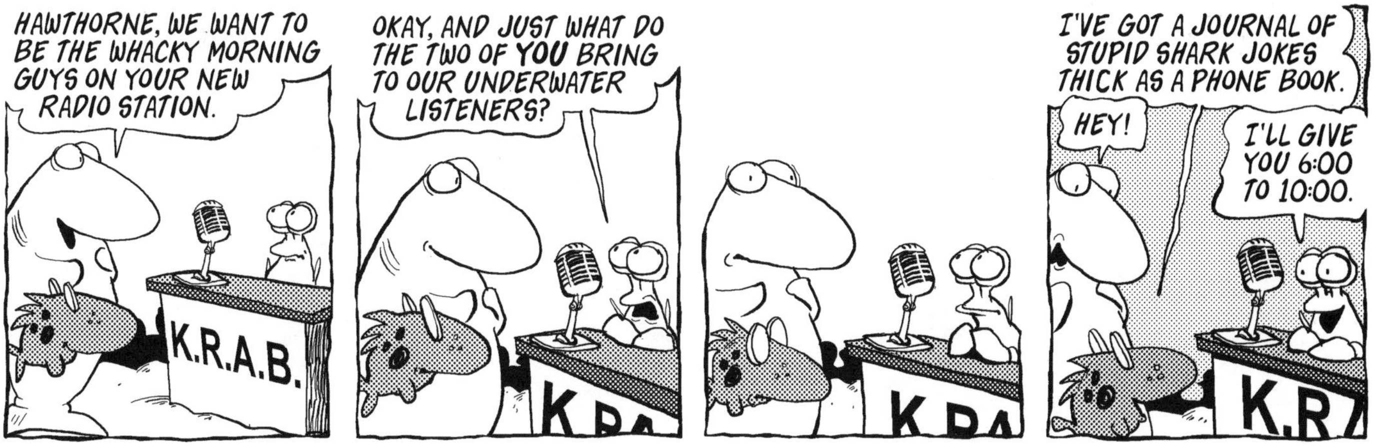
HAWTHORNE, WE WANT TO BE THE WHACKY MORNING GUYS ON YOUR NEW RADIO STATION.
K.R.A.B.
OKAY, AND JUST WHAT DO THE TWO OF **YOU** BRING TO OUR UNDERWATER LISTENERS?
I'VE GOT A JOURNAL OF STUPID SHARK JOKES THICK AS A PHONE BOOK.
HEY!
I'LL GIVE YOU 6:00 TO 10:00.

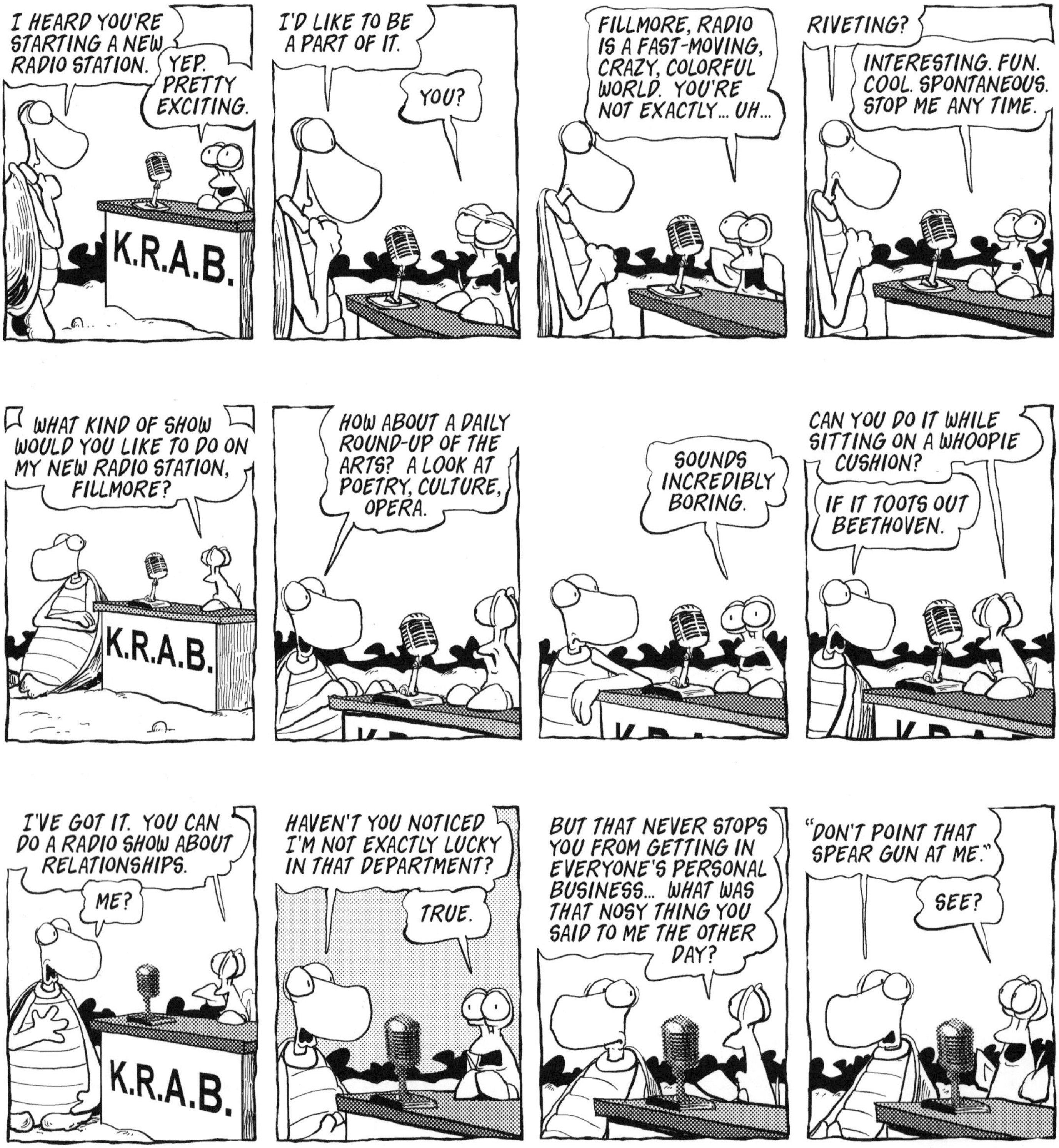
I HEARD YOU'RE STARTING A NEW RADIO STATION.
YEP. PRETTY EXCITING.
K.R.A.B.
I'D LIKE TO BE A PART OF IT.
YOU?
FILLMORE, RADIO IS A FAST-MOVING, CRAZY, COLORFUL WORLD. YOU'RE NOT EXACTLY... UH...
RIVETING?
INTERESTING. FUN. COOL. SPONTANEOUS. STOP ME ANY TIME.
WHAT KIND OF SHOW WOULD YOU LIKE TO DO ON MY NEW RADIO STATION, FILLMORE?
K.R.A.B.
HOW ABOUT A DAILY ROUND-UP OF THE ARTS? A LOOK AT POETRY, CULTURE, OPERA.
SOUNDS INCREDIBLY BORING.
CAN YOU DO IT WHILE SITTING ON A WHOOPIE CUSHION?
IF IT TOOTS OUT BEETHOVEN.
I'VE GOT IT. YOU CAN DO A RADIO SHOW ABOUT RELATIONSHIPS.
ME?
K.R.A.B.
HAVEN'T YOU NOTICED I'M NOT EXACTLY LUCKY IN THAT DEPARTMENT?
TRUE.
BUT THAT NEVER STOPS YOU FROM GETTING IN EVERYONE'S PERSONAL BUSINESS... WHAT WAS THAT NOSY THING YOU SAID TO ME THE OTHER DAY?
"DON'T POINT THAT SPEAR GUN AT ME."
SEE?

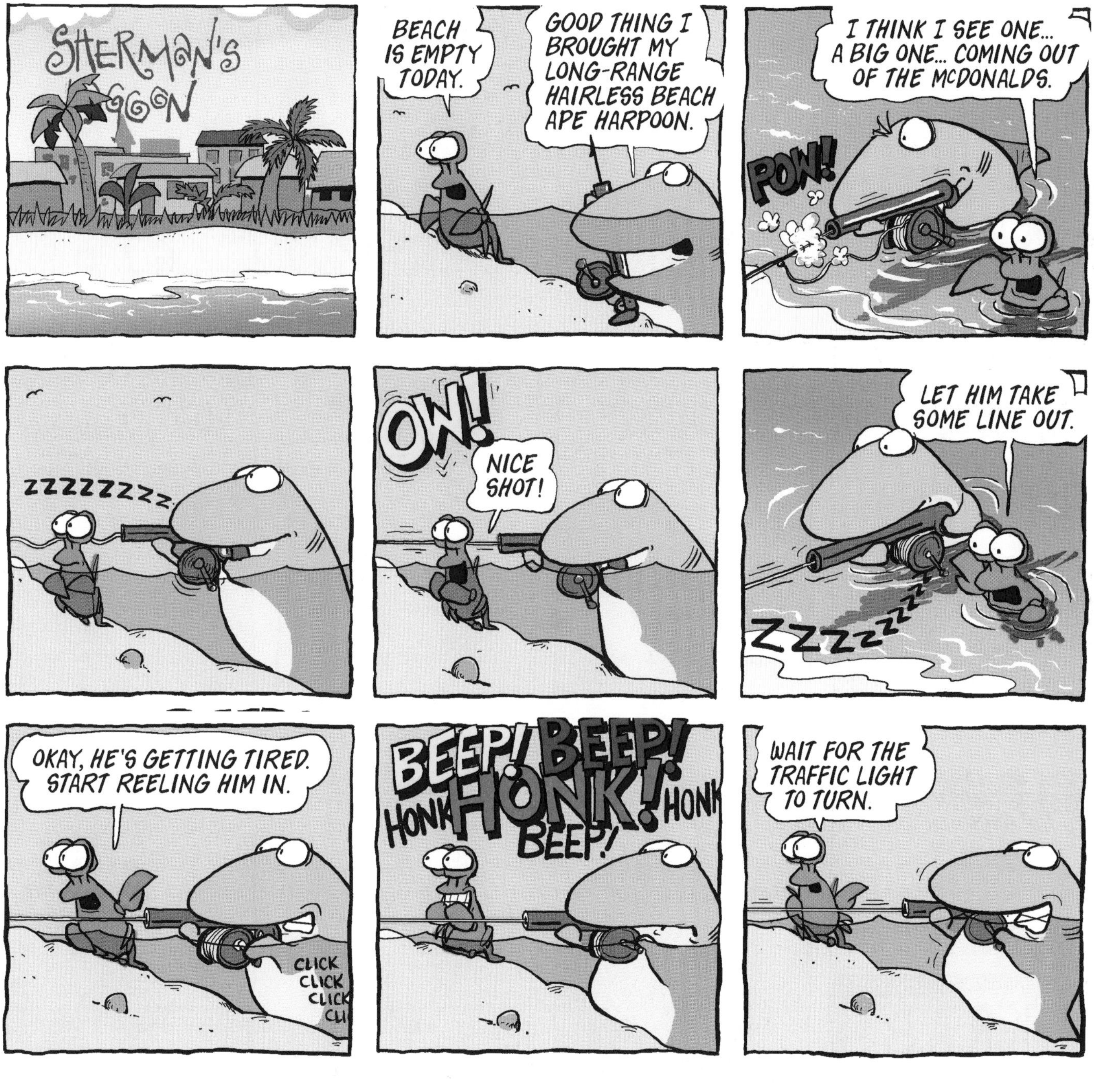
SHERMAN'S LAGOON
BEACH IS EMPTY TODAY.
GOOD THING I BROUGHT MY LONG-RANGE HAIRLESS BEACH APE HARPOON.
I THINK I SEE ONE... A BIG ONE... COMING OUT OF THE McDONALDS.
POW!
ZZZZZZZZ
OW!
NICE SHOT!
LET HIM TAKE SOME LINE OUT.
ZZZZZZZ
OKAY, HE'S GETTING TIRED. START REELING HIM IN.
CLICK CLICK CLICK CLI
BEEP! BEEP! HONK HONK! HONK BEEP!
WAIT FOR THE TRAFFIC LIGHT TO TURN.

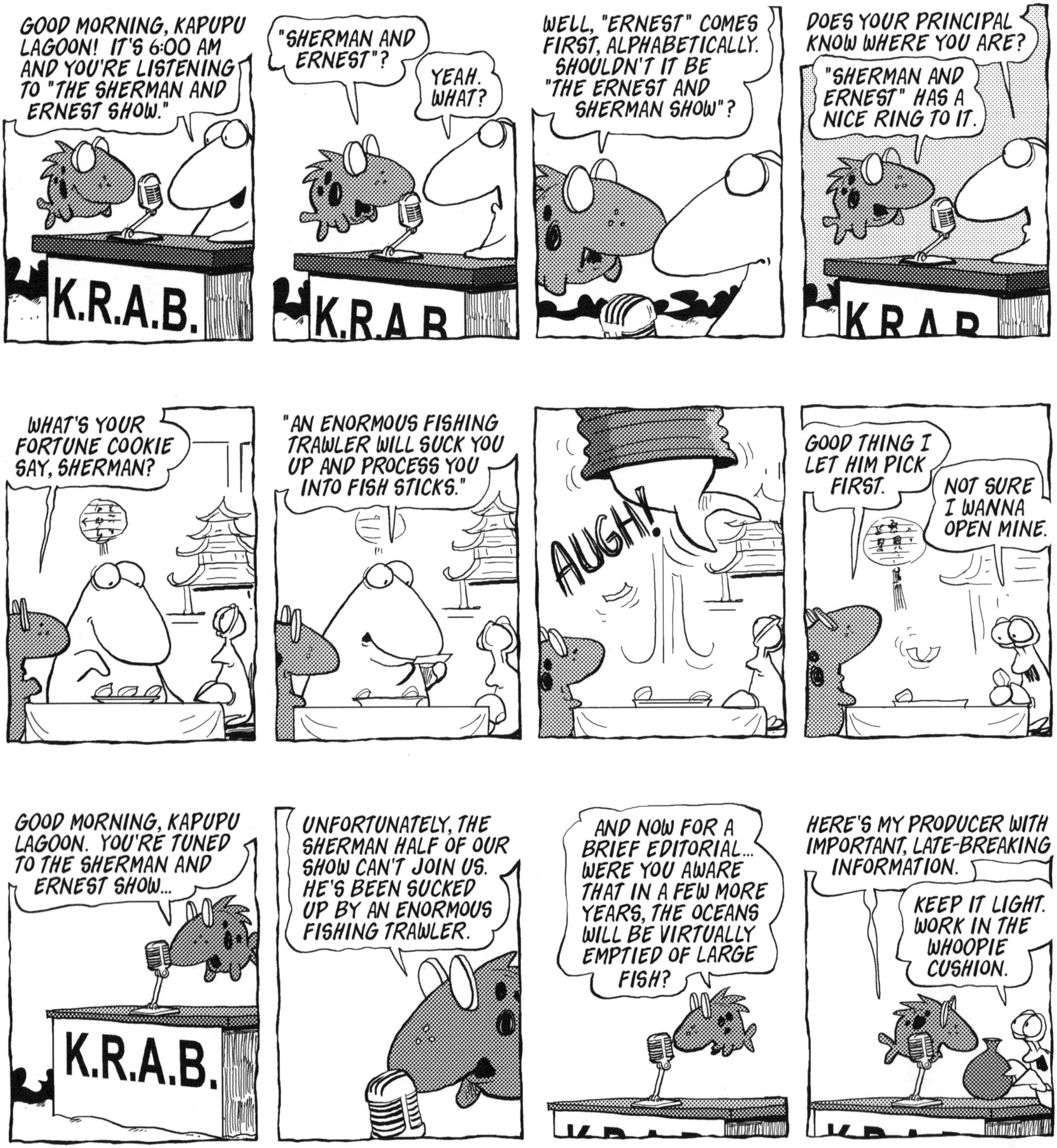
GOOD MORNING, KAPUPU LAGOON! IT'S 6:00 AM AND YOU'RE LISTENING TO "THE SHERMAN AND ERNEST SHOW."
K.R.A.B.
"SHERMAN AND ERNEST"?
YEAH. WHAT?
K.R.A.B
WELL, "ERNEST" COMES FIRST, ALPHABETICALLY. SHOULDN'T IT BE "THE ERNEST AND SHERMAN SHOW"?
DOES YOUR PRINCIPAL KNOW WHERE YOU ARE?
"SHERMAN AND ERNEST" HAS A NICE RING TO IT.
WHAT'S YOUR FORTUNE COOKIE SAY, SHERMAN?
"AN ENORMOUS FISHING TRAWLER WILL SUCK YOU UP AND PROCESS YOU INTO FISH STICKS."
AUGH!
GOOD THING I LET HIM PICK FIRST.
NOT SURE I WANNA OPEN MINE.
GOOD MORNING, KAPUPU LAGOON. YOU'RE TUNED TO THE SHERMAN AND ERNEST SHOW...
K.R.A.B.
UNFORTUNATELY, THE SHERMAN HALF OF OUR SHOW CAN'T JOIN US. HE'S BEEN SUCKED UP BY AN ENORMOUS FISHING TRAWLER.
AND NOW FOR A BRIEF EDITORIAL... WERE YOU AWARE THAT IN A FEW MORE YEARS, THE OCEANS WILL BE VIRTUALLY EMPTIED OF LARGE FISH?
HERE'S MY PRODUCER WITH IMPORTANT, LATE-BREAKING INFORMATION.
KEEP IT LIGHT. WORK IN THE WHOOPIE CUSHION.

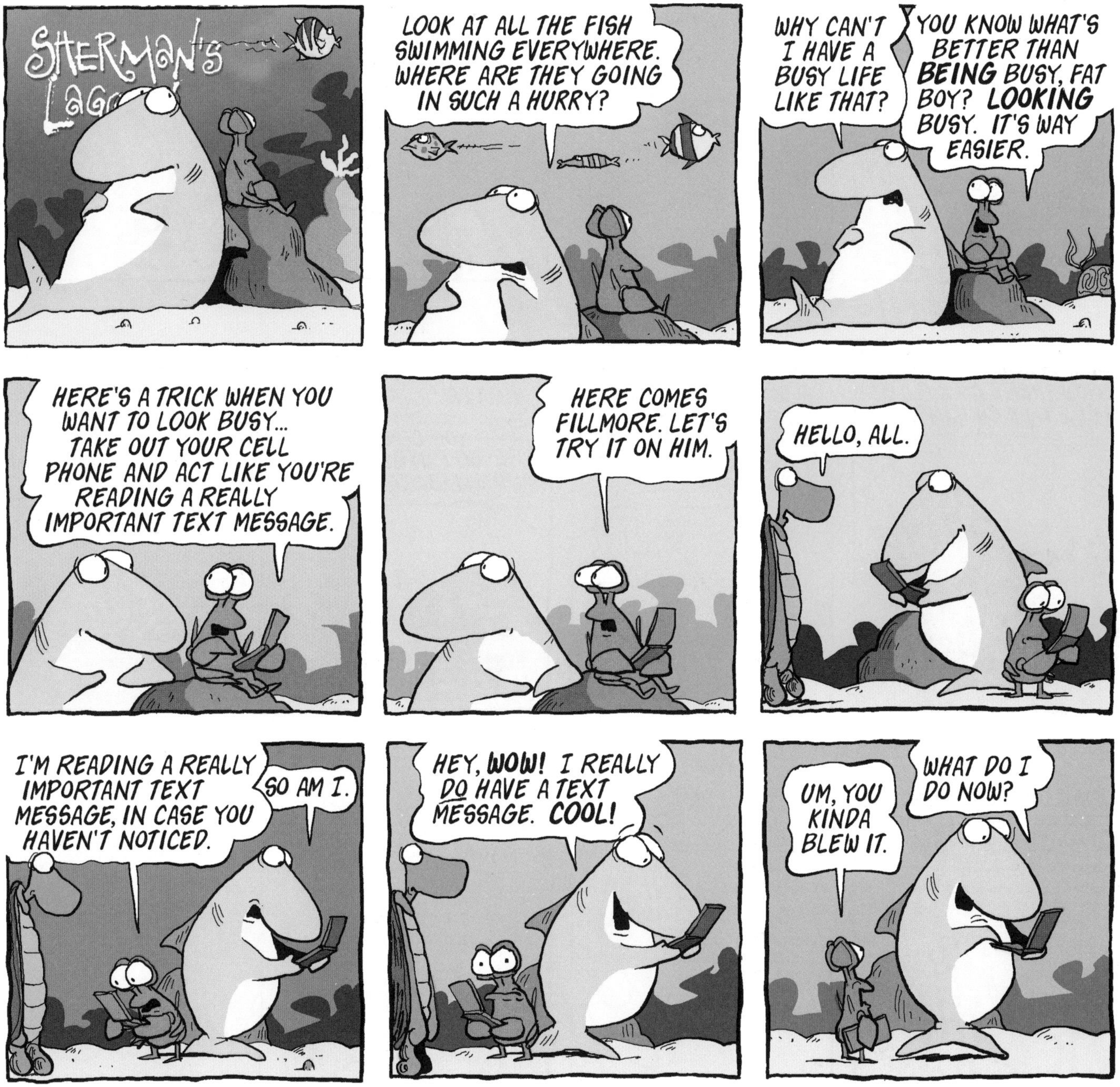
SHERMAN'S LAGOON
LOOK AT ALL THE FISH SWIMMING EVERYWHERE. WHERE ARE THEY GOING IN SUCH A HURRY?
WHY CAN'T I HAVE A BUSY LIFE LIKE THAT?
YOU KNOW WHAT'S BETTER THAN BEING BUSY, FAT BOY? LOOKING BUSY. IT'S WAY EASIER.
HERE'S A TRICK WHEN YOU WANT TO LOOK BUSY... TAKE OUT YOUR CELL PHONE AND ACT LIKE YOU'RE READING A REALLY IMPORTANT TEXT MESSAGE.
HERE COMES FILLMORE. LET'S TRY IT ON HIM.
HELLO, ALL.
I'M READING A REALLY IMPORTANT TEXT MESSAGE, IN CASE YOU HAVEN'T NOTICED.
SO AM I.
HEY, WOW! I REALLY DO HAVE A TEXT MESSAGE. COOL!
UM, YOU KINDA BLEW IT.
WHAT DO I DO NOW?

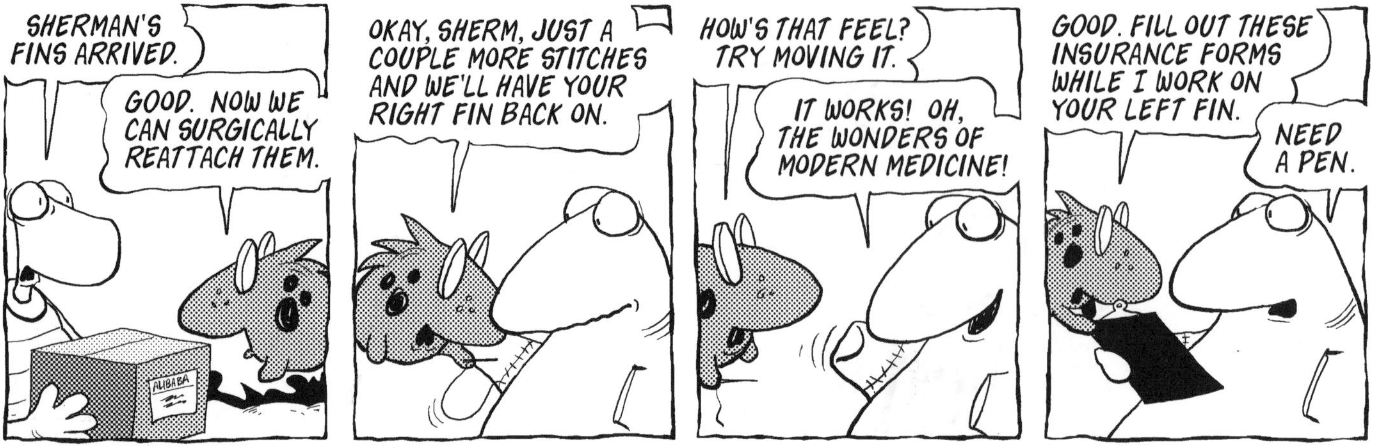
SHERMAN'S FINS ARRIVED.
GOOD. NOW WE CAN SURGICALLY REATTACH THEM.
OKAY, SHERM, JUST A COUPLE MORE STITCHES AND WE'LL HAVE YOUR RIGHT FIN BACK ON.
HOW'S THAT FEEL? TRY MOVING IT.
IT WORKS! OH, THE WONDERS OF MODERN MEDICINE!
GOOD. FILL OUT THESE INSURANCE FORMS WHILE I WORK ON YOUR LEFT FIN.
NEED A PEN.

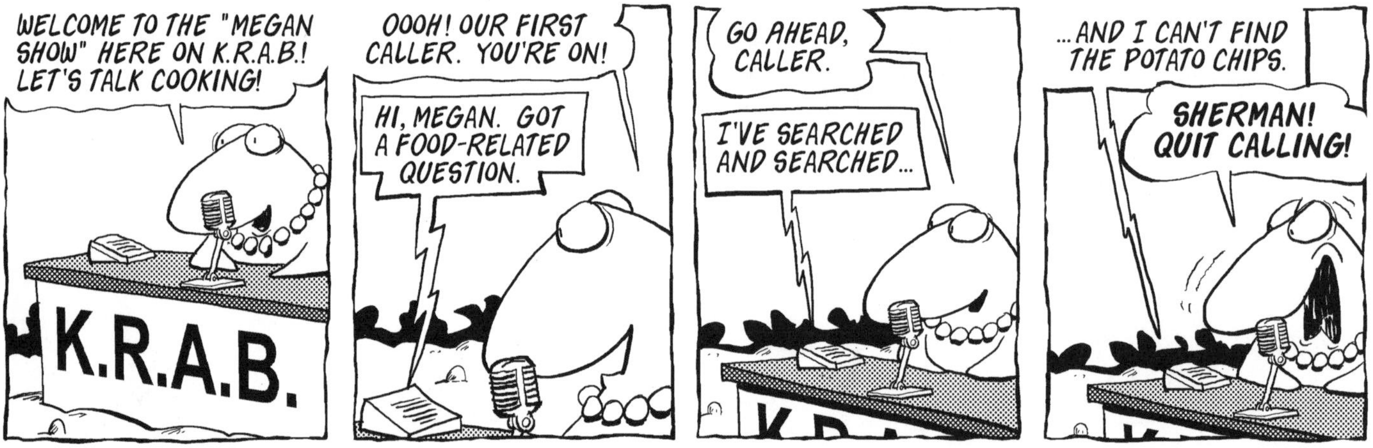
WELCOME TO THE "MEGAN SHOW" HERE ON K.R.A.B.! LET'S TALK COOKING!
K.R.A.B.
OOOH! OUR FIRST CALLER. YOU'RE ON!
HI, MEGAN. GOT A FOOD-RELATED QUESTION.
GO AHEAD, CALLER.
I'VE SEARCHED AND SEARCHED...
...AND I CAN'T FIND THE POTATO CHIPS.
SHERMAN! QUIT CALLING!

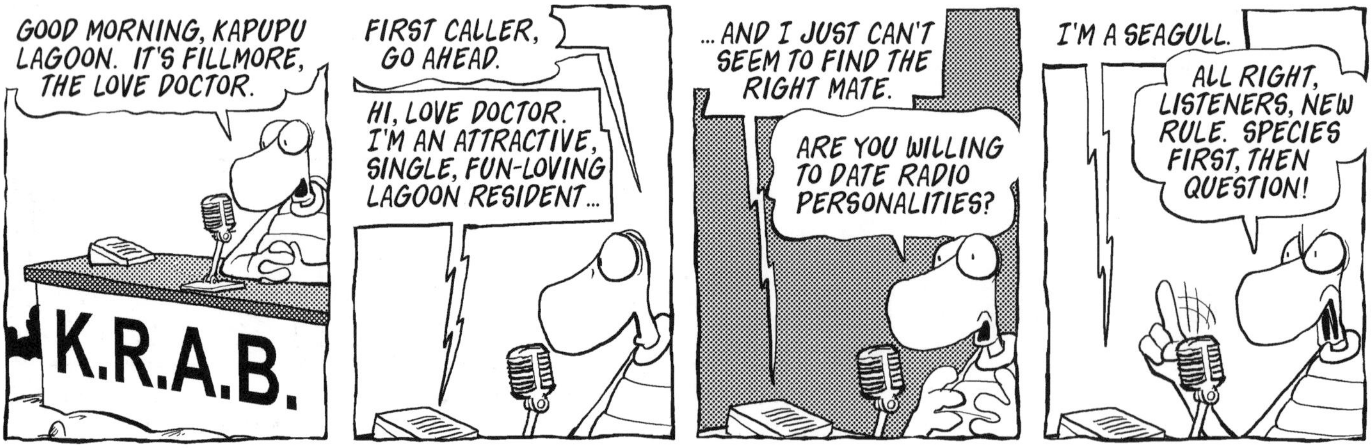
GOOD MORNING, KAPUPU LAGOON. IT'S FILLMORE, THE LOVE DOCTOR.
K.R.A.B.
FIRST CALLER, GO AHEAD.
HI, LOVE DOCTOR. I'M AN ATTRACTIVE, SINGLE, FUN-LOVING LAGOON RESIDENT...
...AND I JUST CAN'T SEEM TO FIND THE RIGHT MATE.
ARE YOU WILLING TO DATE RADIO PERSONALITIES?
I'M A SEAGULL.
ALL RIGHT, LISTENERS, NEW RULE. SPECIES FIRST, THEN QUESTION!

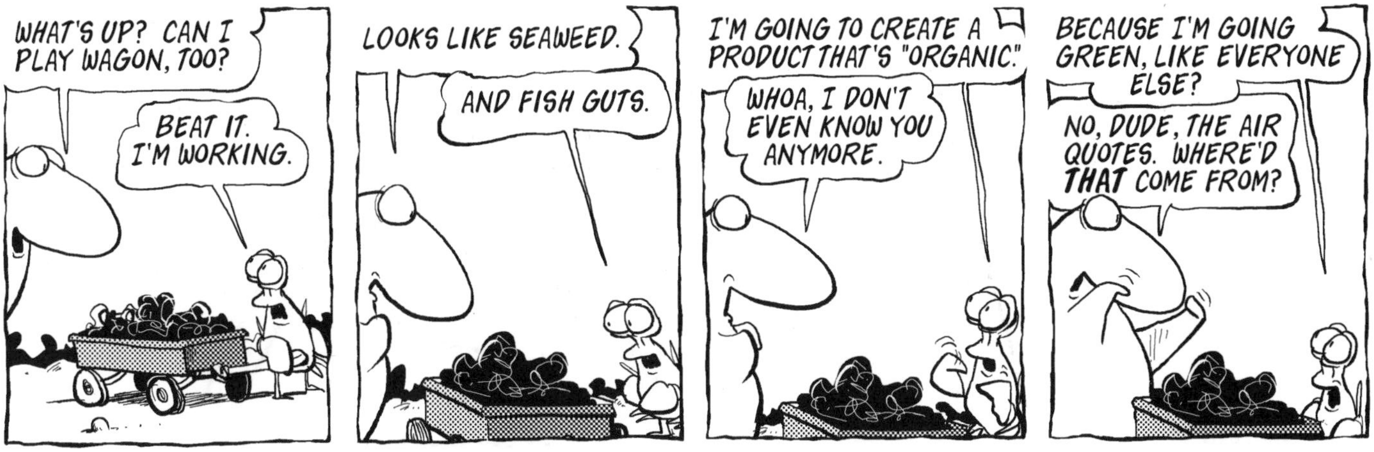
WHAT'S UP? CAN I PLAY WAGON, TOO?
BEAT IT. I'M WORKING.
LOOKS LIKE SEAWEED.
AND FISH GUTS.
I'M GOING TO CREATE A PRODUCT THAT'S "ORGANIC."
WHOA, I DON'T EVEN KNOW YOU ANYMORE.
BECAUSE I'M GOING GREEN, LIKE EVERYONE ELSE?
NO, DUDE, THE AIR QUOTES. WHERE'D **THAT** COME FROM?

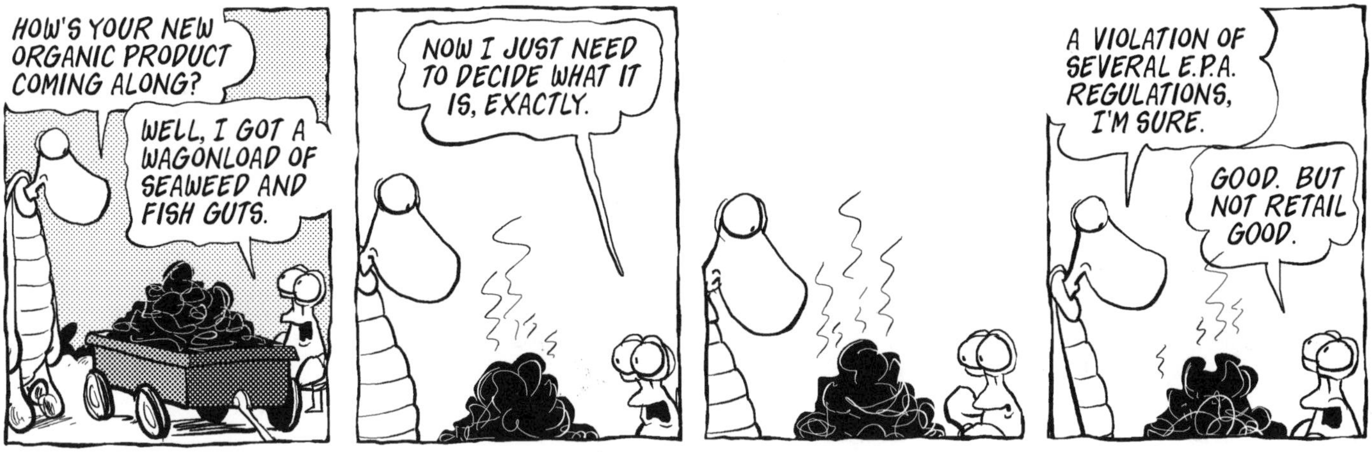
HOW'S YOUR NEW ORGANIC PRODUCT COMING ALONG?
WELL, I GOT A WAGONLOAD OF SEAWEED AND FISH GUTS.
NOW I JUST NEED TO DECIDE WHAT IT IS, EXACTLY.
A VIOLATION OF SEVERAL E.P.A. REGULATIONS, I'M SURE.
GOOD. BUT NOT RETAIL GOOD.

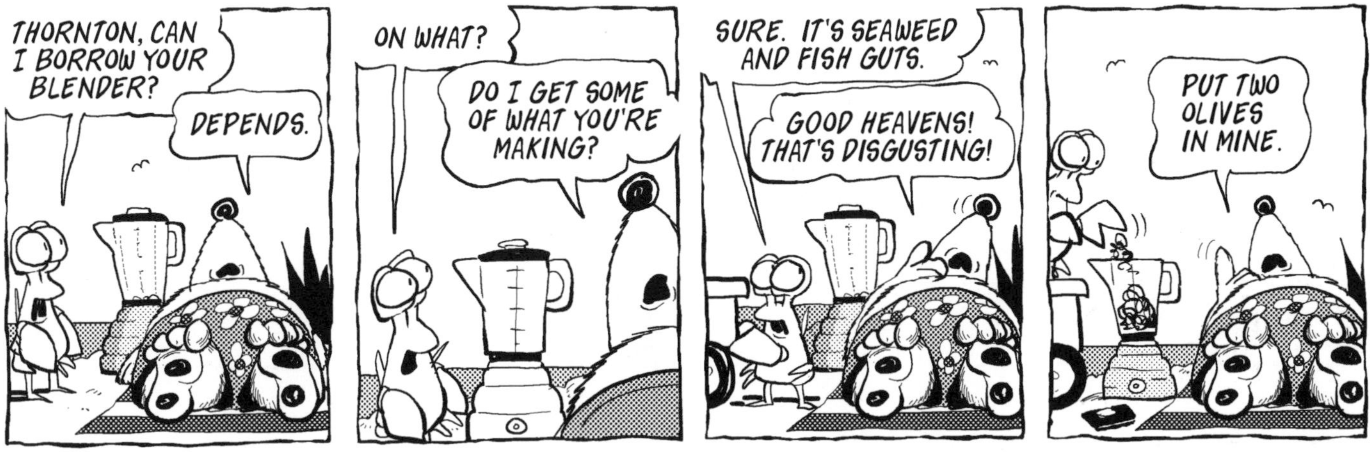
THORNTON, CAN I BORROW YOUR BLENDER?
DEPENDS.
ON WHAT?
DO I GET SOME OF WHAT YOU'RE MAKING?
SURE. IT'S SEAWEED AND FISH GUTS.
GOOD HEAVENS! THAT'S DISGUSTING!
PUT TWO OLIVES IN MINE.

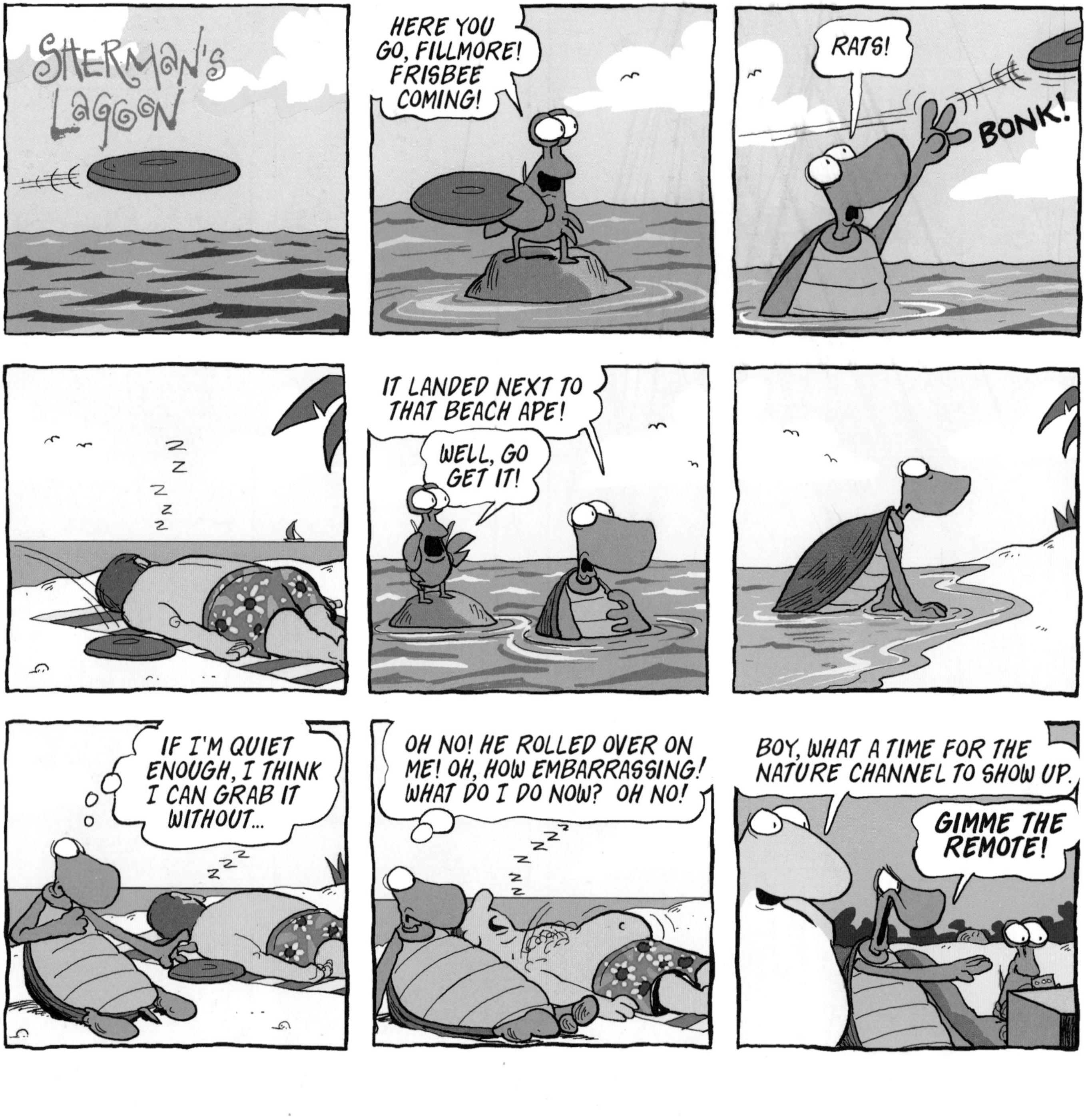
SHERMAN'S LAGOON
HERE YOU GO, FILLMORE! FRISBEE COMING!
RATS!
BONK!
IT LANDED NEXT TO THAT BEACH APE!
WELL, GO GET IT!
IF I'M QUIET ENOUGH, I THINK I CAN GRAB IT WITHOUT...
OH NO! HE ROLLED OVER ON ME! OH, HOW EMBARRASSING! WHAT DO I DO NOW? OH NO!
BOY, WHAT A TIME FOR THE NATURE CHANNEL TO SHOW UP.
GIMME THE REMOTE!

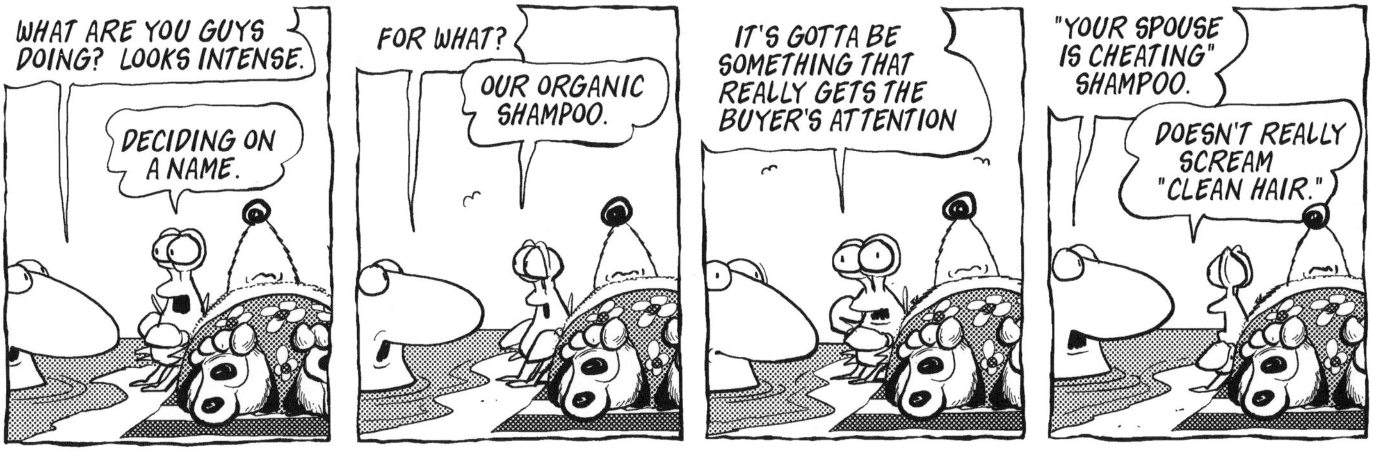
WHAT ARE YOU GUYS DOING? LOOKS INTENSE.
DECIDING ON A NAME.
FOR WHAT?
OUR ORGANIC SHAMPOO.
IT'S GOTTA BE SOMETHING THAT REALLY GETS THE BUYER'S ATTENTION
"YOUR SPOUSE IS CHEATING" SHAMPOO.
DOESN'T REALLY SCREAM "CLEAN HAIR."

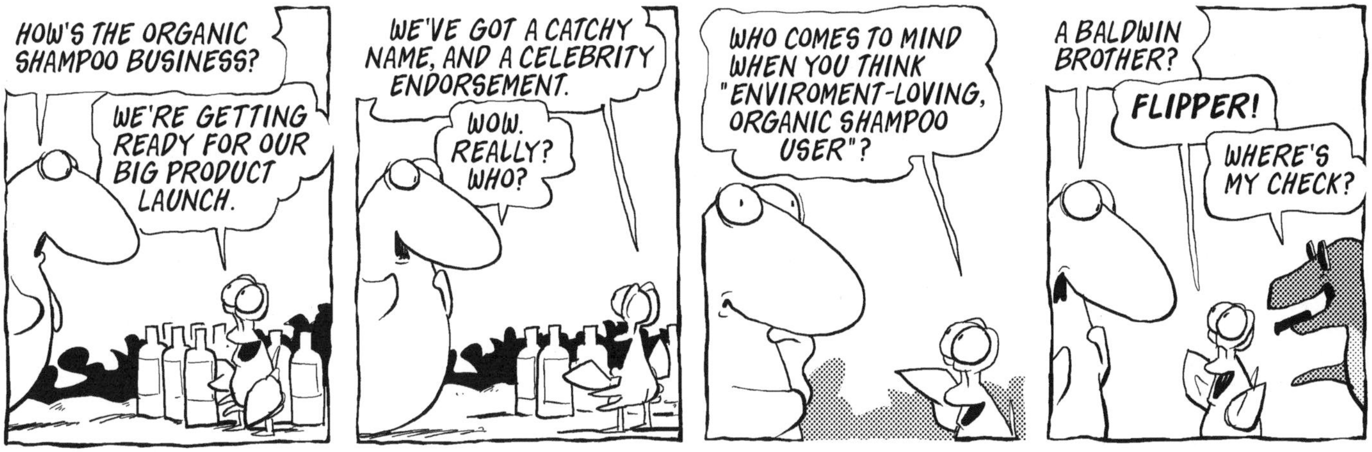
HOW'S THE ORGANIC SHAMPOO BUSINESS?
WE'RE GETTING READY FOR OUR BIG PRODUCT LAUNCH.
WE'VE GOT A CATCHY NAME, AND A CELEBRITY ENDORSEMENT.
WOW. REALLY? WHO?
WHO COMES TO MIND WHEN YOU THINK "ENVIROMENT-LOVING, ORGANIC SHAMPOO USER"?
A BALDWIN BROTHER?
FLIPPER!
WHERE'S MY CHECK?

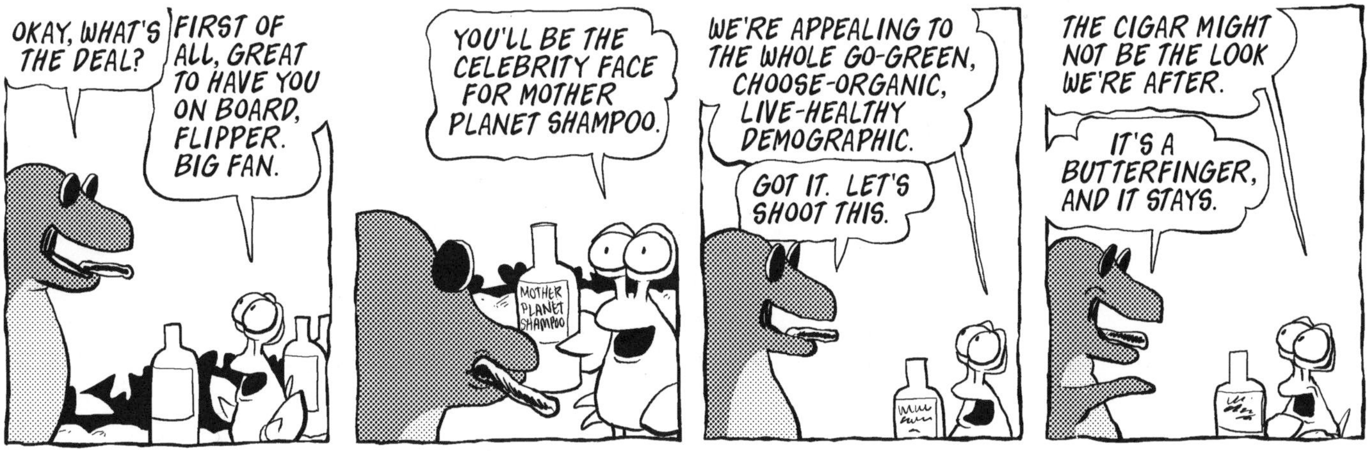
OKAY, WHAT'S THE DEAL?
FIRST OF ALL, GREAT TO HAVE YOU ON BOARD, FLIPPER. BIG FAN.
YOU'LL BE THE CELEBRITY FACE FOR MOTHER PLANET SHAMPOO.
MOTHER PLANET SHAMPOO
WE'RE APPEALING TO THE WHOLE GO-GREEN, CHOOSE-ORGANIC, LIVE-HEALTHY DEMOGRAPHIC.
GOT IT. LET'S SHOOT THIS.
THE CIGAR MIGHT NOT BE THE LOOK WE'RE AFTER.
IT'S A BUTTERFINGER, AND IT STAYS.

BAD NEWS, THORNTON. OUR ORGANIC SHAMPOO BUSINESS IS KAPUT.

HUH? NO!

YEAH. APPARENTLY IT EATS THROUGH YOUR SKULL IF YOU LEAVE IT ON A LITTLE TOO LONG.

HMMMM... THERE MUST BE A WAY TO MAKE LEMONADE OUT OF THIS LEMON.

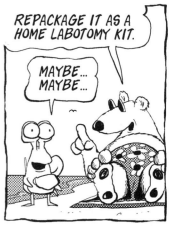

REPACKAGE IT AS A HOME LABOTOMY KIT.

MAYBE... MAYBE...

WHAT'S FILLMORE DOING INSIDE THAT OLD VW VAN?

RELIVING THE SIXTIES.

NEVER LET FILLMORE FANTASIZE LIKE THAT.

TOO LATE.

FILLMORE'S TAKEN QUITE A LIKING TO IT. I THINK HE'S DEVELOPING HIPPY TRAITS.

PEACE, MY BROTHERS.

THIS IS BAD. GO FETCH MY RIOT GEAR.

NICE FLOWER CHILD OUTFIT. WHERE ARE YOU OFF TO?

I'M GOING TO HANG OUT WITH FILLMORE IN THE HIPPIE VAN.

MAYBE I SHOULD TAKE SOME MUSIC WITH ME. SOMETHING WITH A LITTLE SOUL.

...SOMETHING THAT STANDS FOR REBELLION, AND GOES AGAINST THE PRE-PACKAGED CORPORATE ESTABLISHMENT.

POTTERY BARN "SONGS OF THE SIXTIES"?

PERFECT.

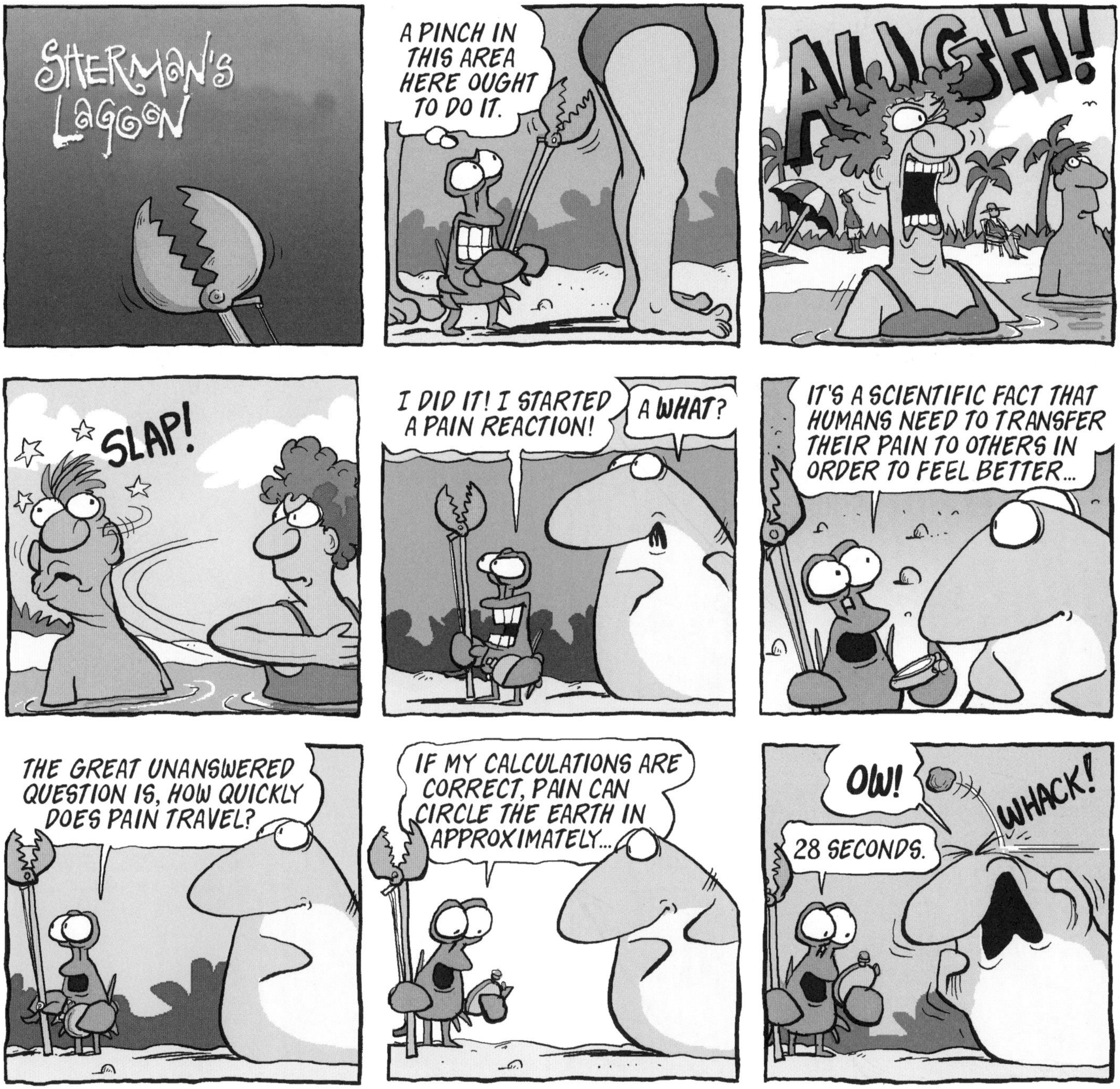
SHERMAN'S LAGOON
A PINCH IN THIS AREA HERE OUGHT TO DO IT.
AUGH!
SLAP!
I DID IT! I STARTED A PAIN REACTION!
A WHAT?
IT'S A SCIENTIFIC FACT THAT HUMANS NEED TO TRANSFER THEIR PAIN TO OTHERS IN ORDER TO FEEL BETTER...
THE GREAT UNANSWERED QUESTION IS, HOW QUICKLY DOES PAIN TRAVEL?
IF MY CALCULATIONS ARE CORRECT, PAIN CAN CIRCLE THE EARTH IN APPROXIMATELY...
OW!
WHACK!
28 SECONDS.

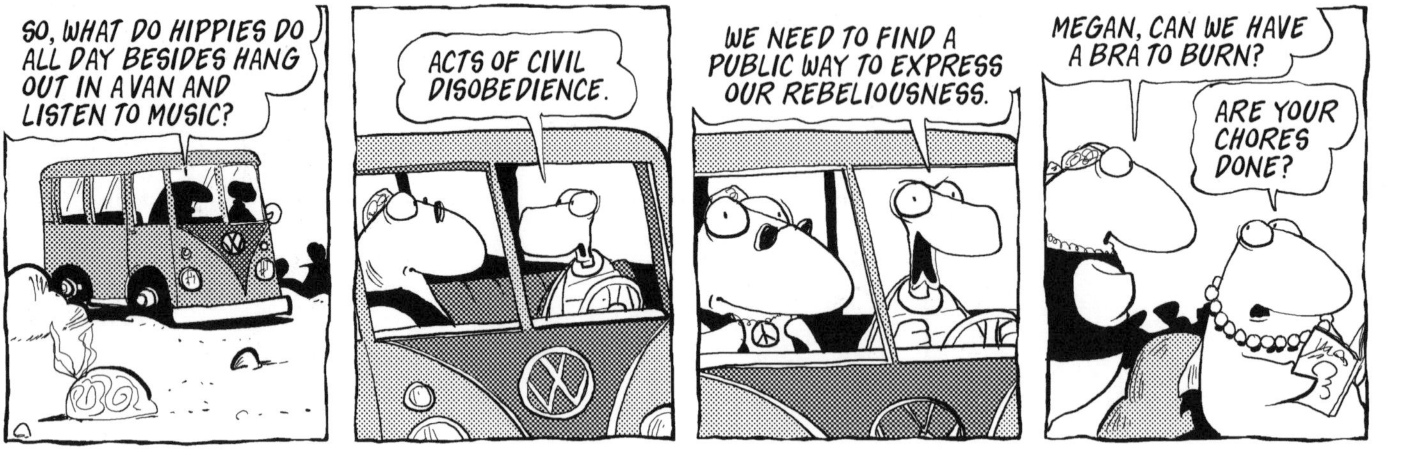
SO, WHAT DO HIPPIES DO ALL DAY BESIDES HANG OUT IN A VAN AND LISTEN TO MUSIC?
ACTS OF CIVIL DISOBEDIENCE.
WE NEED TO FIND A PUBLIC WAY TO EXPRESS OUR REBELIOUSNESS.
MEGAN, CAN WE HAVE A BRA TO BURN?
ARE YOUR CHORES DONE?

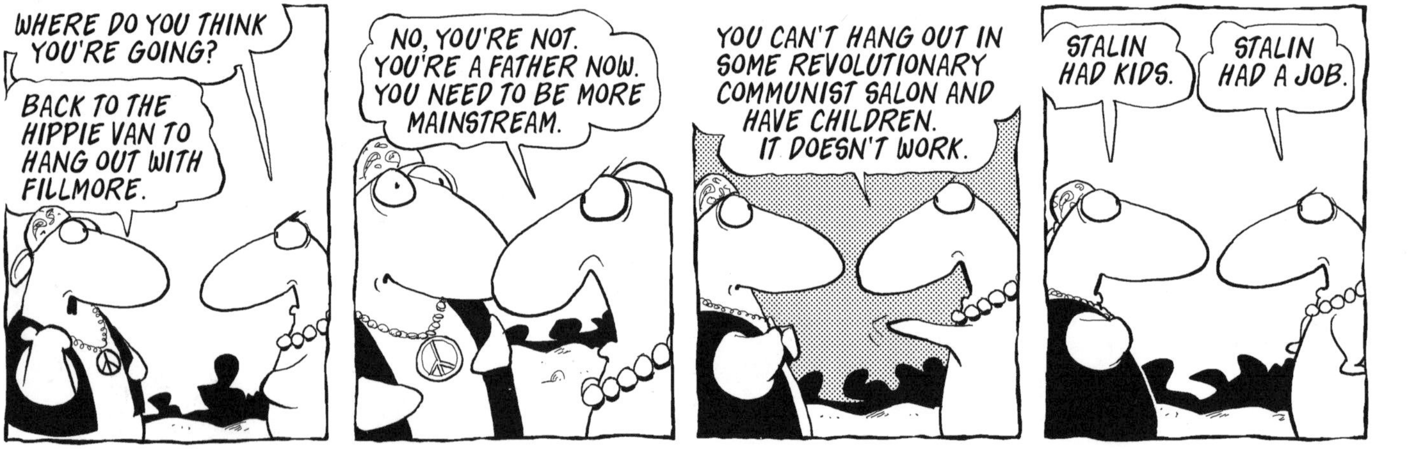
WHERE DO YOU THINK YOU'RE GOING?
BACK TO THE HIPPIE VAN TO HANG OUT WITH FILLMORE.
NO, YOU'RE NOT. YOU'RE A FATHER NOW. YOU NEED TO BE MORE MAINSTREAM.
YOU CAN'T HANG OUT IN SOME REVOLUTIONARY COMMUNIST SALON AND HAVE CHILDREN. IT DOESN'T WORK.
STALIN HAD KIDS.
STALIN HAD A JOB.

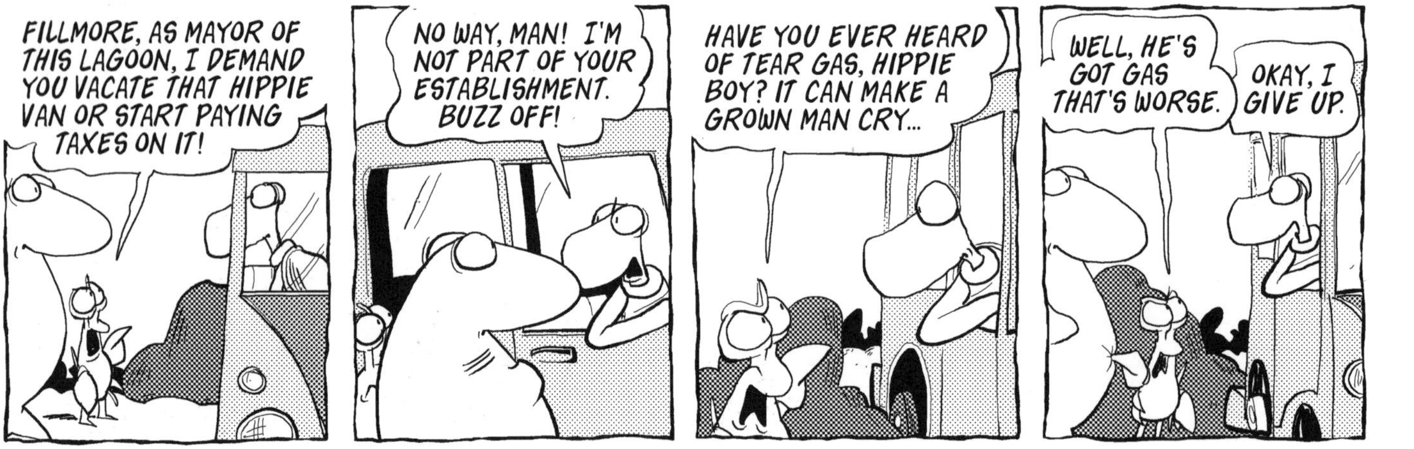
FILLMORE, AS MAYOR OF THIS LAGOON, I DEMAND YOU VACATE THAT HIPPIE VAN OR START PAYING TAXES ON IT!
NO WAY, MAN! I'M NOT PART OF YOUR ESTABLISHMENT. BUZZ OFF!
HAVE YOU EVER HEARD OF TEAR GAS, HIPPIE BOY? IT CAN MAKE A GROWN MAN CRY...
WELL, HE'S GOT GAS THAT'S WORSE.
OKAY, I GIVE UP.

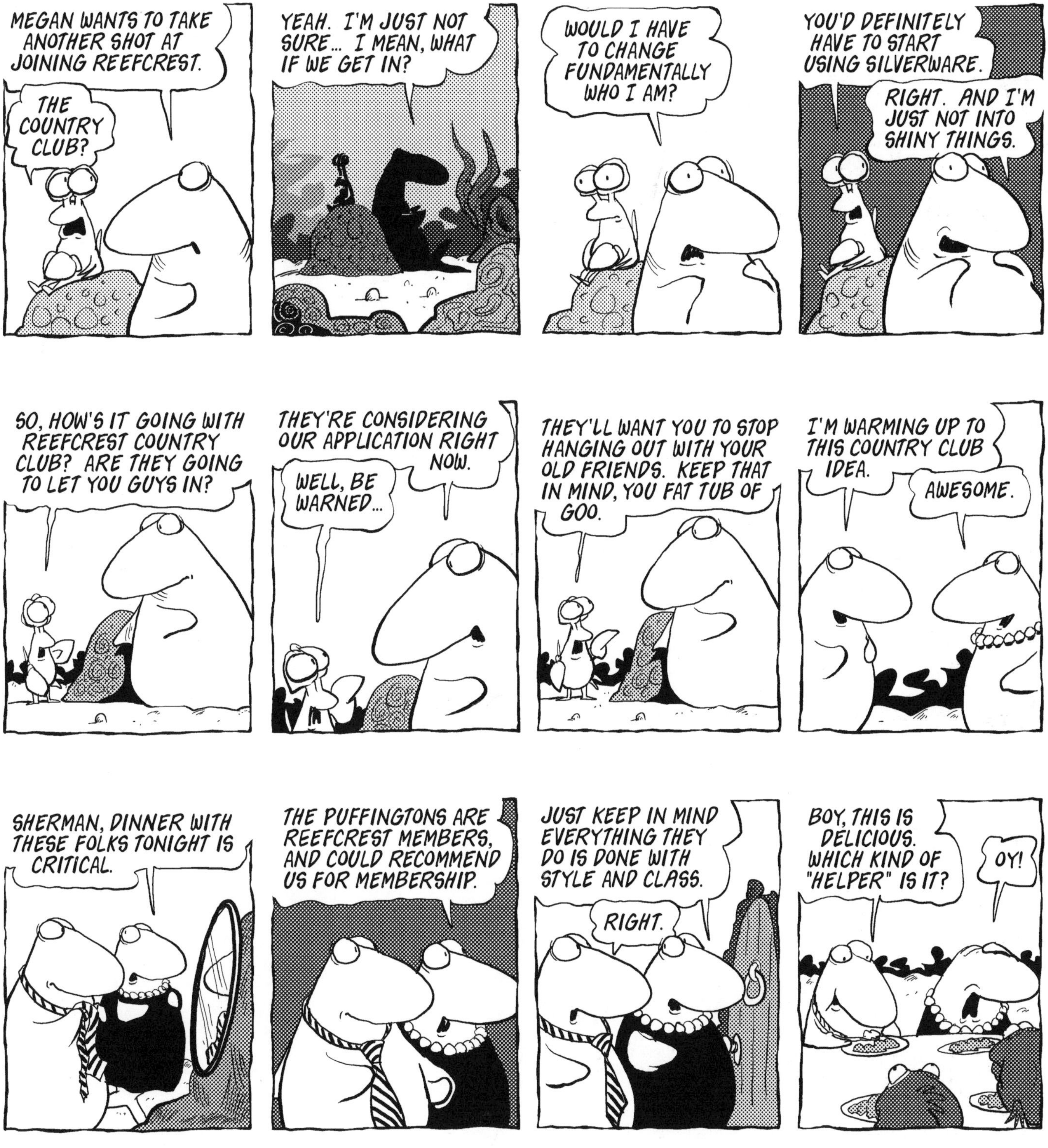
MEGAN WANTS TO TAKE ANOTHER SHOT AT JOINING REEFCREST.
THE COUNTRY CLUB?
YEAH. I'M JUST NOT SURE... I MEAN, WHAT IF WE GET IN?
WOULD I HAVE TO CHANGE FUNDAMENTALLY WHO I AM?
YOU'D DEFINITELY HAVE TO START USING SILVERWARE.
RIGHT. AND I'M JUST NOT INTO SHINY THINGS.
SO, HOW'S IT GOING WITH REEFCREST COUNTRY CLUB? ARE THEY GOING TO LET YOU GUYS IN?
THEY'RE CONSIDERING OUR APPLICATION RIGHT NOW.
WELL, BE WARNED...
THEY'LL WANT YOU TO STOP HANGING OUT WITH YOUR OLD FRIENDS. KEEP THAT IN MIND, YOU FAT TUB OF GOO.
I'M WARMING UP TO THIS COUNTRY CLUB IDEA.
AWESOME.
SHERMAN, DINNER WITH THESE FOLKS TONIGHT IS CRITICAL.
THE PUFFINGTONS ARE REEFCREST MEMBERS, AND COULD RECOMMEND US FOR MEMBERSHIP.
JUST KEEP IN MIND EVERYTHING THEY DO IS DONE WITH STYLE AND CLASS.
RIGHT.
BOY, THIS IS DELICIOUS. WHICH KIND OF "HELPER" IS IT?
OY!

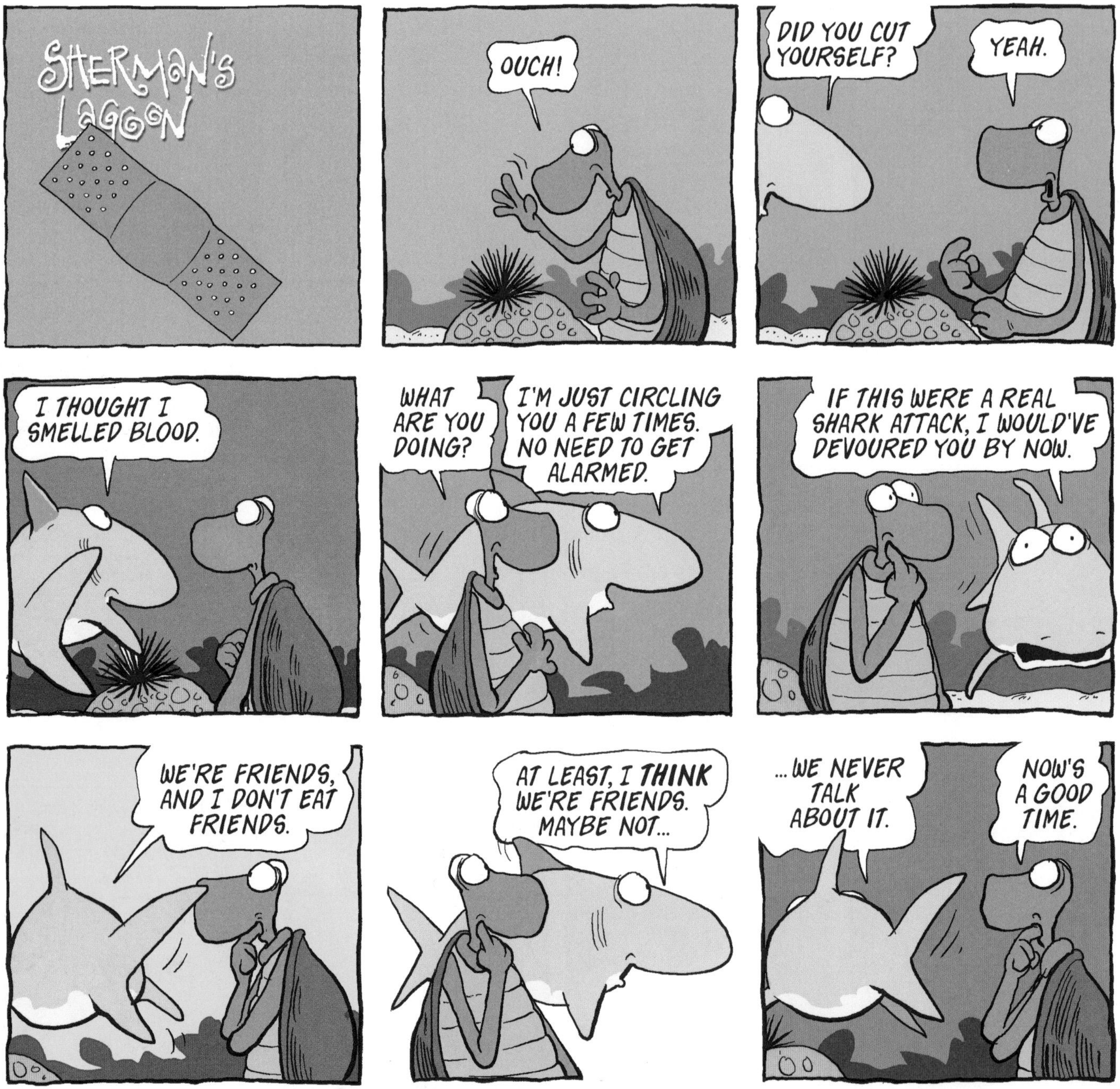
SHERMAN'S LAGOON
OUCH!
DID YOU CUT YOURSELF?
YEAH.
I THOUGHT I SMELLED BLOOD.
WHAT ARE YOU DOING?
I'M JUST CIRCLING YOU A FEW TIMES. NO NEED TO GET ALARMED.
IF THIS WERE A REAL SHARK ATTACK, I WOULD'VE DEVOURED YOU BY NOW.
WE'RE FRIENDS, AND I DON'T EAT FRIENDS.
AT LEAST, I **THINK** WE'RE FRIENDS. MAYBE NOT...
...WE NEVER TALK ABOUT IT.
NOW'S A GOOD TIME.

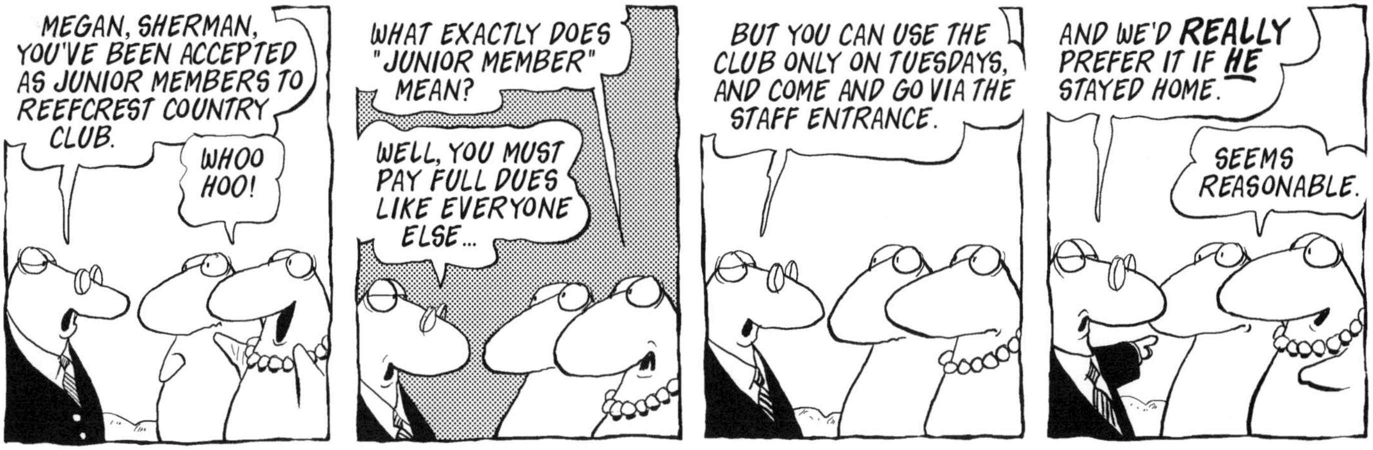
MEGAN, SHERMAN, YOU'VE BEEN ACCEPTED AS JUNIOR MEMBERS TO REEFCREST COUNTRY CLUB.
WHOO HOO!
WHAT EXACTLY DOES "JUNIOR MEMBER" MEAN?
WELL, YOU MUST PAY FULL DUES LIKE EVERYONE ELSE...
BUT YOU CAN USE THE CLUB ONLY ON TUESDAYS, AND COME AND GO VIA THE STAFF ENTRANCE.
AND WE'D REALLY PREFER IT IF HE STAYED HOME.
SEEMS REASONABLE.

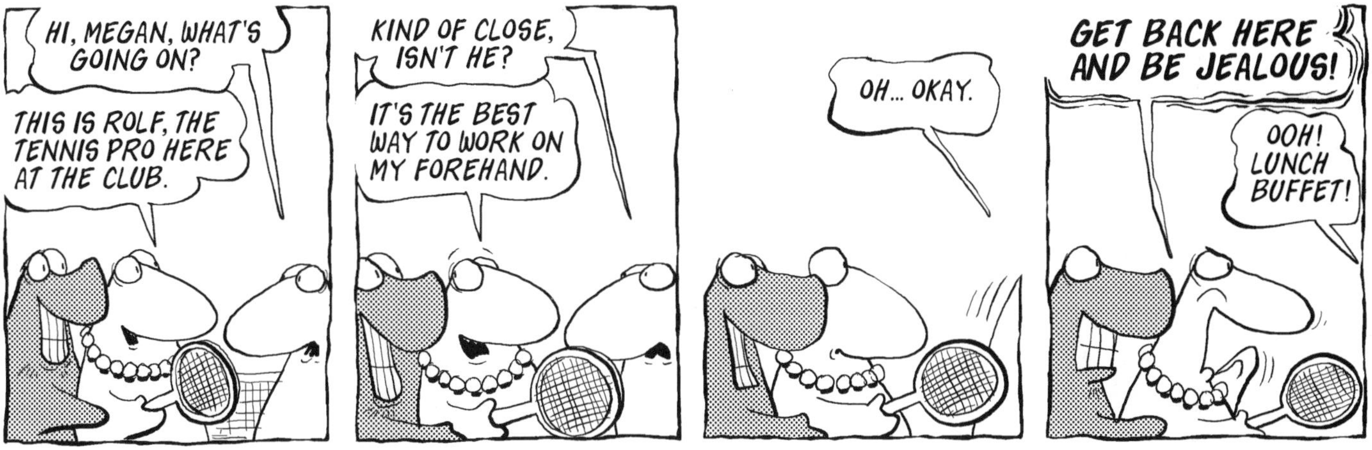
HI, MEGAN, WHAT'S GOING ON?
THIS IS ROLF, THE TENNIS PRO HERE AT THE CLUB.
KIND OF CLOSE, ISN'T HE?
IT'S THE BEST WAY TO WORK ON MY FOREHAND.
OH... OKAY.
GET BACK HERE AND BE JEALOUS!
OOH! LUNCH BUFFET!

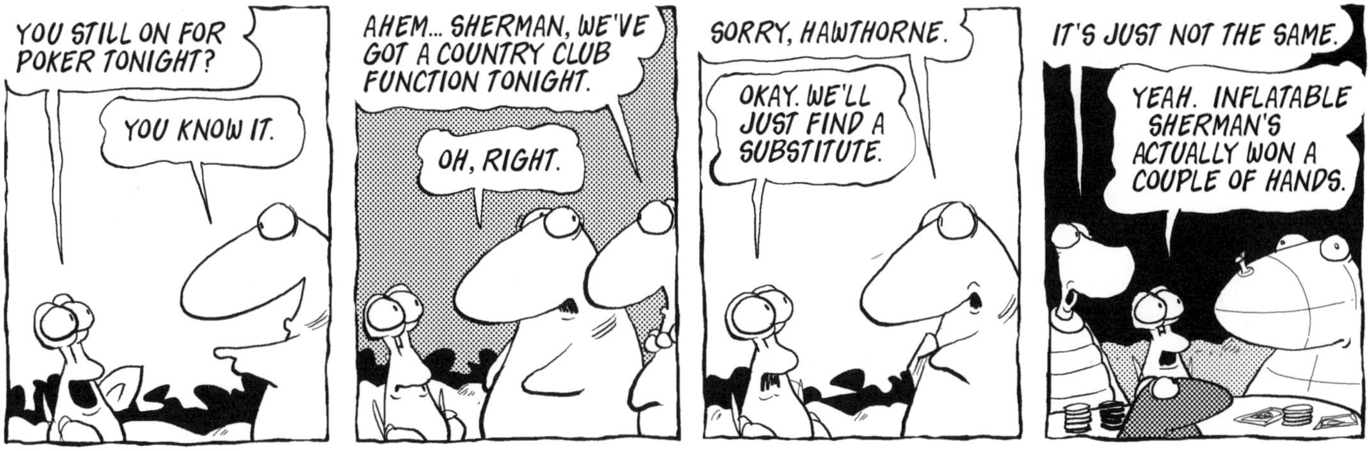
YOU STILL ON FOR POKER TONIGHT?
YOU KNOW IT.
AHEM... SHERMAN, WE'VE GOT A COUNTRY CLUB FUNCTION TONIGHT.
OH, RIGHT.
SORRY, HAWTHORNE.
OKAY. WE'LL JUST FIND A SUBSTITUTE.
IT'S JUST NOT THE SAME.
YEAH. INFLATABLE SHERMAN'S ACTUALLY WON A COUPLE OF HANDS.

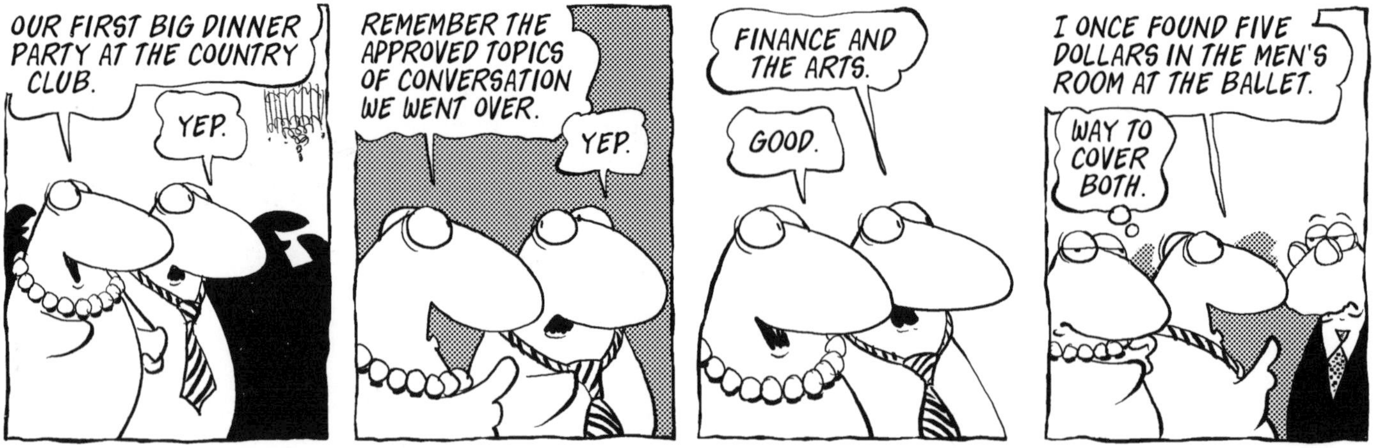
OUR FIRST BIG DINNER PARTY AT THE COUNTRY CLUB.
YEP.
REMEMBER THE APPROVED TOPICS OF CONVERSATION WE WENT OVER.
YEP.
FINANCE AND THE ARTS.
GOOD.
I ONCE FOUND FIVE DOLLARS IN THE MEN'S ROOM AT THE BALLET.
WAY TO COVER BOTH.

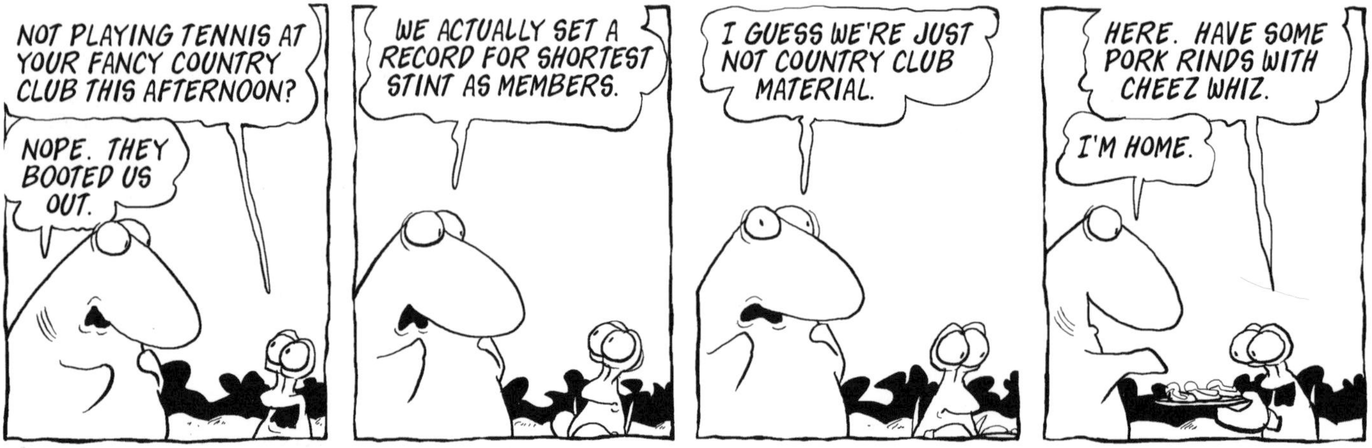
NOT PLAYING TENNIS AT YOUR FANCY COUNTRY CLUB THIS AFTERNOON?
NOPE. THEY BOOTED US OUT.
WE ACTUALLY SET A RECORD FOR SHORTEST STINT AS MEMBERS.
I GUESS WE'RE JUST NOT COUNTRY CLUB MATERIAL.
HERE. HAVE SOME PORK RINDS WITH CHEEZ WHIZ.
I'M HOME.

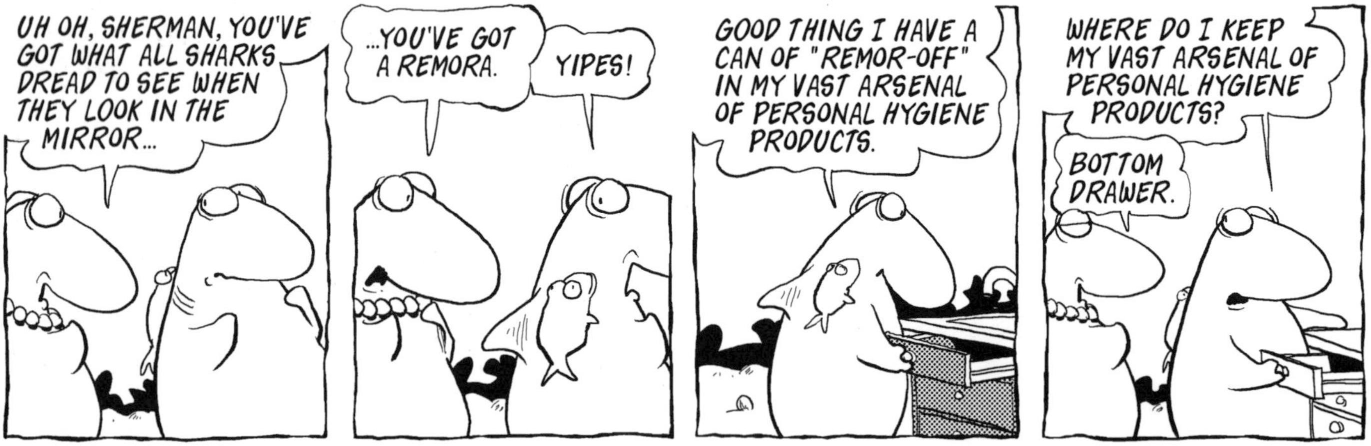
UH OH, SHERMAN, YOU'VE GOT WHAT ALL SHARKS DREAD TO SEE WHEN THEY LOOK IN THE MIRROR...
...YOU'VE GOT A REMORA.
YIPES!
GOOD THING I HAVE A CAN OF "REMOR-OFF" IN MY VAST ARSENAL OF PERSONAL HYGIENE PRODUCTS.
WHERE DO I KEEP MY VAST ARSENAL OF PERSONAL HYGIENE PRODUCTS?
BOTTOM DRAWER.

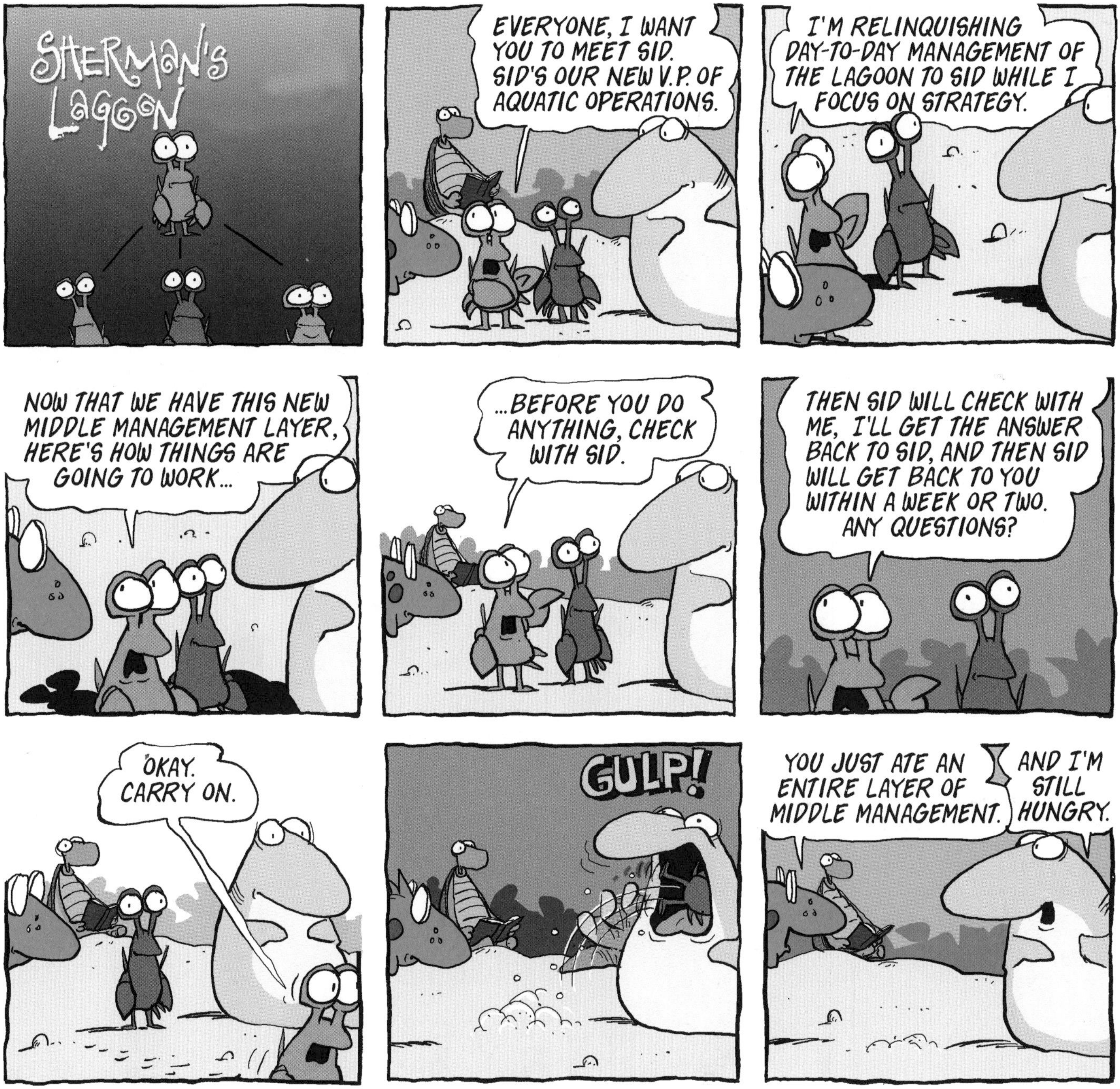
SHERMAN'S LAGOON
EVERYONE, I WANT YOU TO MEET SID. SID'S OUR NEW V.P. OF AQUATIC OPERATIONS.
I'M RELINQUISHING DAY-TO-DAY MANAGEMENT OF THE LAGOON TO SID WHILE I FOCUS ON STRATEGY.
NOW THAT WE HAVE THIS NEW MIDDLE MANAGEMENT LAYER, HERE'S HOW THINGS ARE GOING TO WORK...
...BEFORE YOU DO ANYTHING, CHECK WITH SID.
THEN SID WILL CHECK WITH ME, I'LL GET THE ANSWER BACK TO SID, AND THEN SID WILL GET BACK TO YOU WITHIN A WEEK OR TWO. ANY QUESTIONS?
OKAY. CARRY ON.
GULP!
YOU JUST ATE AN ENTIRE LAYER OF MIDDLE MANAGEMENT.
AND I'M STILL HUNGRY.

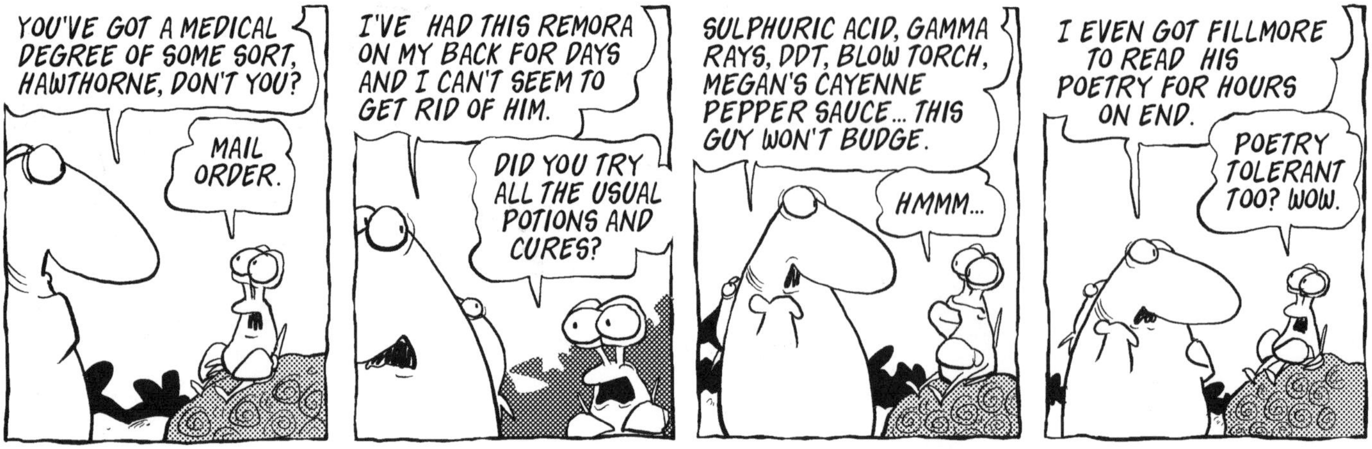
YOU'VE GOT A MEDICAL DEGREE OF SOME SORT, HAWTHORNE, DON'T YOU?
MAIL ORDER.
I'VE HAD THIS REMORA ON MY BACK FOR DAYS AND I CAN'T SEEM TO GET RID OF HIM.
DID YOU TRY ALL THE USUAL POTIONS AND CURES?
SULPHURIC ACID, GAMMA RAYS, DDT, BLOW TORCH, MEGAN'S CAYENNE PEPPER SAUCE... THIS GUY WON'T BUDGE.
HMMM...
I EVEN GOT FILLMORE TO READ HIS POETRY FOR HOURS ON END.
POETRY TOLERANT TOO? WOW.

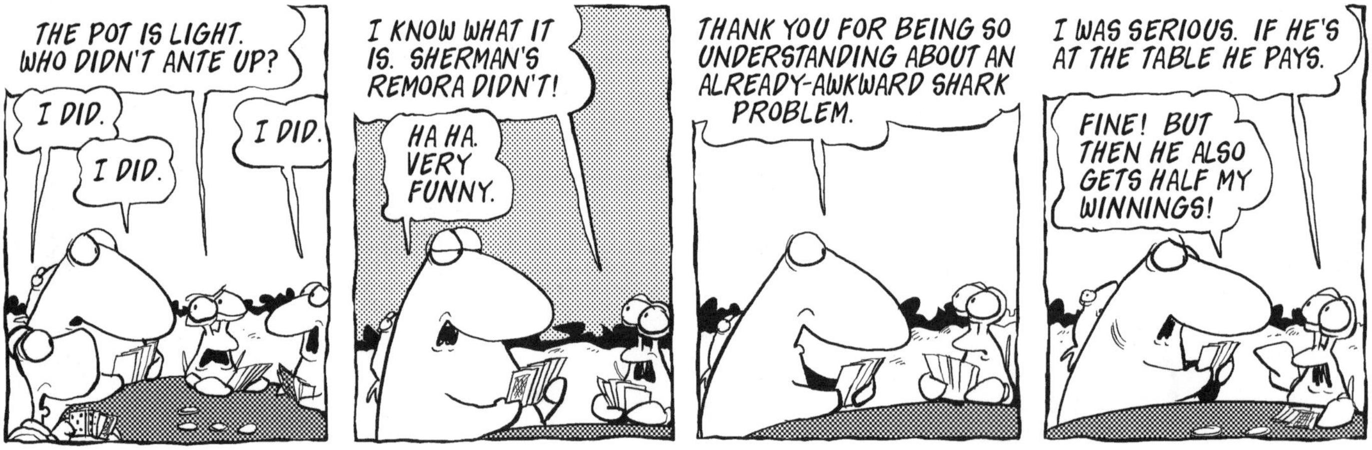
THE POT IS LIGHT. WHO DIDN'T ANTE UP?
I DID.
I DID.
I DID.
I KNOW WHAT IT IS. SHERMAN'S REMORA DIDN'T!
HA HA. VERY FUNNY.
THANK YOU FOR BEING SO UNDERSTANDING ABOUT AN ALREADY-AWKWARD SHARK PROBLEM.
I WAS SERIOUS. IF HE'S AT THE TABLE HE PAYS.
FINE! BUT THEN HE ALSO GETS HALF MY WINNINGS!

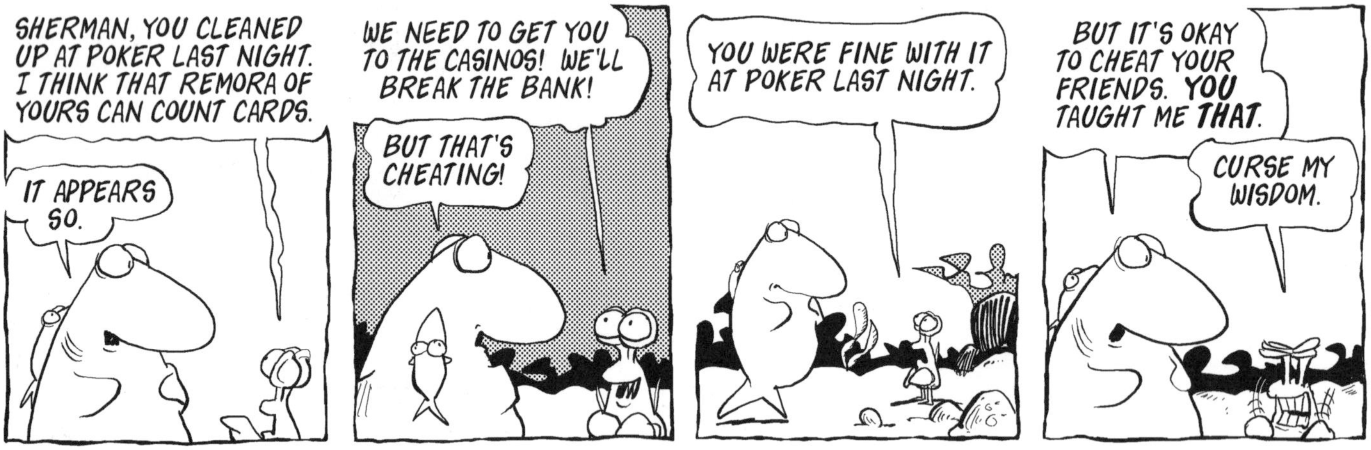
SHERMAN, YOU CLEANED UP AT POKER LAST NIGHT. I THINK THAT REMORA OF YOURS CAN COUNT CARDS.
IT APPEARS SO.
WE NEED TO GET YOU TO THE CASINOS! WE'LL BREAK THE BANK!
BUT THAT'S CHEATING!
YOU WERE FINE WITH IT AT POKER LAST NIGHT.
BUT IT'S OKAY TO CHEAT YOUR FRIENDS. YOU TAUGHT ME THAT.
CURSE MY WISDOM.

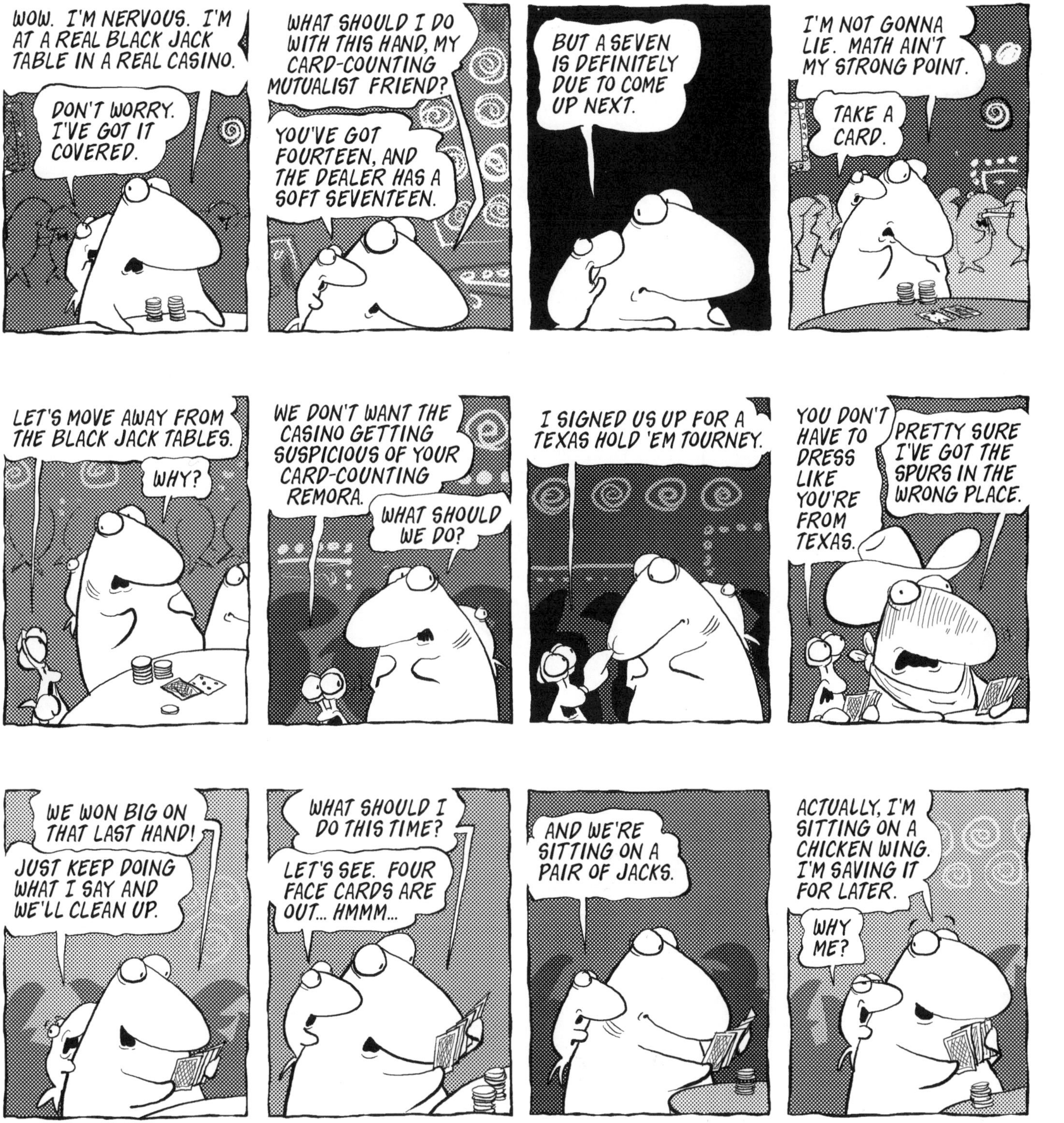
WOW. I'M NERVOUS. I'M AT A REAL BLACK JACK TABLE IN A REAL CASINO.
DON'T WORRY. I'VE GOT IT COVERED.
WHAT SHOULD I DO WITH THIS HAND, MY CARD-COUNTING MUTUALIST FRIEND?
YOU'VE GOT FOURTEEN, AND THE DEALER HAS A SOFT SEVENTEEN.
BUT A SEVEN IS DEFINITELY DUE TO COME UP NEXT.
I'M NOT GONNA LIE. MATH AIN'T MY STRONG POINT.
TAKE A CARD.
LET'S MOVE AWAY FROM THE BLACK JACK TABLES.
WHY?
WE DON'T WANT THE CASINO GETTING SUSPICIOUS OF YOUR CARD-COUNTING REMORA.
WHAT SHOULD WE DO?
I SIGNED US UP FOR A TEXAS HOLD 'EM TOURNEY.
YOU DON'T HAVE TO DRESS LIKE YOU'RE FROM TEXAS.
PRETTY SURE I'VE GOT THE SPURS IN THE WRONG PLACE.
WE WON BIG ON THAT LAST HAND!
JUST KEEP DOING WHAT I SAY AND WE'LL CLEAN UP.
WHAT SHOULD I DO THIS TIME?
LET'S SEE. FOUR FACE CARDS ARE OUT... HMMM...
AND WE'RE SITTING ON A PAIR OF JACKS.
ACTUALLY, I'M SITTING ON A CHICKEN WING. I'M SAVING IT FOR LATER.
WHY ME?

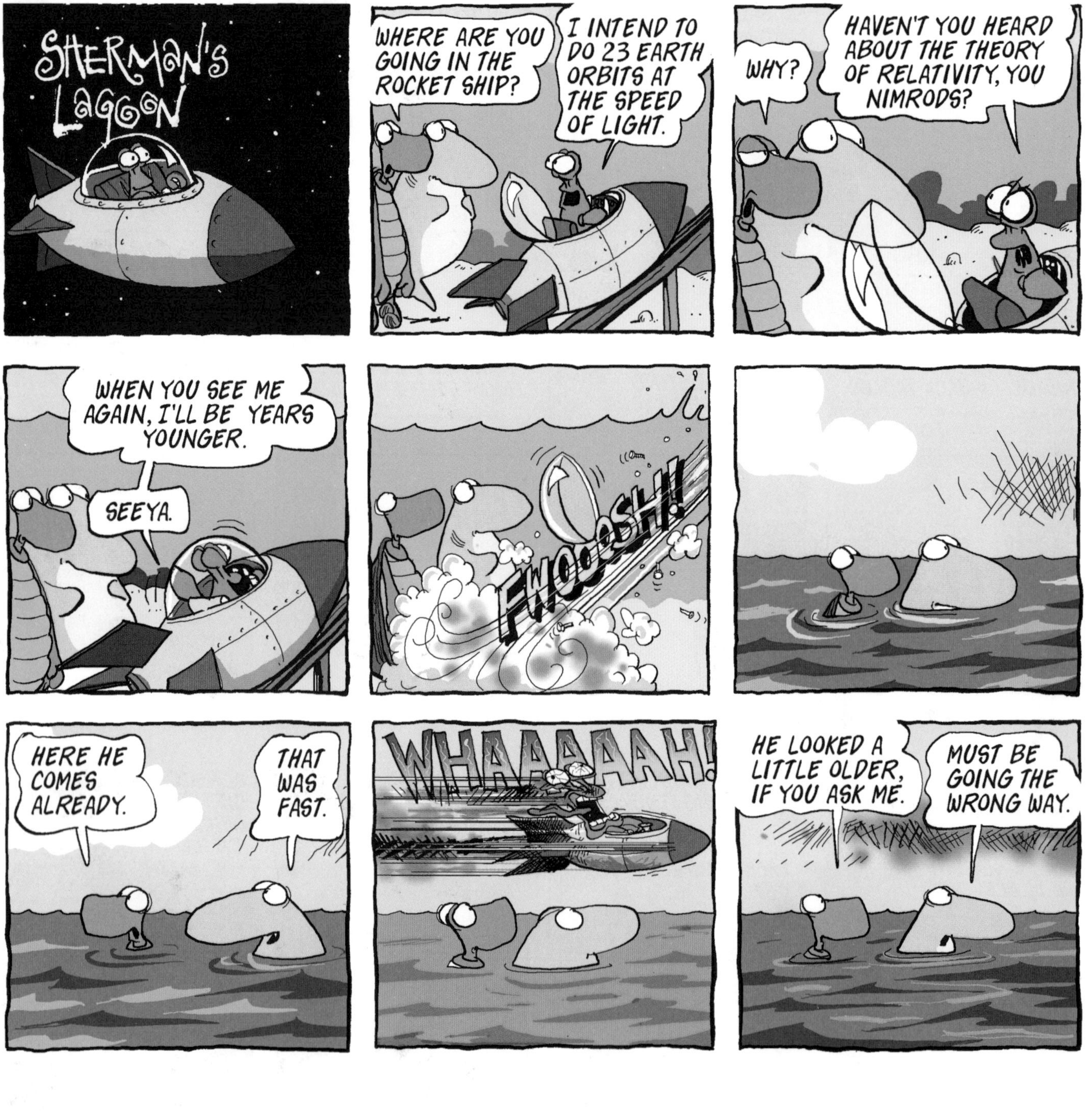
SHERMAN'S LAGOON
WHERE ARE YOU GOING IN THE ROCKET SHIP?
I INTEND TO DO 23 EARTH ORBITS AT THE SPEED OF LIGHT.
WHY?
HAVEN'T YOU HEARD ABOUT THE THEORY OF RELATIVITY, YOU NIMRODS?
WHEN YOU SEE ME AGAIN, I'LL BE YEARS YOUNGER.
SEEYA.
FWOOOSH!
HERE HE COMES ALREADY.
THAT WAS FAST.
WHAAAAAH!
HE LOOKED A LITTLE OLDER, IF YOU ASK ME.
MUST BE GOING THE WRONG WAY.

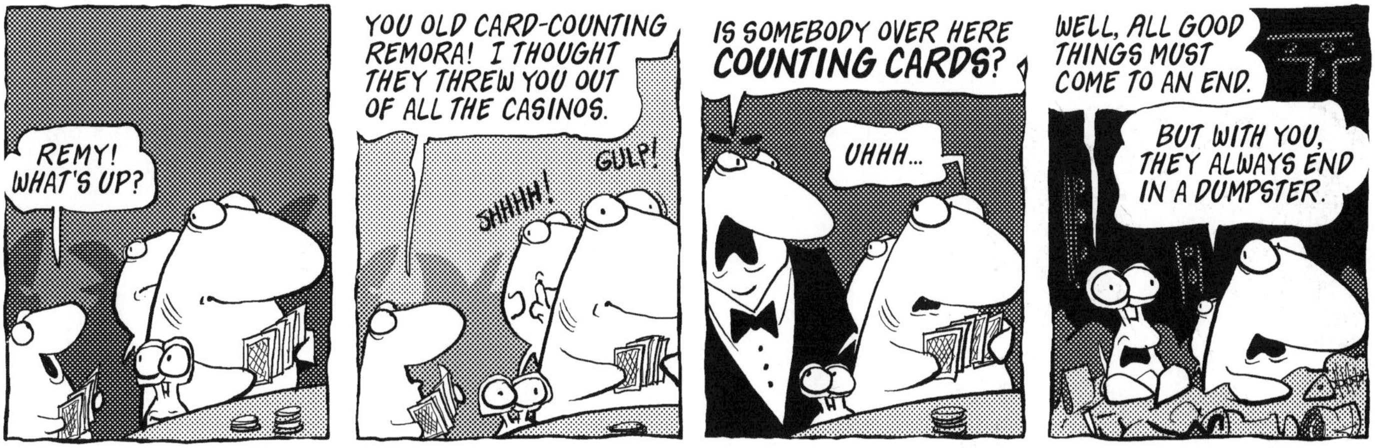
REMY! WHAT'S UP?
YOU OLD CARD-COUNTING REMORA! I THOUGHT THEY THREW YOU OUT OF ALL THE CASINOS.
SHHHH!
GULP!
IS SOMEBODY OVER HERE **COUNTING CARDS?**
UHHH...
WELL, ALL GOOD THINGS MUST COME TO AN END.
BUT WITH YOU, THEY ALWAYS END IN A DUMPSTER.

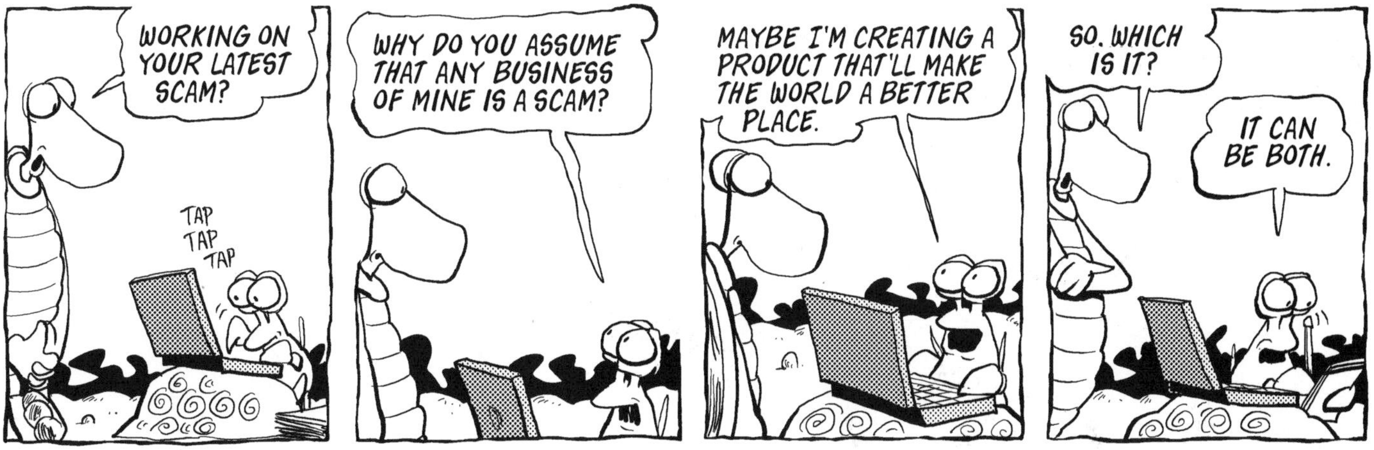
WORKING ON YOUR LATEST SCAM?
TAP TAP TAP
WHY DO YOU ASSUME THAT ANY *BUSINESS* OF MINE IS A SCAM?
MAYBE I'M CREATING A PRODUCT THAT'LL MAKE THE WORLD A BETTER PLACE.
SO. WHICH IS IT?
IT CAN BE BOTH.

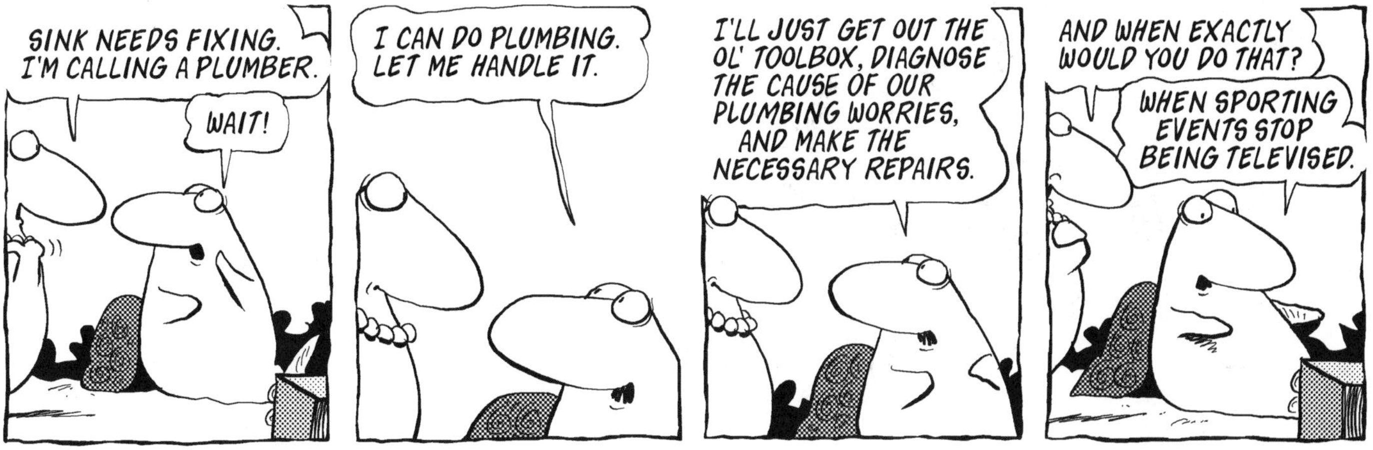
SINK NEEDS FIXING. I'M CALLING A PLUMBER.
WAIT!
I CAN DO PLUMBING. LET ME HANDLE IT.
I'LL JUST GET OUT THE OL' TOOLBOX, DIAGNOSE THE CAUSE OF OUR PLUMBING WORRIES, AND MAKE THE NECESSARY REPAIRS.
AND WHEN EXACTLY WOULD YOU DO THAT?
WHEN SPORTING EVENTS STOP BEING TELEVISED.

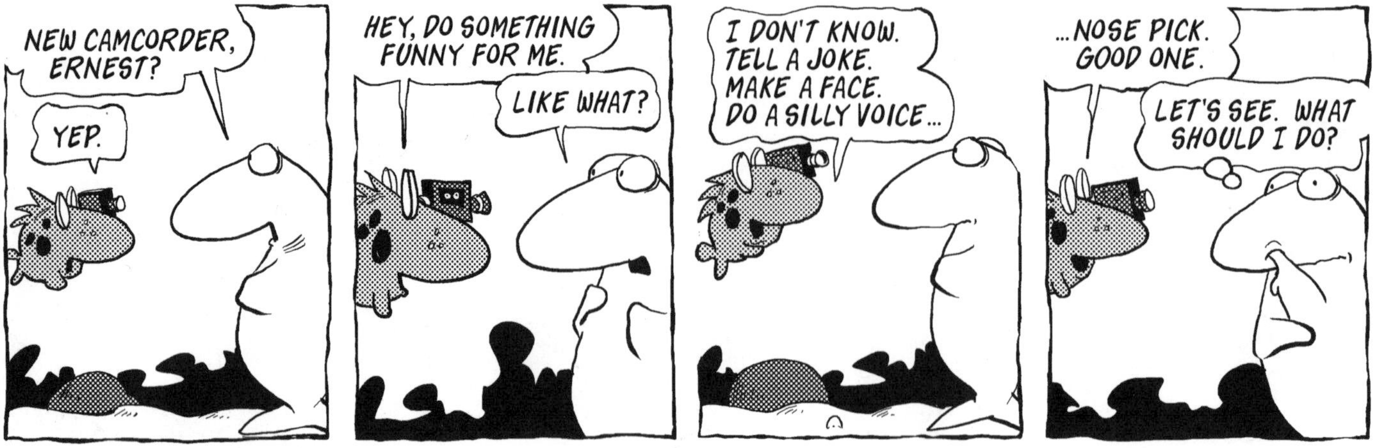
NEW CAMCORDER, ERNEST?
YEP.
HEY, DO SOMETHING FUNNY FOR ME.
LIKE WHAT?
I DON'T KNOW. TELL A JOKE. MAKE A FACE. DO A SILLY VOICE...
...NOSE PICK. GOOD ONE.
LET'S SEE. WHAT SHOULD I DO?

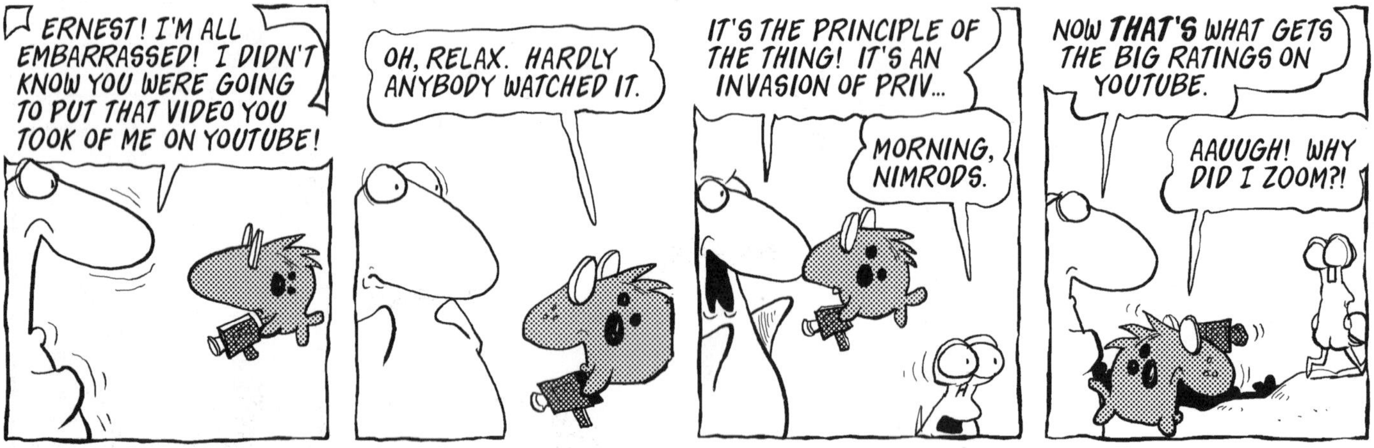
ERNEST! I'M ALL EMBARRASSED! I DIDN'T KNOW YOU WERE GOING TO PUT THAT VIDEO YOU TOOK OF ME ON YOUTUBE!
OH, RELAX. HARDLY ANYBODY WATCHED IT.
IT'S THE PRINCIPLE OF THE THING! IT'S AN INVASION OF PRIV...
MORNING, NIMRODS.
NOW THAT'S WHAT GETS THE BIG RATINGS ON YOUTUBE.
AAUUGH! WHY DID I ZOOM?!

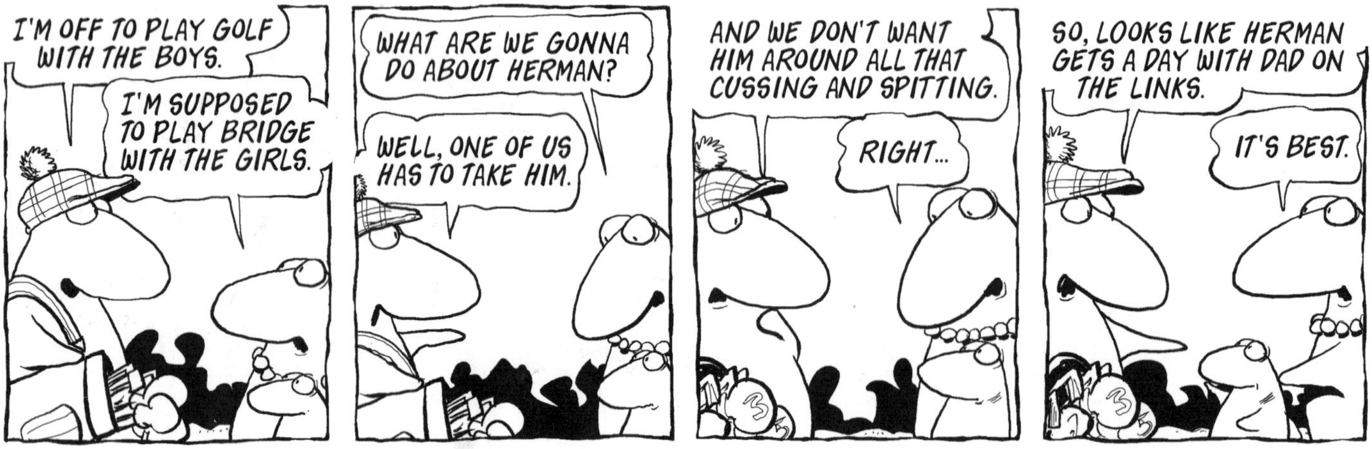
I'M OFF TO PLAY GOLF WITH THE BOYS.
I'M SUPPOSED TO PLAY BRIDGE WITH THE GIRLS.
WHAT ARE WE GONNA DO ABOUT HERMAN?
WELL, ONE OF US HAS TO TAKE HIM.
AND WE DON'T WANT HIM AROUND ALL THAT CUSSING AND SPITTING.
RIGHT...
SO, LOOKS LIKE HERMAN GETS A DAY WITH DAD ON THE LINKS.
IT'S BEST.

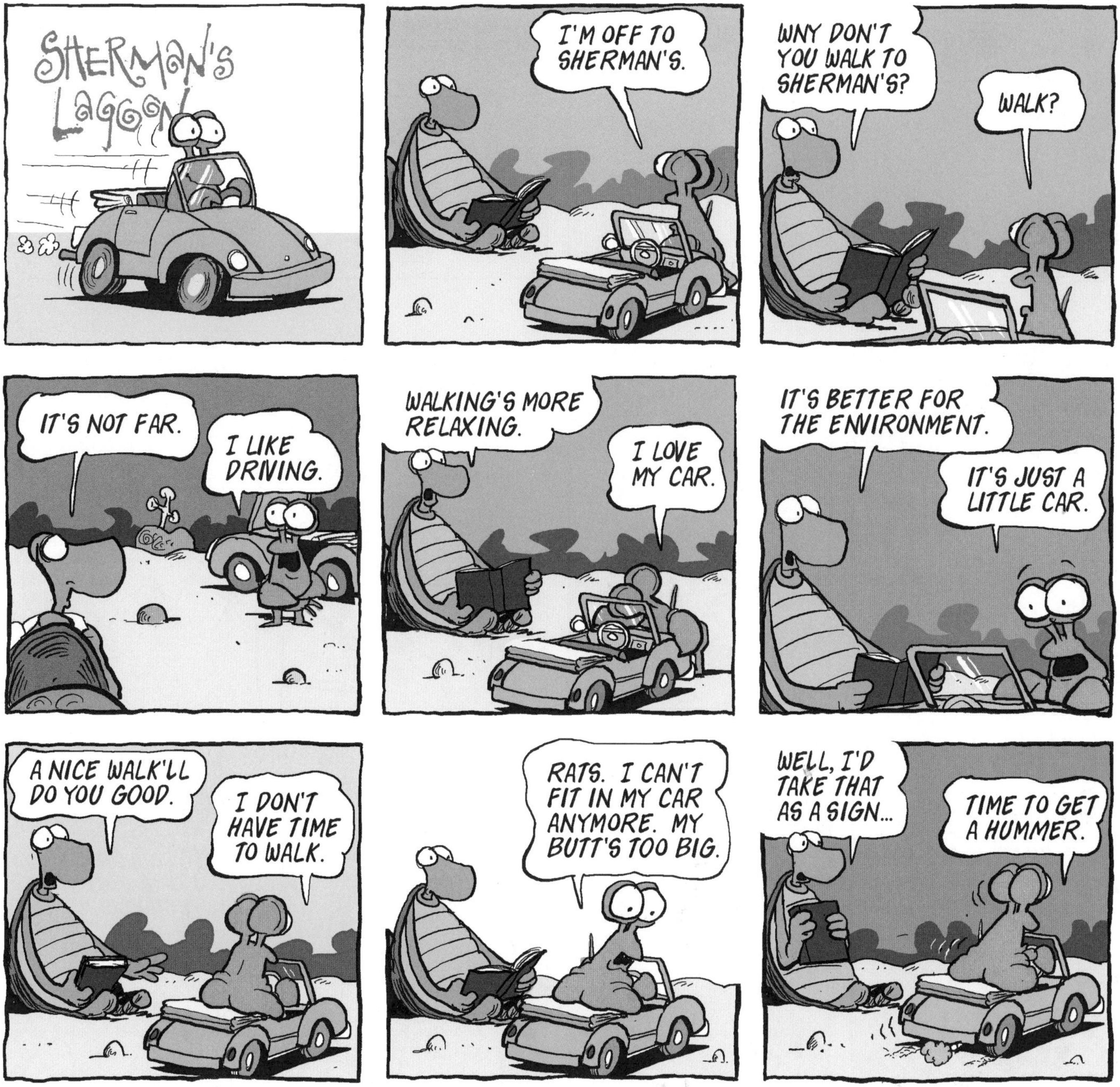
SHERMAN'S LAGOON
I'M OFF TO SHERMAN'S.
WHY DON'T YOU WALK TO SHERMAN'S?
WALK?
IT'S NOT FAR.
I LIKE DRIVING.
WALKING'S MORE RELAXING.
I LOVE MY CAR.
IT'S BETTER FOR THE ENVIRONMENT.
IT'S JUST A LITTLE CAR.
A NICE WALK'LL DO YOU GOOD.
I DON'T HAVE TIME TO WALK.
RATS. I CAN'T FIT IN MY CAR ANYMORE. MY BUTT'S TOO BIG.
WELL, I'D TAKE THAT AS A SIGN...
TIME TO GET A HUMMER.

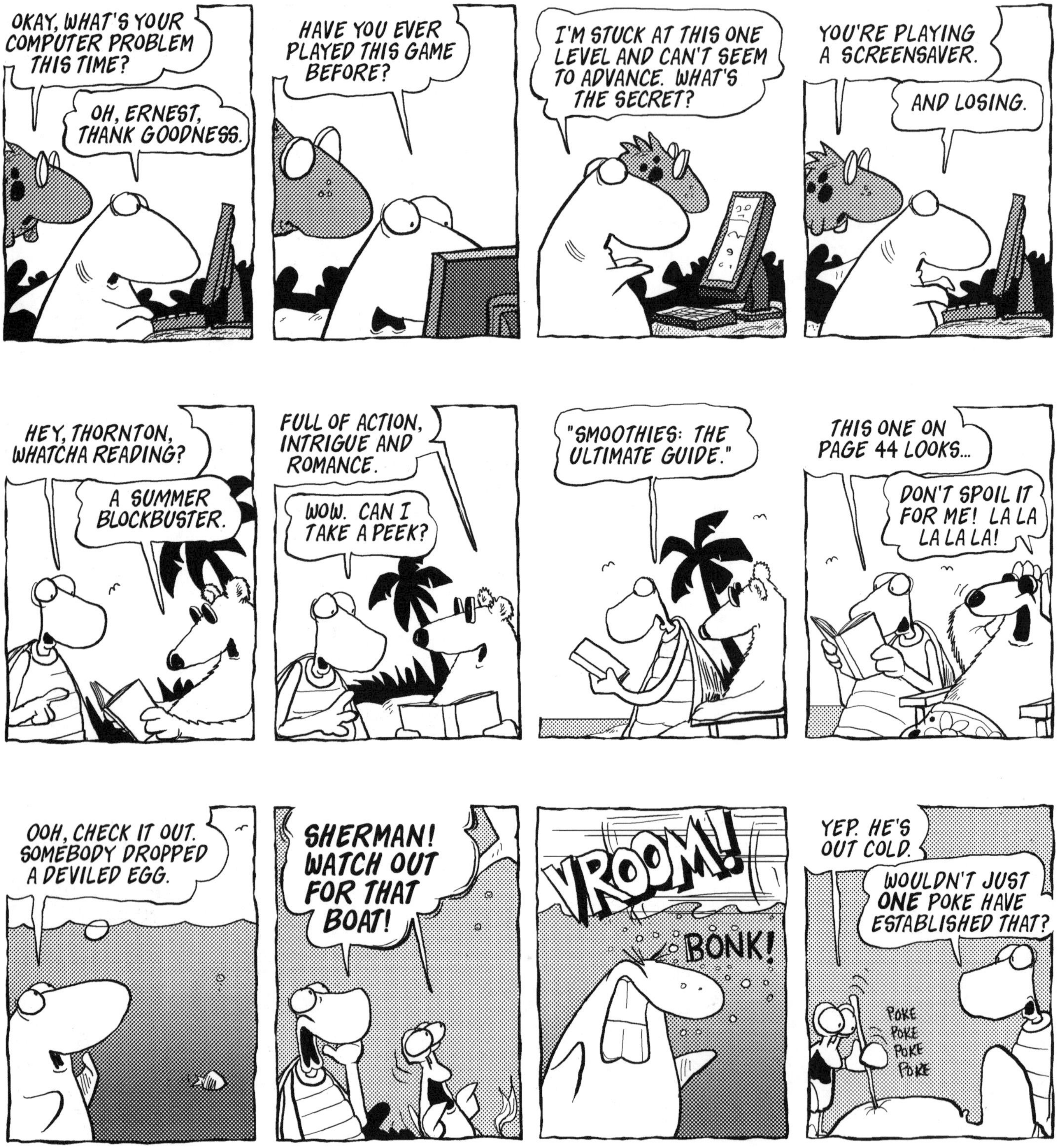

OKAY, WHAT'S YOUR COMPUTER PROBLEM THIS TIME?
OH, ERNEST, THANK GOODNESS.
HAVE YOU EVER PLAYED THIS GAME BEFORE?
I'M STUCK AT THIS ONE LEVEL AND CAN'T SEEM TO ADVANCE. WHAT'S THE SECRET?
YOU'RE PLAYING A SCREENSAVER.
AND LOSING.
HEY, THORNTON, WHATCHA READING?
A SUMMER BLOCKBUSTER.
FULL OF ACTION, INTRIGUE AND ROMANCE.
WOW. CAN I TAKE A PEEK?
"SMOOTHIES: THE ULTIMATE GUIDE."
THIS ONE ON PAGE 44 LOOKS...
DON'T SPOIL IT FOR ME! LA LA LA LA LA!
OOH, CHECK IT OUT. SOMEBODY DROPPED A DEVILED EGG.
SHERMAN! WATCH OUT FOR THAT BOAT!
VROOM!
BONK!
YEP. HE'S OUT COLD.
WOULDN'T JUST ONE POKE HAVE ESTABLISHED THAT?
POKE
POKE
POKE
POKE

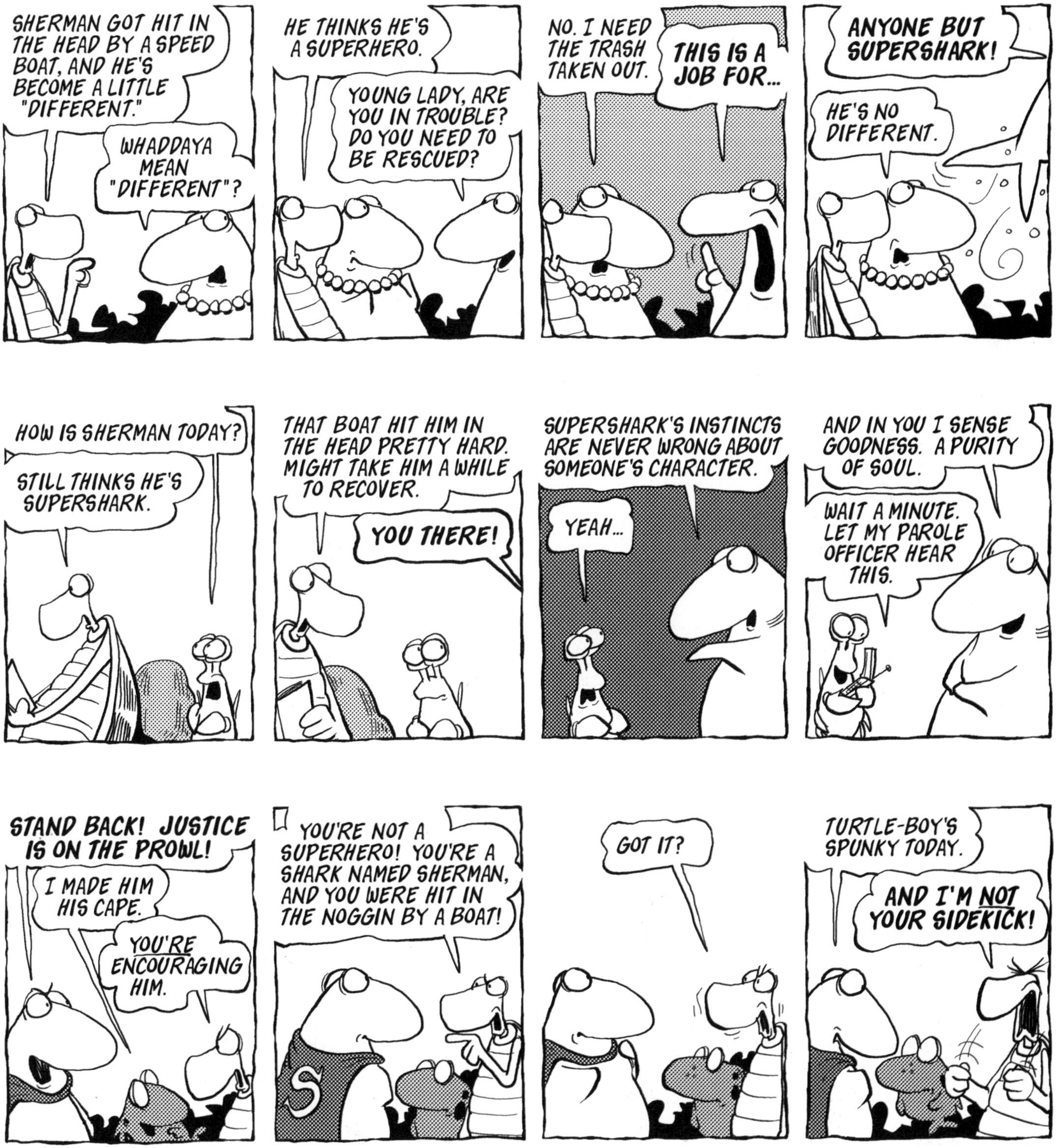
SHERMAN GOT HIT IN THE HEAD BY A SPEED BOAT, AND HE'S BECOME A LITTLE "DIFFERENT."
WHADDAYA MEAN "DIFFERENT"?
HE THINKS HE'S A SUPERHERO.
YOUNG LADY, ARE YOU IN TROUBLE? DO YOU NEED TO BE RESCUED?
NO. I NEED THE TRASH TAKEN OUT.
THIS IS A JOB FOR...
ANYONE BUT SUPERSHARK!
HE'S NO DIFFERENT.
HOW IS SHERMAN TODAY?
STILL THINKS HE'S SUPERSHARK.
THAT BOAT HIT HIM IN THE HEAD PRETTY HARD. MIGHT TAKE HIM A WHILE TO RECOVER.
YOU THERE!
SUPERSHARK'S INSTINCTS ARE NEVER WRONG ABOUT SOMEONE'S CHARACTER.
YEAH...
AND IN YOU I SENSE GOODNESS. A PURITY OF SOUL.
WAIT A MINUTE. LET MY PAROLE OFFICER HEAR THIS.
STAND BACK! JUSTICE IS ON THE PROWL!
I MADE HIM HIS CAPE.
YOU'RE ENCOURAGING HIM.
YOU'RE NOT A SUPERHERO! YOU'RE A SHARK NAMED SHERMAN, AND YOU WERE HIT IN THE NOGGIN BY A BOAT!
GOT IT?
TURTLE-BOY'S SPUNKY TODAY.
AND I'M NOT YOUR SIDEKICK!

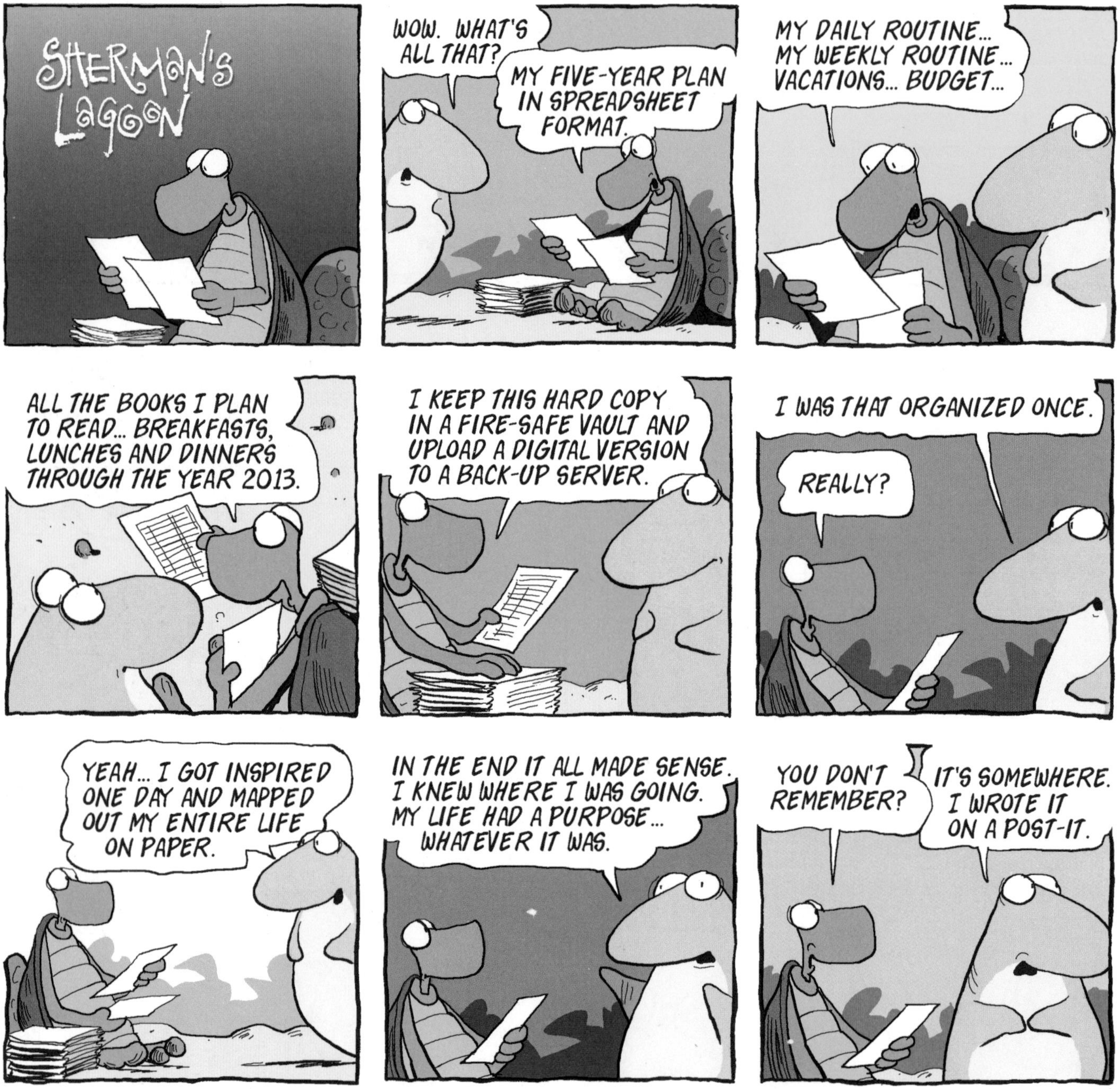
SHERMAN'S LAGOON
WOW. WHAT'S ALL THAT?
MY FIVE-YEAR PLAN IN SPREADSHEET FORMAT.
MY DAILY ROUTINE... MY WEEKLY ROUTINE... VACATIONS... BUDGET...
ALL THE BOOKS I PLAN TO READ... BREAKFASTS, LUNCHES AND DINNERS THROUGH THE YEAR 2013.
I KEEP THIS HARD COPY IN A FIRE-SAFE VAULT AND UPLOAD A DIGITAL VERSION TO A BACK-UP SERVER.
I WAS THAT ORGANIZED ONCE.
REALLY?
YEAH... I GOT INSPIRED ONE DAY AND MAPPED OUT MY ENTIRE LIFE ON PAPER.
IN THE END IT ALL MADE SENSE. I KNEW WHERE I WAS GOING. MY LIFE HAD A PURPOSE... WHATEVER IT WAS.
YOU DON'T REMEMBER?
IT'S SOMEWHERE. I WROTE IT ON A POST-IT.

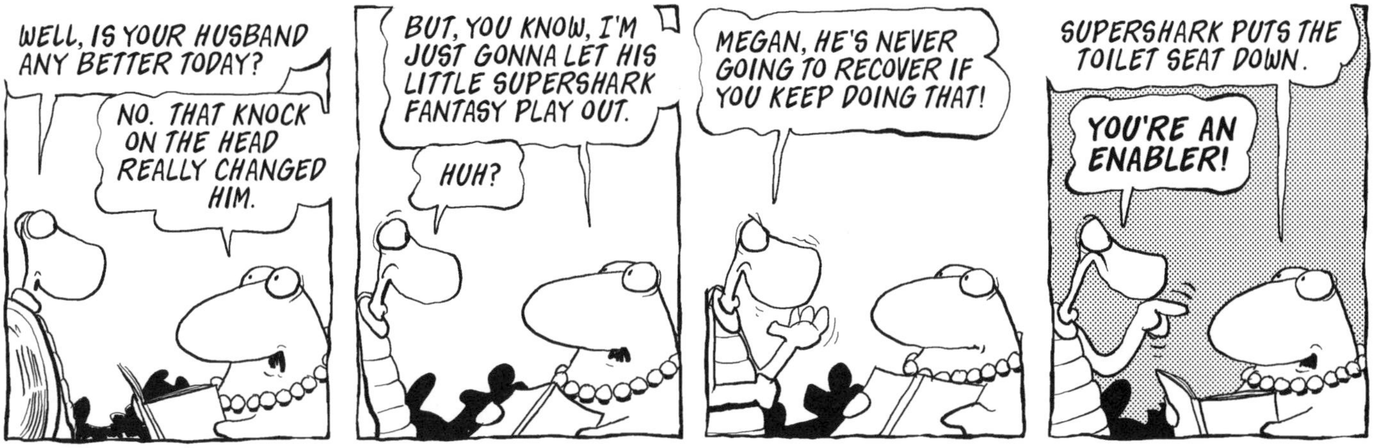
WELL, IS YOUR HUSBAND ANY BETTER TODAY?
NO. THAT KNOCK ON THE HEAD REALLY CHANGED HIM.
BUT, YOU KNOW, I'M JUST GONNA LET HIS LITTLE SUPERSHARK FANTASY PLAY OUT.
HUH?
MEGAN, HE'S NEVER GOING TO RECOVER IF YOU KEEP DOING THAT!
SUPERSHARK PUTS THE TOILET SEAT DOWN.
YOU'RE AN ENABLER!

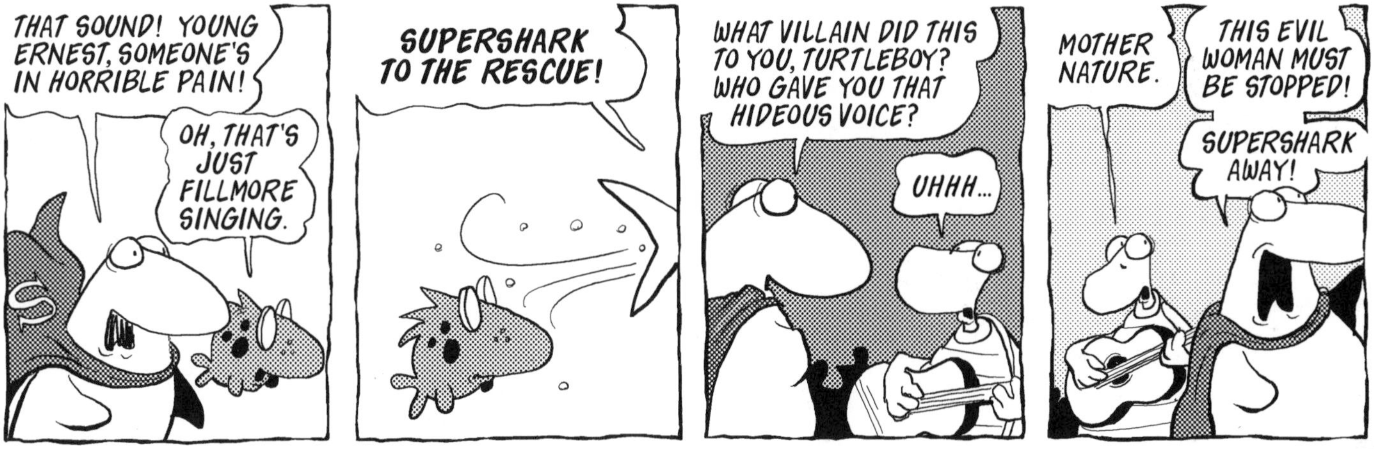
THAT SOUND! YOUNG ERNEST, SOMEONE'S IN HORRIBLE PAIN!
OH, THAT'S JUST FILLMORE SINGING.
SUPERSHARK TO THE RESCUE!
WHAT VILLAIN DID THIS TO YOU, TURTLEBOY? WHO GAVE YOU THAT HIDEOUS VOICE?
UHHH...
MOTHER NATURE.
THIS EVIL WOMAN MUST BE STOPPED!
SUPERSHARK AWAY!

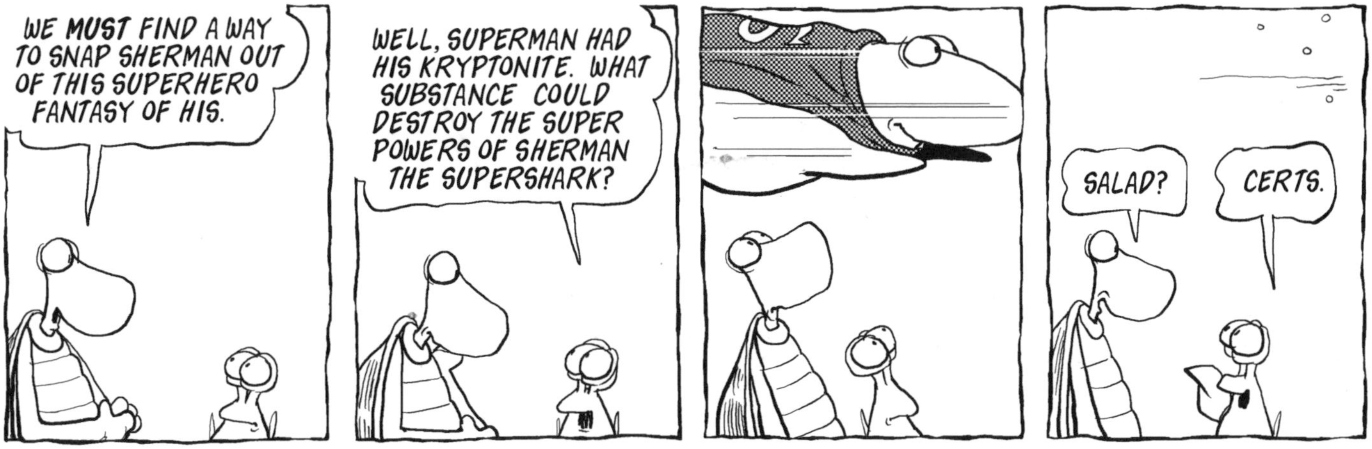
WE MUST FIND A WAY TO SNAP SHERMAN OUT OF THIS SUPERHERO FANTASY OF HIS.
WELL, SUPERMAN HAD HIS KRYPTONITE. WHAT SUBSTANCE COULD DESTROY THE SUPER POWERS OF SHERMAN THE SUPERSHARK?
SALAD?
CERTS.

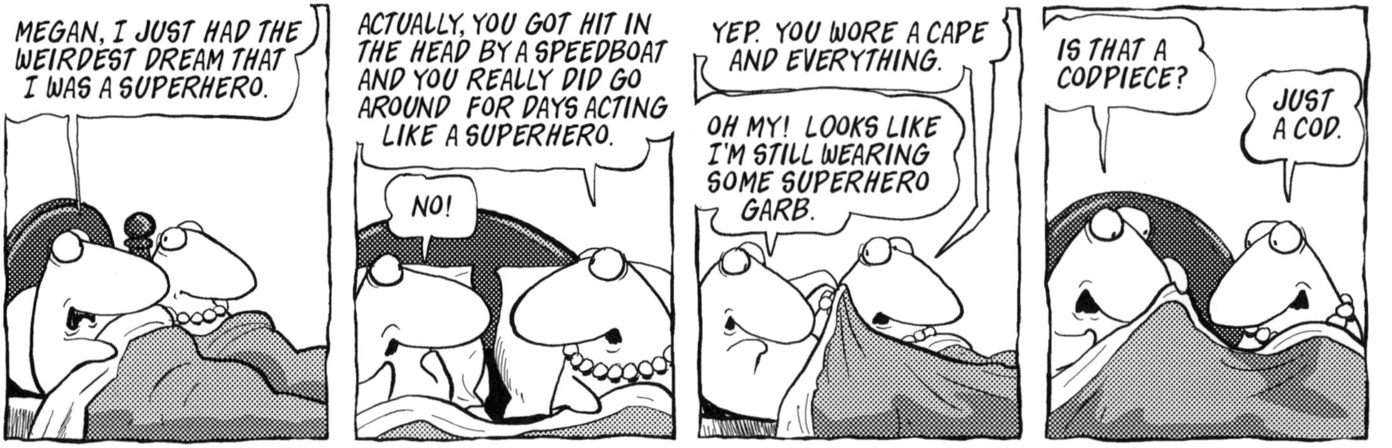
MEGAN, I JUST HAD THE WEIRDEST DREAM THAT I WAS A SUPERHERO.
ACTUALLY, YOU GOT HIT IN THE HEAD BY A SPEEDBOAT AND YOU REALLY DID GO AROUND FOR DAYS ACTING LIKE A SUPERHERO.
NO!
YEP. YOU WORE A CAPE AND EVERYTHING.
OH MY! LOOKS LIKE I'M STILL WEARING SOME SUPERHERO GARB.
IS THAT A CODPIECE?
JUST A COD.

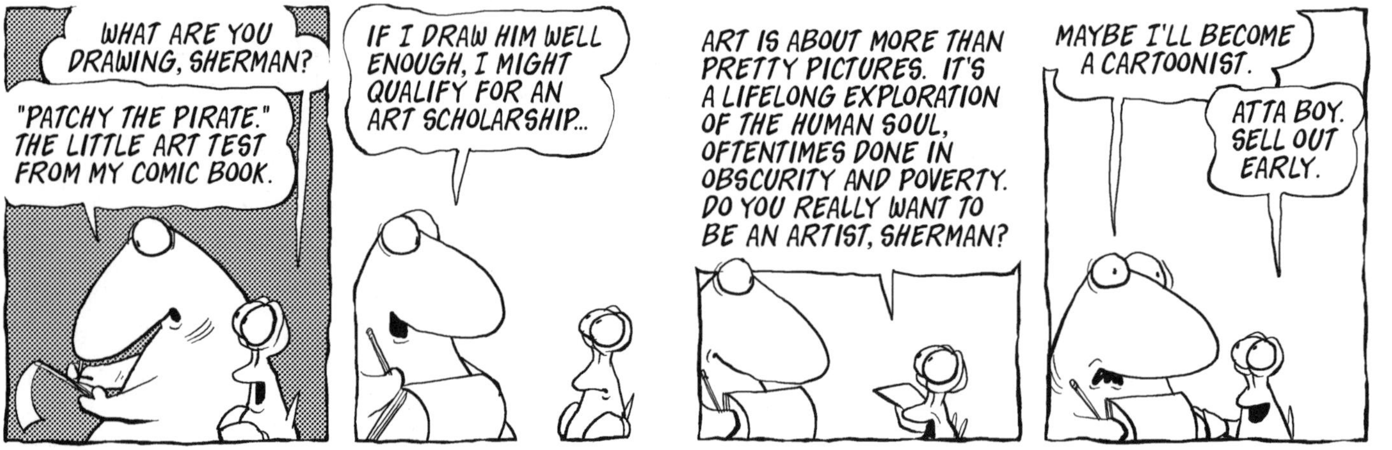
WHAT ARE YOU DRAWING, SHERMAN?
"PATCHY THE PIRATE." THE LITTLE ART TEST FROM MY COMIC BOOK.
IF I DRAW HIM WELL ENOUGH, I MIGHT QUALIFY FOR AN ART SCHOLARSHIP...
ART IS ABOUT MORE THAN PRETTY PICTURES. IT'S A LIFELONG EXPLORATION OF THE HUMAN SOUL, OFTENTIMES DONE IN OBSCURITY AND POVERTY. DO YOU REALLY WANT TO BE AN ARTIST, SHERMAN?
MAYBE I'LL BECOME A CARTOONIST.
ATTA BOY. SELL OUT EARLY.

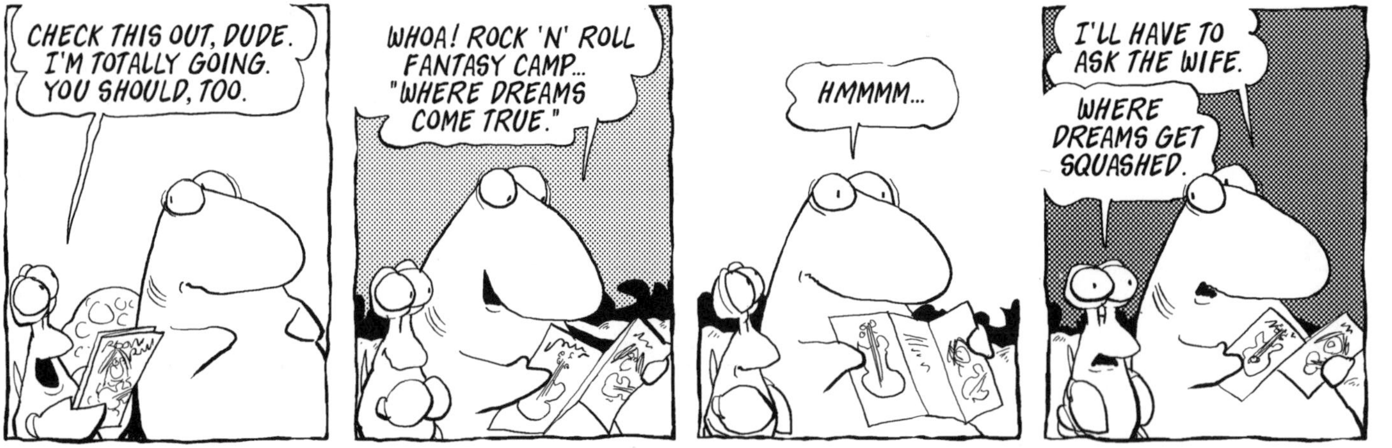
CHECK THIS OUT, DUDE. I'M TOTALLY GOING. YOU SHOULD, TOO.
WHOA! ROCK 'N' ROLL FANTASY CAMP... "WHERE DREAMS COME TRUE."
HMMMM...
I'LL HAVE TO ASK THE WIFE.
WHERE DREAMS GET SQUASHED.

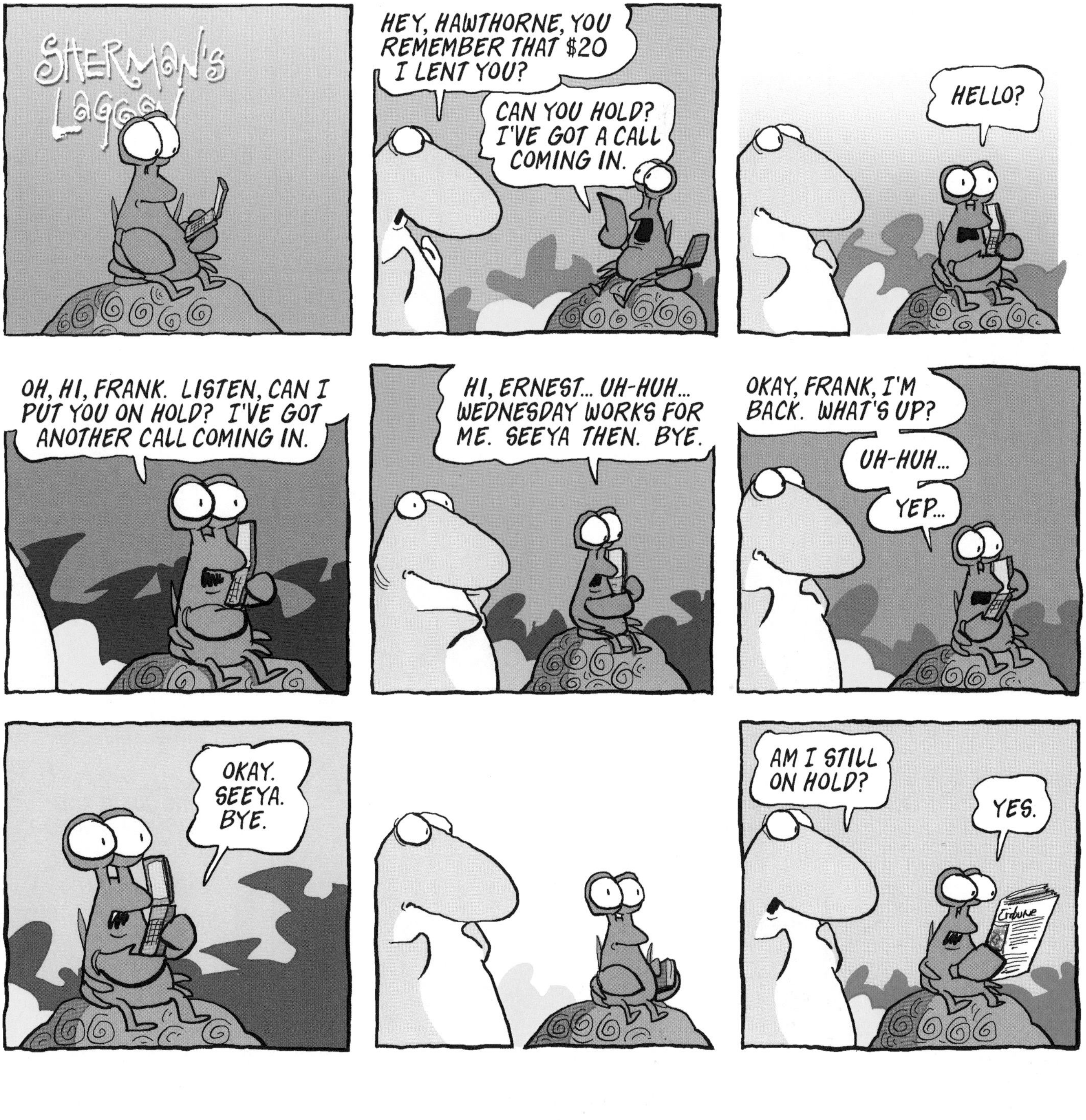
SHERMAN'S LAGOON
HEY, HAWTHORNE, YOU REMEMBER THAT $20 I LENT YOU?
CAN YOU HOLD? I'VE GOT A CALL COMING IN.
HELLO?
OH, HI, FRANK. LISTEN, CAN I PUT YOU ON HOLD? I'VE GOT ANOTHER CALL COMING IN.
HI, ERNEST... UH-HUH... WEDNESDAY WORKS FOR ME. SEEYA THEN. BYE.
OKAY, FRANK, I'M BACK. WHAT'S UP?
UH-HUH...
YEP...
OKAY. SEEYA. BYE.
AM I STILL ON HOLD?
YES.
Tribune

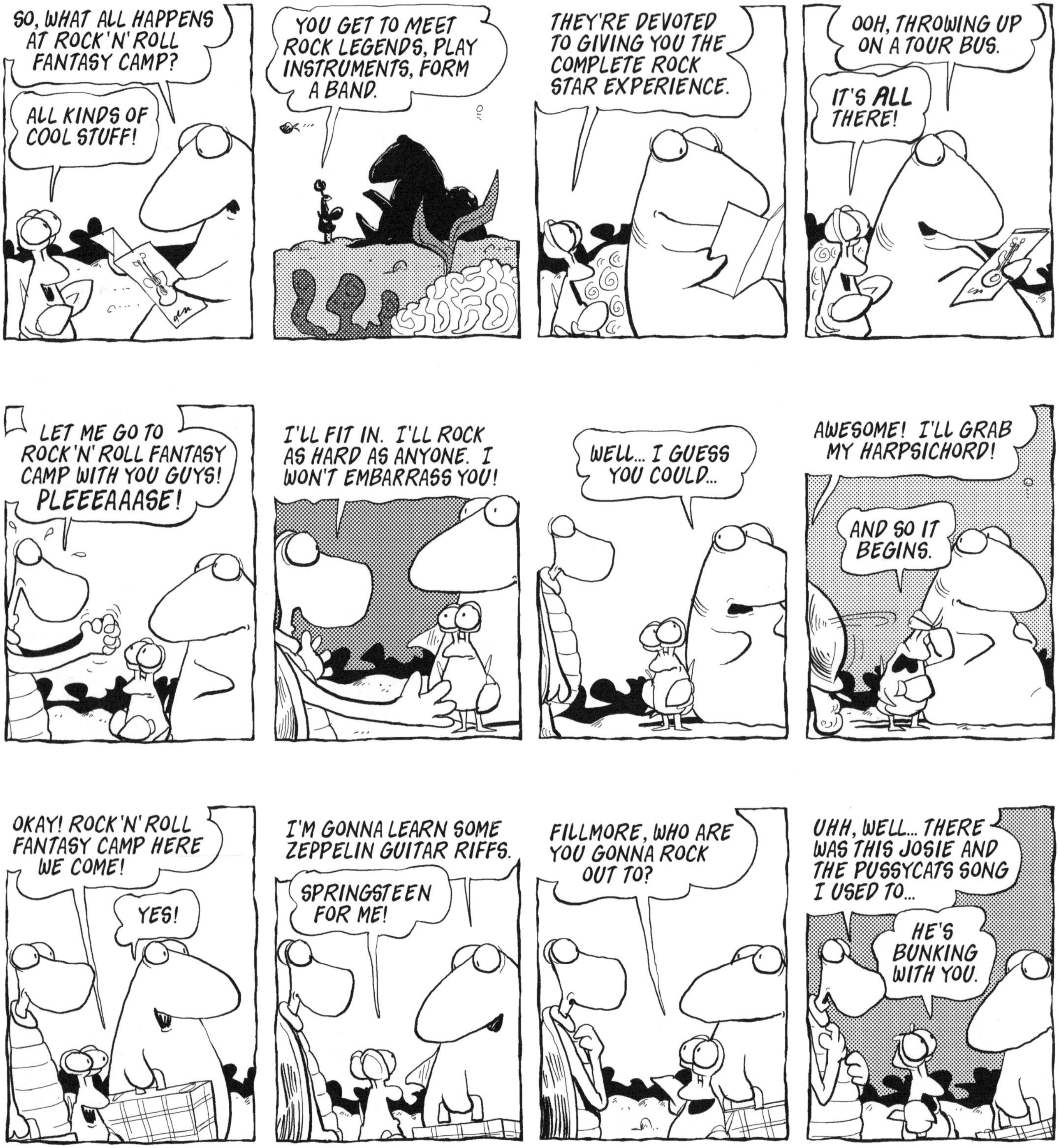
SO, WHAT ALL HAPPENS AT ROCK 'N' ROLL FANTASY CAMP?
ALL KINDS OF COOL STUFF!
YOU GET TO MEET ROCK LEGENDS, PLAY INSTRUMENTS, FORM A BAND.
THEY'RE DEVOTED TO GIVING YOU THE COMPLETE ROCK STAR EXPERIENCE.
OOH, THROWING UP ON A TOUR BUS.
IT'S ALL THERE!
LET ME GO TO ROCK 'N' ROLL FANTASY CAMP WITH YOU GUYS! PLEEEAAASE!
I'LL FIT IN. I'LL ROCK AS HARD AS ANYONE. I WON'T EMBARRASS YOU!
WELL... I GUESS YOU COULD...
AWESOME! I'LL GRAB MY HARPSICHORD!
AND SO IT BEGINS.
OKAY! ROCK 'N' ROLL FANTASY CAMP HERE WE COME!
YES!
I'M GONNA LEARN SOME ZEPPELIN GUITAR RIFFS.
SPRINGSTEEN FOR ME!
FILLMORE, WHO ARE YOU GONNA ROCK OUT TO?
UHH, WELL... THERE WAS THIS JOSIE AND THE PUSSYCATS SONG I USED TO...
HE'S BUNKING WITH YOU.

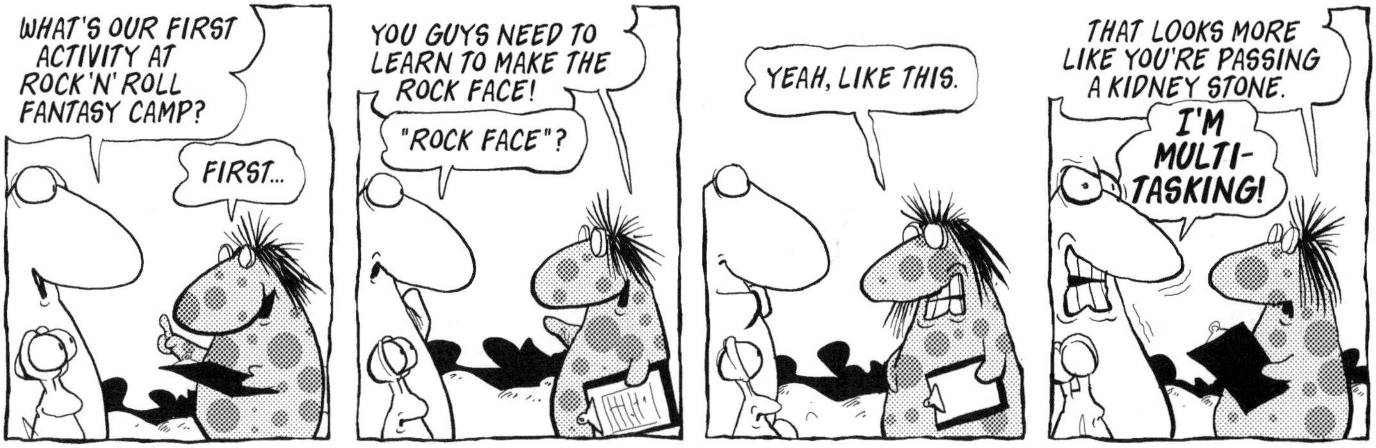
WHAT'S OUR FIRST ACTIVITY AT ROCK 'N' ROLL FANTASY CAMP?
FIRST...
YOU GUYS NEED TO LEARN TO MAKE THE ROCK FACE!
"ROCK FACE"?
YEAH, LIKE THIS.
THAT LOOKS MORE LIKE YOU'RE PASSING A KIDNEY STONE.
I'M MULTI-TASKING!

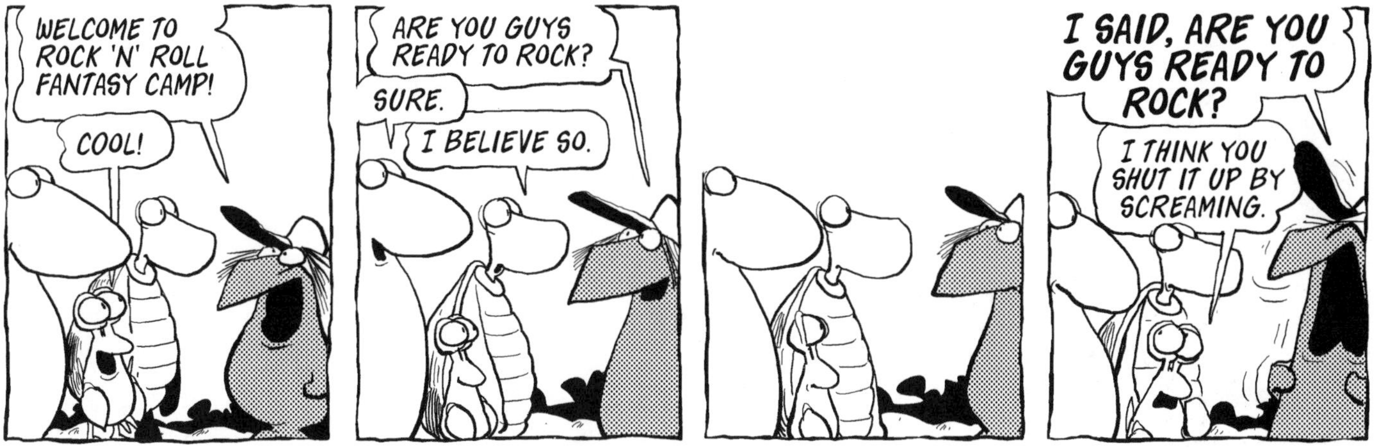
WELCOME TO ROCK 'N' ROLL FANTASY CAMP!
COOL!
ARE YOU GUYS READY TO ROCK?
SURE.
I BELIEVE SO.
I SAID, ARE YOU GUYS READY TO ROCK?
I THINK YOU SHUT IT UP BY SCREAMING.

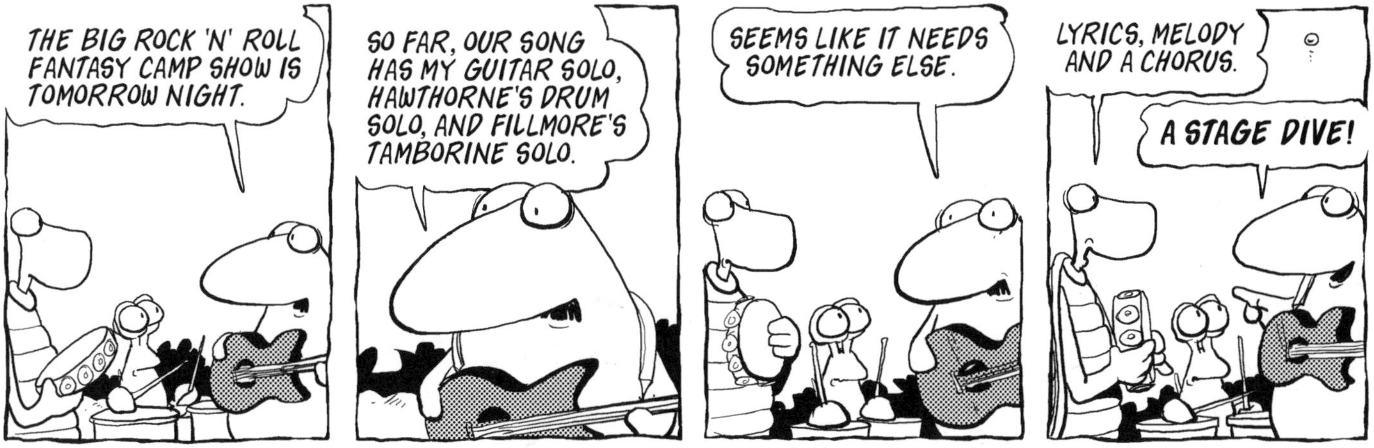
THE BIG ROCK 'N' ROLL FANTASY CAMP SHOW IS TOMORROW NIGHT.
SO FAR, OUR SONG HAS MY GUITAR SOLO, HAWTHORNE'S DRUM SOLO, AND FILLMORE'S TAMBORINE SOLO.
SEEMS LIKE IT NEEDS SOMETHING ELSE.
LYRICS, MELODY AND A CHORUS.
A STAGE DIVE!

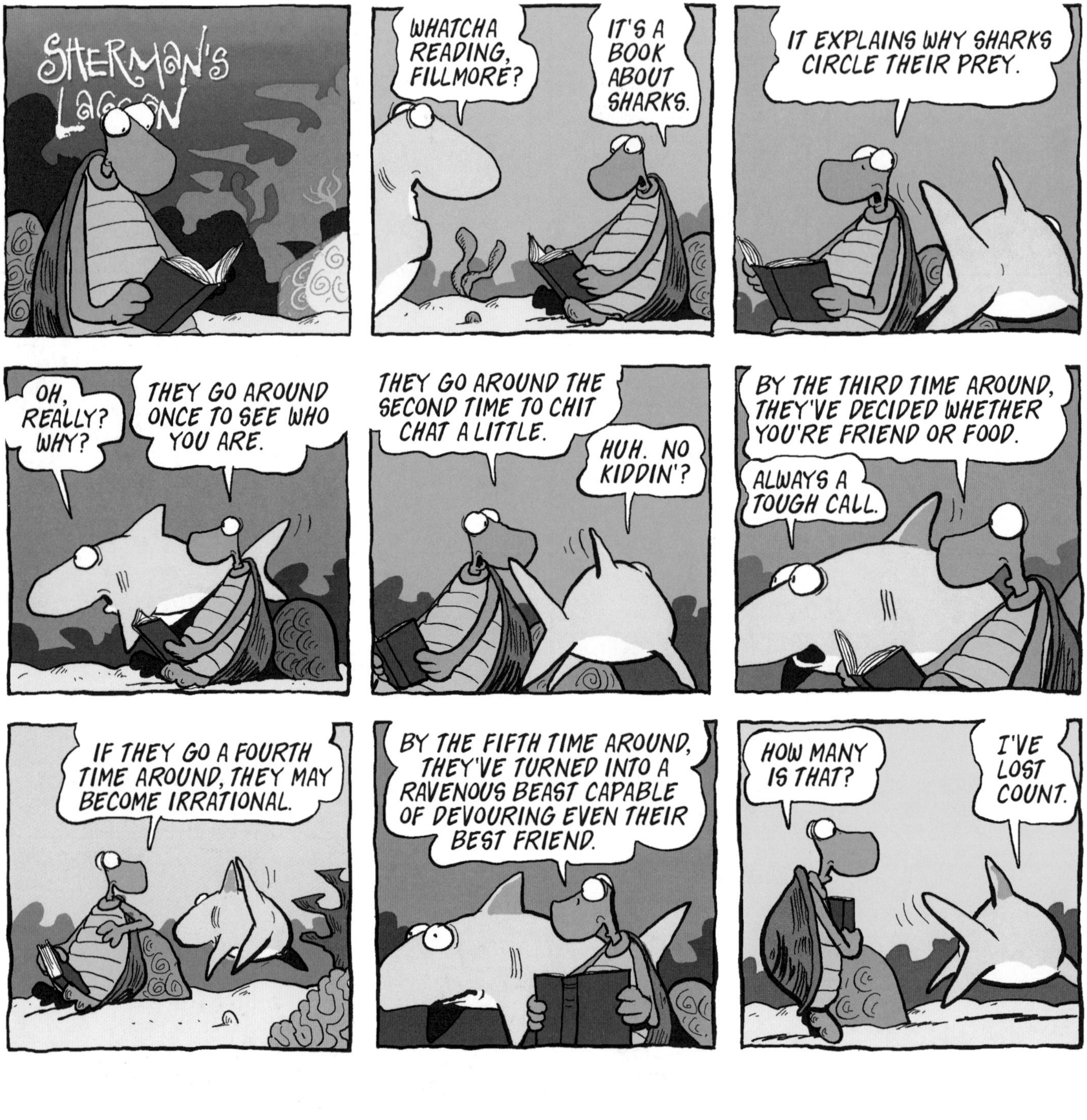
SHERMAN'S LAGOON
WHATCHA READING, FILLMORE?
IT'S A BOOK ABOUT SHARKS.
IT EXPLAINS WHY SHARKS CIRCLE THEIR PREY.
OH, REALLY? WHY?
THEY GO AROUND ONCE TO SEE WHO YOU ARE.
THEY GO AROUND THE SECOND TIME TO CHIT CHAT A LITTLE.
HUH. NO KIDDIN'?
BY THE THIRD TIME AROUND, THEY'VE DECIDED WHETHER YOU'RE FRIEND OR FOOD.
ALWAYS A TOUGH CALL.
IF THEY GO A FOURTH TIME AROUND, THEY MAY BECOME IRRATIONAL.
BY THE FIFTH TIME AROUND, THEY'VE TURNED INTO A RAVENOUS BEAST CAPABLE OF DEVOURING EVEN THEIR BEST FRIEND.
HOW MANY IS THAT?
I'VE LOST COUNT.

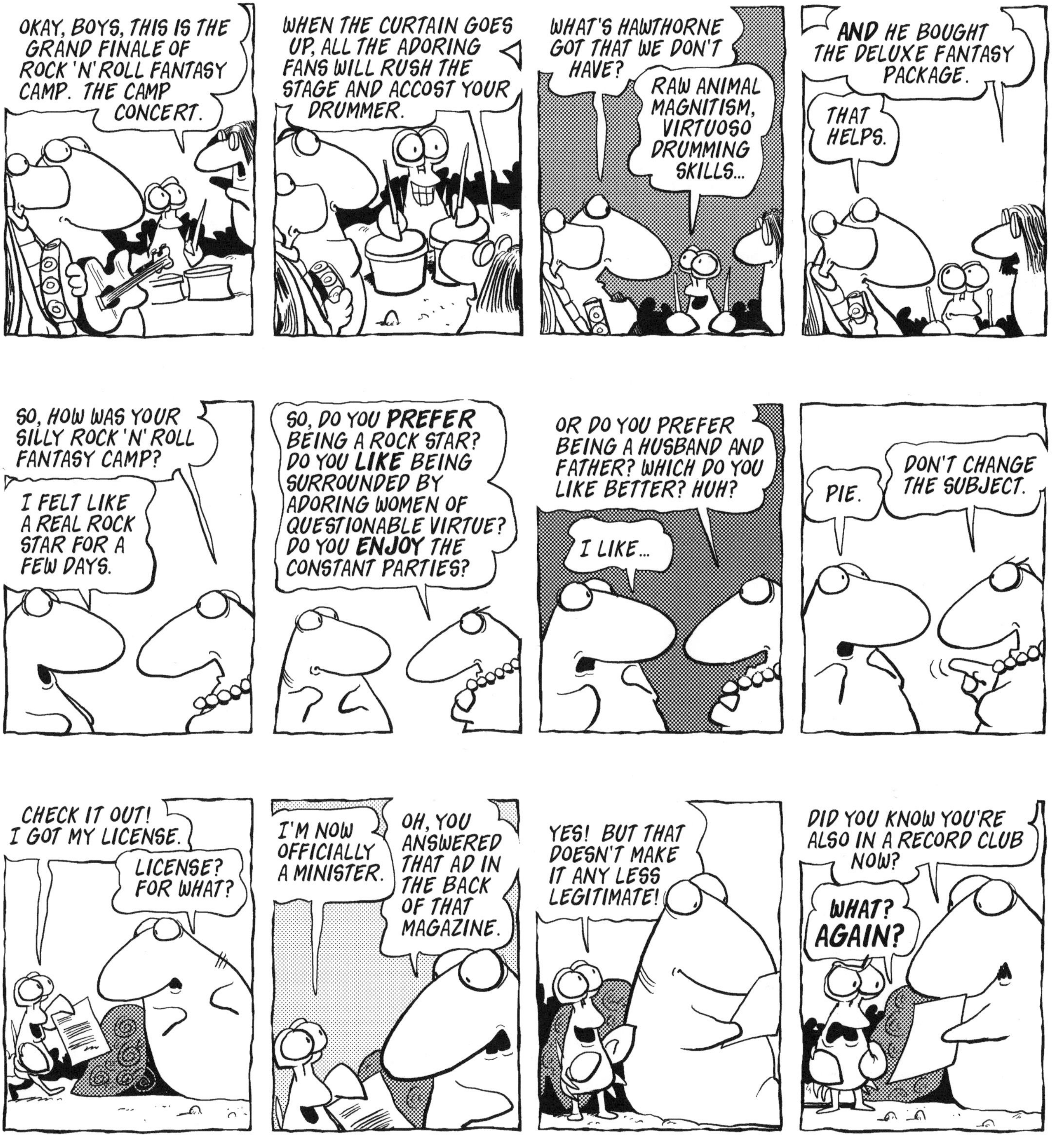
OKAY, BOYS, THIS IS THE GRAND FINALE OF ROCK 'N' ROLL FANTASY CAMP. THE CAMP CONCERT.
WHEN THE CURTAIN GOES UP, ALL THE ADORING FANS WILL RUSH THE STAGE AND ACCOST YOUR DRUMMER.
WHAT'S HAWTHORNE GOT THAT WE DON'T HAVE?
RAW ANIMAL MAGNITISM, VIRTUOSO DRUMMING SKILLS...
AND HE BOUGHT THE DELUXE FANTASY PACKAGE.
THAT HELPS.
SO, HOW WAS YOUR SILLY ROCK 'N' ROLL FANTASY CAMP?
I FELT LIKE A REAL ROCK STAR FOR A FEW DAYS.
SO, DO YOU PREFER BEING A ROCK STAR? DO YOU LIKE BEING SURROUNDED BY ADORING WOMEN OF QUESTIONABLE VIRTUE? DO YOU ENJOY THE CONSTANT PARTIES?
OR DO YOU PREFER BEING A HUSBAND AND FATHER? WHICH DO YOU LIKE BETTER? HUH?
I LIKE...
PIE.
DON'T CHANGE THE SUBJECT.
CHECK IT OUT! I GOT MY LICENSE.
LICENSE? FOR WHAT?
I'M NOW OFFICIALLY A MINISTER.
OH, YOU ANSWERED THAT AD IN THE BACK OF THAT MAGAZINE.
YES! BUT THAT DOESN'T MAKE IT ANY LESS LEGITIMATE!
DID YOU KNOW YOU'RE ALSO IN A RECORD CLUB NOW?
WHAT? AGAIN?

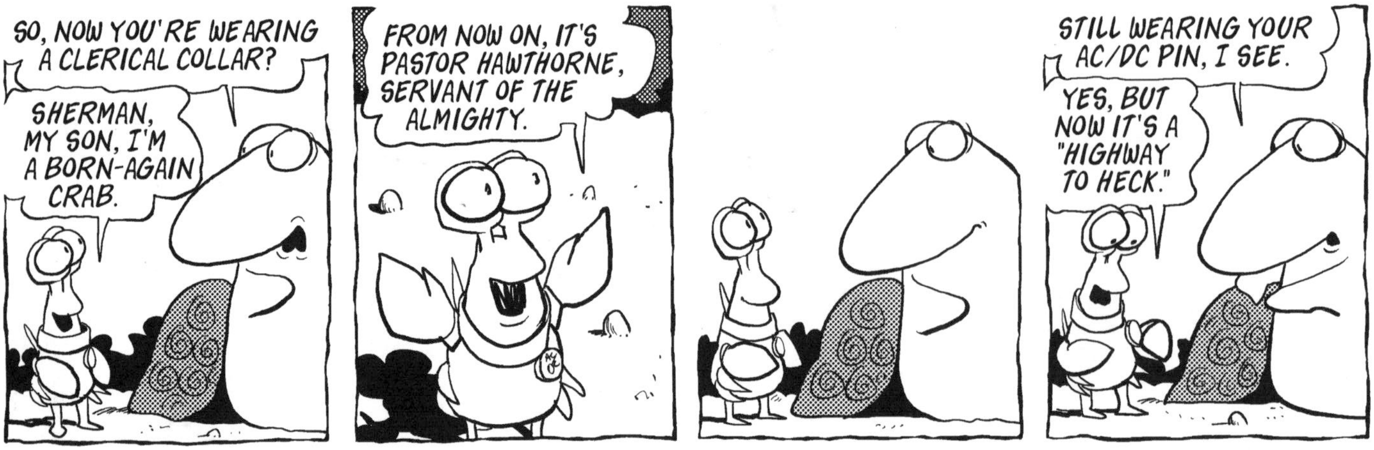
SO, NOW YOU'RE WEARING A CLERICAL COLLAR?
SHERMAN, MY SON, I'M A BORN-AGAIN CRAB.
FROM NOW ON, IT'S PASTOR HAWTHORNE, SERVANT OF THE ALMIGHTY.
STILL WEARING YOUR AC/DC PIN, I SEE.
YES, BUT NOW IT'S A "HIGHWAY TO HECK."

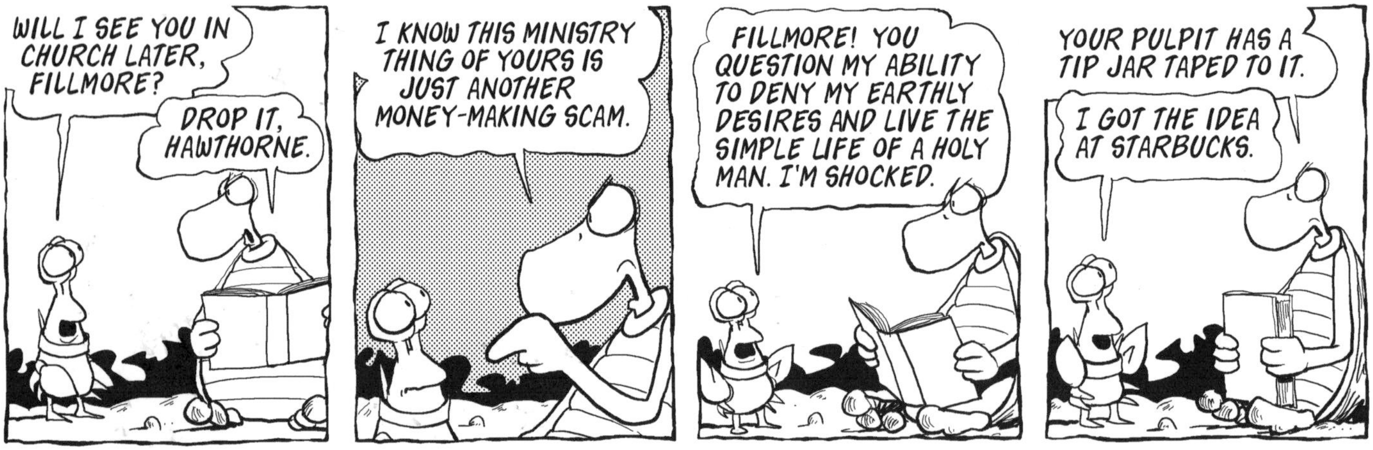
WILL I SEE YOU IN CHURCH LATER, FILLMORE?
DROP IT, HAWTHORNE.
I KNOW THIS MINISTRY THING OF YOURS IS JUST ANOTHER MONEY-MAKING SCAM.
FILLMORE! YOU QUESTION MY ABILITY TO DENY MY EARTHLY DESIRES AND LIVE THE SIMPLE LIFE OF A HOLY MAN. I'M SHOCKED.
YOUR PULPIT HAS A TIP JAR TAPED TO IT.
I GOT THE IDEA AT STARBUCKS.

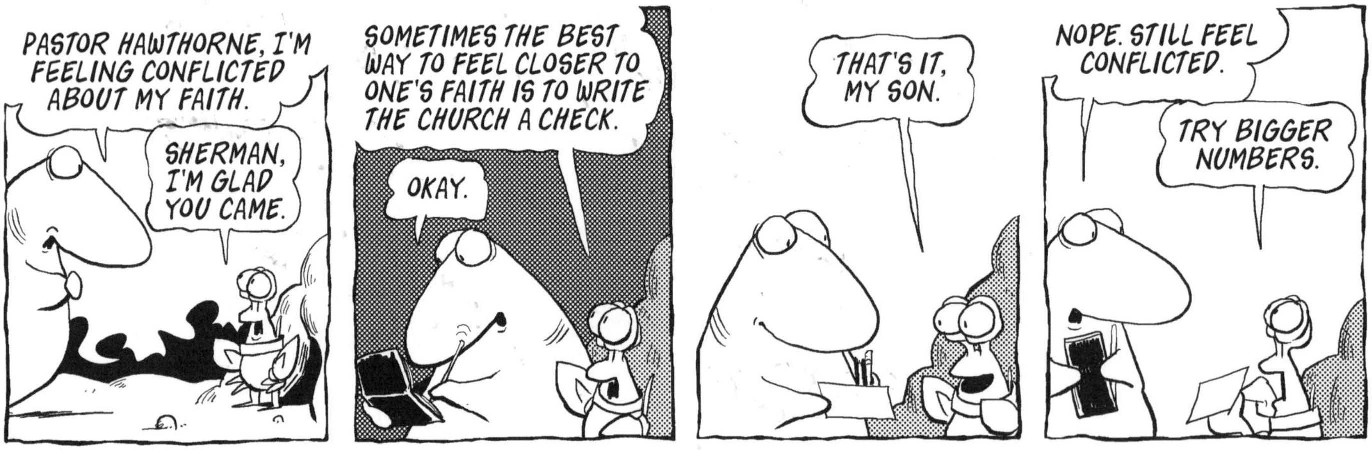
PASTOR HAWTHORNE, I'M FEELING CONFLICTED ABOUT MY FAITH.
SHERMAN, I'M GLAD YOU CAME.
SOMETIMES THE BEST WAY TO FEEL CLOSER TO ONE'S FAITH IS TO WRITE THE CHURCH A CHECK.
OKAY.
THAT'S IT, MY SON.
NOPE. STILL FEEL CONFLICTED.
TRY BIGGER NUMBERS.

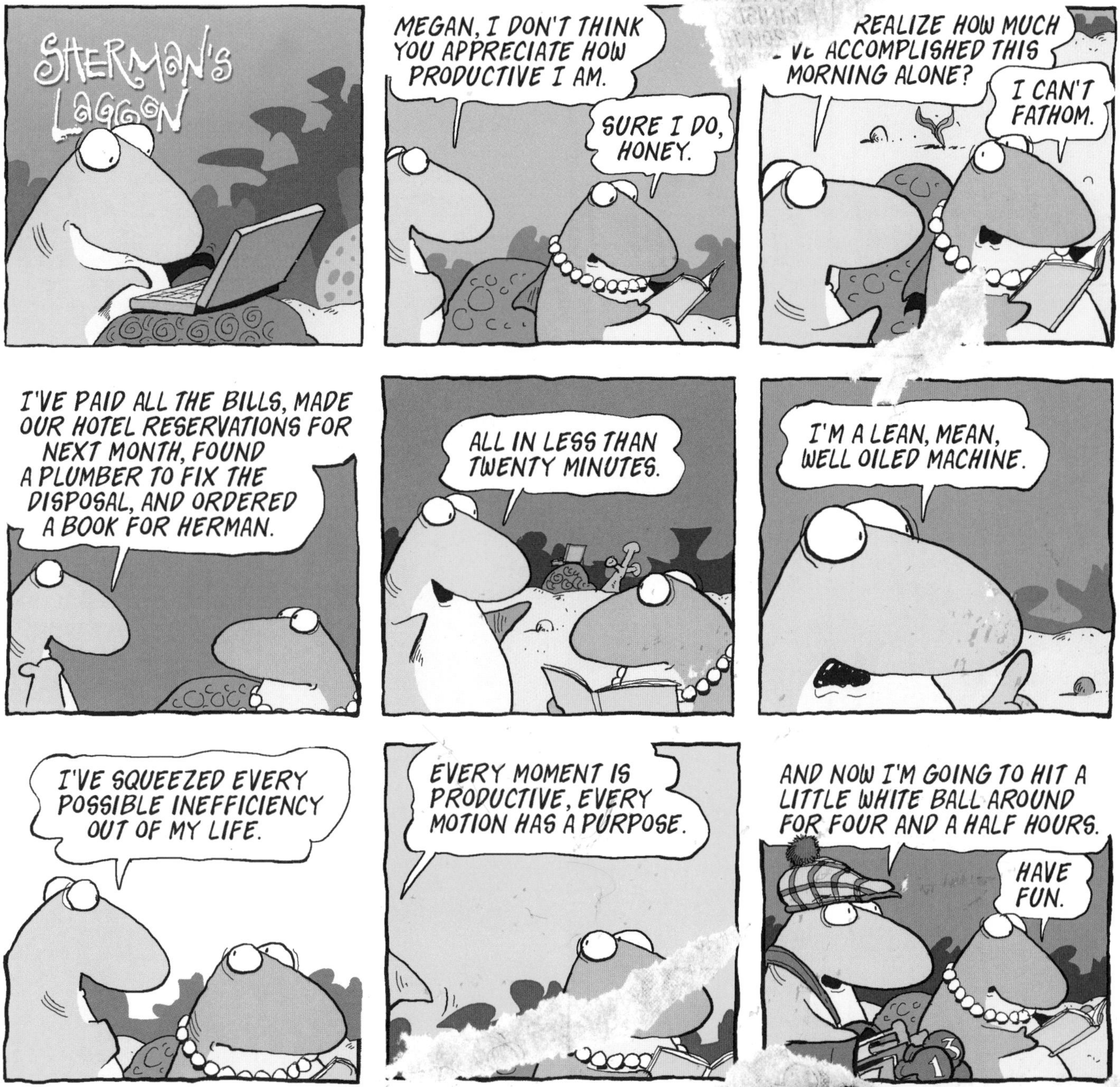
SHERMAN'S LAGOON
MEGAN, I DON'T THINK YOU APPRECIATE HOW PRODUCTIVE I AM.
SURE I DO, HONEY.
REALIZE HOW MUCH
ACCOMPLISHED THIS MORNING ALONE?
I CAN'T FATHOM.
I'VE PAID ALL THE BILLS, MADE OUR HOTEL RESERVATIONS FOR NEXT MONTH, FOUND A PLUMBER TO FIX THE DISPOSAL, AND ORDERED A BOOK FOR HERMAN.
ALL IN LESS THAN TWENTY MINUTES.
I'M A LEAN, MEAN, WELL OILED MACHINE.
I'VE SQUEEZED EVERY POSSIBLE INEFFICIENCY OUT OF MY LIFE.
EVERY MOMENT IS PRODUCTIVE, EVERY MOTION HAS A PURPOSE.
AND NOW I'M GOING TO HIT A LITTLE WHITE BALL AROUND FOR FOUR AND A HALF HOURS.
HAVE FUN.

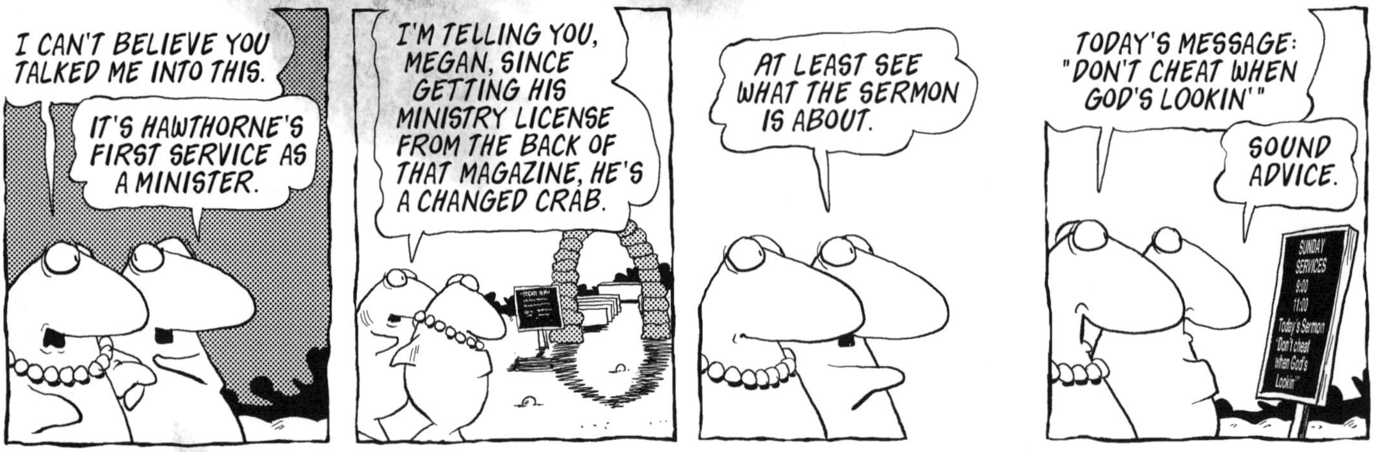
I CAN'T BELIEVE YOU TALKED ME INTO THIS.
IT'S HAWTHORNE'S FIRST SERVICE AS A MINISTER.
I'M TELLING YOU, MEGAN, SINCE GETTING HIS MINISTRY LICENSE FROM THE BACK OF THAT MAGAZINE, HE'S A CHANGED CRAB.
AT LEAST SEE WHAT THE SERMON IS ABOUT.
TODAY'S MESSAGE: "DON'T CHEAT WHEN GOD'S LOOKIN'"
SOUND ADVICE.
SUNDAY SERVICES 9:00 11:00 Today's Sermon "Don't cheat when God's Lookin'"

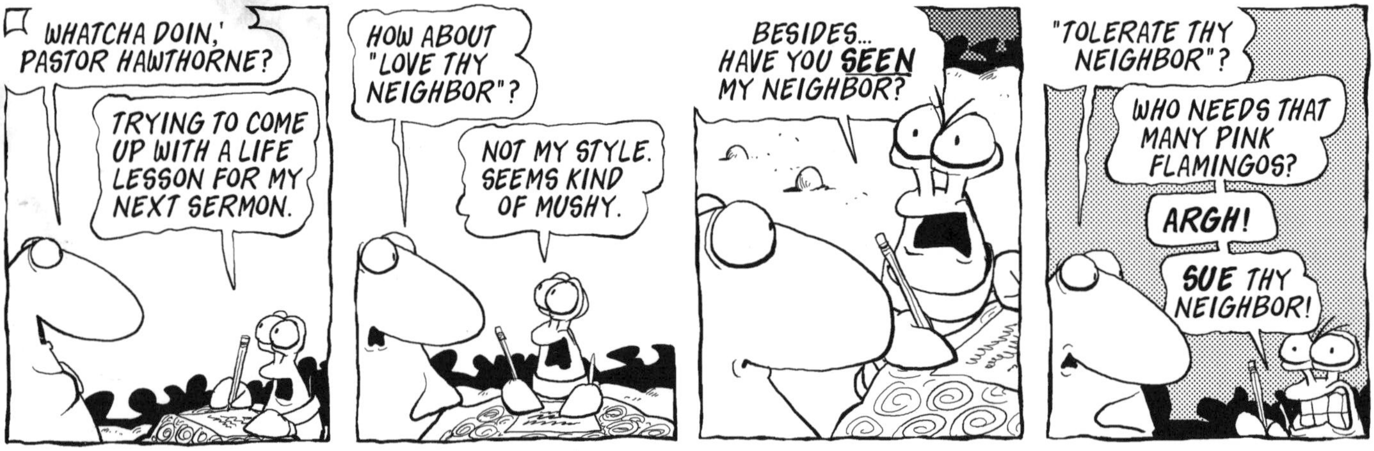
WHATCHA DOIN,' PASTOR HAWTHORNE?
TRYING TO COME UP WITH A LIFE LESSON FOR MY NEXT SERMON.
HOW ABOUT "LOVE THY NEIGHBOR"?
NOT MY STYLE. SEEMS KIND OF MUSHY.
BESIDES... HAVE YOU SEEN MY NEIGHBOR?
"TOLERATE THY NEIGHBOR"?
WHO NEEDS THAT MANY PINK FLAMINGOS?
ARGH!
SUE THY NEIGHBOR!

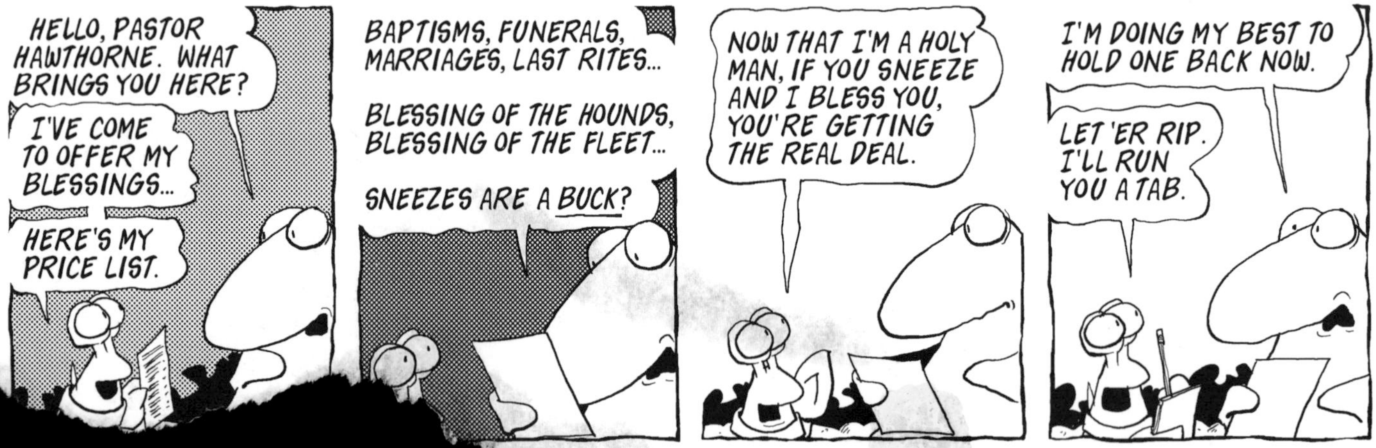
HELLO, PASTOR HAWTHORNE. WHAT BRINGS YOU HERE?
I'VE COME TO OFFER MY BLESSINGS...
HERE'S MY PRICE LIST.
BAPTISMS, FUNERALS, MARRIAGES, LAST RITES...
BLESSING OF THE HOUNDS, BLESSING OF THE FLEET...
SNEEZES ARE A BUCK?
NOW THAT I'M A HOLY MAN, IF YOU SNEEZE AND I BLESS YOU, YOU'RE GETTING THE REAL DEAL.
I'M DOING MY BEST TO HOLD ONE BACK NOW.
LET 'ER RIP. I'LL RUN YOU A TAB.

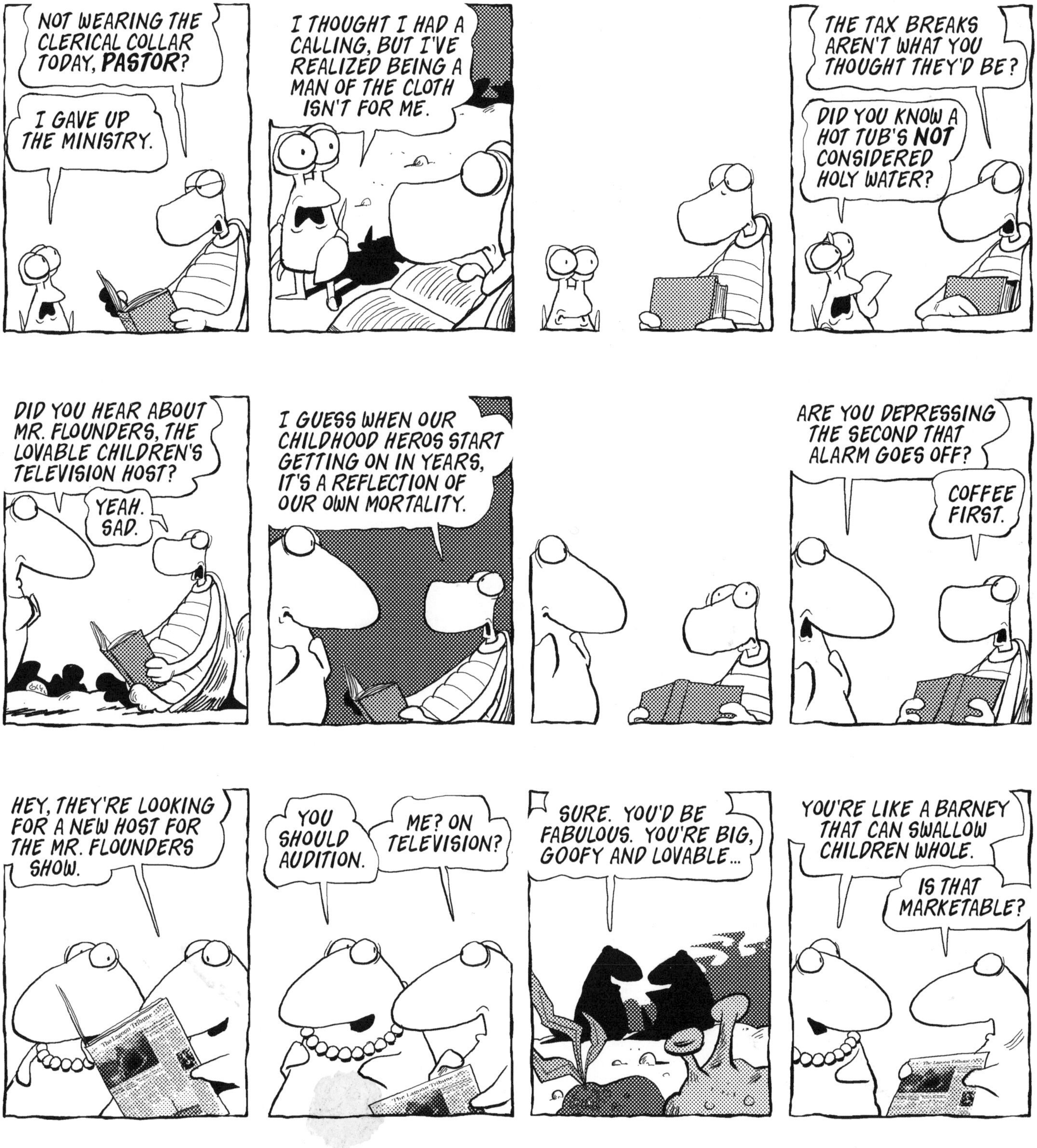
NOT WEARING THE CLERICAL COLLAR TODAY, **PASTOR**?
I GAVE UP THE MINISTRY.
I THOUGHT I HAD A CALLING, BUT I'VE REALIZED BEING A MAN OF THE CLOTH ISN'T FOR ME.
THE TAX BREAKS AREN'T WHAT YOU THOUGHT THEY'D BE?
DID YOU KNOW A HOT TUB'S **NOT** CONSIDERED HOLY WATER?
DID YOU HEAR ABOUT MR. FLOUNDERS, THE LOVABLE CHILDREN'S TELEVISION HOST?
YEAH. SAD.
I GUESS WHEN OUR CHILDHOOD HEROS START GETTING ON IN YEARS, IT'S A REFLECTION OF OUR OWN MORTALITY.
ARE YOU DEPRESSING THE SECOND THAT ALARM GOES OFF?
COFFEE FIRST.
HEY, THEY'RE LOOKING FOR A NEW HOST FOR THE MR. FLOUNDERS SHOW.
YOU SHOULD AUDITION.
ME? ON TELEVISION?
SURE. YOU'D BE FABULOUS. YOU'RE BIG, GOOFY AND LOVABLE...
YOU'RE LIKE A BARNEY THAT CAN SWALLOW CHILDREN WHOLE.
IS THAT MARKETABLE?

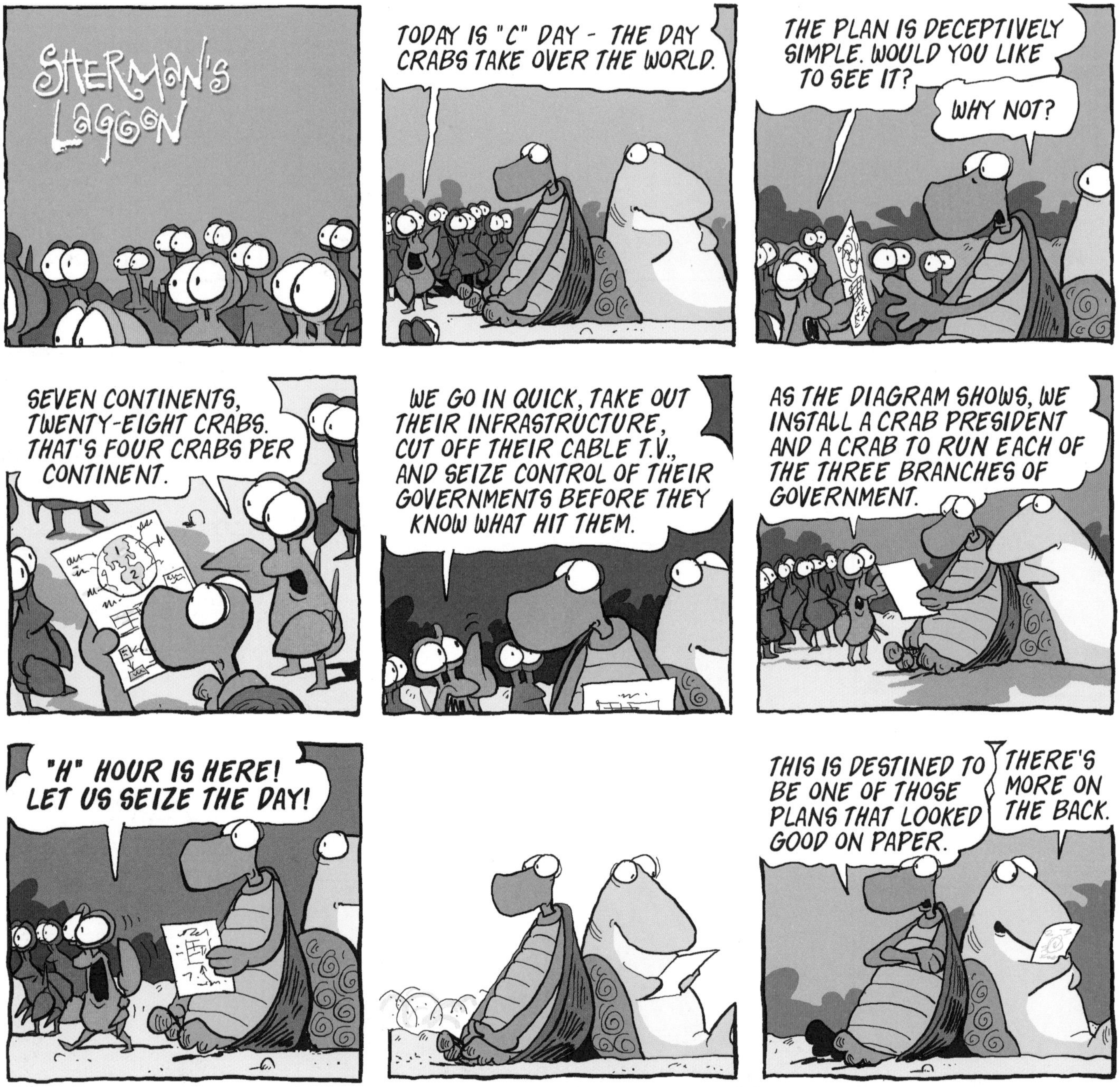
SHERMAN'S LAGOON
TODAY IS "C" DAY - THE DAY CRABS TAKE OVER THE WORLD.
THE PLAN IS DECEPTIVELY SIMPLE. WOULD YOU LIKE TO SEE IT?
WHY NOT?
SEVEN CONTINENTS, TWENTY-EIGHT CRABS. THAT'S FOUR CRABS PER CONTINENT.
WE GO IN QUICK, TAKE OUT THEIR INFRASTRUCTURE, CUT OFF THEIR CABLE T.V., AND SEIZE CONTROL OF THEIR GOVERNMENTS BEFORE THEY KNOW WHAT HIT THEM.
AS THE DIAGRAM SHOWS, WE INSTALL A CRAB PRESIDENT AND A CRAB TO RUN EACH OF THE THREE BRANCHES OF GOVERNMENT.
"H" HOUR IS HERE! LET US SEIZE THE DAY!
THIS IS DESTINED TO BE ONE OF THOSE PLANS THAT LOOKED GOOD ON PAPER.
THERE'S MORE ON THE BACK.

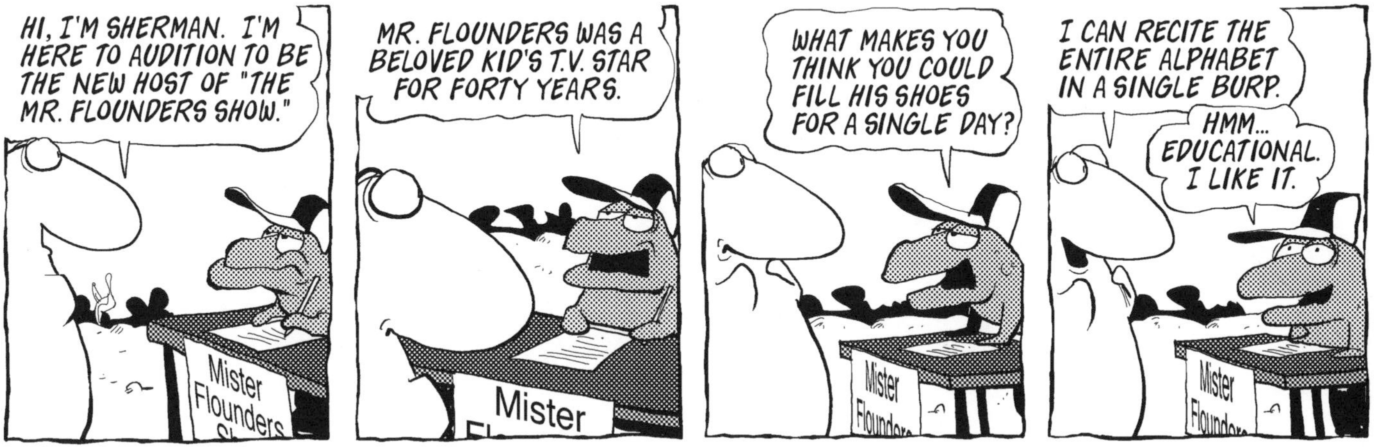
HI, I'M SHERMAN. I'M HERE TO AUDITION TO BE THE NEW HOST OF "THE MR. FLOUNDERS SHOW."
Mister Flounders
MR. FLOUNDERS WAS A BELOVED KID'S T.V. STAR FOR FORTY YEARS.
Mister
WHAT MAKES YOU THINK YOU COULD FILL HIS SHOES FOR A SINGLE DAY?
Mister
I CAN RECITE THE ENTIRE ALPHABET IN A SINGLE BURP.
HMM... EDUCATIONAL. I LIKE IT.
Mister

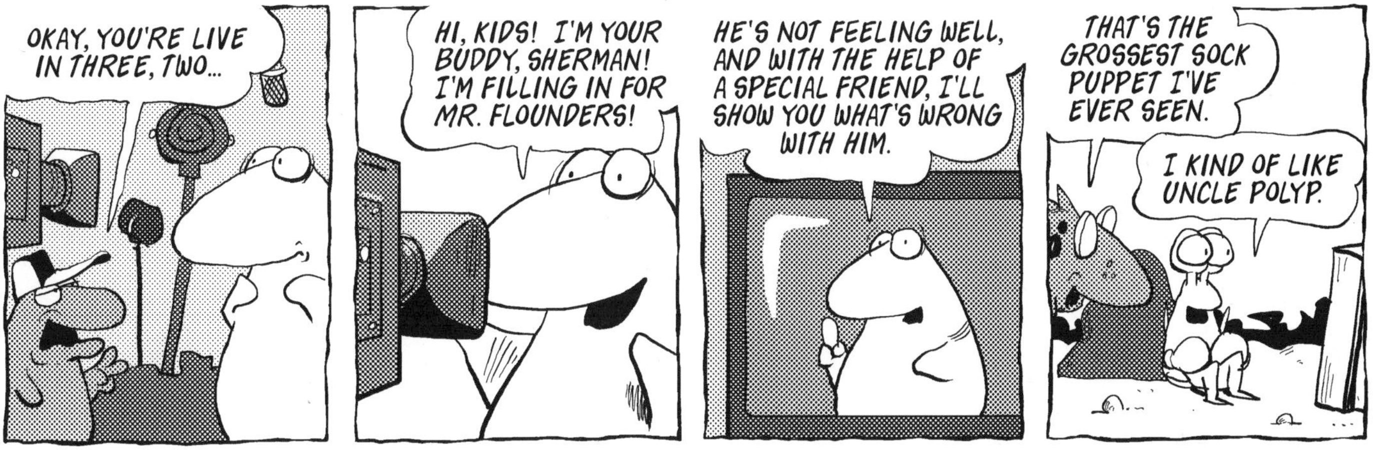
OKAY, YOU'RE LIVE IN THREE, TWO...
HI, KIDS! I'M YOUR BUDDY, SHERMAN! I'M FILLING IN FOR MR. FLOUNDERS!
HE'S NOT FEELING WELL, AND WITH THE HELP OF A SPECIAL FRIEND, I'LL SHOW YOU WHAT'S WRONG WITH HIM.
THAT'S THE GROSSEST SOCK PUPPET I'VE EVER SEEN.
I KIND OF LIKE UNCLE POLYP.

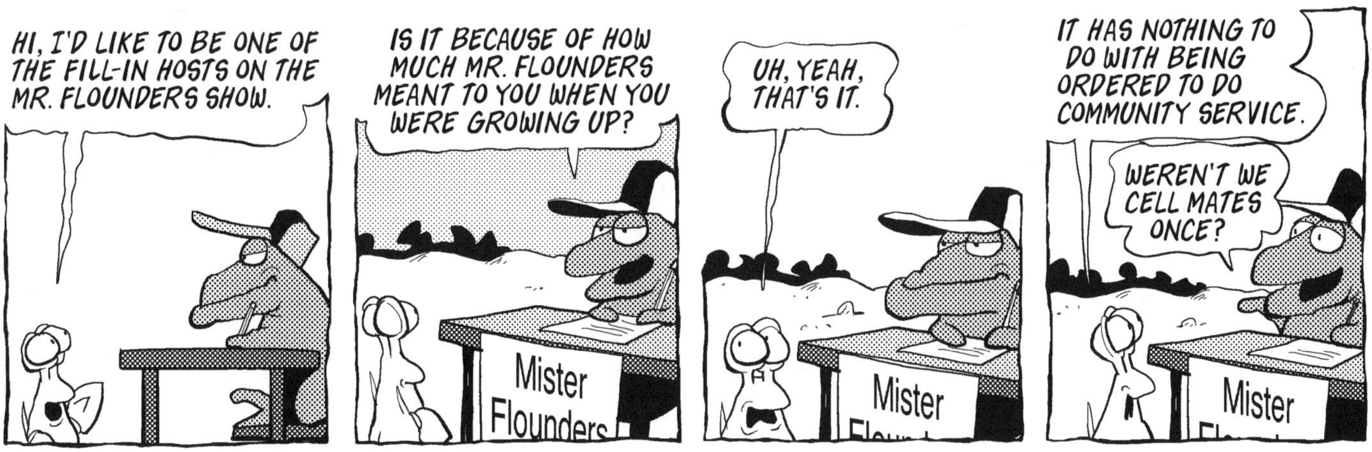
HI, I'D LIKE TO BE ONE OF THE FILL-IN HOSTS ON THE MR. FLOUNDERS SHOW.
IS IT BECAUSE OF HOW MUCH MR. FLOUNDERS MEANT TO YOU WHEN YOU WERE GROWING UP?
Mister
UH, YEAH, THAT'S IT.
Mister
IT HAS NOTHING TO DO WITH BEING ORDERED TO DO COMMUNITY SERVICE.
WEREN'T WE CELL MATES ONCE?
Mister

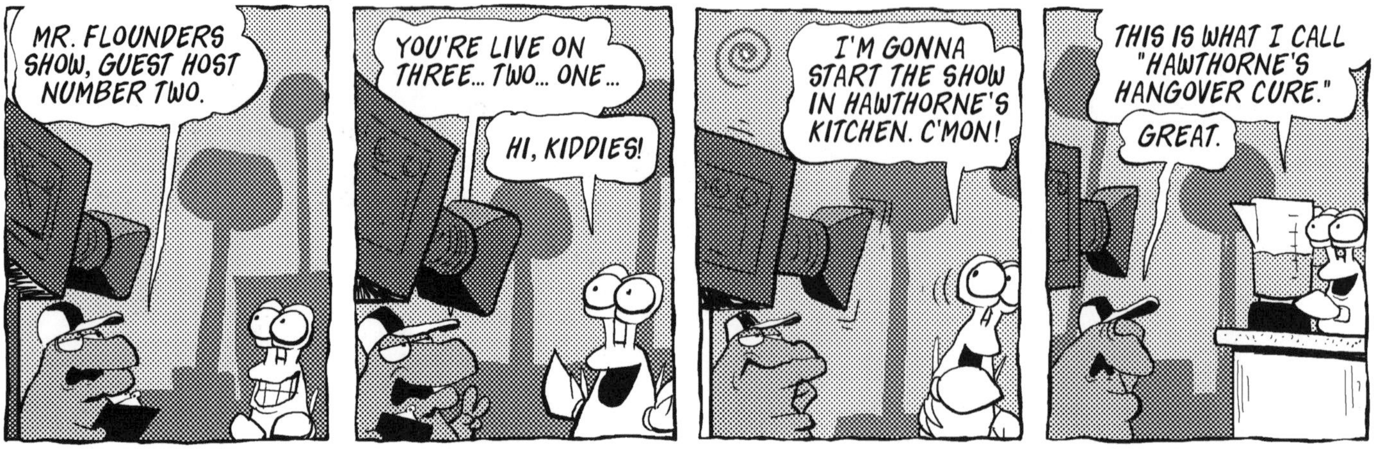
MR. FLOUNDERS SHOW, GUEST HOST NUMBER TWO.
YOU'RE LIVE ON THREE... TWO... ONE...
HI, KIDDIES!
I'M GONNA START THE SHOW IN HAWTHORNE'S KITCHEN. C'MON!
THIS IS WHAT I CALL "HAWTHORNE'S HANGOVER CURE."
GREAT.

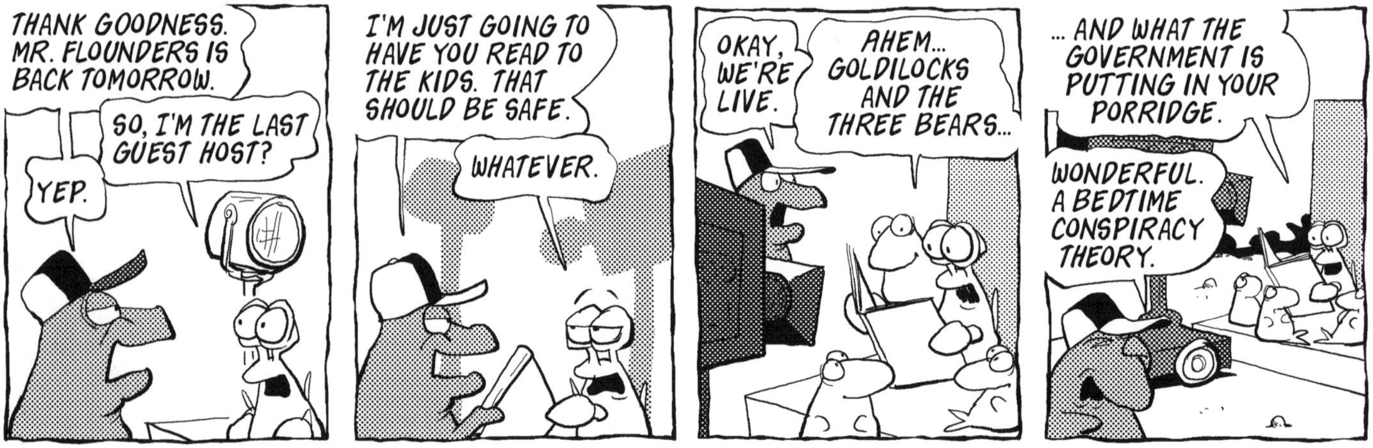
THANK GOODNESS. MR. FLOUNDERS IS BACK TOMORROW.
SO, I'M THE LAST GUEST HOST?
YEP.
I'M JUST GOING TO HAVE YOU READ TO THE KIDS. THAT SHOULD BE SAFE.
WHATEVER.
OKAY, WE'RE LIVE.
AHEM... GOLDILOCKS AND THE THREE BEARS...
... AND WHAT THE GOVERNMENT IS PUTTING IN YOUR PORRIDGE.
WONDERFUL. A BEDTIME CONSPIRACY THEORY.

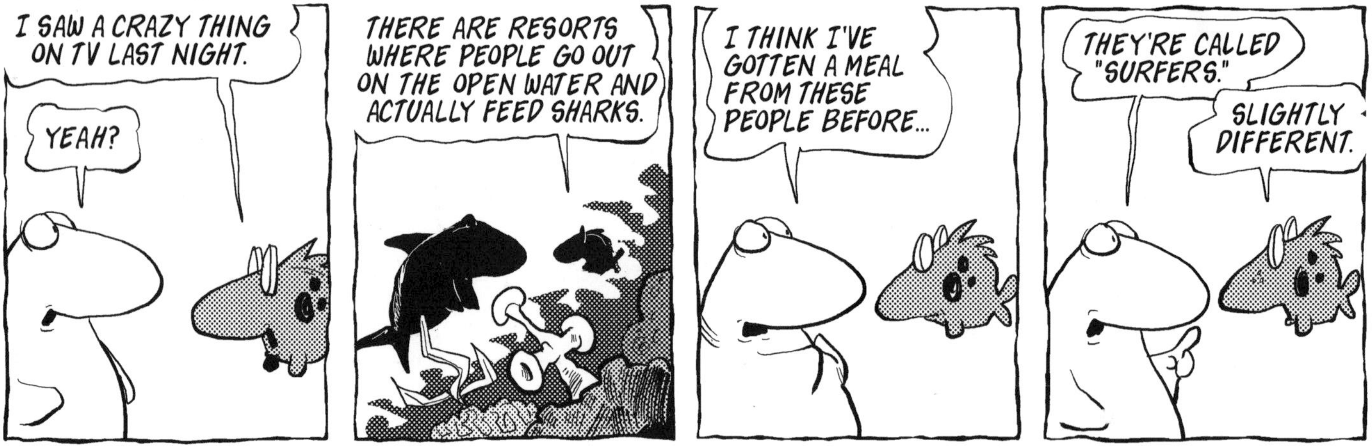
I SAW A CRAZY THING ON TV LAST NIGHT.
YEAH?
THERE ARE RESORTS WHERE PEOPLE GO OUT ON THE OPEN WATER AND ACTUALLY FEED SHARKS.
I THINK I'VE GOTTEN A MEAL FROM THESE PEOPLE BEFORE...
THEY'RE CALLED "SURFERS."
SLIGHTLY DIFFERENT.

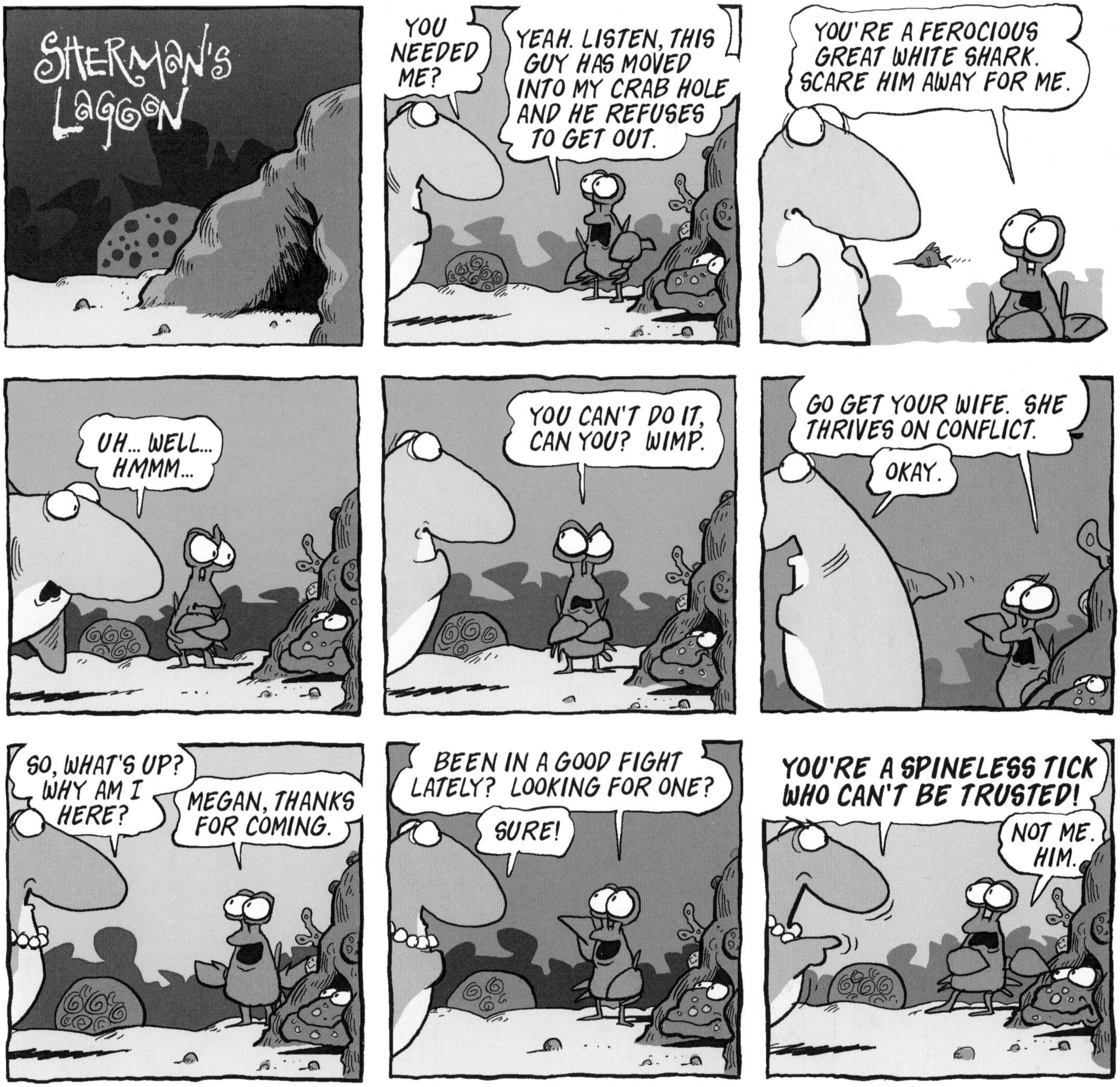
SHERMAN'S LAGOON
YOU NEEDED ME?
YEAH. LISTEN, THIS GUY HAS MOVED INTO MY CRAB HOLE AND HE REFUSES TO GET OUT.
YOU'RE A FEROCIOUS GREAT WHITE SHARK. SCARE HIM AWAY FOR ME.
UH... WELL... HMMM...
YOU CAN'T DO IT, CAN YOU? WIMP.
GO GET YOUR WIFE. SHE THRIVES ON CONFLICT.
OKAY.
SO, WHAT'S UP? WHY AM I HERE?
MEGAN, THANKS FOR COMING.
BEEN IN A GOOD FIGHT LATELY? LOOKING FOR ONE?
SURE!
YOU'RE A SPINELESS TICK WHO CAN'T BE TRUSTED!
NOT ME. HIM.

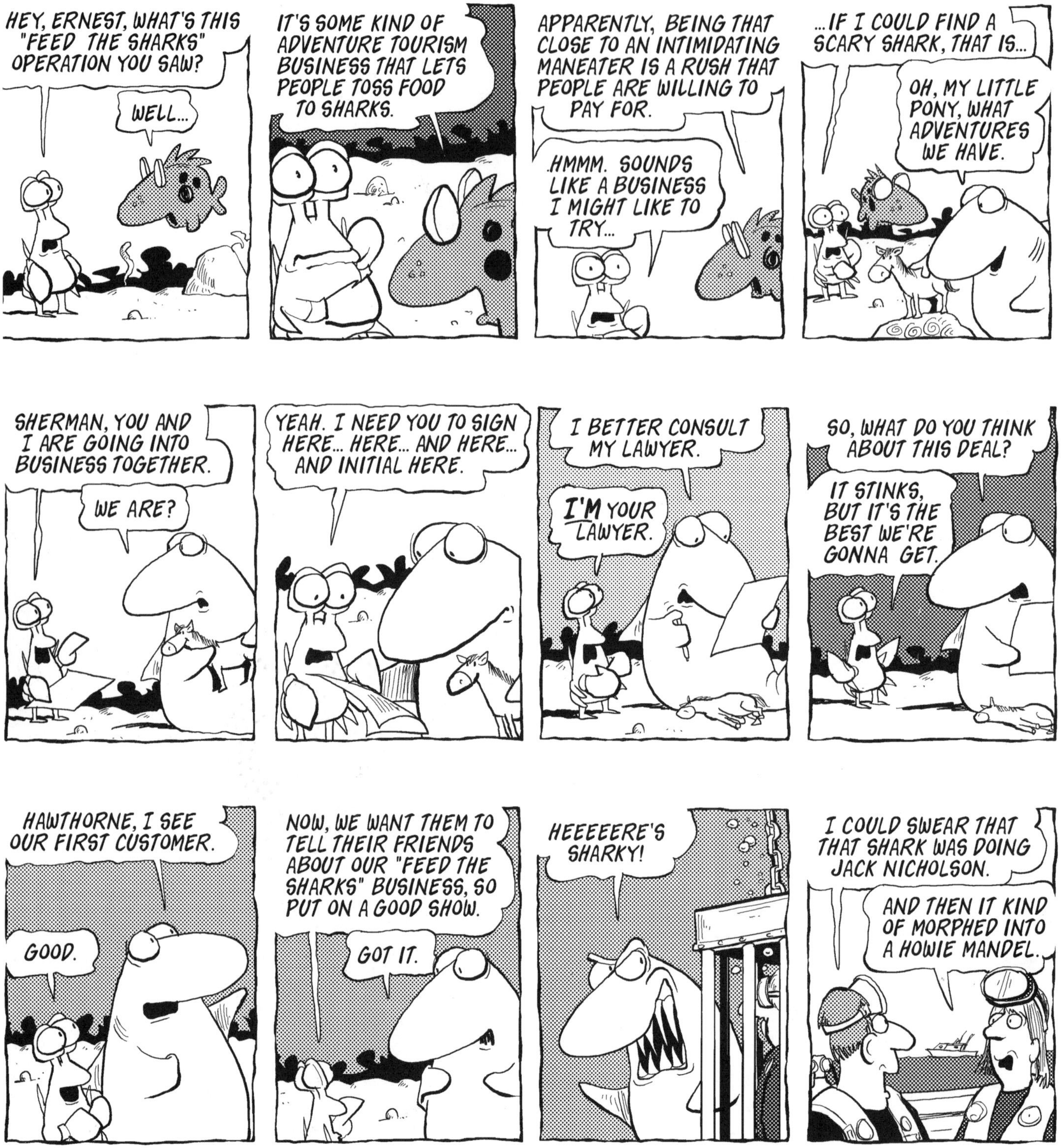
HEY, ERNEST, WHAT'S THIS "FEED THE SHARKS" OPERATION YOU SAW?
WELL...
IT'S SOME KIND OF ADVENTURE TOURISM BUSINESS THAT LETS PEOPLE TOSS FOOD TO SHARKS.
APPARENTLY, BEING THAT CLOSE TO AN INTIMIDATING MANEATER IS A RUSH THAT PEOPLE ARE WILLING TO PAY FOR.
HMMM. SOUNDS LIKE A BUSINESS I MIGHT LIKE TO TRY...
...IF I COULD FIND A SCARY SHARK, THAT IS...
OH, MY LITTLE PONY, WHAT ADVENTURES WE HAVE.
SHERMAN, YOU AND I ARE GOING INTO BUSINESS TOGETHER.
WE ARE?
YEAH. I NEED YOU TO SIGN HERE... HERE... AND HERE... AND INITIAL HERE.
I BETTER CONSULT MY LAWYER.
I'M YOUR LAWYER.
SO, WHAT DO YOU THINK ABOUT THIS DEAL?
IT STINKS, BUT IT'S THE BEST WE'RE GONNA GET.
HAWTHORNE, I SEE OUR FIRST CUSTOMER.
GOOD.
NOW, WE WANT THEM TO TELL THEIR FRIENDS ABOUT OUR "FEED THE SHARKS" BUSINESS, SO PUT ON A GOOD SHOW.
GOT IT.
HEEEEERE'S SHARKY!
I COULD SWEAR THAT THAT SHARK WAS DOING JACK NICHOLSON.
AND THEN IT KIND OF MORPHED INTO A HOWIE MANDEL.

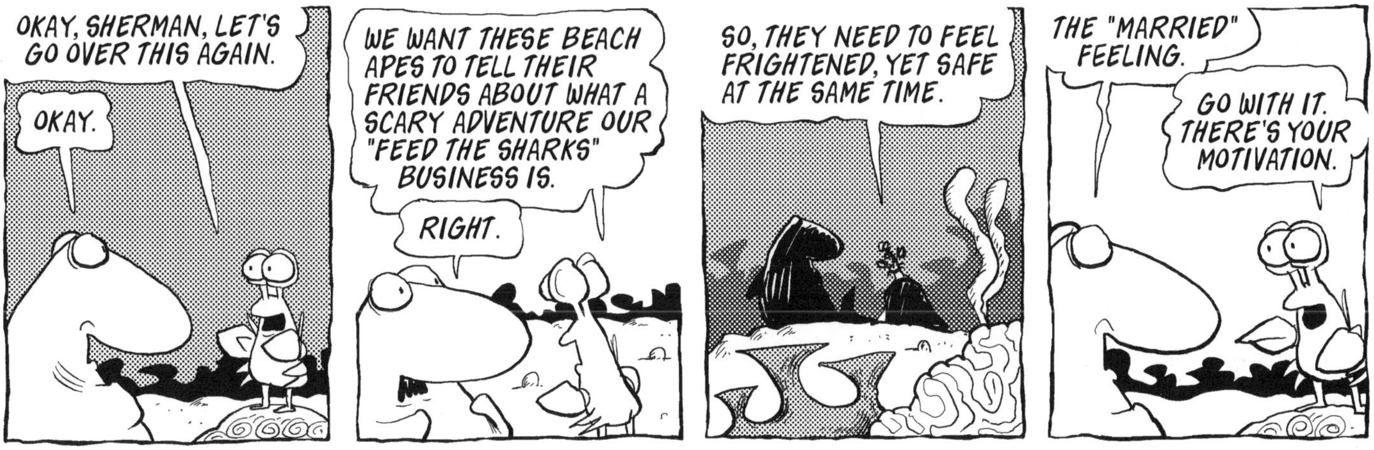
OKAY, SHERMAN, LET'S GO OVER THIS AGAIN.
OKAY.
WE WANT THESE BEACH APES TO TELL THEIR FRIENDS ABOUT WHAT A SCARY ADVENTURE OUR "FEED THE SHARKS" BUSINESS IS.
RIGHT.
SO, THEY NEED TO FEEL FRIGHTENED, YET SAFE AT THE SAME TIME.
THE "MARRIED" FEELING.
GO WITH IT. THERE'S YOUR MOTIVATION.

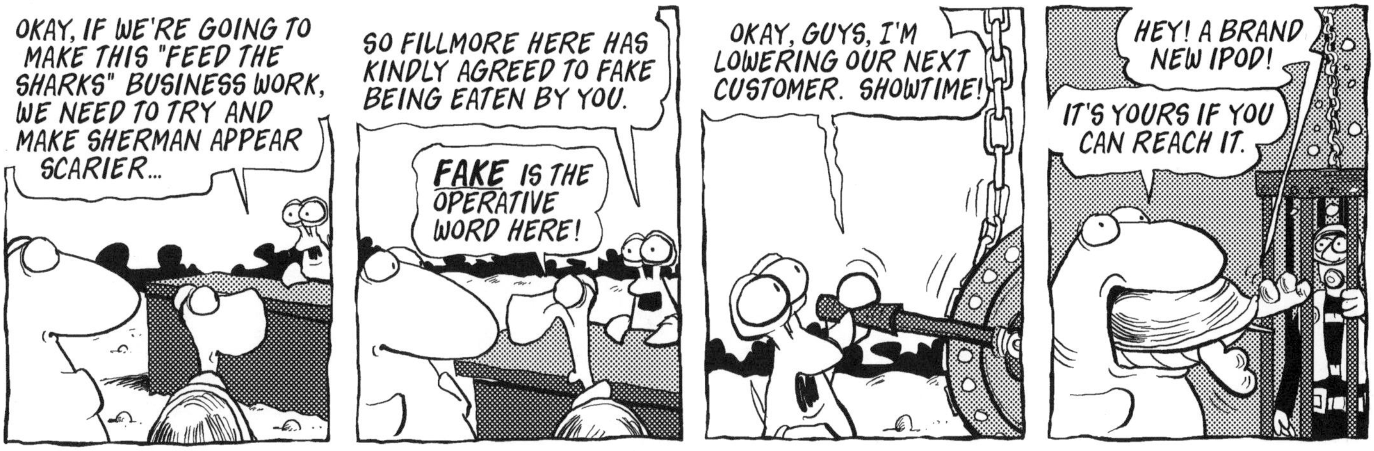
OKAY, IF WE'RE GOING TO MAKE THIS "FEED THE SHARKS" BUSINESS WORK, WE NEED TO TRY AND MAKE SHERMAN APPEAR SCARIER...
SO FILLMORE HERE HAS KINDLY AGREED TO FAKE BEING EATEN BY YOU.
FAKE IS THE OPERATIVE WORD HERE!
OKAY, GUYS, I'M LOWERING OUR NEXT CUSTOMER. SHOWTIME!
HEY! A BRAND NEW IPOD!
IT'S YOURS IF YOU CAN REACH IT.

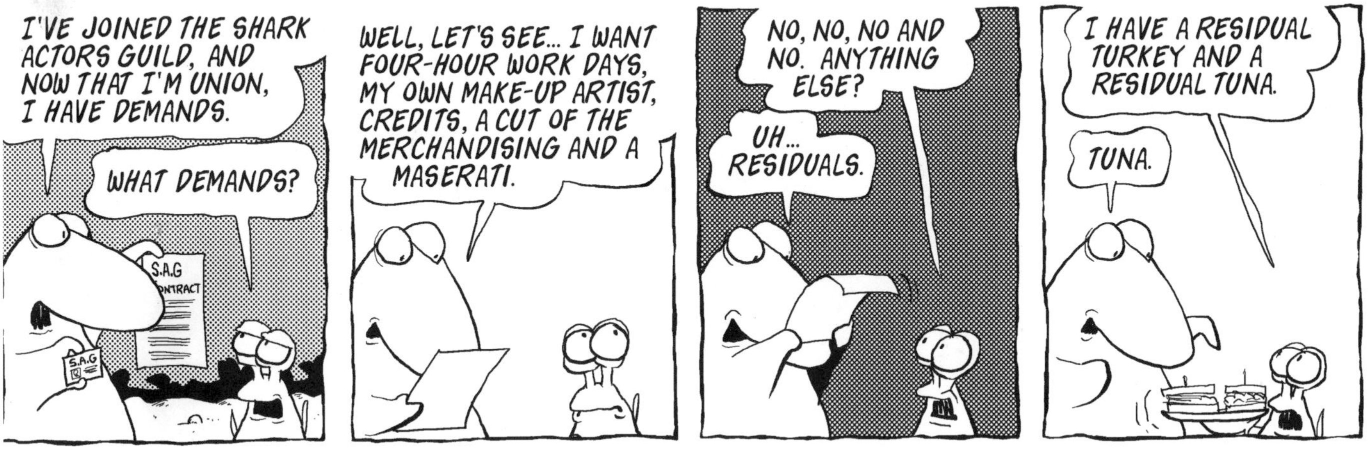
I'VE JOINED THE SHARK ACTORS GUILD, AND NOW THAT I'M UNION, I HAVE DEMANDS.
WHAT DEMANDS?
S.A.G
S.A.G CONTRACT
WELL, LET'S SEE... I WANT FOUR-HOUR WORK DAYS, MY OWN MAKE-UP ARTIST, CREDITS, A CUT OF THE MERCHANDISING AND A MASERATI.
NO, NO, NO AND NO. ANYTHING ELSE?
UH... RESIDUALS.
I HAVE A RESIDUAL TURKEY AND A RESIDUAL TUNA.
TUNA.

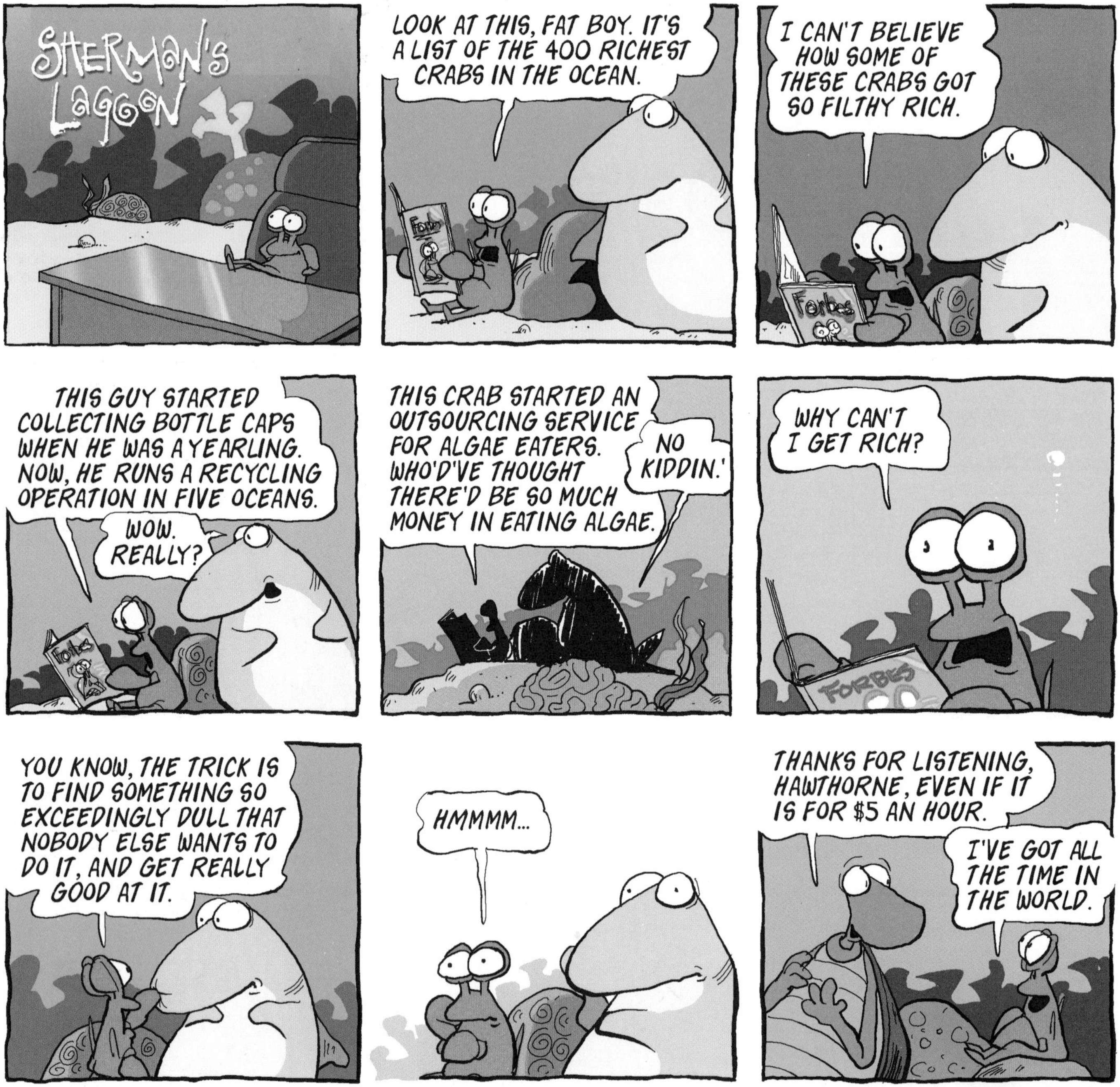
SHERMAN'S LAGOON
LOOK AT THIS, FAT BOY. IT'S A LIST OF THE 400 RICHEST CRABS IN THE OCEAN.
Forbes
I CAN'T BELIEVE HOW SOME OF THESE CRABS GOT SO FILTHY RICH.
Forbes
THIS GUY STARTED COLLECTING BOTTLE CAPS WHEN HE WAS A YEARLING. NOW, HE RUNS A RECYCLING OPERATION IN FIVE OCEANS.
WOW. REALLY?
Forbes
THIS CRAB STARTED AN OUTSOURCING SERVICE FOR ALGAE EATERS. WHO'D'VE THOUGHT THERE'D BE SO MUCH MONEY IN EATING ALGAE.
NO KIDDIN.'
WHY CAN'T I GET RICH?
FORBES
YOU KNOW, THE TRICK IS TO FIND SOMETHING SO EXCEEDINGLY DULL THAT NOBODY ELSE WANTS TO DO IT, AND GET REALLY GOOD AT IT.
HMMMM...
THANKS FOR LISTENING, HAWTHORNE, EVEN IF IT IS FOR $5 AN HOUR.
I'VE GOT ALL THE TIME IN THE WORLD.

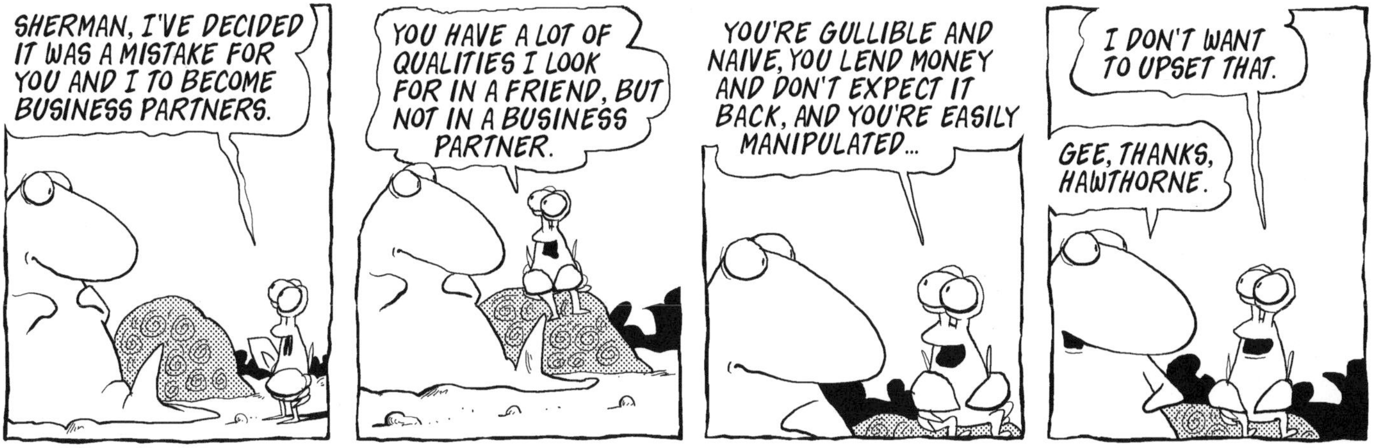
SHERMAN, I'VE DECIDED IT WAS A MISTAKE FOR YOU AND I TO BECOME BUSINESS PARTNERS.
YOU HAVE A LOT OF QUALITIES I LOOK FOR IN A FRIEND, BUT NOT IN A BUSINESS PARTNER.
YOU'RE GULLIBLE AND NAIVE, YOU LEND MONEY AND DON'T EXPECT IT BACK, AND YOU'RE EASILY MANIPULATED...
GEE, THANKS, HAWTHORNE.
I DON'T WANT TO UPSET THAT.

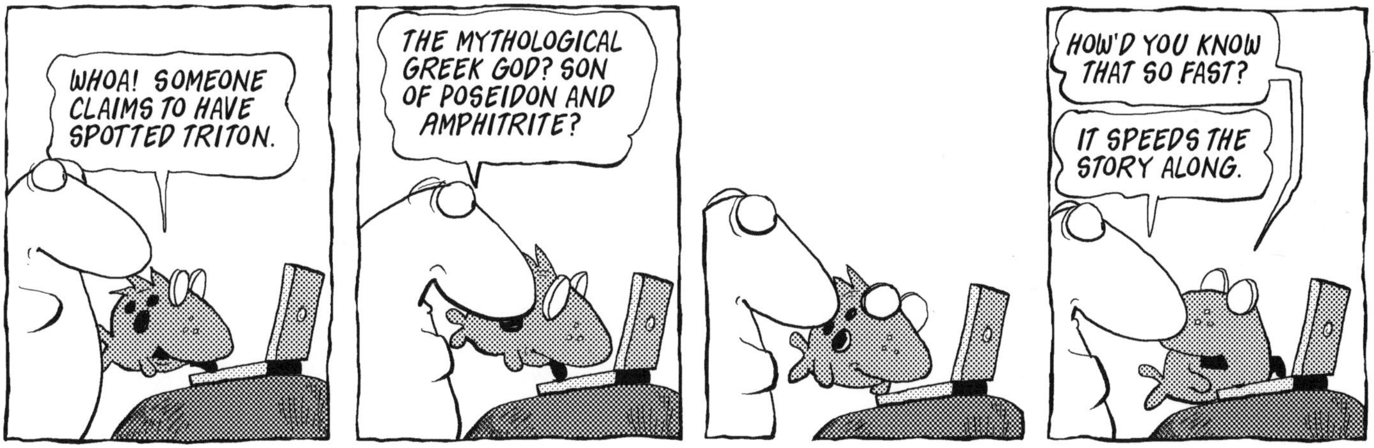
WHOA! SOMEONE CLAIMS TO HAVE SPOTTED TRITON.
THE MYTHOLOGICAL GREEK GOD? SON OF POSEIDON AND AMPHITRITE?
HOW'D YOU KNOW THAT SO FAST?
IT SPEEDS THE STORY ALONG.

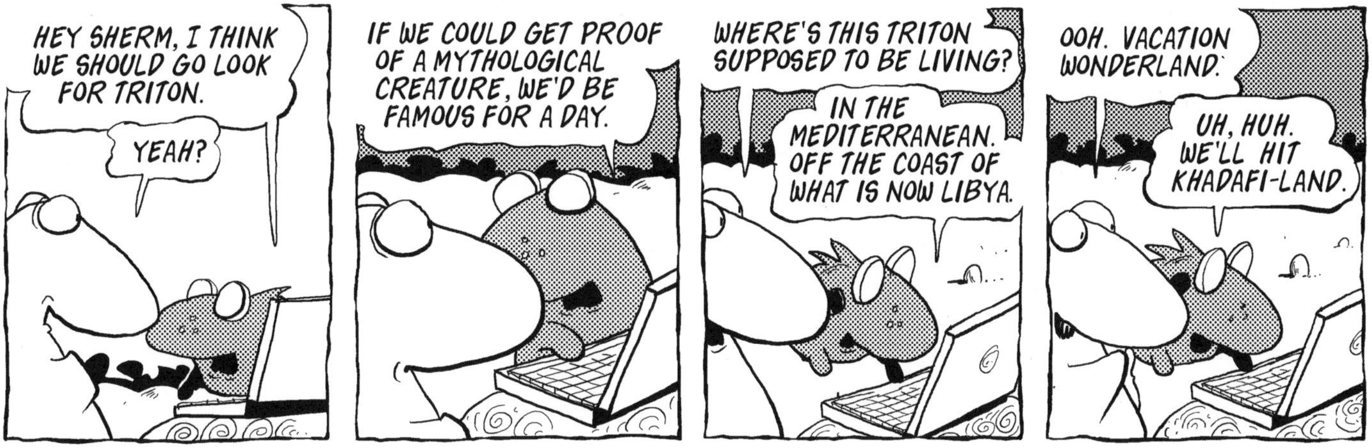
HEY SHERM, I THINK WE SHOULD GO LOOK FOR TRITON.
YEAH?
IF WE COULD GET PROOF OF A MYTHOLOGICAL CREATURE, WE'D BE FAMOUS FOR A DAY.
WHERE'S THIS TRITON SUPPOSED TO BE LIVING?
IN THE MEDITERRANEAN. OFF THE COAST OF WHAT IS NOW LIBYA.
OOH. VACATION WONDERLAND.
UH, HUH. WE'LL HIT KHADAFI-LAND.

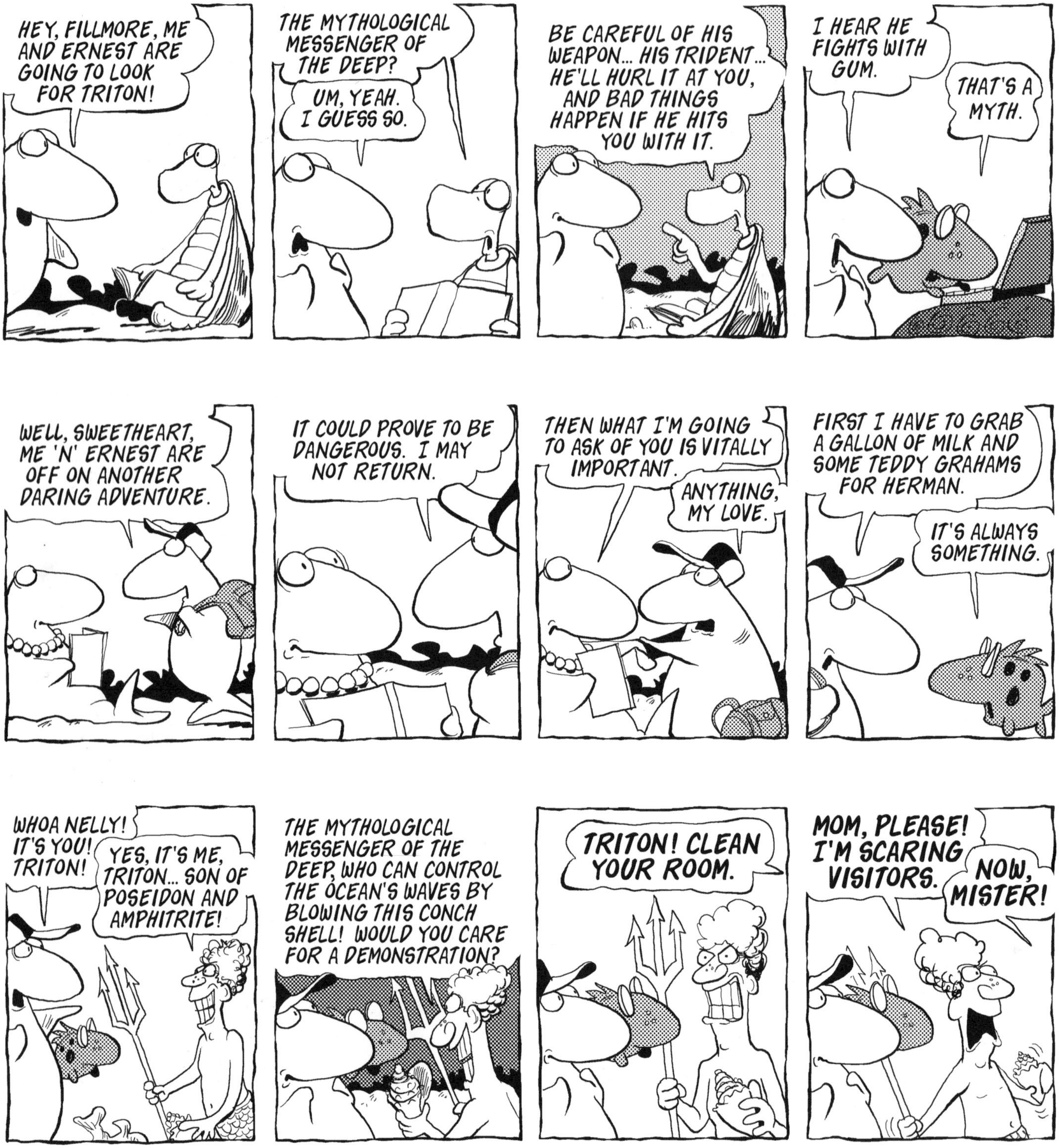
HEY, FILLMORE, ME AND ERNEST ARE GOING TO LOOK FOR TRITON!
THE MYTHOLOGICAL MESSENGER OF THE DEEP?
UM, YEAH. I GUESS SO.
BE CAREFUL OF HIS WEAPON... HIS TRIDENT... HE'LL HURL IT AT YOU, AND BAD THINGS HAPPEN IF HE HITS YOU WITH IT.
I HEAR HE FIGHTS WITH GUM.
THAT'S A MYTH.
WELL, SWEETHEART, ME 'N' ERNEST ARE OFF ON ANOTHER DARING ADVENTURE.
IT COULD PROVE TO BE DANGEROUS. I MAY NOT RETURN.
THEN WHAT I'M GOING TO ASK OF YOU IS VITALLY IMPORTANT.
ANYTHING, MY LOVE.
FIRST I HAVE TO GRAB A GALLON OF MILK AND SOME TEDDY GRAHAMS FOR HERMAN.
IT'S ALWAYS SOMETHING.
WHOA NELLY! IT'S YOU! TRITON!
YES, IT'S ME, TRITON... SON OF POSEIDON AND AMPHITRITE!
THE MYTHOLOGICAL MESSENGER OF THE DEEP, WHO CAN CONTROL THE OCEAN'S WAVES BY BLOWING THIS CONCH SHELL! WOULD YOU CARE FOR A DEMONSTRATION?
TRITON! CLEAN YOUR ROOM.
MOM, PLEASE! I'M SCARING VISITORS.
NOW, MISTER!

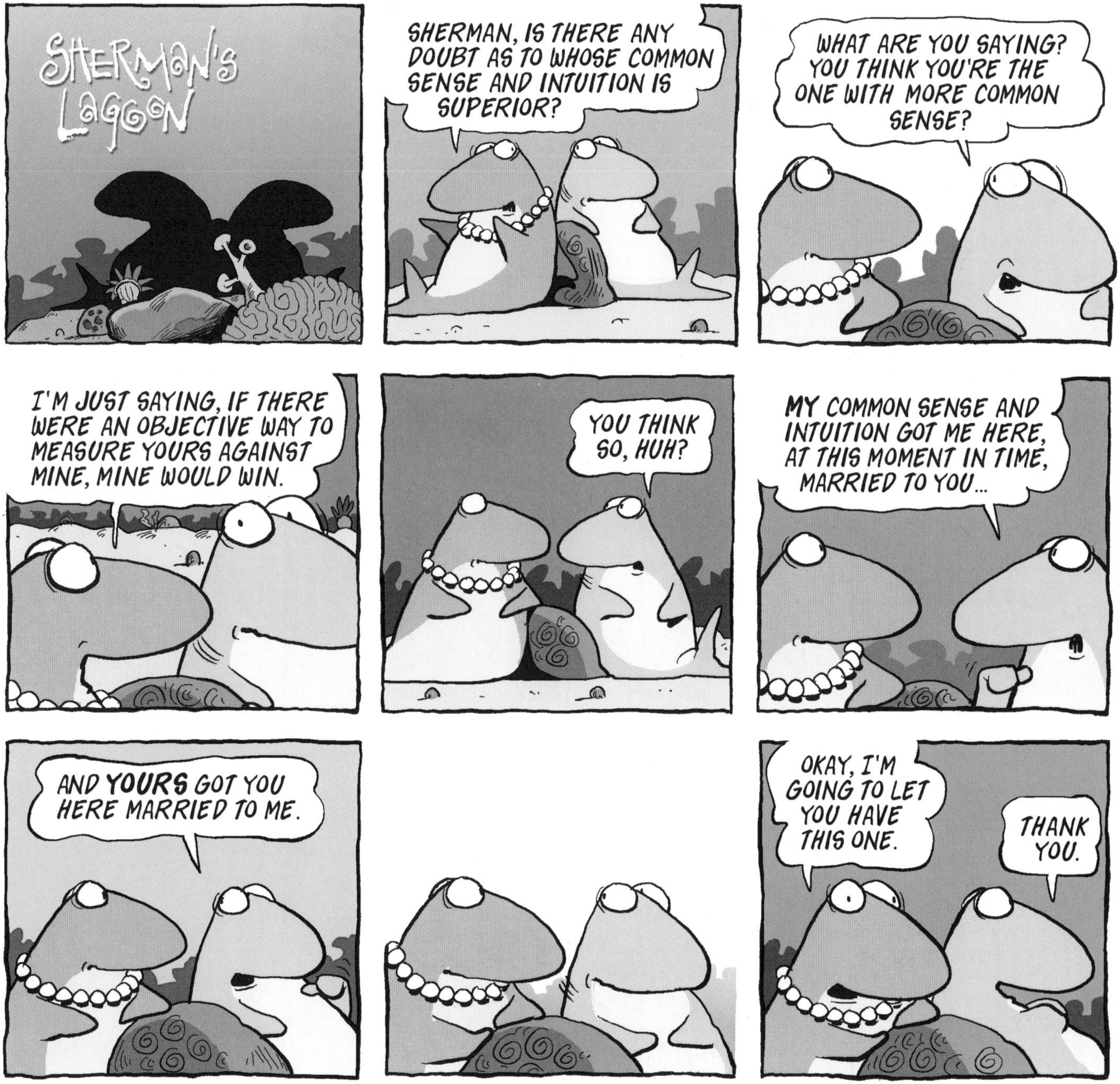
SHERMAN'S LAGOON
SHERMAN, IS THERE ANY DOUBT AS TO WHOSE COMMON SENSE AND INTUITION IS SUPERIOR?
WHAT ARE YOU SAYING? YOU THINK YOU'RE THE ONE WITH MORE COMMON SENSE?
I'M JUST SAYING, IF THERE WERE AN OBJECTIVE WAY TO MEASURE YOURS AGAINST MINE, MINE WOULD WIN.
YOU THINK SO, HUH?
MY COMMON SENSE AND INTUITION GOT ME HERE, AT THIS MOMENT IN TIME, MARRIED TO YOU...
AND YOURS GOT YOU HERE MARRIED TO ME.
OKAY, I'M GOING TO LET YOU HAVE THIS ONE.
THANK YOU.

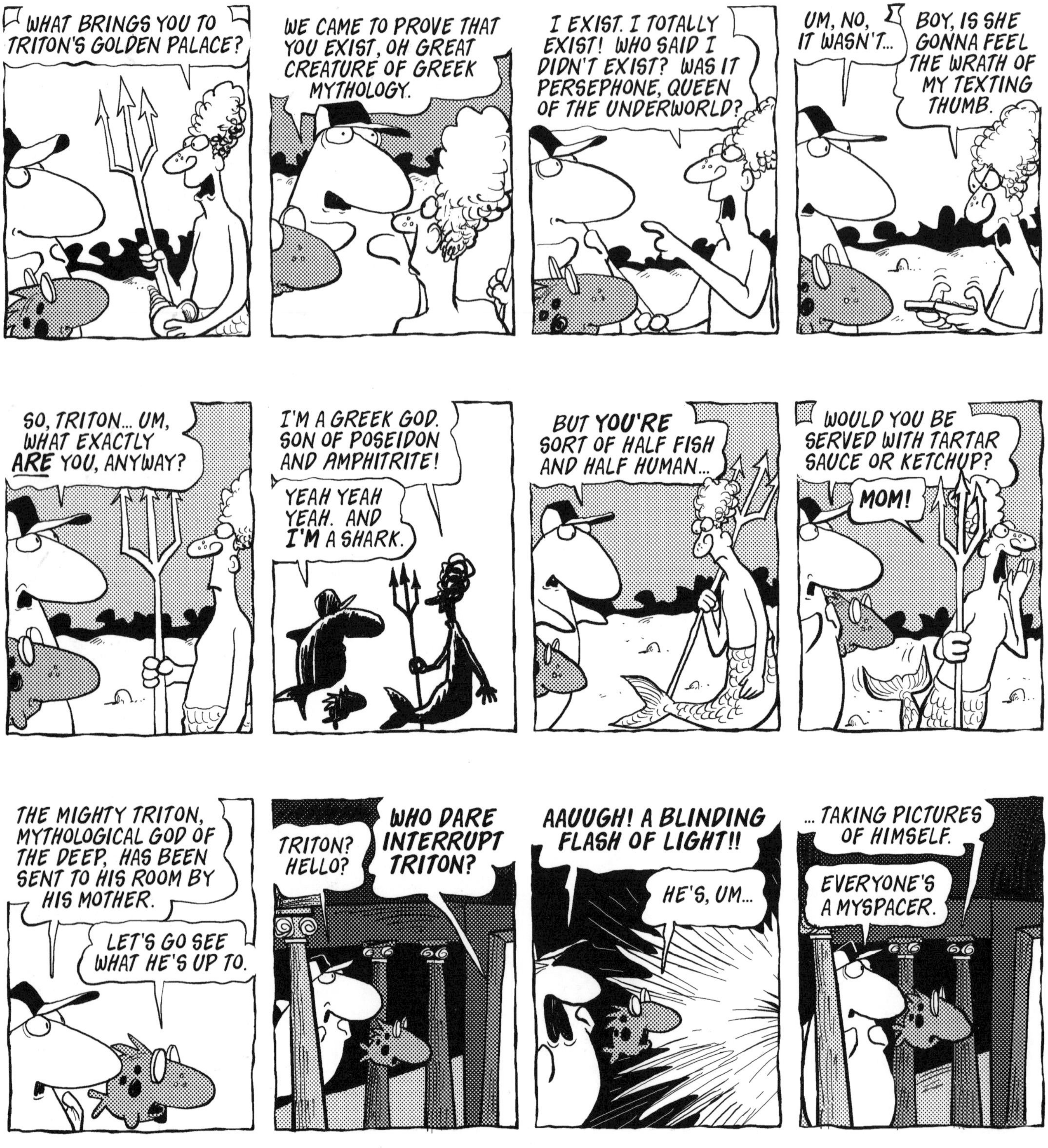
WHAT BRINGS YOU TO TRITON'S GOLDEN PALACE?
WE CAME TO PROVE THAT YOU EXIST, OH GREAT CREATURE OF GREEK MYTHOLOGY.
I EXIST. I TOTALLY EXIST! WHO SAID I DIDN'T EXIST? WAS IT PERSEPHONE, QUEEN OF THE UNDERWORLD?
UM, NO, IT WASN'T...
BOY, IS SHE GONNA FEEL THE WRATH OF MY TEXTING THUMB.
SO, TRITON... UM, WHAT EXACTLY ARE YOU, ANYWAY?
I'M A GREEK GOD. SON OF POSEIDON AND AMPHITRITE!
YEAH YEAH YEAH. AND I'M A SHARK.
BUT YOU'RE SORT OF HALF FISH AND HALF HUMAN...
WOULD YOU BE SERVED WITH TARTAR SAUCE OR KETCHUP?
MOM!
THE MIGHTY TRITON, MYTHOLOGICAL GOD OF THE DEEP, HAS BEEN SENT TO HIS ROOM BY HIS MOTHER.
LET'S GO SEE WHAT HE'S UP TO.
TRITON? HELLO?
WHO DARE INTERRUPT TRITON?
AAUUGH! A BLINDING FLASH OF LIGHT!!
HE'S, UM...
... TAKING PICTURES OF HIMSELF.
EVERYONE'S A MYSPACER.

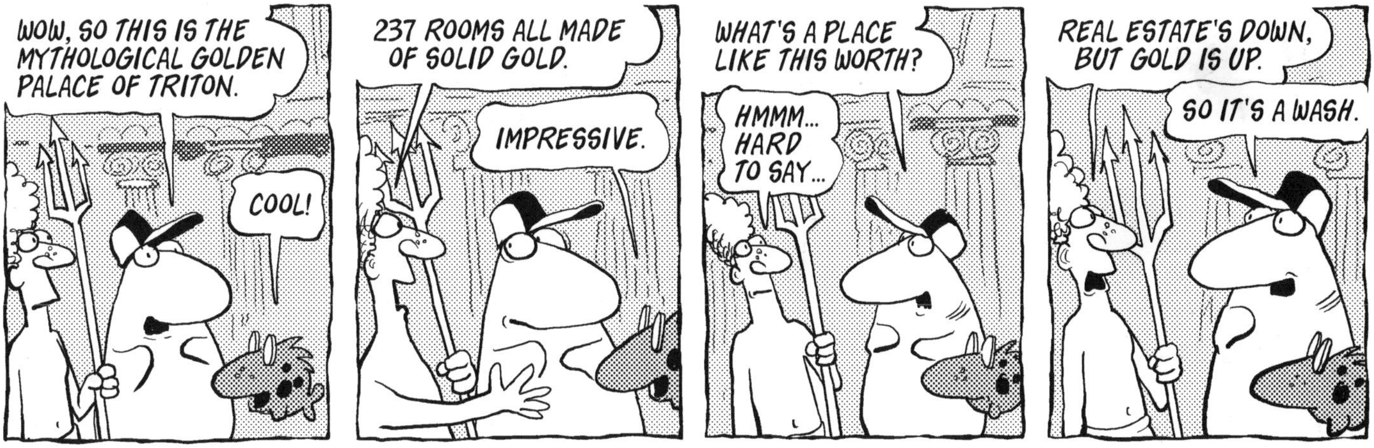
WOW, SO THIS IS THE MYTHOLOGICAL GOLDEN PALACE OF TRITON.
COOL!
237 ROOMS ALL MADE OF SOLID GOLD.
IMPRESSIVE.
WHAT'S A PLACE LIKE THIS WORTH?
HMMM... HARD TO SAY...
REAL ESTATE'S DOWN, BUT GOLD IS UP.
SO IT'S A WASH.

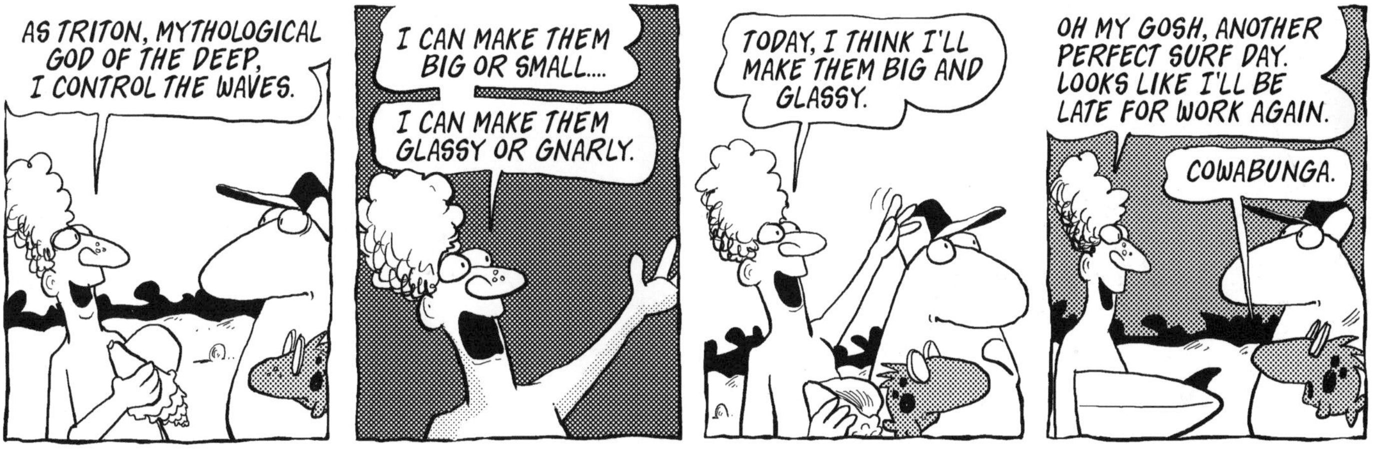
AS TRITON, MYTHOLOGICAL GOD OF THE DEEP, I CONTROL THE WAVES.
I CAN MAKE THEM BIG OR SMALL....
I CAN MAKE THEM GLASSY OR GNARLY.
TODAY, I THINK I'LL MAKE THEM BIG AND GLASSY.
OH MY GOSH, ANOTHER PERFECT SURF DAY. LOOKS LIKE I'LL BE LATE FOR WORK AGAIN.
COWABUNGA.

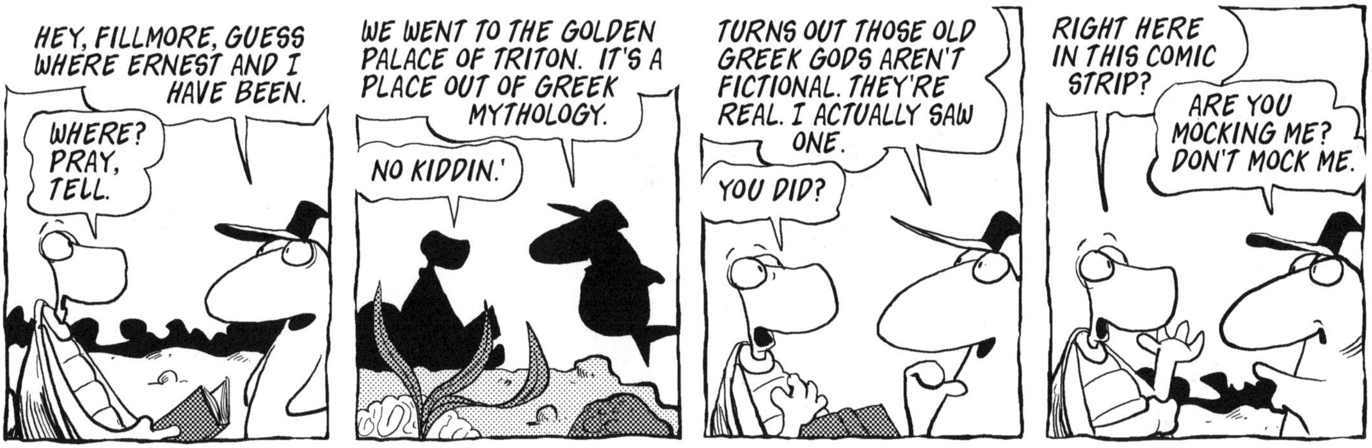
HEY, FILLMORE, GUESS WHERE ERNEST AND I HAVE BEEN.
WHERE? PRAY, TELL.
WE WENT TO THE GOLDEN PALACE OF TRITON. IT'S A PLACE OUT OF GREEK MYTHOLOGY.
NO KIDDIN.'
TURNS OUT THOSE OLD GREEK GODS AREN'T FICTIONAL. THEY'RE REAL. I ACTUALLY SAW ONE.
YOU DID?
RIGHT HERE IN THIS COMIC STRIP?
ARE YOU MOCKING ME? DON'T MOCK ME.

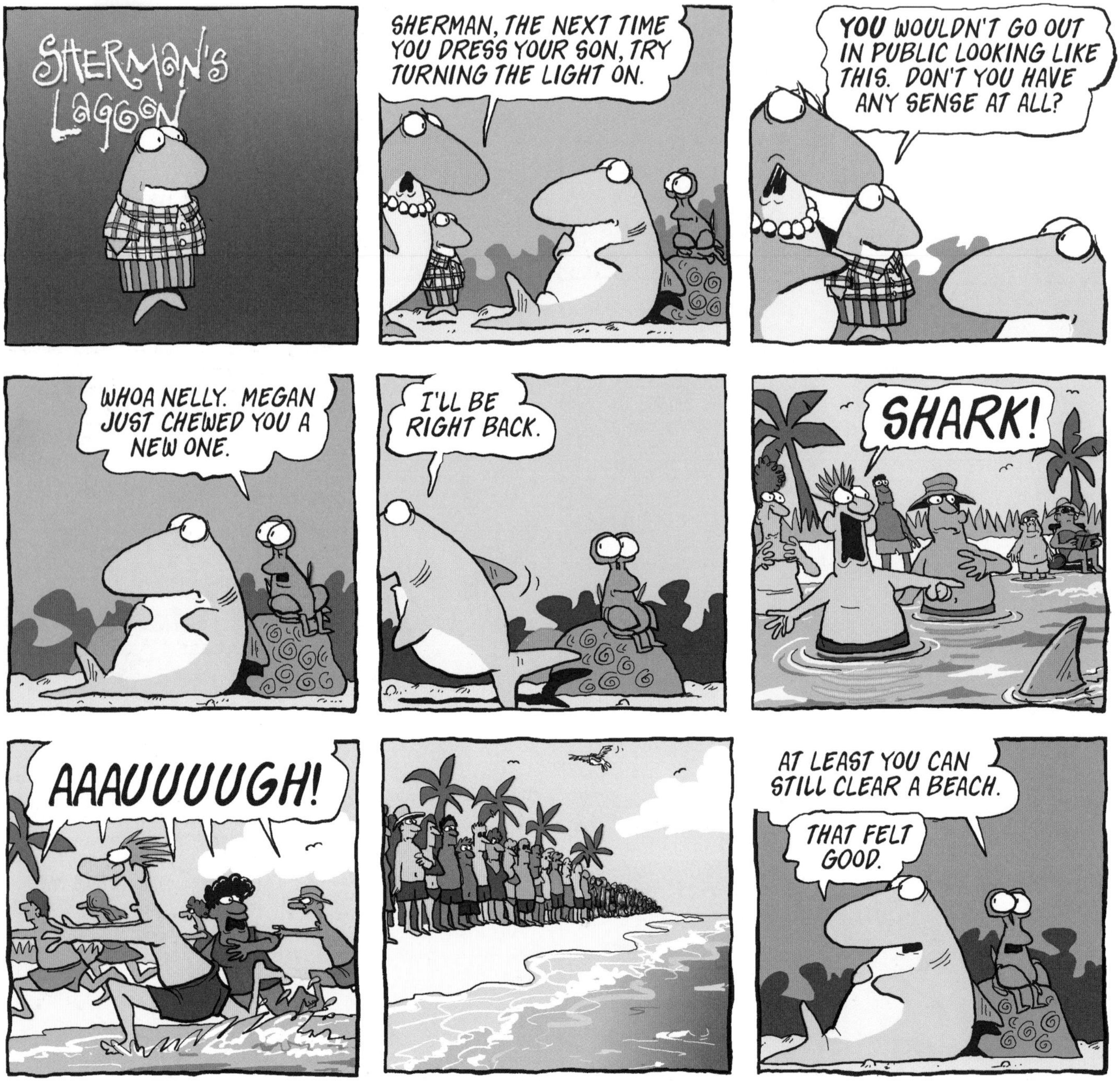
SHERMAN'S LAGOON
SHERMAN, THE NEXT TIME YOU DRESS YOUR SON, TRY TURNING THE LIGHT ON.
YOU WOULDN'T GO OUT IN PUBLIC LOOKING LIKE THIS. DON'T YOU HAVE ANY SENSE AT ALL?
WHOA NELLY. MEGAN JUST CHEWED YOU A NEW ONE.
I'LL BE RIGHT BACK.
SHARK!
AAAUUUUGH!
AT LEAST YOU CAN STILL CLEAR A BEACH.
THAT FELT GOOD.

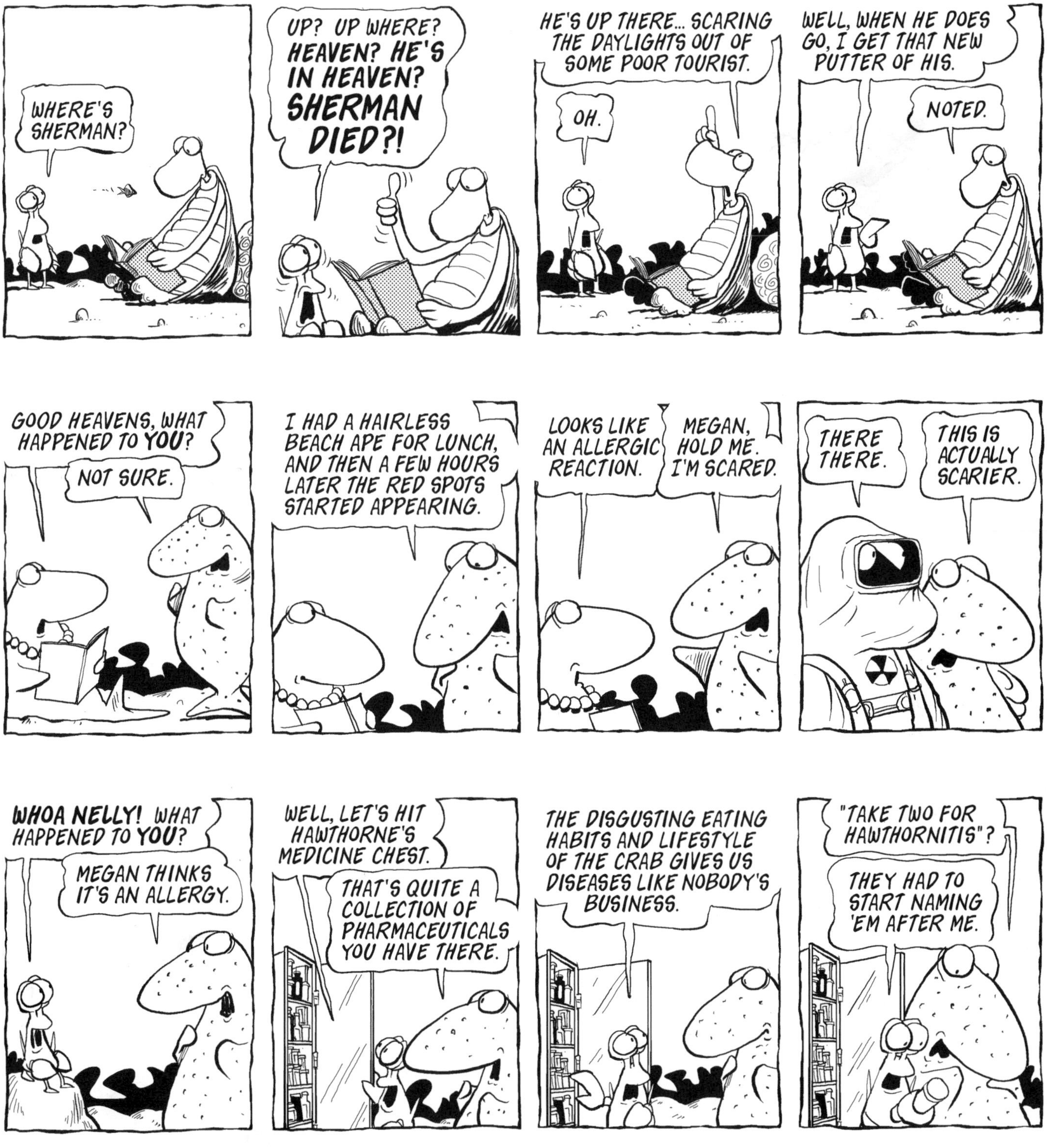
WHERE'S SHERMAN?
UP? UP WHERE? HEAVEN? HE'S IN HEAVEN? SHERMAN DIED?!
HE'S UP THERE... SCARING THE DAYLIGHTS OUT OF SOME POOR TOURIST.
OH.
WELL, WHEN HE DOES GO, I GET THAT NEW PUTTER OF HIS.
NOTED.
GOOD HEAVENS, WHAT HAPPENED TO YOU?
NOT SURE.
I HAD A HAIRLESS BEACH APE FOR LUNCH, AND THEN A FEW HOURS LATER THE RED SPOTS STARTED APPEARING.
LOOKS LIKE AN ALLERGIC REACTION.
MEGAN, HOLD ME. I'M SCARED.
THERE THERE.
THIS IS ACTUALLY SCARIER.
WHOA NELLY! WHAT HAPPENED TO YOU?
MEGAN THINKS IT'S AN ALLERGY.
WELL, LET'S HIT HAWTHORNE'S MEDICINE CHEST.
THAT'S QUITE A COLLECTION OF PHARMACEUTICALS YOU HAVE THERE.
THE DISGUSTING EATING HABITS AND LIFESTYLE OF THE CRAB GIVES US DISEASES LIKE NOBODY'S BUSINESS.
"TAKE TWO FOR HAWTHORNITIS"?
THEY HAD TO START NAMING 'EM AFTER ME.

OH, GROSS!

WHAT KIND OF MUTANT FREAK HAVE YOU BECOME? BACK! BACK!

OKAY, SORRY.

LET'S CHECK THIS OUT, SICKO.

YOUR BEDSIDE MANNER NEEDS WORK.

MEGAN! THE DOCTOR TOLD ME THAT I'M ALLERGIC TO MEAT! A SHARK!

IT'S OKAY, SHERMAN. IT DOESN'T MAKE YOU ANY LESS OF A MAN.

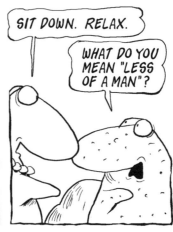

SIT DOWN. RELAX.

WHAT DO YOU MEAN "LESS OF A MAN"?

LET'S FIND YOU SOME ICE DANCING TO WATCH.

I NEED FOOTBALL, NOW MORE THAN EVER!

SHERMAN, I'VE BEEN GROCERY SHOPPING.

YEAH?

I'VE DECIDED IF YOU'VE GOT A MEAT ALLERGY, WE'LL DEAL WITH IT TOGETHER. I'LL BE A VEGETARIAN, TOO.

REALLY?

HEY, WAIT A MINUTE... YOU SMELL LIKE ANOTHER GUY.

WHAT? THAT'S, UH, RIDICULOUS!

IT'S HIM! YOU'VE BEEN WITH THE BURGER KING!

ALRIGHT! I'M WEAK!

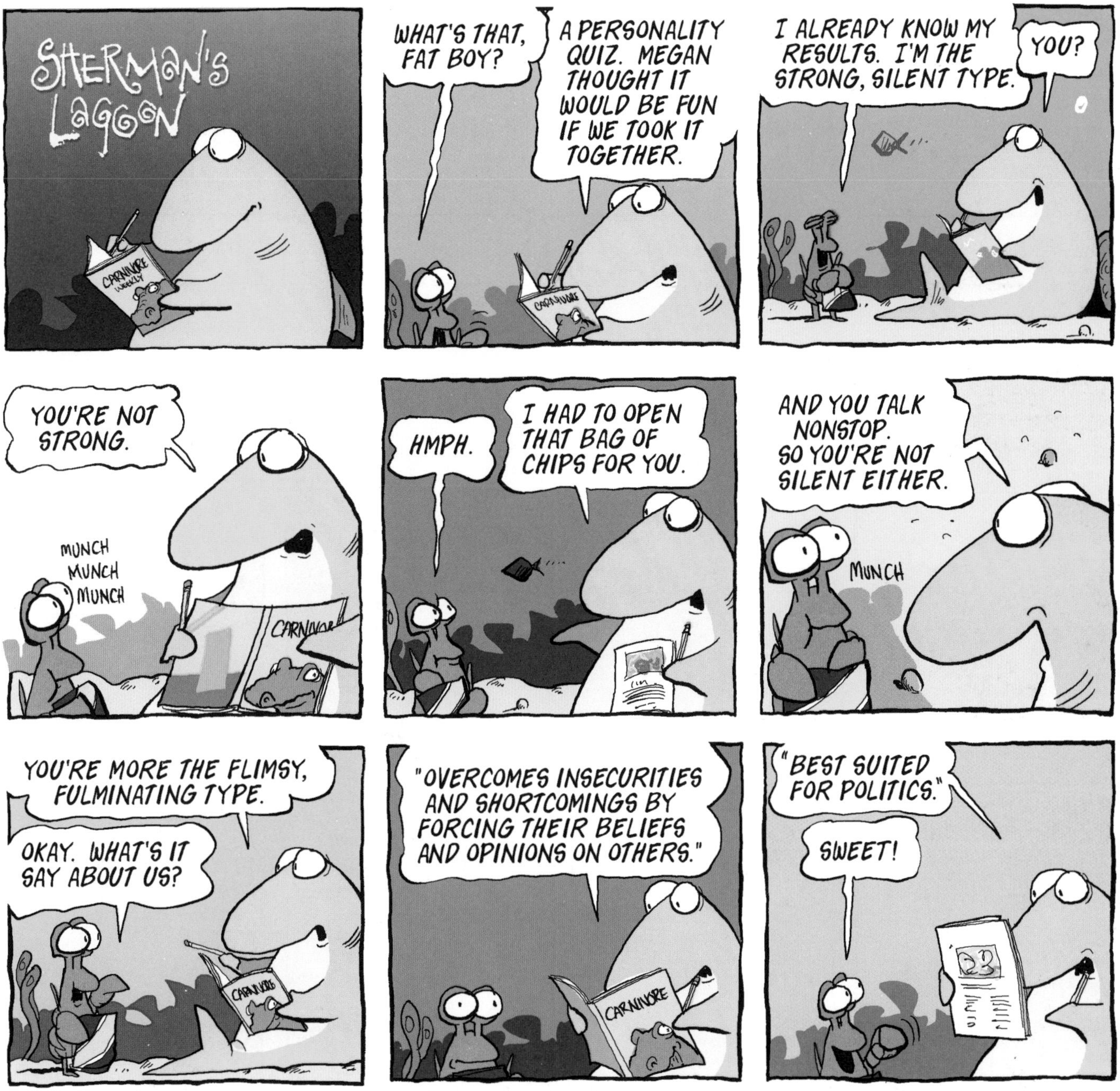
SHERMAN'S LAGOON
CARNIVORE WEEKLY
WHAT'S THAT, FAT BOY?
A PERSONALITY QUIZ. MEGAN THOUGHT IT WOULD BE FUN IF WE TOOK IT TOGETHER.
I ALREADY KNOW MY RESULTS. I'M THE STRONG, SILENT TYPE.
YOU?
YOU'RE NOT STRONG.
MUNCH MUNCH MUNCH
HMPH.
I HAD TO OPEN THAT BAG OF CHIPS FOR YOU.
AND YOU TALK NONSTOP. SO YOU'RE NOT SILENT EITHER.
MUNCH
YOU'RE MORE THE FLIMSY, FULMINATING TYPE.
OKAY. WHAT'S IT SAY ABOUT US?
"OVERCOMES INSECURITIES AND SHORTCOMINGS BY FORCING THEIR BELIEFS AND OPINIONS ON OTHERS."
CARNIVORE
"BEST SUITED FOR POLITICS."
SWEET!

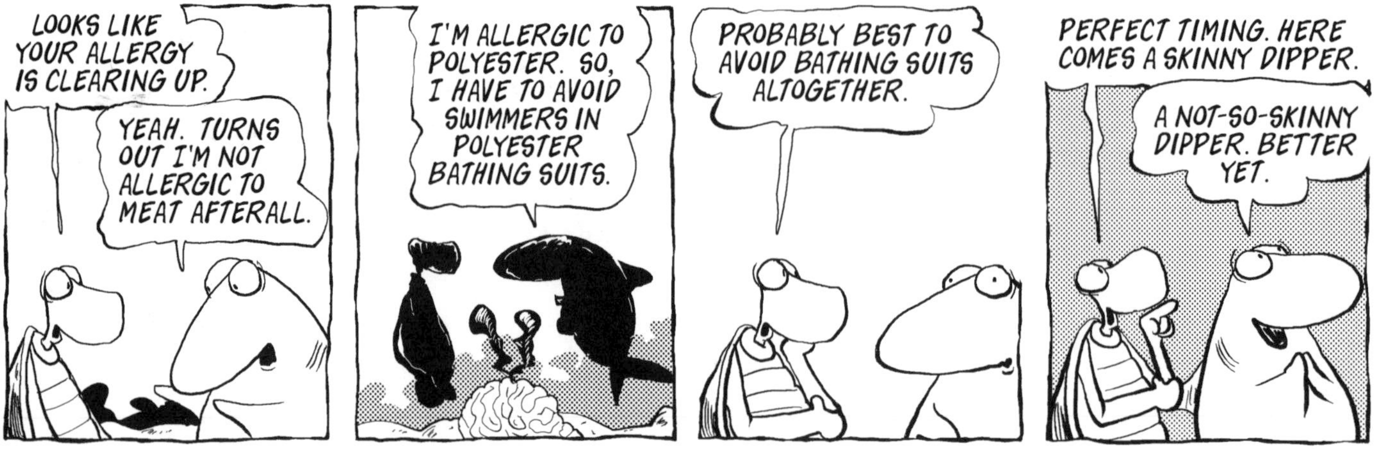
LOOKS LIKE YOUR ALLERGY IS CLEARING UP.
YEAH. TURNS OUT I'M NOT ALLERGIC TO MEAT AFTERALL.
I'M ALLERGIC TO POLYESTER. SO, I HAVE TO AVOID SWIMMERS IN POLYESTER BATHING SUITS.
PROBABLY BEST TO AVOID BATHING SUITS ALTOGETHER.
PERFECT TIMING. HERE COMES A SKINNY DIPPER.
A NOT-SO-SKINNY DIPPER. BETTER YET.

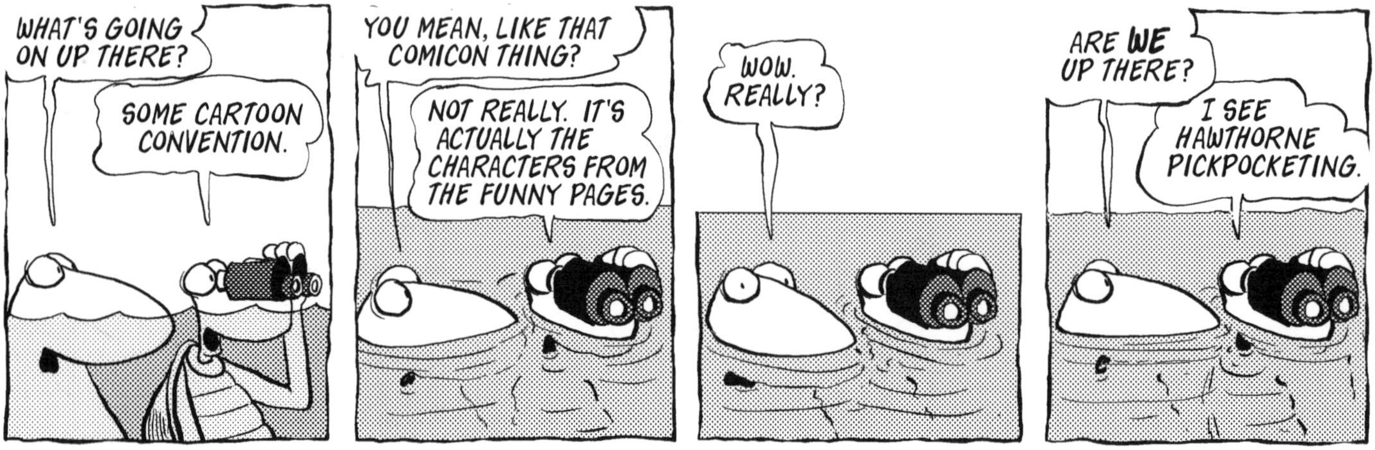
WHAT'S GOING ON UP THERE?
SOME CARTOON CONVENTION.
YOU MEAN, LIKE THAT COMICON THING?
NOT REALLY. IT'S ACTUALLY THE CHARACTERS FROM THE FUNNY PAGES.
WOW. REALLY?
ARE WE UP THERE?
I SEE HAWTHORNE PICKPOCKETING.

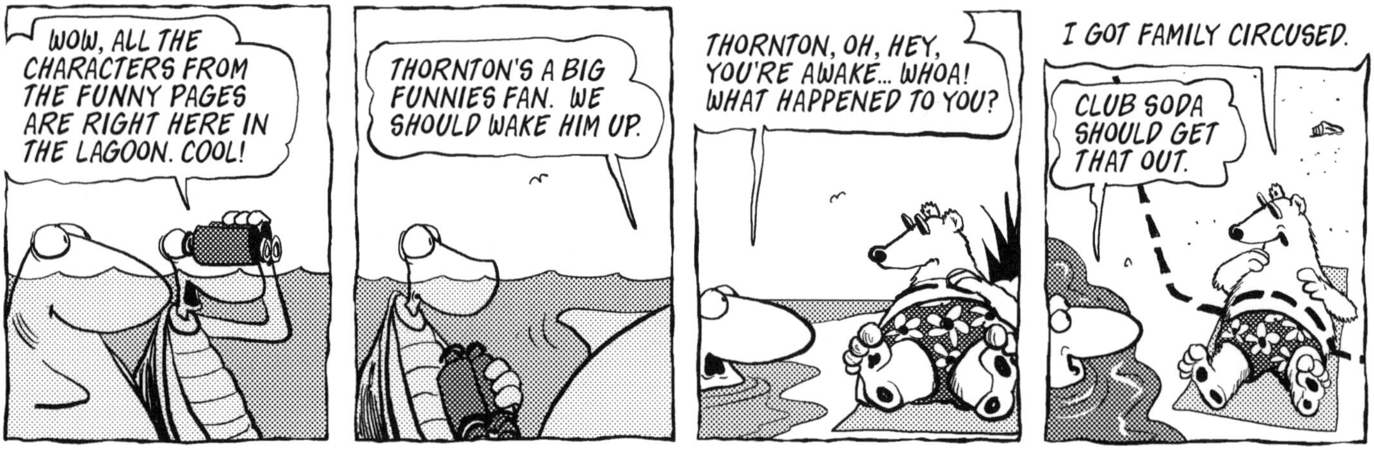
WOW, ALL THE CHARACTERS FROM THE FUNNY PAGES ARE RIGHT HERE IN THE LAGOON. COOL!
THORNTON'S A BIG FUNNIES FAN. WE SHOULD WAKE HIM UP.
THORNTON, OH, HEY, YOU'RE AWAKE... WHOA! WHAT HAPPENED TO YOU?
I GOT FAMILY CIRCUSED.
CLUB SODA SHOULD GET THAT OUT.

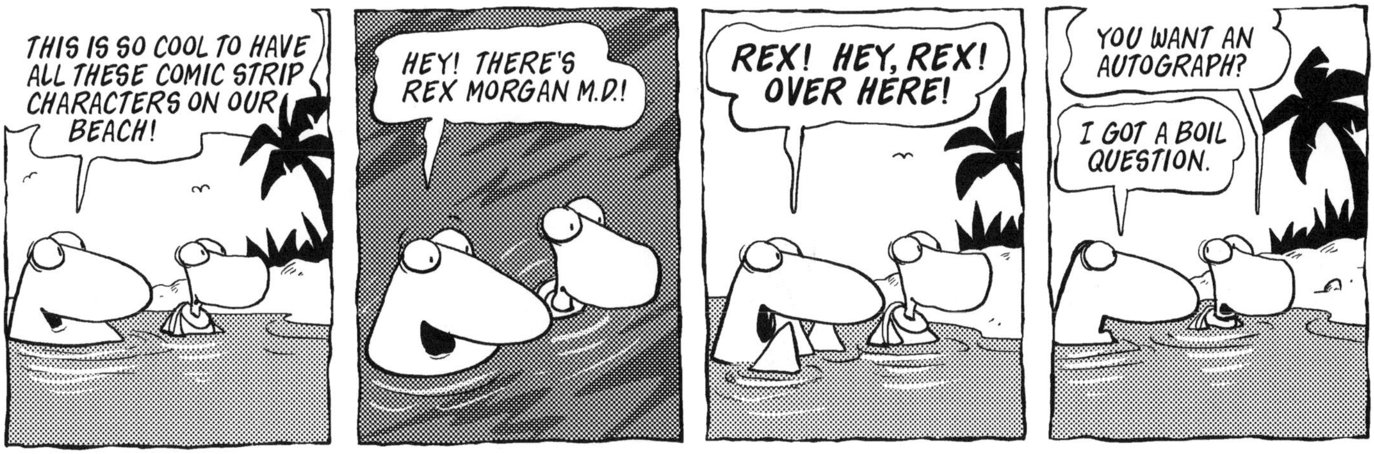
THIS IS SO COOL TO HAVE ALL THESE COMIC STRIP CHARACTERS ON OUR BEACH!
HEY! THERE'S REX MORGAN M.D.!
REX! HEY, REX! OVER HERE!
YOU WANT AN AUTOGRAPH?
I GOT A BOIL QUESTION.

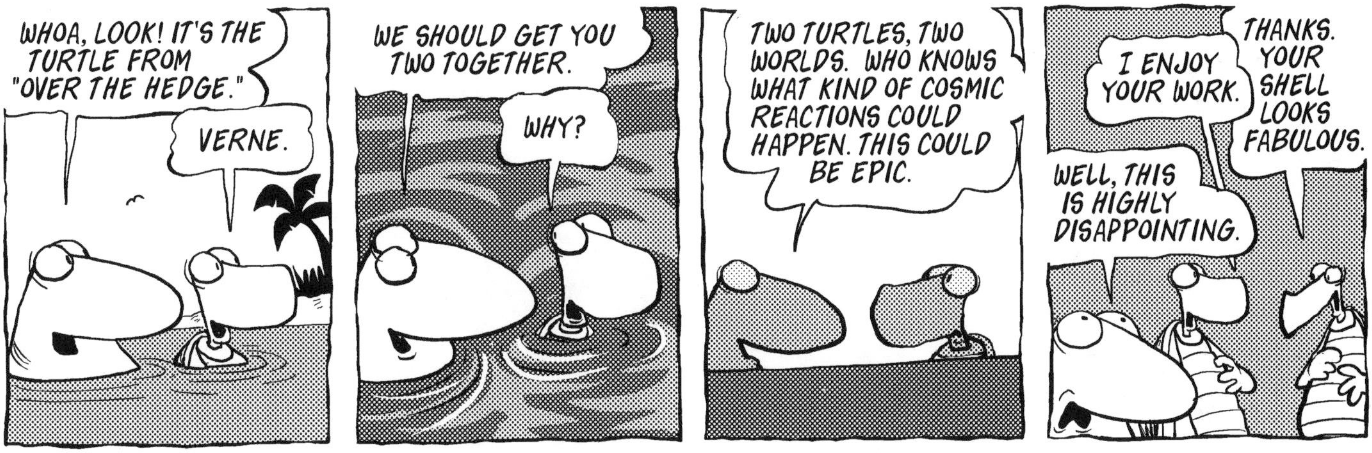
WHOA, LOOK! IT'S THE TURTLE FROM "OVER THE HEDGE."
VERNE.
WE SHOULD GET YOU TWO TOGETHER.
WHY?
TWO TURTLES, TWO WORLDS. WHO KNOWS WHAT KIND OF COSMIC REACTIONS COULD HAPPEN. THIS COULD BE EPIC.
I ENJOY YOUR WORK.
THANKS. YOUR SHELL LOOKS FABULOUS.
WELL, THIS IS HIGHLY DISAPPOINTING.

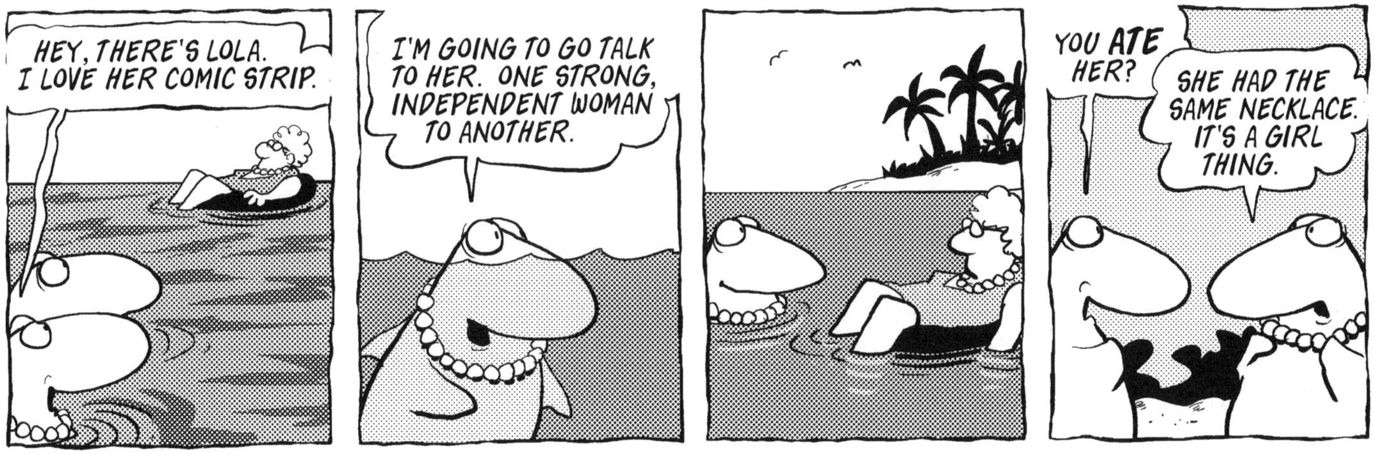
HEY, THERE'S LOLA. I LOVE HER COMIC STRIP.
I'M GOING TO GO TALK TO HER. ONE STRONG, INDEPENDENT WOMAN TO ANOTHER.
YOU ATE HER?
SHE HAD THE SAME NECKLACE. IT'S A GIRL THING.

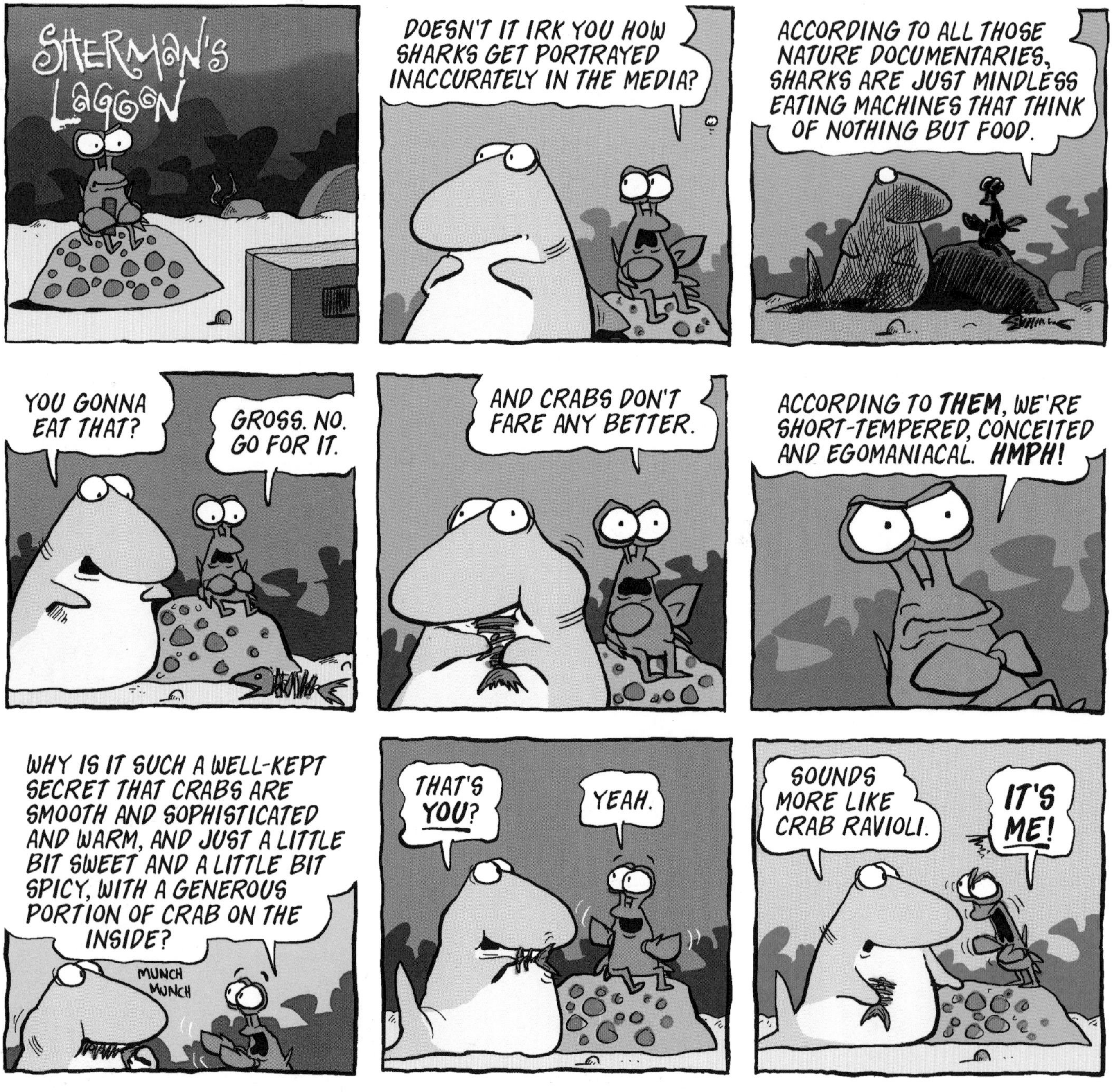

SHERMAN'S LAGOON
DOESN'T IT IRK YOU HOW SHARKS GET PORTRAYED INACCURATELY IN THE MEDIA?
ACCORDING TO ALL THOSE NATURE DOCUMENTARIES, SHARKS ARE JUST MINDLESS EATING MACHINES THAT THINK OF NOTHING BUT FOOD.
YOU GONNA EAT THAT?
GROSS. NO. GO FOR IT.
AND CRABS DON'T FARE ANY BETTER.
ACCORDING TO THEM, WE'RE SHORT-TEMPERED, CONCEITED AND EGOMANIACAL. HMPH!
WHY IS IT SUCH A WELL-KEPT SECRET THAT CRABS ARE SMOOTH AND SOPHISTICATED AND WARM, AND JUST A LITTLE BIT SWEET AND A LITTLE BIT SPICY, WITH A GENEROUS PORTION OF CRAB ON THE INSIDE?
MUNCH MUNCH
THAT'S YOU?
YEAH.
SOUNDS MORE LIKE CRAB RAVIOLI.
IT'S ME!

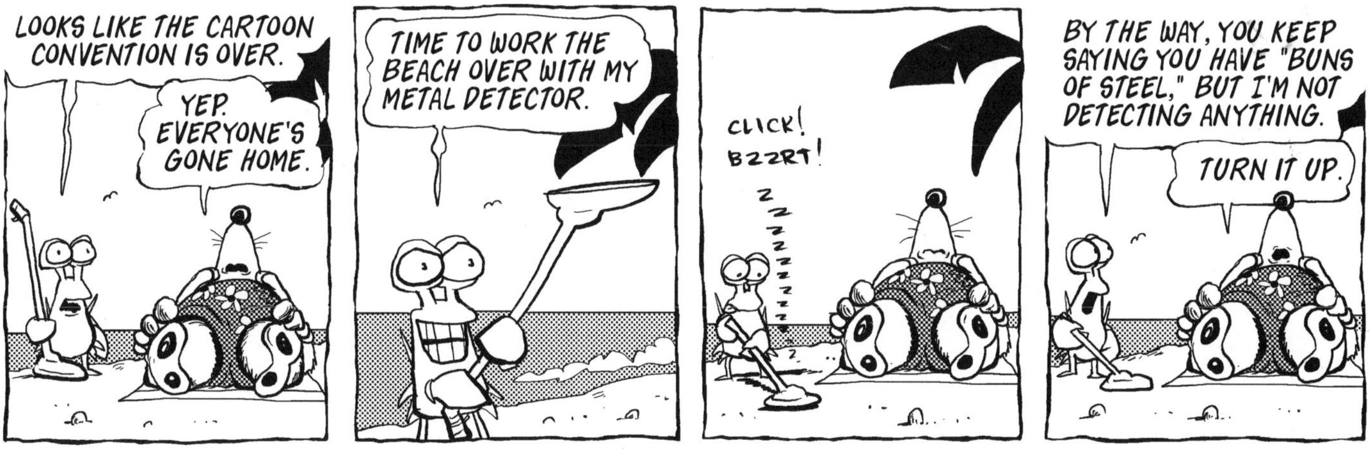
LOOKS LIKE THE CARTOON CONVENTION IS OVER.
YEP. EVERYONE'S GONE HOME.
TIME TO WORK THE BEACH OVER WITH MY METAL DETECTOR.
CLICK! BZZRT!
BY THE WAY, YOU KEEP SAYING YOU HAVE "BUNS OF STEEL," BUT I'M NOT DETECTING ANYTHING.
TURN IT UP.

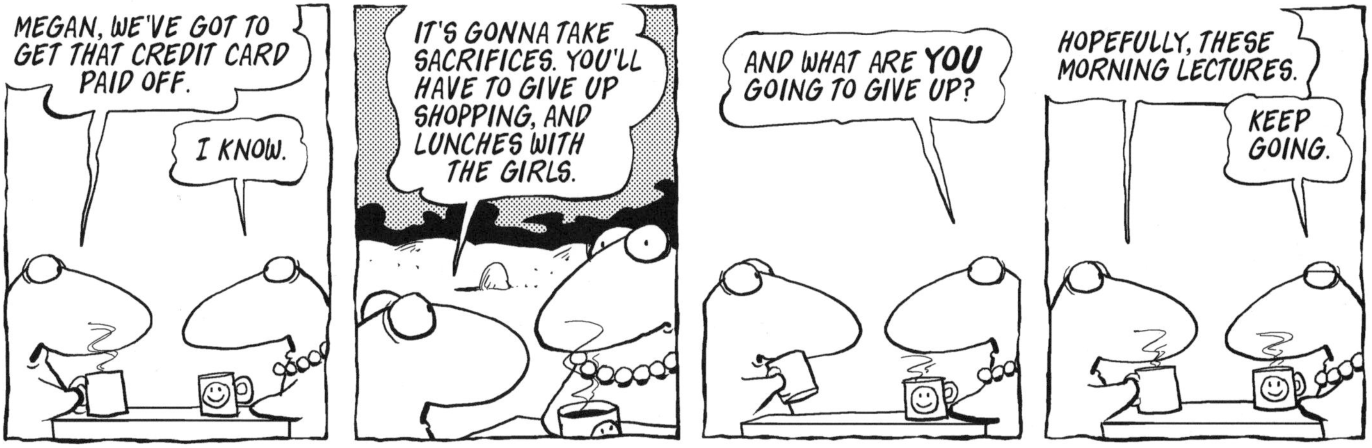
MEGAN, WE'VE GOT TO GET THAT CREDIT CARD PAID OFF.
I KNOW.
IT'S GONNA TAKE SACRIFICES. YOU'LL HAVE TO GIVE UP SHOPPING, AND LUNCHES WITH THE GIRLS.
AND WHAT ARE **YOU** GOING TO GIVE UP?
HOPEFULLY, THESE MORNING LECTURES.
KEEP GOING.

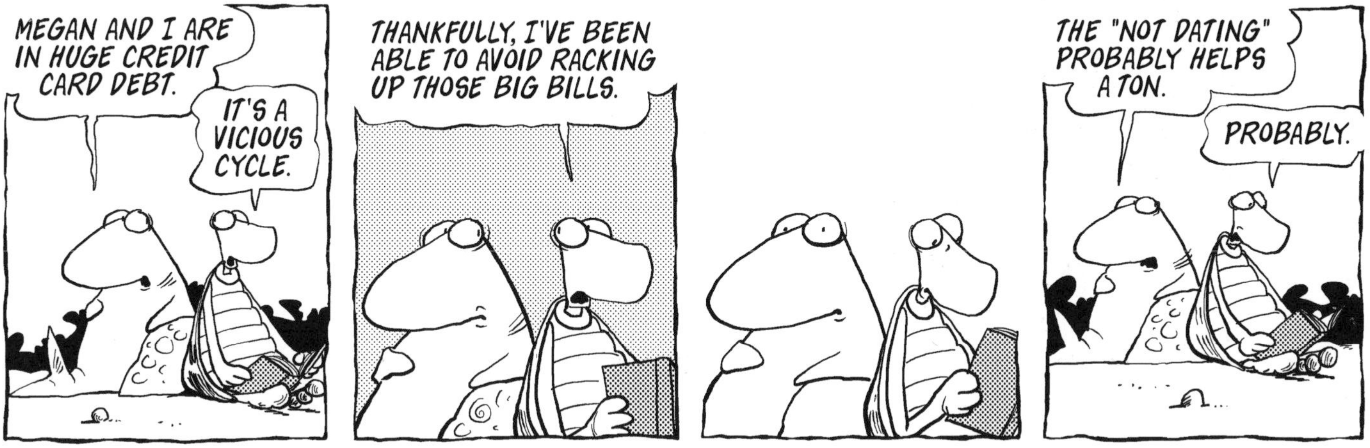
MEGAN AND I ARE IN HUGE CREDIT CARD DEBT.
IT'S A VICIOUS CYCLE.
THANKFULLY, I'VE BEEN ABLE TO AVOID RACKING UP THOSE BIG BILLS.
THE "NOT DATING" PROBABLY HELPS A TON.
PROBABLY.

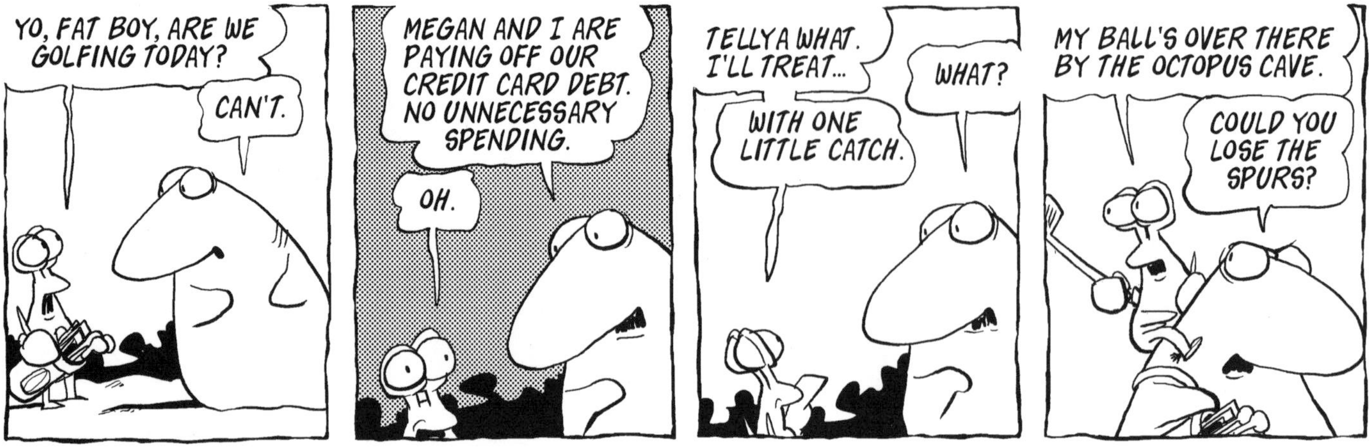
YO, FAT BOY, ARE WE GOLFING TODAY?
CAN'T.
MEGAN AND I ARE PAYING OFF OUR CREDIT CARD DEBT. NO UNNECESSARY SPENDING.
OH.
TELLYA WHAT. I'LL TREAT...
WHAT?
WITH ONE LITTLE CATCH.
MY BALL'S OVER THERE BY THE OCTOPUS CAVE.
COULD YOU LOSE THE SPURS?

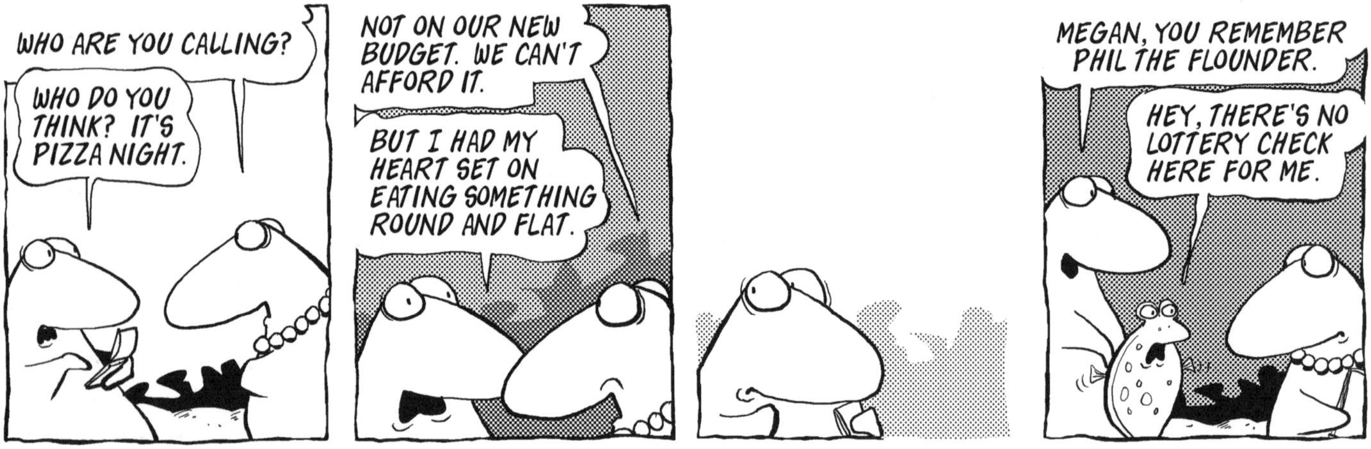
WHO ARE YOU CALLING?
WHO DO YOU THINK? IT'S PIZZA NIGHT.
NOT ON OUR NEW BUDGET. WE CAN'T AFFORD IT.
BUT I HAD MY HEART SET ON EATING SOMETHING ROUND AND FLAT.
MEGAN, YOU REMEMBER PHIL THE FLOUNDER.
HEY, THERE'S NO LOTTERY CHECK HERE FOR ME.

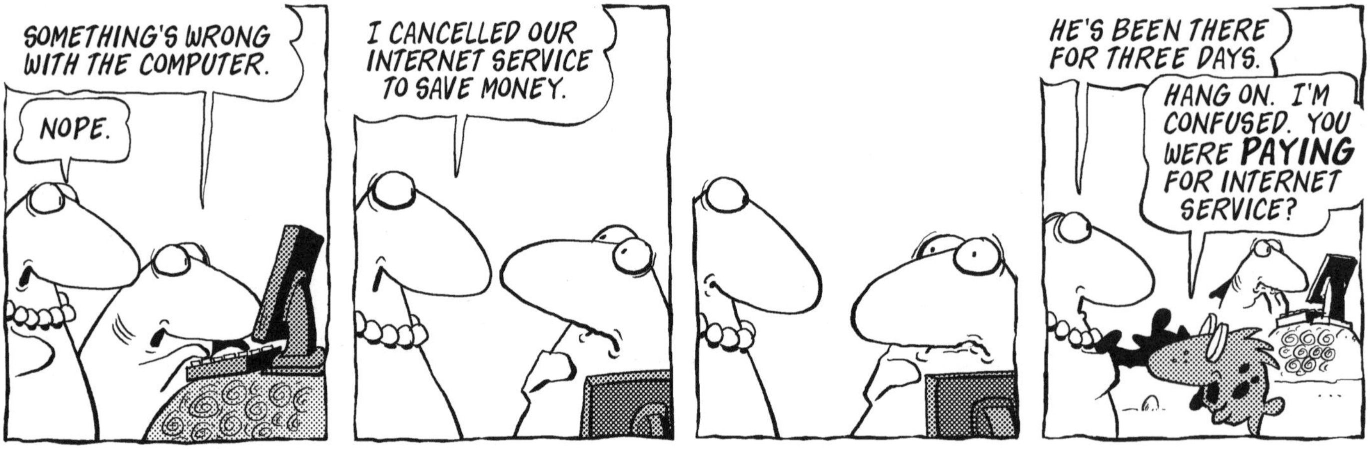
SOMETHING'S WRONG WITH THE COMPUTER.
NOPE.
I CANCELLED OUR INTERNET SERVICE TO SAVE MONEY.
HE'S BEEN THERE FOR THREE DAYS.
HANG ON. I'M CONFUSED. YOU WERE PAYING FOR INTERNET SERVICE?

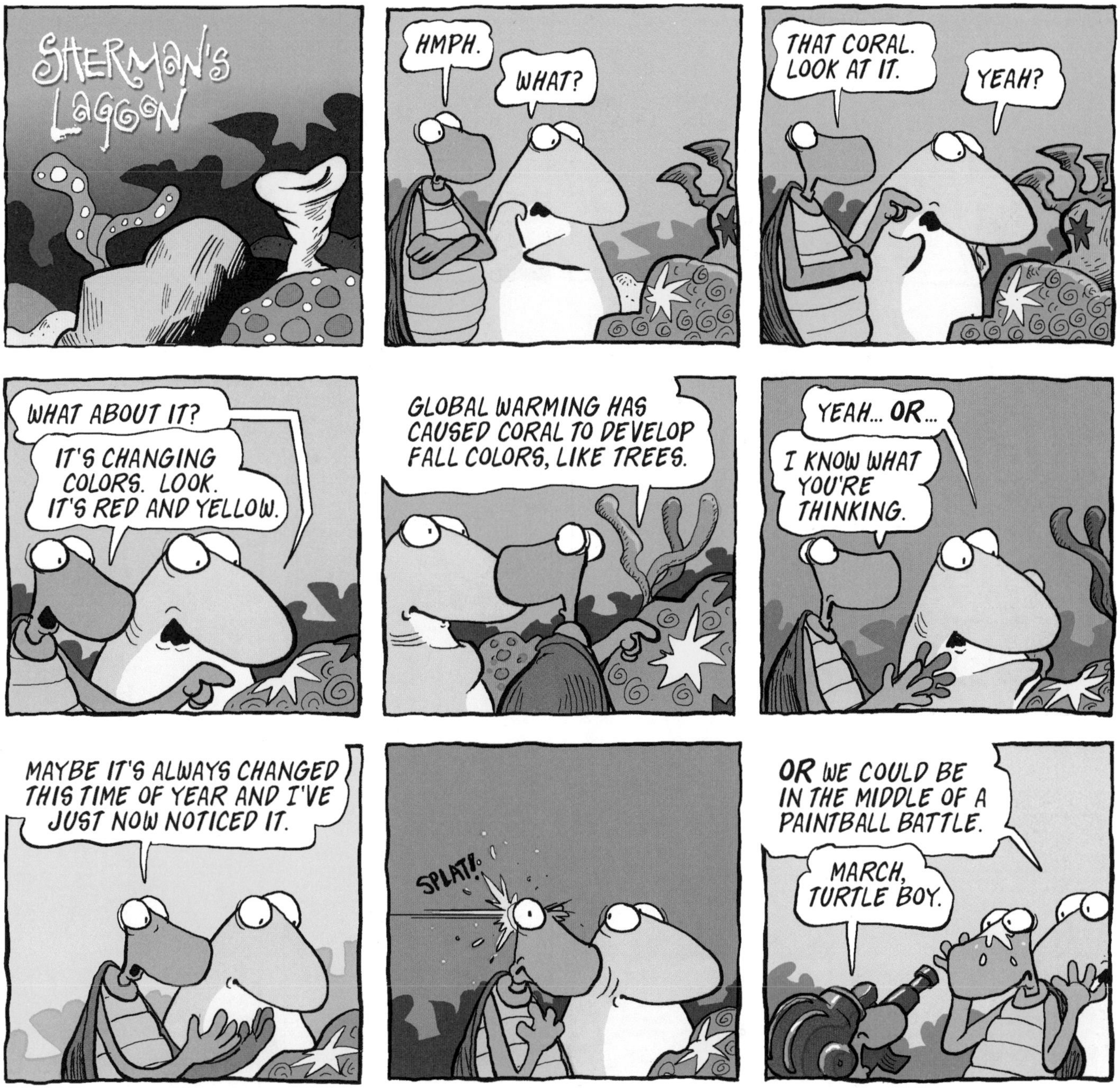
SHERMAN'S LAGOON
HMPH.
WHAT?
THAT CORAL. LOOK AT IT.
YEAH?
WHAT ABOUT IT?
IT'S CHANGING COLORS. LOOK. IT'S RED AND YELLOW.
GLOBAL WARMING HAS CAUSED CORAL TO DEVELOP FALL COLORS, LIKE TREES.
YEAH... OR...
I KNOW WHAT YOU'RE THINKING.
MAYBE IT'S ALWAYS CHANGED THIS TIME OF YEAR AND I'VE JUST NOW NOTICED IT.
SPLAT!
OR WE COULD BE IN THE MIDDLE OF A PAINTBALL BATTLE.
MARCH, TURTLE BOY.

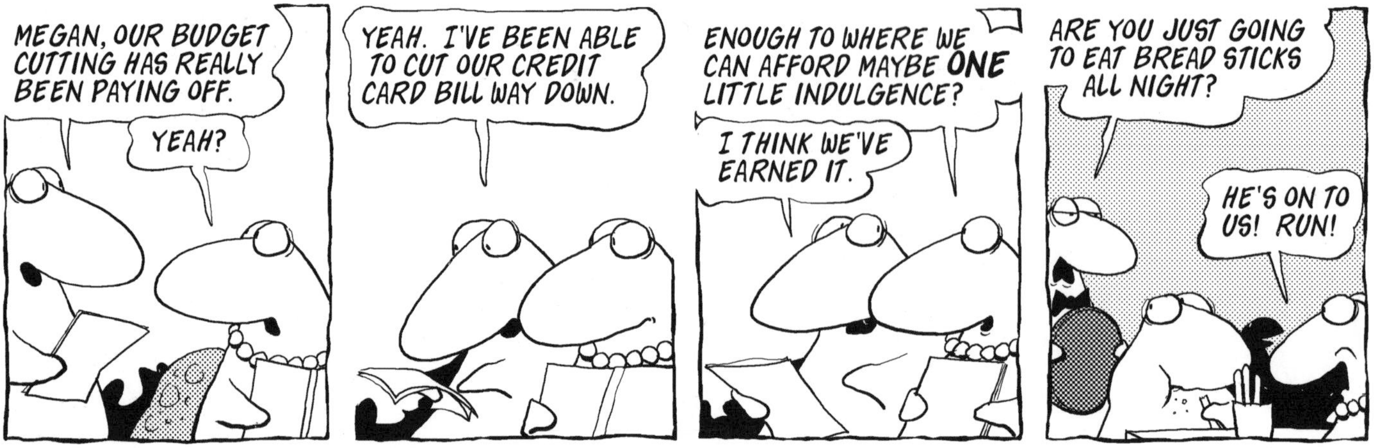
MEGAN, OUR BUDGET CUTTING HAS REALLY BEEN PAYING OFF.
YEAH?
YEAH. I'VE BEEN ABLE TO CUT OUR CREDIT CARD BILL WAY DOWN.
ENOUGH TO WHERE WE CAN AFFORD MAYBE **ONE** LITTLE INDULGENCE?
I THINK WE'VE EARNED IT.
ARE YOU JUST GOING TO EAT BREAD STICKS ALL NIGHT?
HE'S ON TO US! RUN!

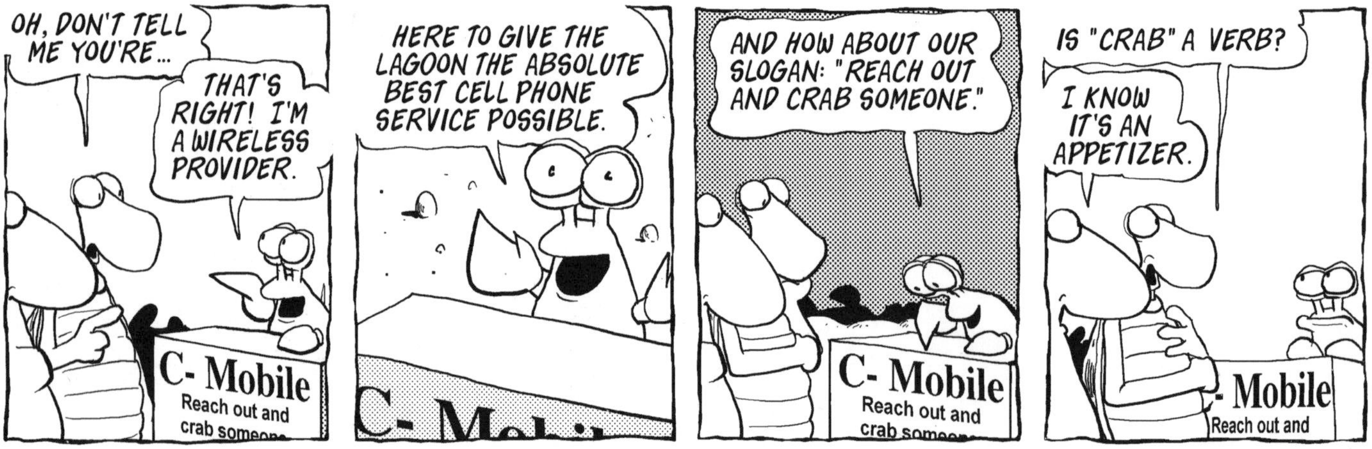
OH, DON'T TELL ME YOU'RE...
THAT'S RIGHT! I'M A WIRELESS PROVIDER.
C- Mobile
Reach out and
HERE TO GIVE THE LAGOON THE ABSOLUTE BEST CELL PHONE SERVICE POSSIBLE.
AND HOW ABOUT OUR SLOGAN: "REACH OUT AND CRAB SOMEONE."
C- Mobile
Reach out and
IS "CRAB" A VERB?
I KNOW IT'S AN APPETIZER.

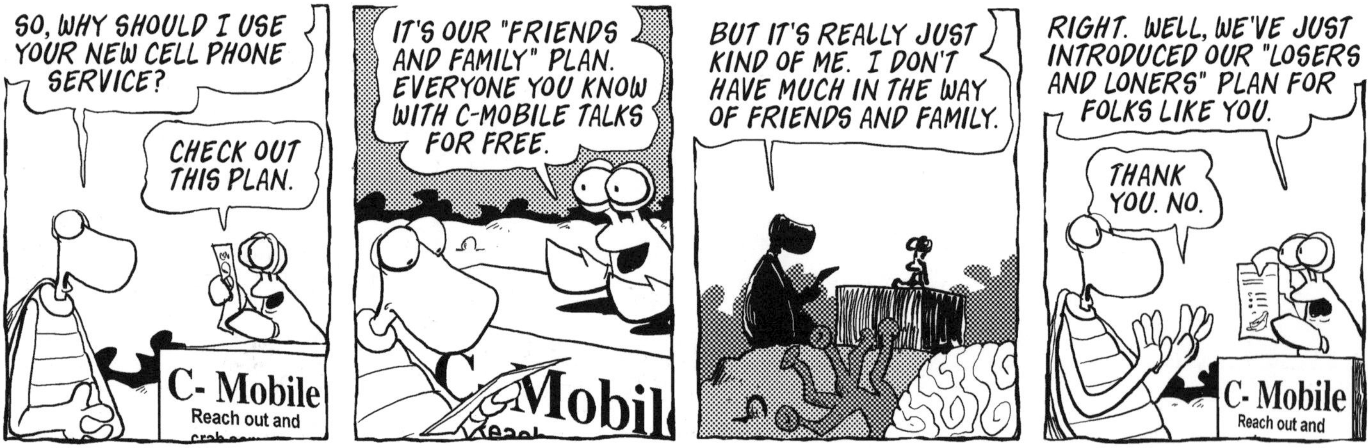
SO, WHY SHOULD I USE YOUR NEW CELL PHONE SERVICE?
CHECK OUT THIS PLAN.
C- Mobile
Reach out and
IT'S OUR "FRIENDS AND FAMILY" PLAN. EVERYONE YOU KNOW WITH C-MOBILE TALKS FOR FREE.
BUT IT'S REALLY JUST KIND OF ME. I DON'T HAVE MUCH IN THE WAY OF FRIENDS AND FAMILY.
RIGHT. WELL, WE'VE JUST INTRODUCED OUR "LOSERS AND LONERS" PLAN FOR FOLKS LIKE YOU.
THANK YOU. NO.
C- Mobile
Reach out and

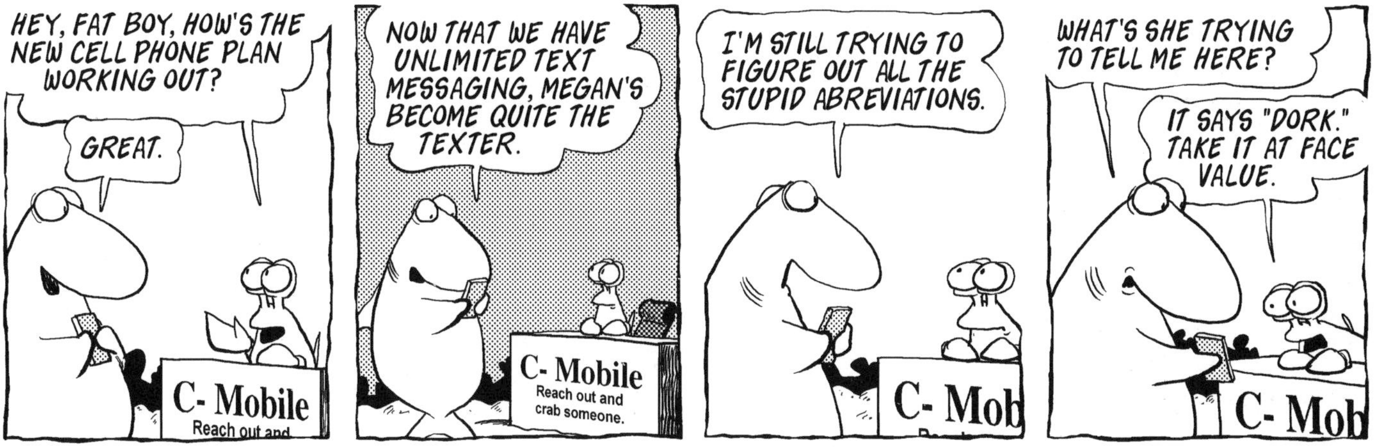
HEY, FAT BOY, HOW'S THE NEW CELL PHONE PLAN WORKING OUT?
GREAT.
C- Mobile
Reach out and
NOW THAT WE HAVE UNLIMITED TEXT MESSAGING, MEGAN'S BECOME QUITE THE TEXTER.
C- Mobile
Reach out and crab someone.
I'M STILL TRYING TO FIGURE OUT ALL THE STUPID ABREVIATIONS.
WHAT'S SHE TRYING TO TELL ME HERE?
IT SAYS "DORK." TAKE IT AT FACE VALUE.

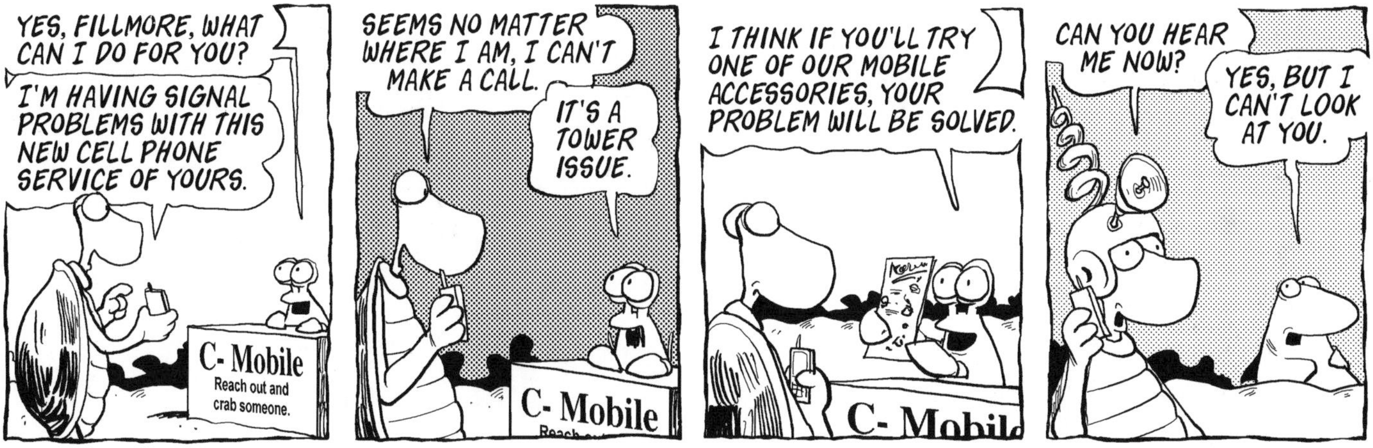
YES, FILLMORE, WHAT CAN I DO FOR YOU?
I'M HAVING SIGNAL PROBLEMS WITH THIS NEW CELL PHONE SERVICE OF YOURS.
C- Mobile
Reach out and crab someone.
SEEMS NO MATTER WHERE I AM, I CAN'T MAKE A CALL.
IT'S A TOWER ISSUE.
C- Mobile
I THINK IF YOU'LL TRY ONE OF OUR MOBILE ACCESSORIES, YOUR PROBLEM WILL BE SOLVED.
CAN YOU HEAR ME NOW?
YES, BUT I CAN'T LOOK AT YOU.

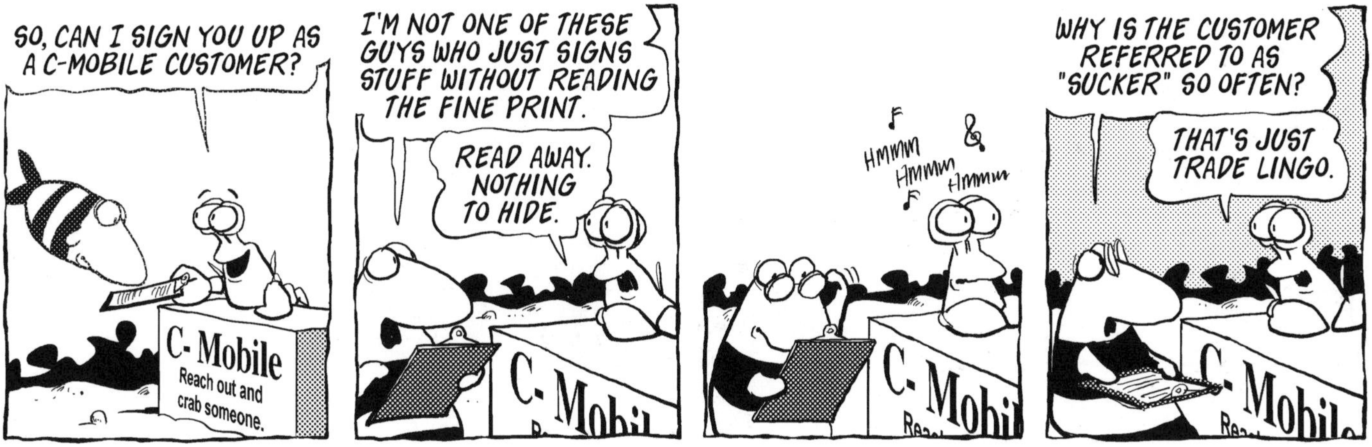
SO, CAN I SIGN YOU UP AS A C-MOBILE CUSTOMER?
C- Mobile
Reach out and crab someone.
I'M NOT ONE OF THESE GUYS WHO JUST SIGNS STUFF WITHOUT READING THE FINE PRINT.
READ AWAY. NOTHING TO HIDE.
HMMM HMMM HMMM
WHY IS THE CUSTOMER REFERRED TO AS "SUCKER" SO OFTEN?
THAT'S JUST TRADE LINGO.

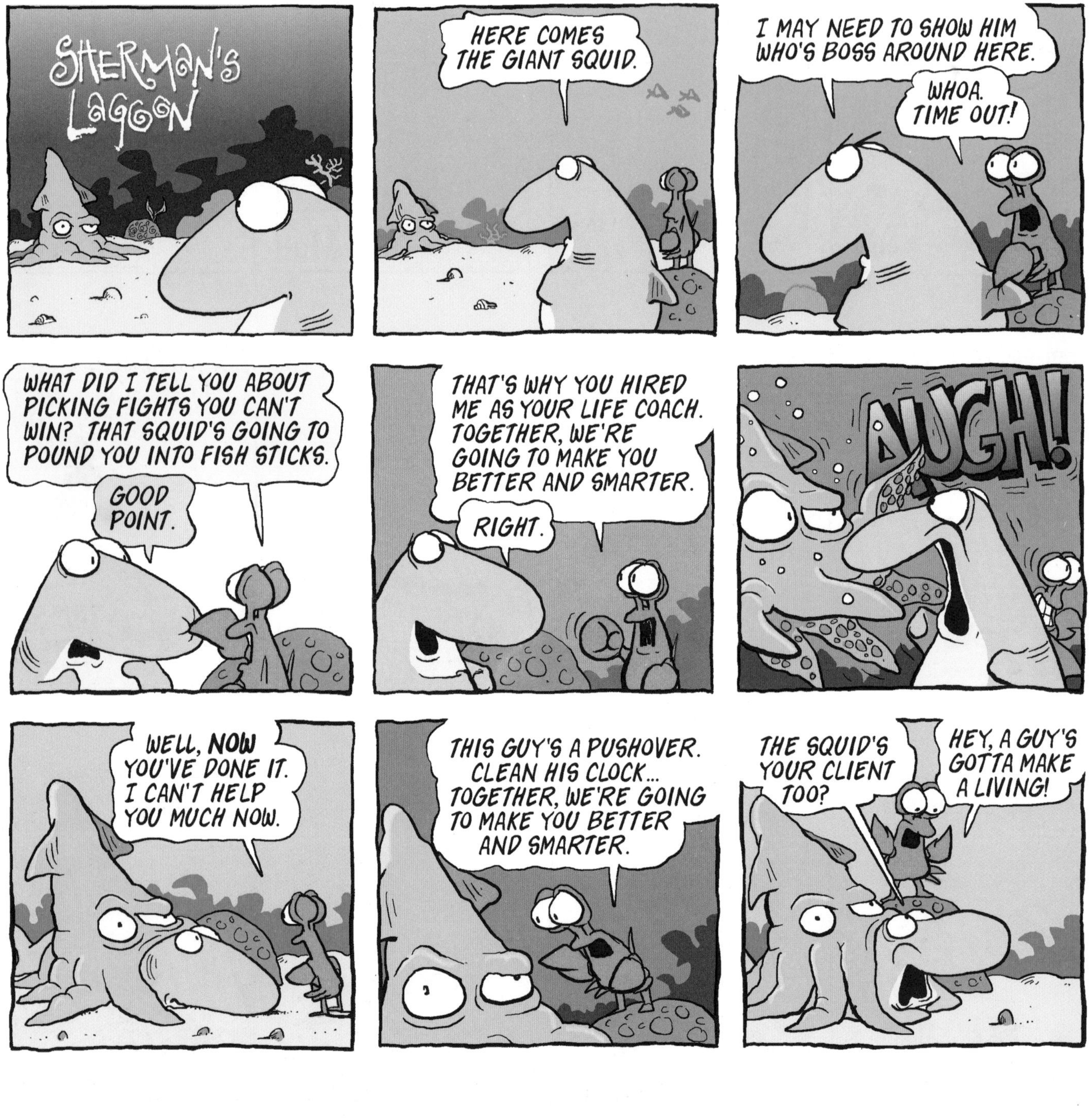
SHERMAN'S LAGOON
HERE COMES THE GIANT SQUID.
I MAY NEED TO SHOW HIM WHO'S BOSS AROUND HERE.
WHOA. TIME OUT!
WHAT DID I TELL YOU ABOUT PICKING FIGHTS YOU CAN'T WIN? THAT SQUID'S GOING TO POUND YOU INTO FISH STICKS.
GOOD POINT.
THAT'S WHY YOU HIRED ME AS YOUR LIFE COACH. TOGETHER, WE'RE GOING TO MAKE YOU BETTER AND SMARTER.
RIGHT.
AUGH!
WELL, NOW YOU'VE DONE IT. I CAN'T HELP YOU MUCH NOW.
THIS GUY'S A PUSHOVER. CLEAN HIS CLOCK... TOGETHER, WE'RE GOING TO MAKE YOU BETTER AND SMARTER.
THE SQUID'S YOUR CLIENT TOO?
HEY, A GUY'S GOTTA MAKE A LIVING!

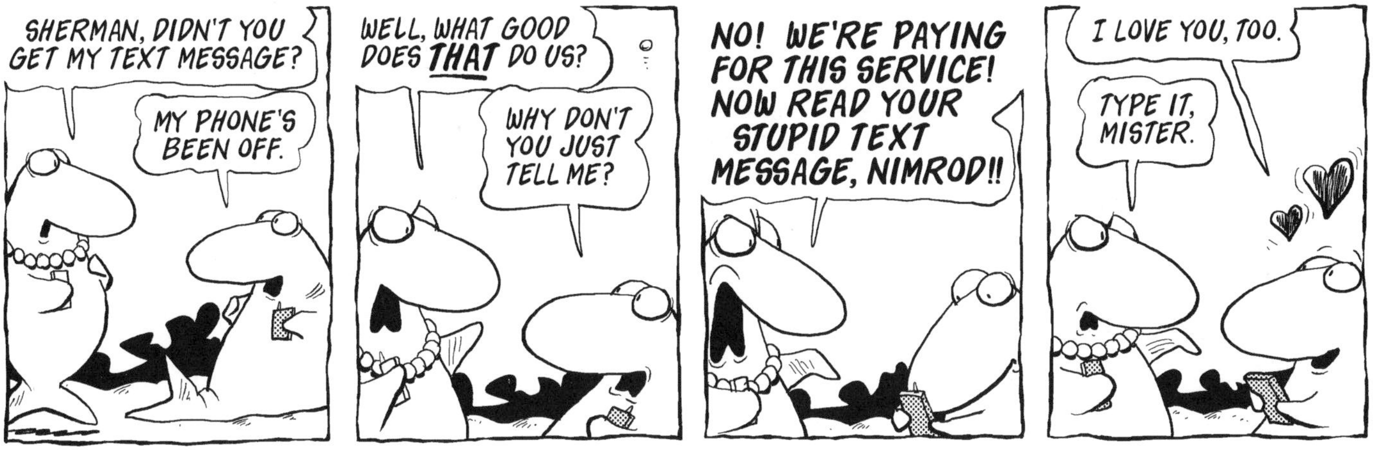
SHERMAN, DIDN'T YOU GET MY TEXT MESSAGE?
MY PHONE'S BEEN OFF.
WELL, WHAT GOOD DOES THAT DO US?
WHY DON'T YOU JUST TELL ME?
NO! WE'RE PAYING FOR THIS SERVICE! NOW READ YOUR STUPID TEXT MESSAGE, NIMROD!!
I LOVE YOU, TOO.
TYPE IT, MISTER.

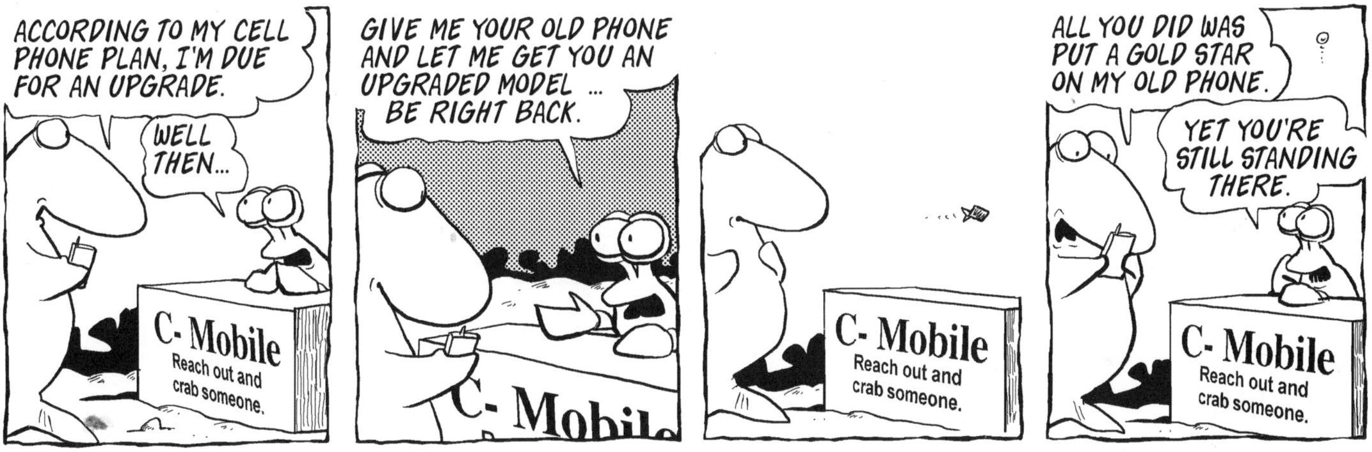
ACCORDING TO MY CELL PHONE PLAN, I'M DUE FOR AN UPGRADE.
WELL THEN...
C- Mobile
Reach out and crab someone.
GIVE ME YOUR OLD PHONE AND LET ME GET YOU AN UPGRADED MODEL ... BE RIGHT BACK.
C- Mobile
Reach out and crab someone.
ALL YOU DID WAS PUT A GOLD STAR ON MY OLD PHONE.
YET YOU'RE STILL STANDING THERE.
C- Mobile
Reach out and crab someone.

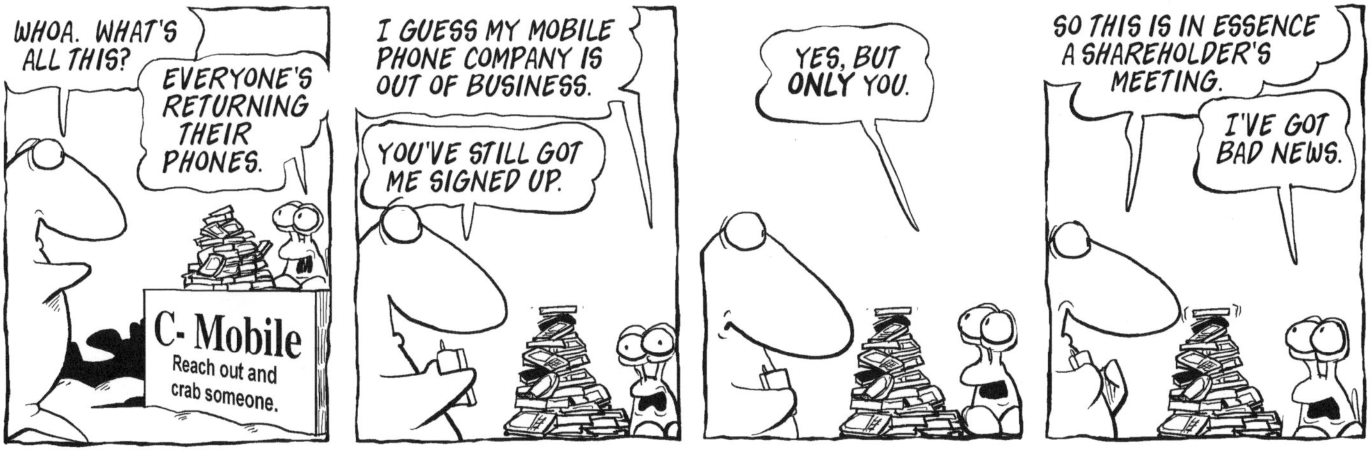
WHOA. WHAT'S ALL THIS?
EVERYONE'S RETURNING THEIR PHONES.
C- Mobile
Reach out and crab someone.
I GUESS MY MOBILE PHONE COMPANY IS OUT OF BUSINESS.
YOU'VE STILL GOT ME SIGNED UP.
YES, BUT ONLY YOU.
SO THIS IS IN ESSENCE A SHAREHOLDER'S MEETING.
I'VE GOT BAD NEWS.

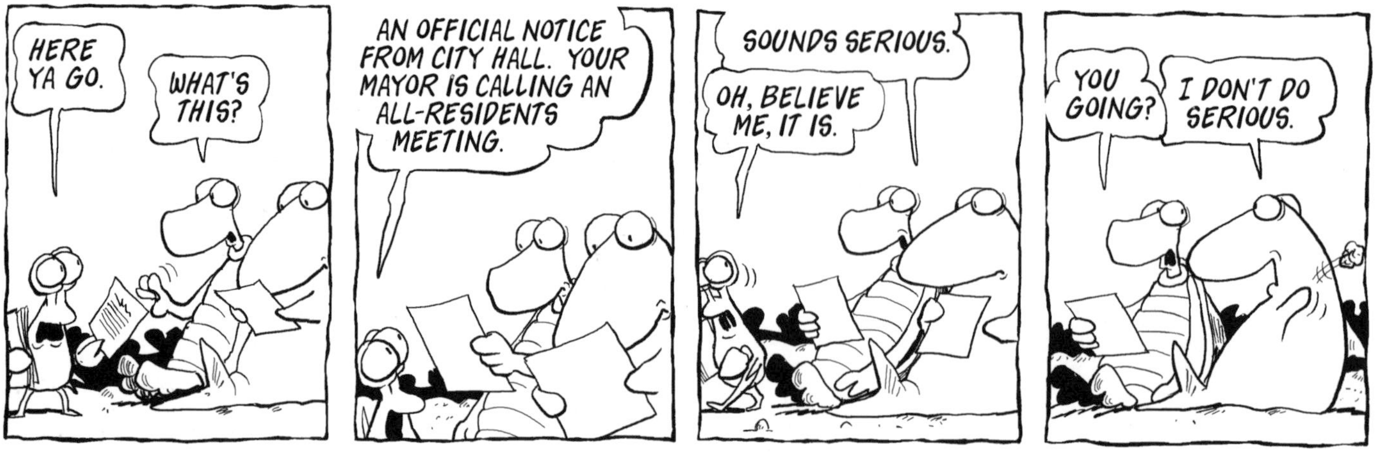
HERE YA GO.
WHAT'S THIS?
AN OFFICIAL NOTICE FROM CITY HALL. YOUR MAYOR IS CALLING AN ALL-RESIDENTS MEETING.
SOUNDS SERIOUS.
OH, BELIEVE ME, IT IS.
YOU GOING?
I DON'T DO SERIOUS.

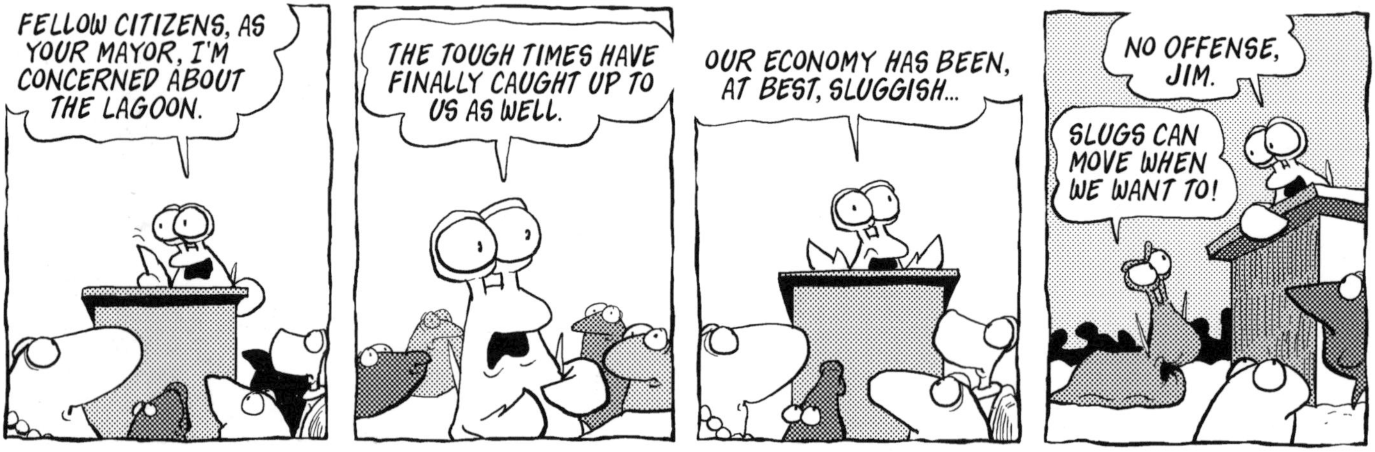
FELLOW CITIZENS, AS YOUR MAYOR, I'M CONCERNED ABOUT THE LAGOON.
THE TOUGH TIMES HAVE FINALLY CAUGHT UP TO US AS WELL.
OUR ECONOMY HAS BEEN, AT BEST, SLUGGISH...
NO OFFENSE, JIM.
SLUGS CAN MOVE WHEN WE WANT TO!

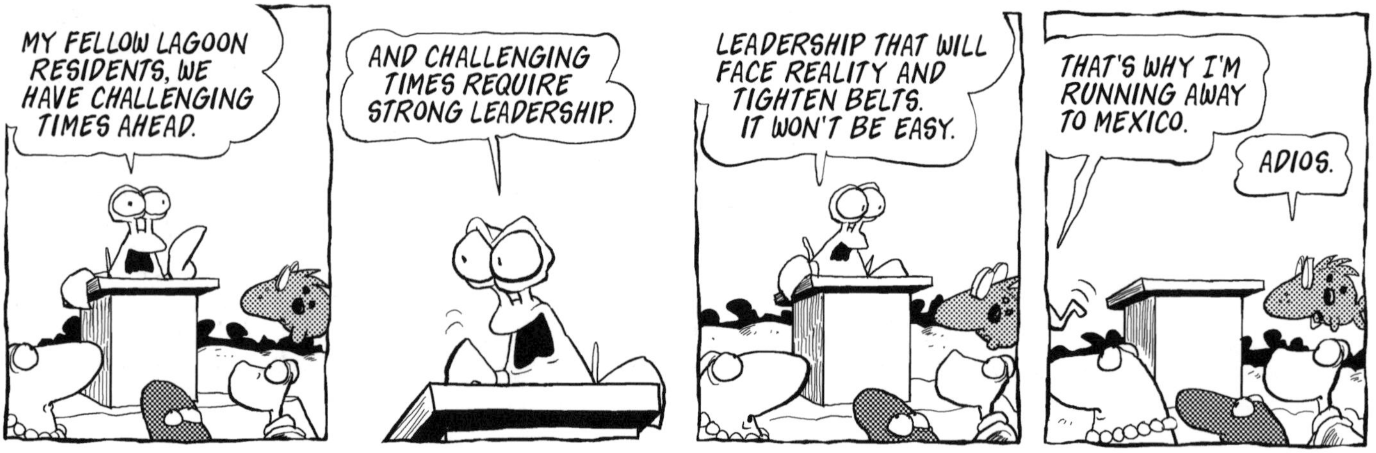
MY FELLOW LAGOON RESIDENTS, WE HAVE CHALLENGING TIMES AHEAD.
AND CHALLENGING TIMES REQUIRE STRONG LEADERSHIP.
LEADERSHIP THAT WILL FACE REALITY AND TIGHTEN BELTS. IT WON'T BE EASY.
THAT'S WHY I'M RUNNING AWAY TO MEXICO.
ADIOS.

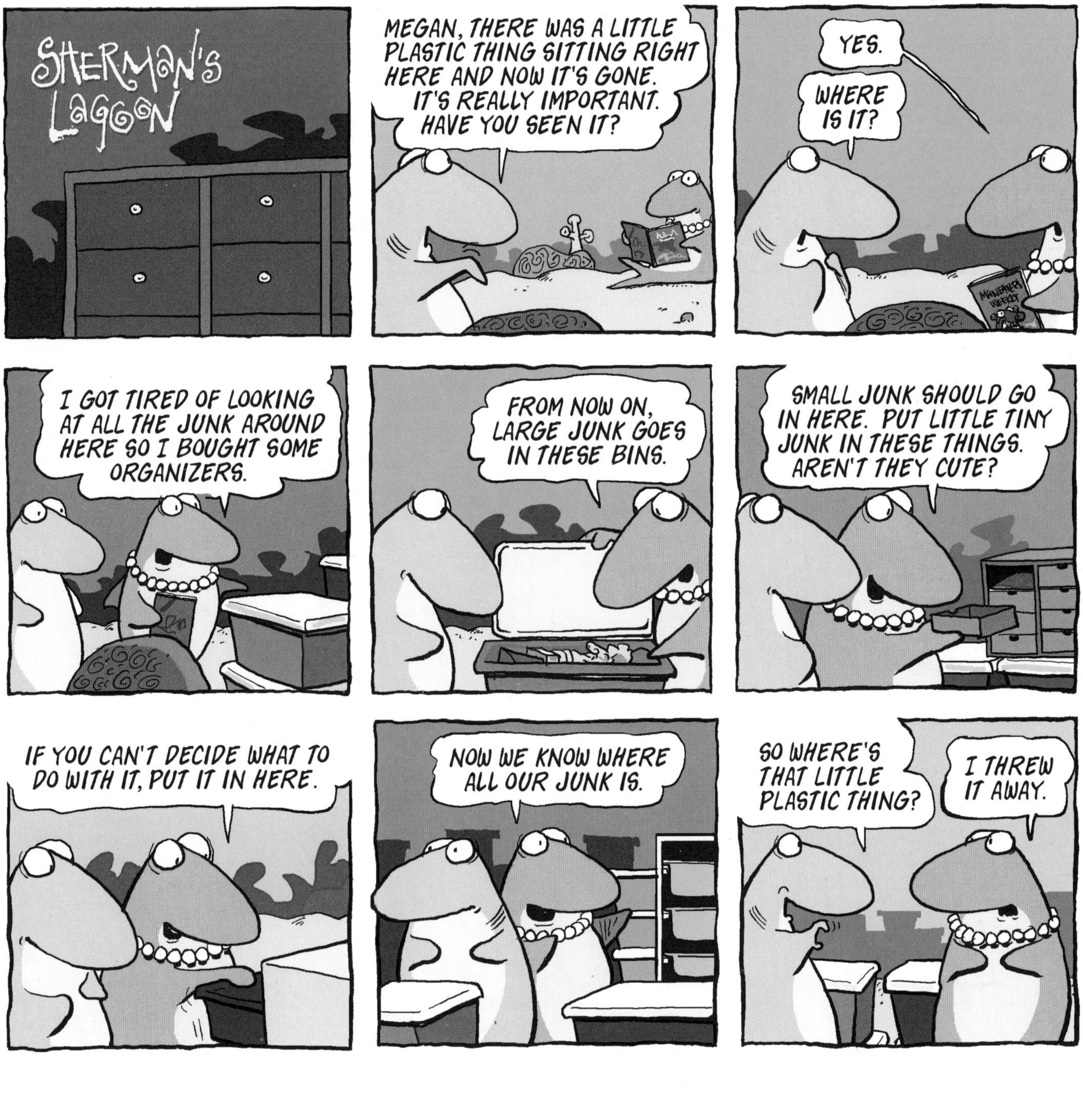
SHERMAN'S LAGOON
MEGAN, THERE WAS A LITTLE PLASTIC THING SITTING RIGHT HERE AND NOW IT'S GONE. IT'S REALLY IMPORTANT. HAVE YOU SEEN IT?
YES.
WHERE IS IT?
I GOT TIRED OF LOOKING AT ALL THE JUNK AROUND HERE SO I BOUGHT SOME ORGANIZERS.
FROM NOW ON, LARGE JUNK GOES IN THESE BINS.
SMALL JUNK SHOULD GO IN HERE. PUT LITTLE TINY JUNK IN THESE THINGS. AREN'T THEY CUTE?
IF YOU CAN'T DECIDE WHAT TO DO WITH IT, PUT IT IN HERE.
NOW WE KNOW WHERE ALL OUR JUNK IS.
SO WHERE'S THAT LITTLE PLASTIC THING?
I THREW IT AWAY.

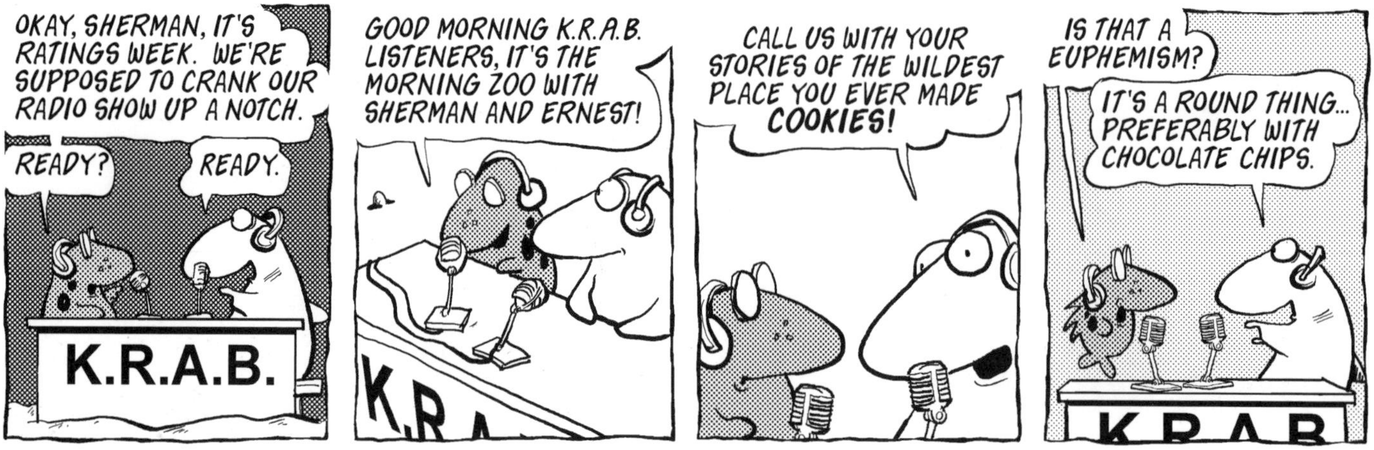
OKAY, SHERMAN, IT'S RATINGS WEEK. WE'RE SUPPOSED TO CRANK OUR RADIO SHOW UP A NOTCH.
READY?
READY.
K.R.A.B.
GOOD MORNING K.R.A.B. LISTENERS, IT'S THE MORNING ZOO WITH SHERMAN AND ERNEST!
CALL US WITH YOUR STORIES OF THE WILDEST PLACE YOU EVER MADE **COOKIES**!
IS THAT A EUPHEMISM?
IT'S A ROUND THING... PREFERABLY WITH CHOCOLATE CHIPS.

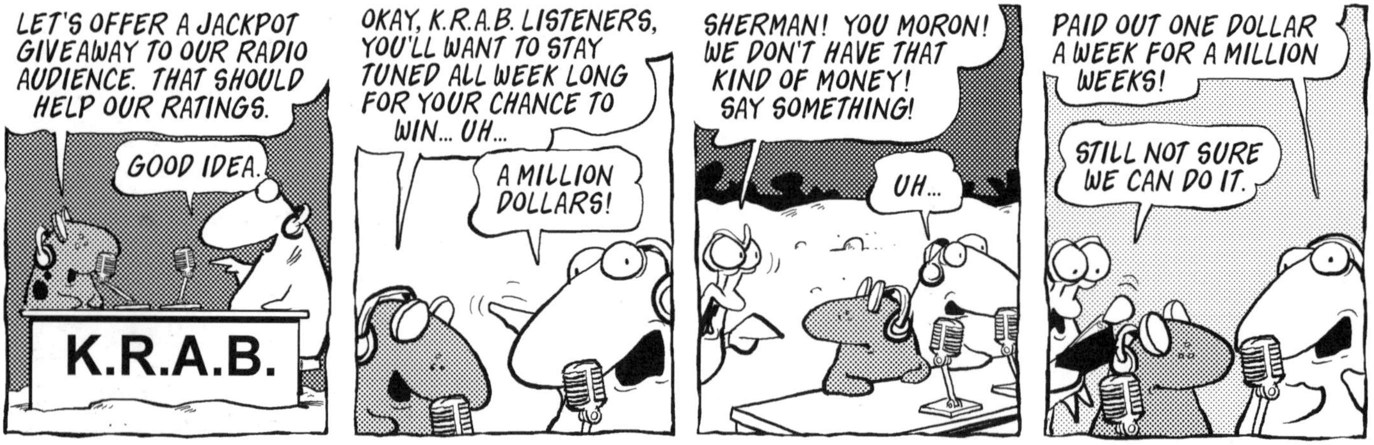
LET'S OFFER A JACKPOT GIVEAWAY TO OUR RADIO AUDIENCE. THAT SHOULD HELP OUR RATINGS.
GOOD IDEA.
K.R.A.B.
OKAY, K.R.A.B. LISTENERS, YOU'LL WANT TO STAY TUNED ALL WEEK LONG FOR YOUR CHANCE TO WIN... UH...
A MILLION DOLLARS!
SHERMAN! YOU MORON! WE DON'T HAVE THAT KIND OF MONEY! SAY SOMETHING!
UH...
PAID OUT ONE DOLLAR A WEEK FOR A MILLION WEEKS!
STILL NOT SURE WE CAN DO IT.

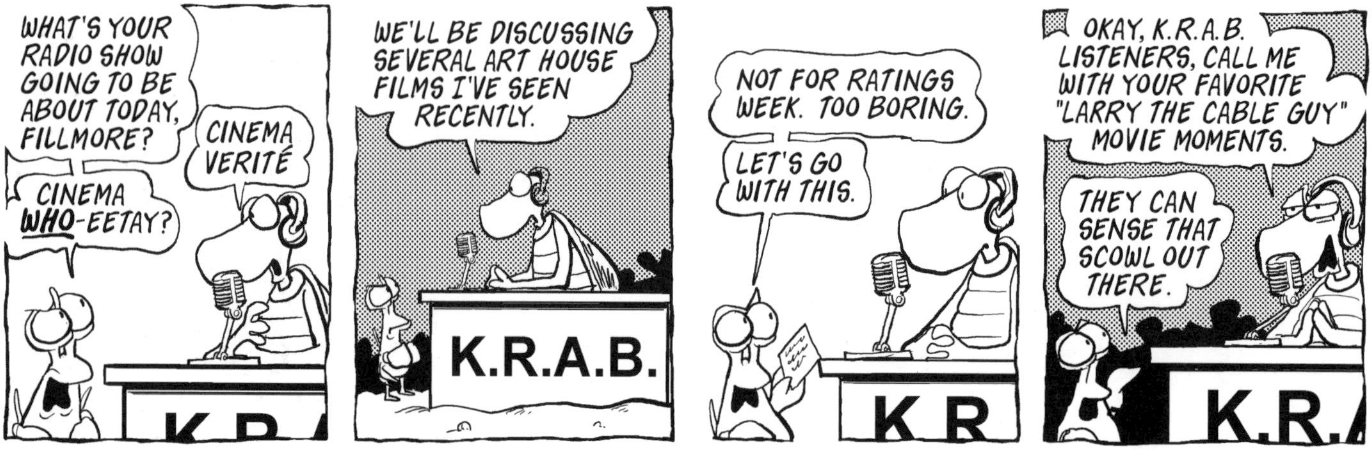
WHAT'S YOUR RADIO SHOW GOING TO BE ABOUT TODAY, FILLMORE?
CINEMA VERITÉ
CINEMA WHO-EETAY?
WE'LL BE DISCUSSING SEVERAL ART HOUSE FILMS I'VE SEEN RECENTLY.
K.R.A.B.
NOT FOR RATINGS WEEK. TOO BORING.
LET'S GO WITH THIS.
OKAY, K.R.A.B. LISTENERS, CALL ME WITH YOUR FAVORITE "LARRY THE CABLE GUY" MOVIE MOMENTS.
THEY CAN SENSE THAT SCOWL OUT THERE.

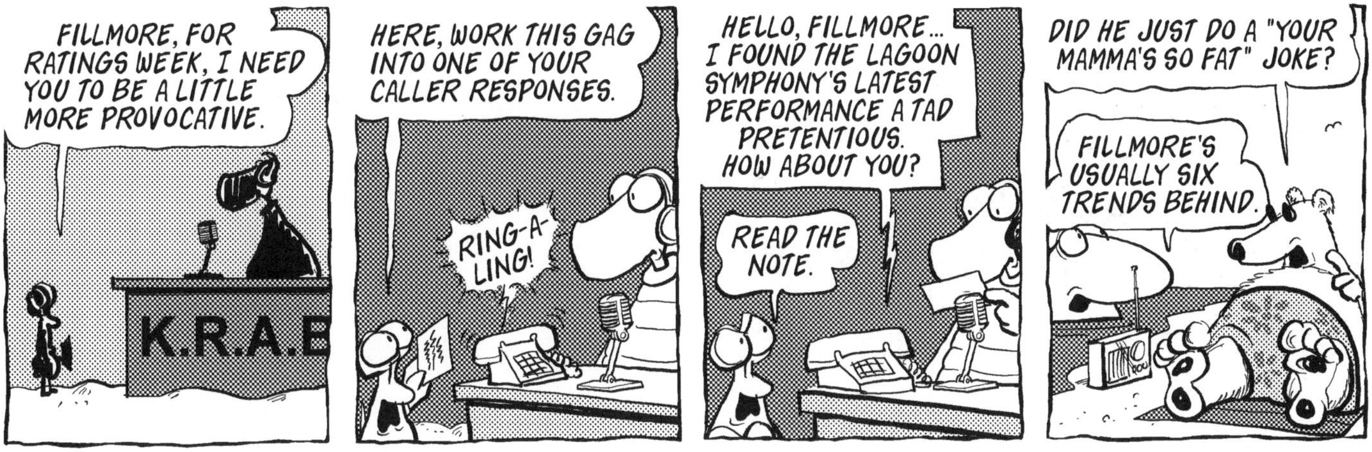
FILLMORE, FOR RATINGS WEEK, I NEED YOU TO BE A LITTLE MORE PROVOCATIVE.
K.R.A.B
HERE, WORK THIS GAG INTO ONE OF YOUR CALLER RESPONSES.
RING-A-LING!
HELLO, FILLMORE... I FOUND THE LAGOON SYMPHONY'S LATEST PERFORMANCE A TAD PRETENTIOUS. HOW ABOUT YOU?
READ THE NOTE.
DID HE JUST DO A "YOUR MAMMA'S SO FAT" JOKE?
FILLMORE'S USUALLY SIX TRENDS BEHIND.

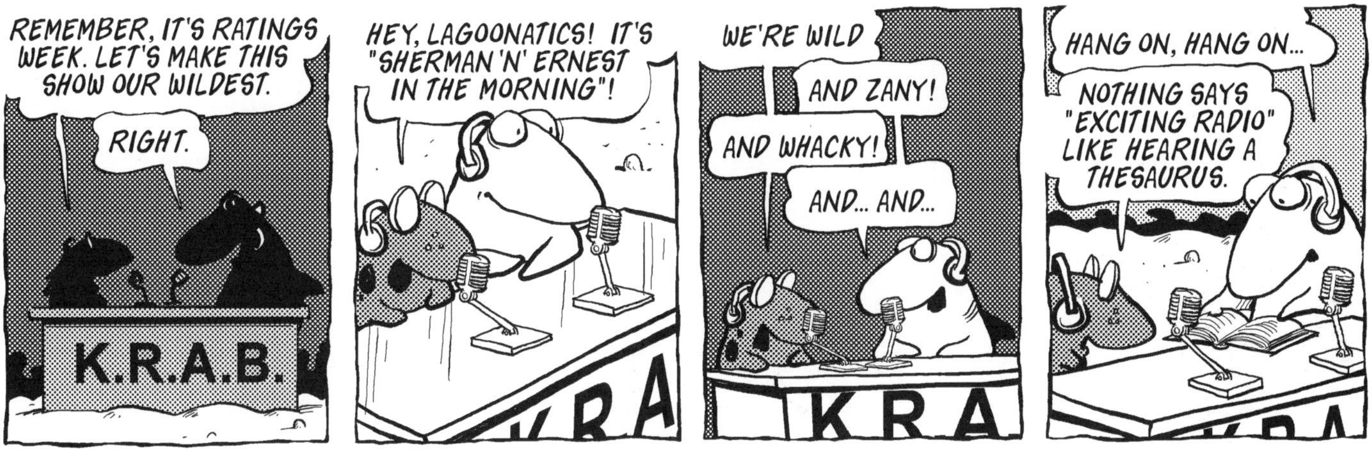
REMEMBER, IT'S RATINGS WEEK. LET'S MAKE THIS SHOW OUR WILDEST.
RIGHT.
K.R.A.B.
HEY, LAGOONATICS! IT'S "SHERMAN 'N' ERNEST IN THE MORNING"!
WE'RE WILD
AND ZANY!
AND WHACKY!
AND... AND...
HANG ON, HANG ON...
NOTHING SAYS "EXCITING RADIO" LIKE HEARING A THESAURUS.

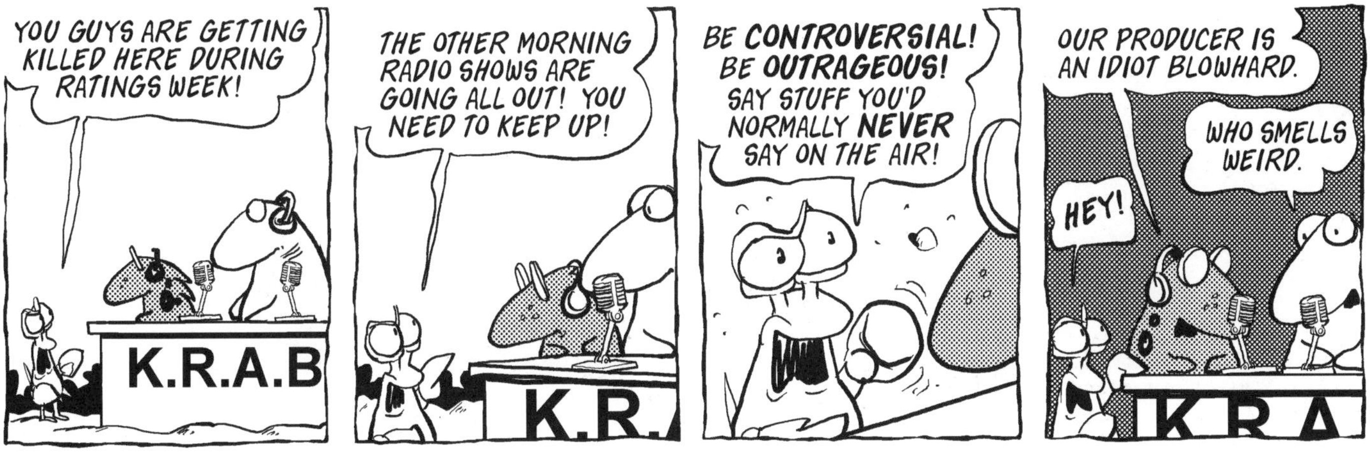
YOU GUYS ARE GETTING KILLED HERE DURING RATINGS WEEK!
K.R.A.B
THE OTHER MORNING RADIO SHOWS ARE GOING ALL OUT! YOU NEED TO KEEP UP!
BE CONTROVERSIAL! BE OUTRAGEOUS! SAY STUFF YOU'D NORMALLY NEVER SAY ON THE AIR!
OUR PRODUCER IS AN IDIOT BLOWHARD.
WHO SMELLS WEIRD.
HEY!

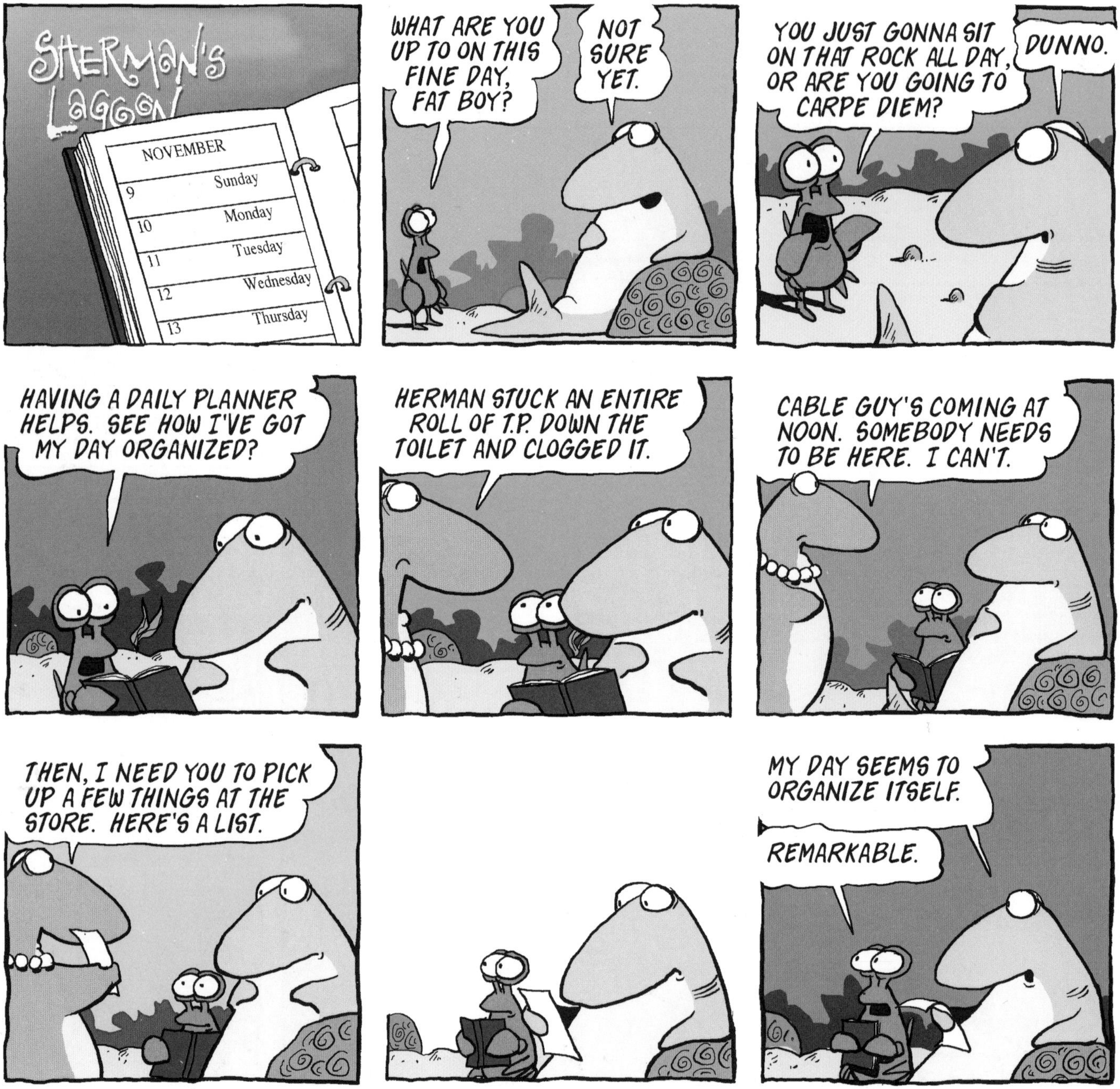
SHERMAN'S LAGOON
NOVEMBER
9 Sunday
10 Monday
11 Tuesday
12 Wednesday
13 Thursday
WHAT ARE YOU UP TO ON THIS FINE DAY, FAT BOY?
NOT SURE YET.
YOU JUST GONNA SIT ON THAT ROCK ALL DAY, OR ARE YOU GOING TO CARPE DIEM?
DUNNO.
HAVING A DAILY PLANNER HELPS. SEE HOW I'VE GOT MY DAY ORGANIZED?
HERMAN STUCK AN ENTIRE ROLL OF T.P. DOWN THE TOILET AND CLOGGED IT.
CABLE GUY'S COMING AT NOON. SOMEBODY NEEDS TO BE HERE. I CAN'T.
THEN, I NEED YOU TO PICK UP A FEW THINGS AT THE STORE. HERE'S A LIST.
MY DAY SEEMS TO ORGANIZE ITSELF.
REMARKABLE.

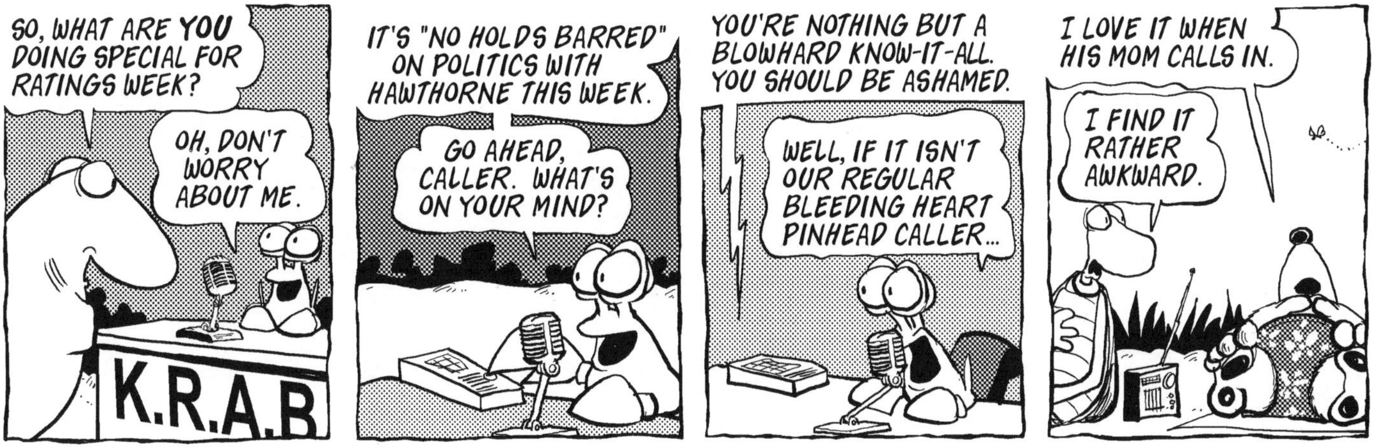
SO, WHAT ARE **YOU** DOING SPECIAL FOR RATINGS WEEK?
OH, DON'T WORRY ABOUT ME.
K.R.A.B
IT'S "NO HOLDS BARRED" ON POLITICS WITH HAWTHORNE THIS WEEK.
GO AHEAD, CALLER. WHAT'S ON YOUR MIND?
YOU'RE NOTHING BUT A BLOWHARD KNOW-IT-ALL. YOU SHOULD BE ASHAMED.
WELL, IF IT ISN'T OUR REGULAR BLEEDING HEART PINHEAD CALLER...
I LOVE IT WHEN HIS MOM CALLS IN.
I FIND IT RATHER AWKWARD.

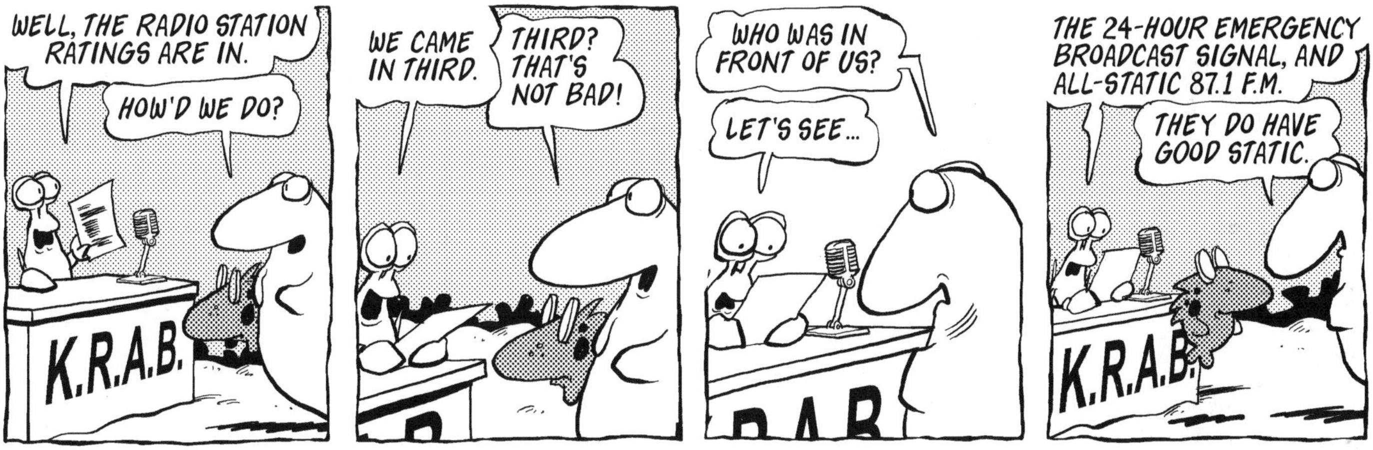
WELL, THE RADIO STATION RATINGS ARE IN.
HOW'D WE DO?
K.R.A.B.
WE CAME IN THIRD.
THIRD? THAT'S NOT BAD!
WHO WAS IN FRONT OF US?
LET'S SEE...
THE 24-HOUR EMERGENCY BROADCAST SIGNAL, AND ALL-STATIC 87.1 F.M.
THEY DO HAVE GOOD STATIC.
K.R.A.B.

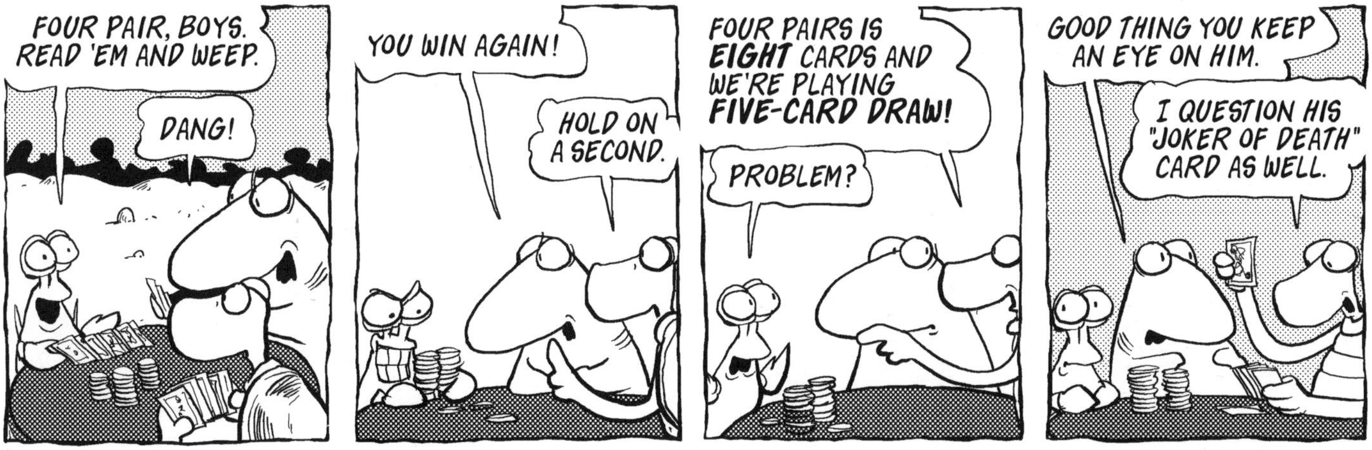
FOUR PAIR, BOYS. READ 'EM AND WEEP.
DANG!
YOU WIN AGAIN!
HOLD ON A SECOND.
FOUR PAIRS IS **EIGHT** CARDS AND WE'RE PLAYING **FIVE-CARD DRAW!**
PROBLEM?
GOOD THING YOU KEEP AN EYE ON HIM.
I QUESTION HIS "JOKER OF DEATH" CARD AS WELL.

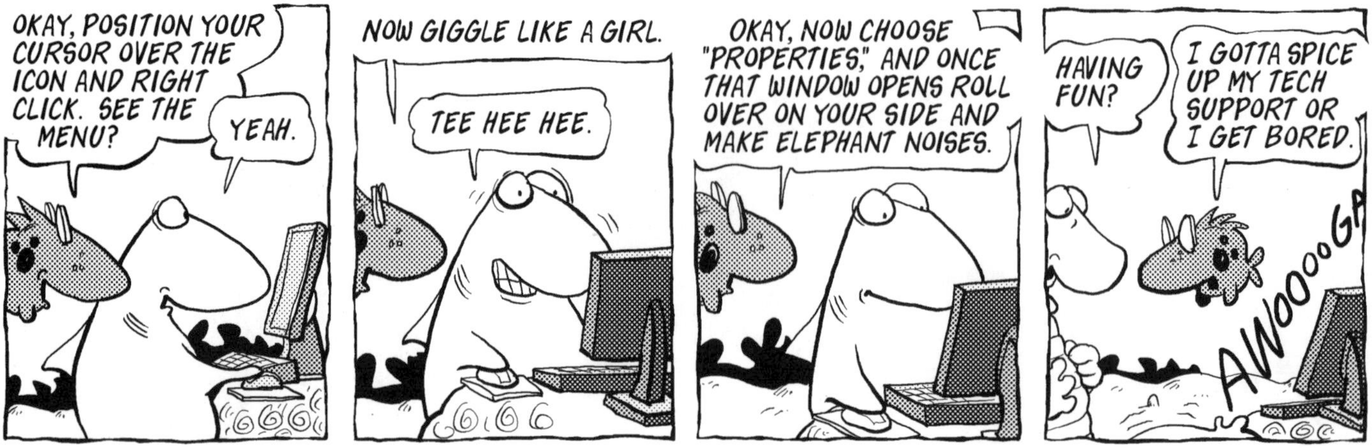
OKAY, POSITION YOUR CURSOR OVER THE ICON AND RIGHT CLICK. SEE THE MENU?
YEAH.
NOW GIGGLE LIKE A GIRL.
TEE HEE HEE.
OKAY, NOW CHOOSE "PROPERTIES," AND ONCE THAT WINDOW OPENS ROLL OVER ON YOUR SIDE AND MAKE ELEPHANT NOISES.
HAVING FUN?
I GOTTA SPICE UP MY TECH SUPPORT OR I GET BORED.
AWOOooGA

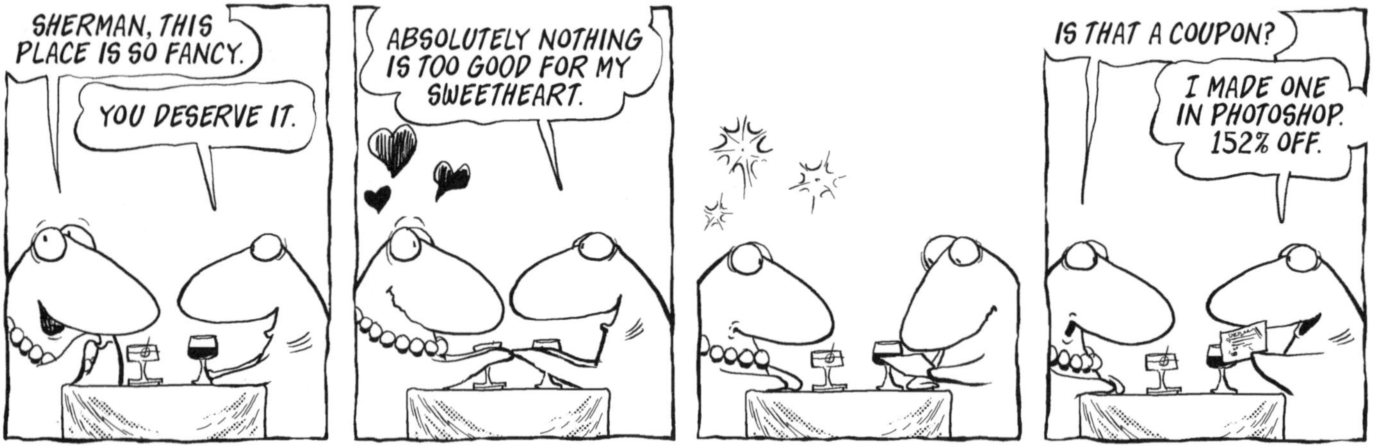
SHERMAN, THIS PLACE IS SO FANCY.
YOU DESERVE IT.
ABSOLUTELY NOTHING IS TOO GOOD FOR MY SWEETHEART.
IS THAT A COUPON?
I MADE ONE IN PHOTOSHOP. 152% OFF.

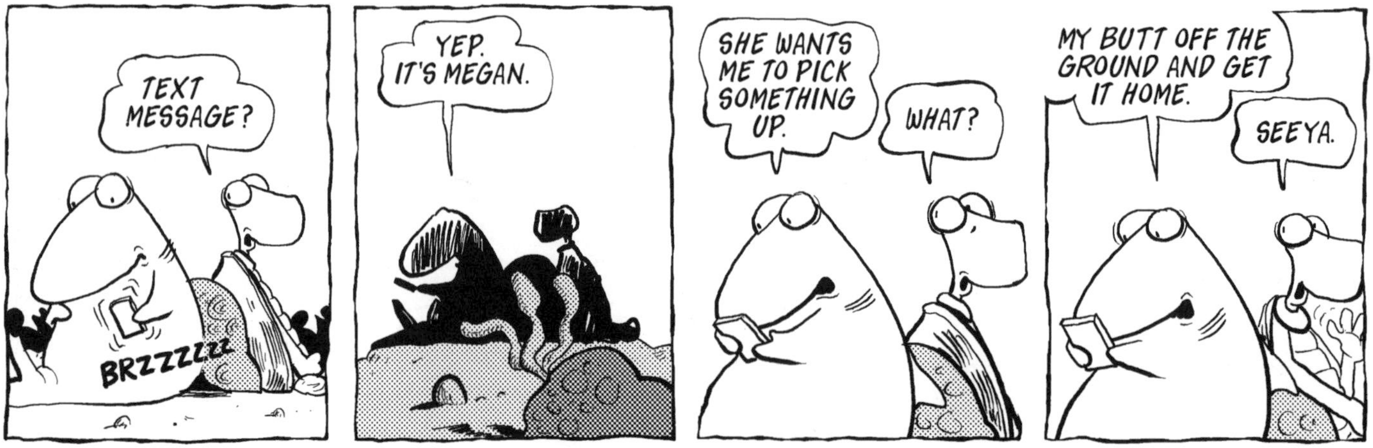
TEXT MESSAGE?
BRZZZZZZ
YEP. IT'S MEGAN.
SHE WANTS ME TO PICK SOMETHING UP.
WHAT?
MY BUTT OFF THE GROUND AND GET IT HOME.
SEEYA.

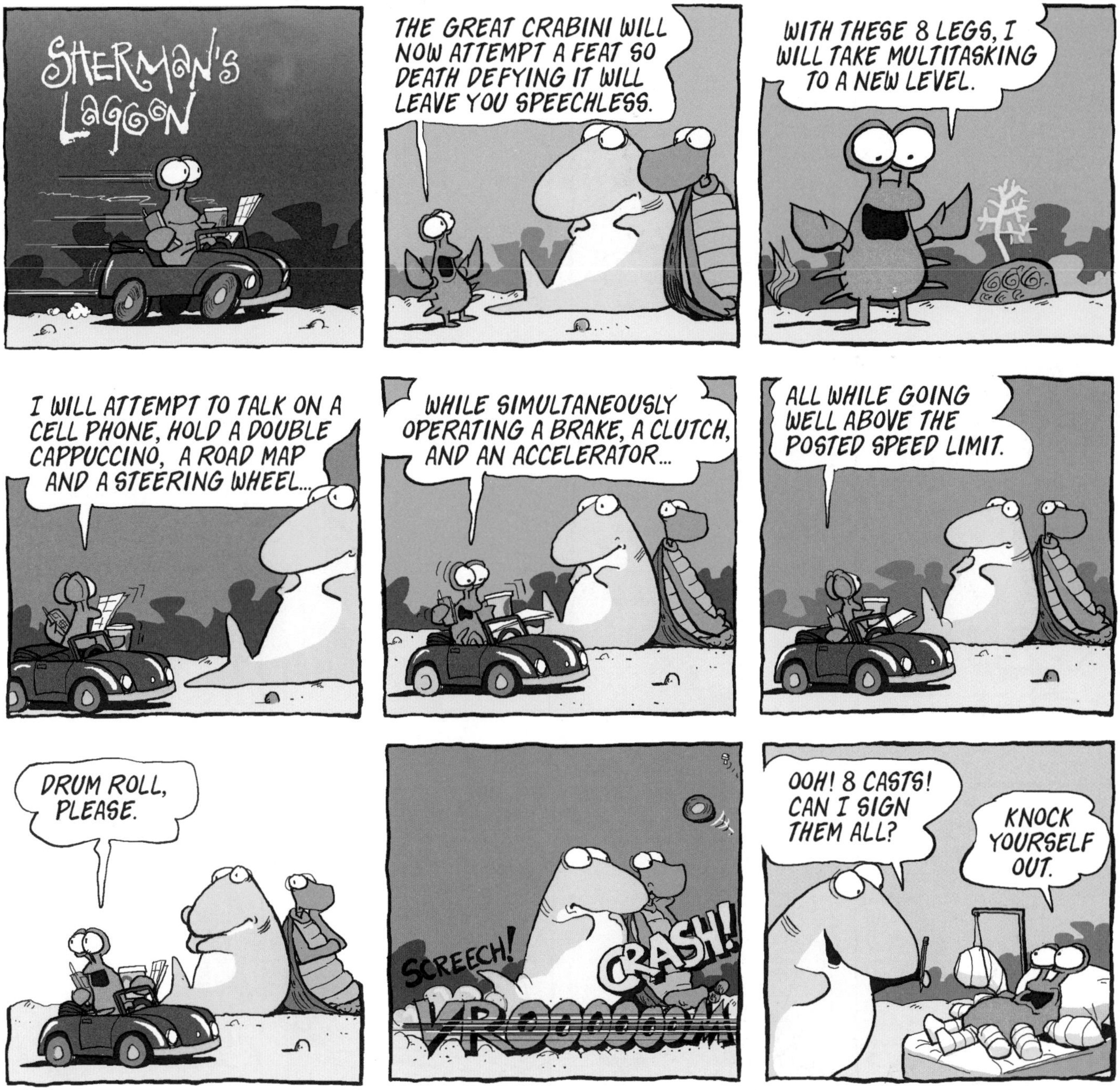
SHERMAN'S LAGOON
THE GREAT CRABINI WILL NOW ATTEMPT A FEAT SO DEATH DEFYING IT WILL LEAVE YOU SPEECHLESS.
WITH THESE 8 LEGS, I WILL TAKE MULTITASKING TO A NEW LEVEL.
I WILL ATTEMPT TO TALK ON A CELL PHONE, HOLD A DOUBLE CAPPUCCINO, A ROAD MAP AND A STEERING WHEEL...
WHILE SIMULTANEOUSLY OPERATING A BRAKE, A CLUTCH, AND AN ACCELERATOR...
ALL WHILE GOING WELL ABOVE THE POSTED SPEED LIMIT.
DRUM ROLL, PLEASE.
SCREECH!
CRASH!
VROOOOOOOM
OOH! 8 CASTS! CAN I SIGN THEM ALL?
KNOCK YOURSELF OUT.

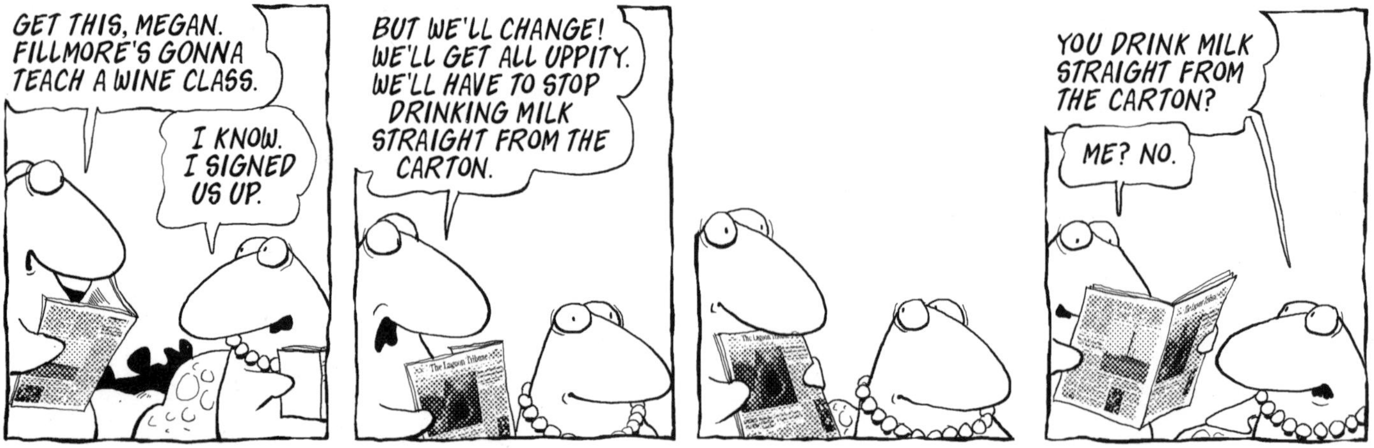
GET THIS, MEGAN. FILLMORE'S GONNA TEACH A WINE CLASS.
I KNOW. I SIGNED US UP.
BUT WE'LL CHANGE! WE'LL GET ALL UPPITY. WE'LL HAVE TO STOP DRINKING MILK STRAIGHT FROM THE CARTON.
YOU DRINK MILK STRAIGHT FROM THE CARTON?
ME? NO.

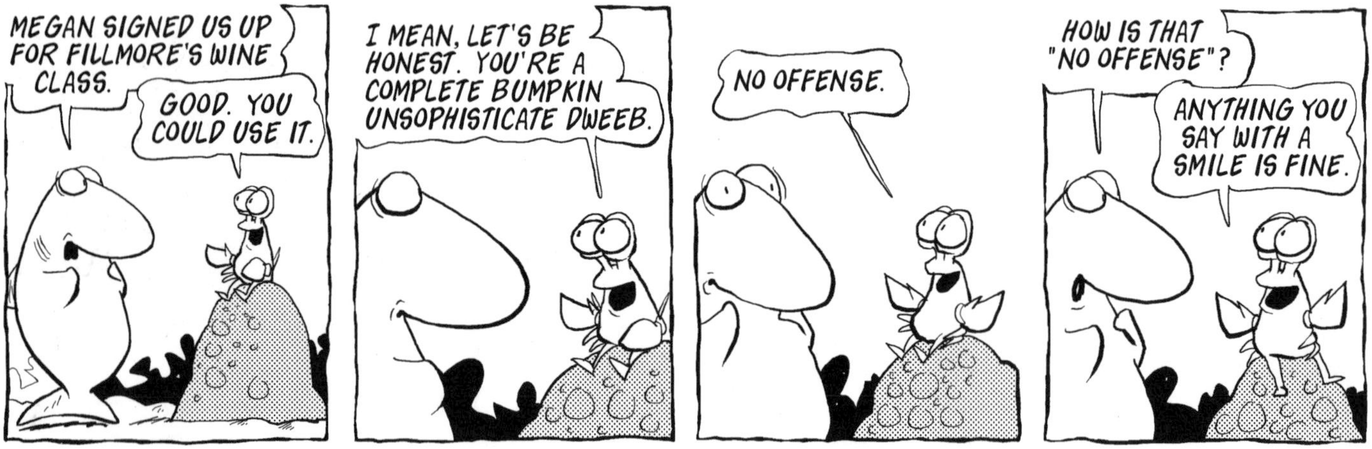
MEGAN SIGNED US UP FOR FILLMORE'S WINE CLASS.
GOOD. YOU COULD USE IT.
I MEAN, LET'S BE HONEST. YOU'RE A COMPLETE BUMPKIN UNSOPHISTICATE DWEEB.
NO OFFENSE.
HOW IS THAT "NO OFFENSE"?
ANYTHING YOU SAY WITH A SMILE IS FINE.

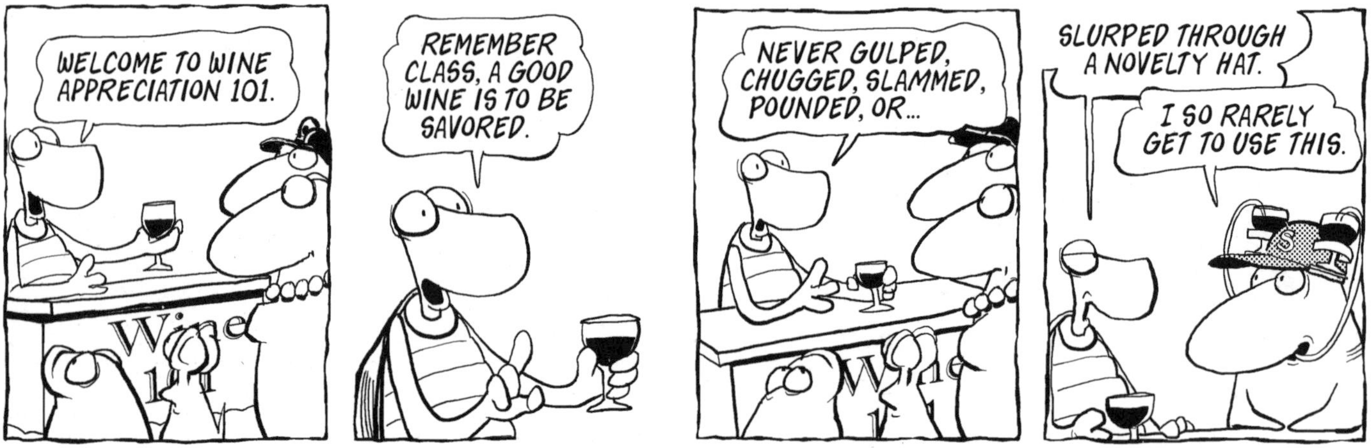
WELCOME TO WINE APPRECIATION 101.
REMEMBER CLASS, A GOOD WINE IS TO BE SAVORED.
NEVER GULPED, CHUGGED, SLAMMED, POUNDED, OR...
SLURPED THROUGH A NOVELTY HAT.
I SO RARELY GET TO USE THIS.

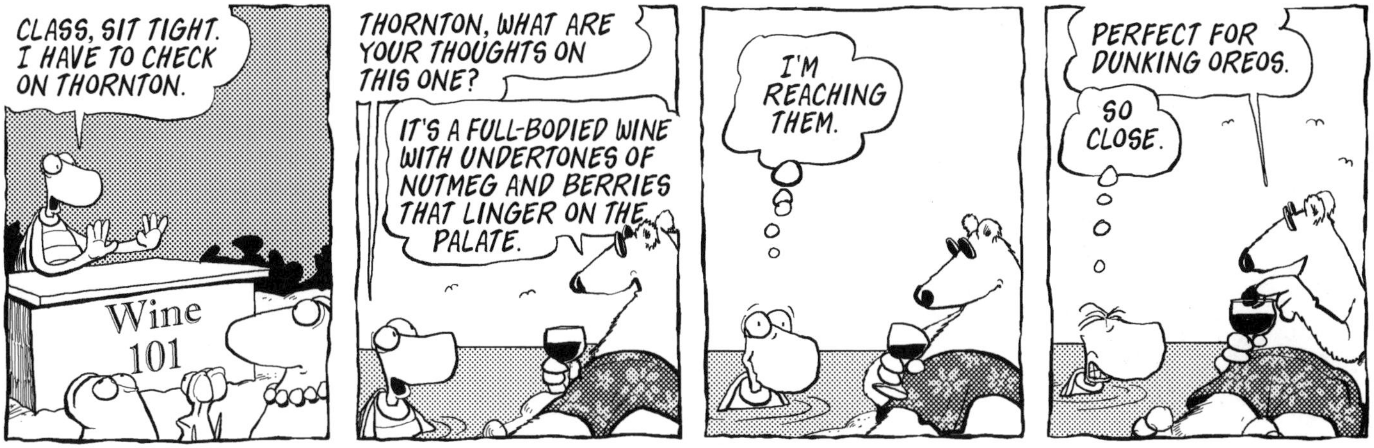
CLASS, SIT TIGHT. I HAVE TO CHECK ON THORNTON.
THORNTON, WHAT ARE YOUR THOUGHTS ON THIS ONE?
IT'S A FULL-BODIED WINE WITH UNDERTONES OF NUTMEG AND BERRIES THAT LINGER ON THE PALATE.
I'M REACHING THEM.
PERFECT FOR DUNKING OREOS.
SO CLOSE.
Wine 101

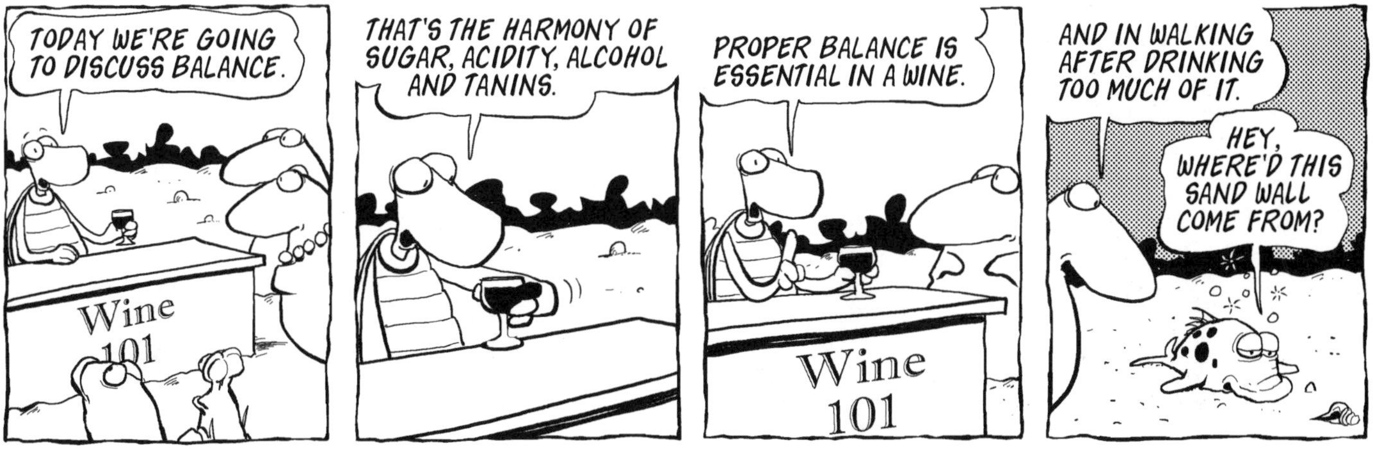
TODAY WE'RE GOING TO DISCUSS BALANCE.
THAT'S THE HARMONY OF SUGAR, ACIDITY, ALCOHOL AND TANINS.
PROPER BALANCE IS ESSENTIAL IN A WINE.
AND IN WALKING AFTER DRINKING TOO MUCH OF IT.
HEY, WHERE'D THIS SAND WALL COME FROM?
Wine 101

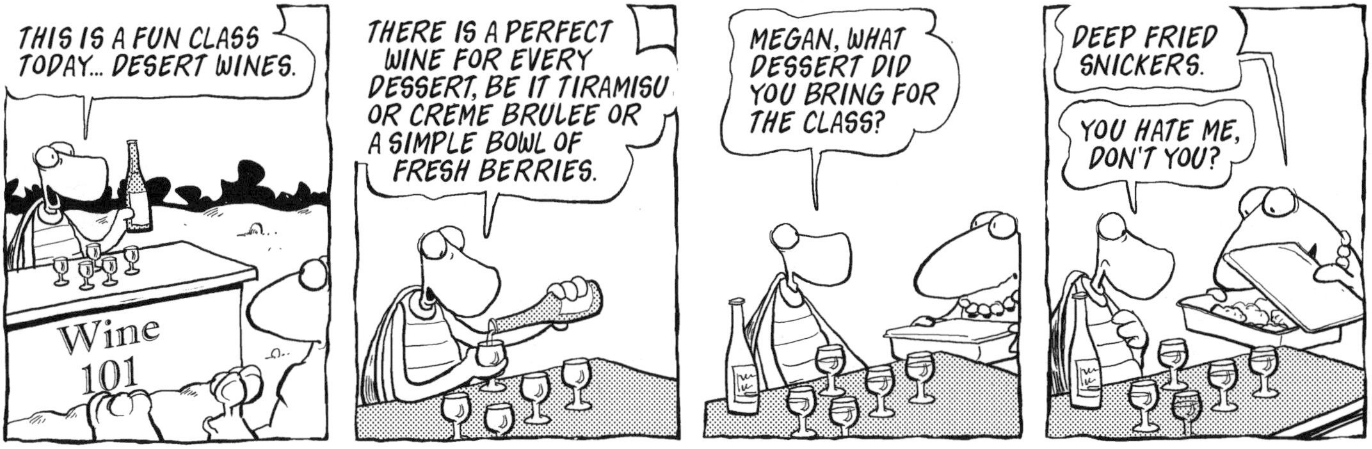
THIS IS A FUN CLASS TODAY... DESERT WINES.
THERE IS A PERFECT WINE FOR EVERY DESSERT, BE IT TIRAMISU OR CREME BRULEE OR A SIMPLE BOWL OF FRESH BERRIES.
MEGAN, WHAT DESSERT DID YOU BRING FOR THE CLASS?
DEEP FRIED SNICKERS.
YOU HATE ME, DON'T YOU?
Wine 101

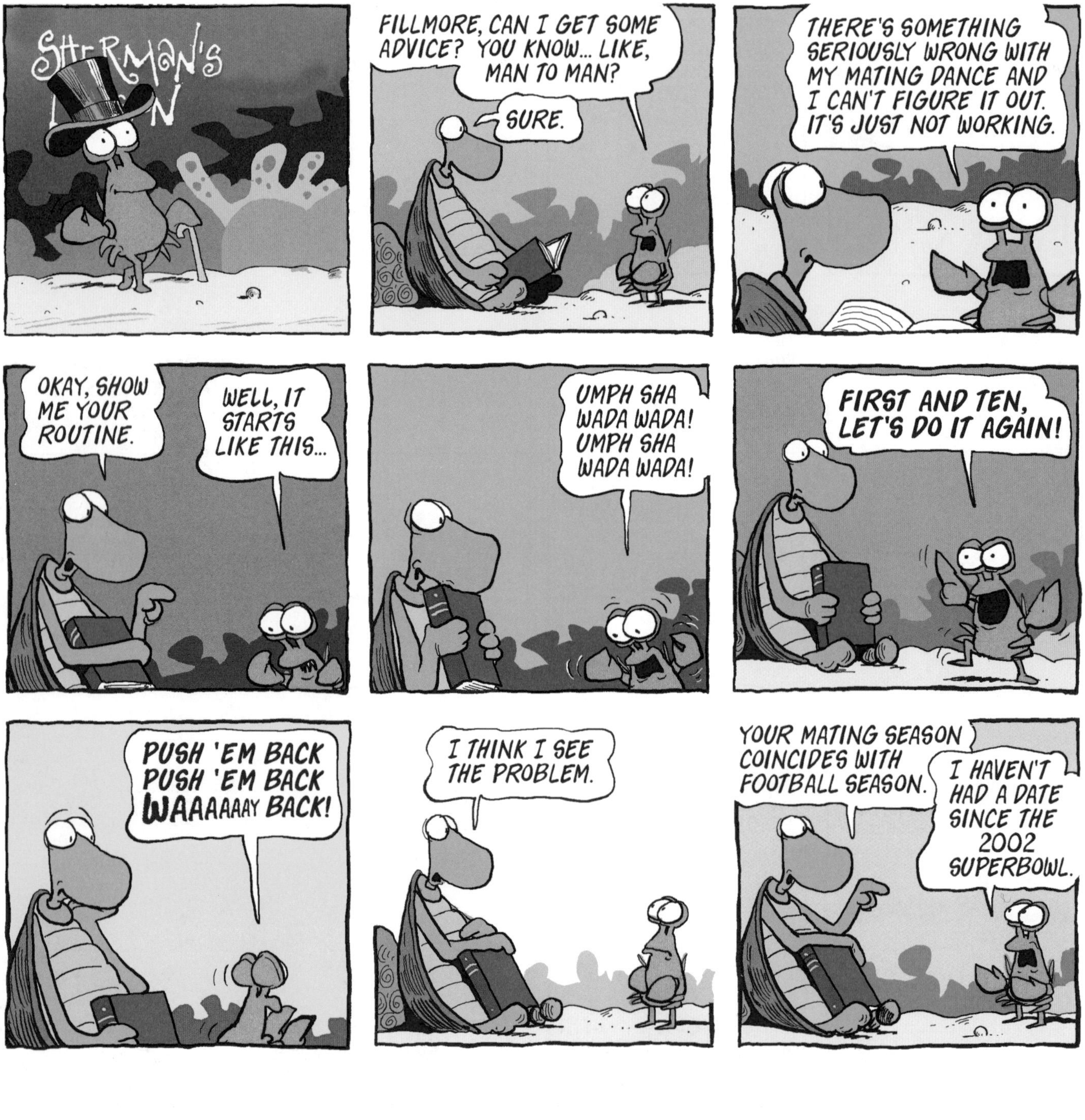
SHERMAN'S LAGOON
FILLMORE, CAN I GET SOME ADVICE? YOU KNOW... LIKE, MAN TO MAN?
SURE.
THERE'S SOMETHING SERIOUSLY WRONG WITH MY MATING DANCE AND I CAN'T FIGURE IT OUT. IT'S JUST NOT WORKING.
OKAY, SHOW ME YOUR ROUTINE.
WELL, IT STARTS LIKE THIS...
UMPH SHA WADA WADA! UMPH SHA WADA WADA!
FIRST AND TEN, LET'S DO IT AGAIN!
PUSH 'EM BACK PUSH 'EM BACK WAAAAAAY BACK!
I THINK I SEE THE PROBLEM.
YOUR MATING SEASON COINCIDES WITH FOOTBALL SEASON.
I HAVEN'T HAD A DATE SINCE THE 2002 SUPERBOWL.

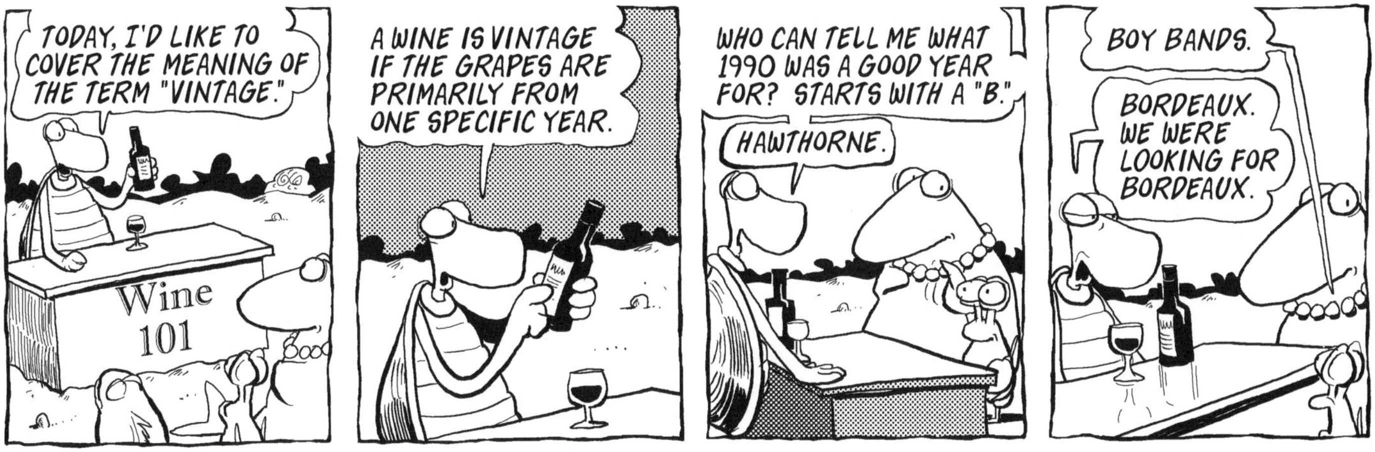
TODAY, I'D LIKE TO COVER THE MEANING OF THE TERM "VINTAGE."
Wine 101
A WINE IS VINTAGE IF THE GRAPES ARE PRIMARILY FROM ONE SPECIFIC YEAR.
WHO CAN TELL ME WHAT 1990 WAS A GOOD YEAR FOR? STARTS WITH A "B."
HAWTHORNE.
BOY BANDS.
BORDEAUX. WE WERE LOOKING FOR BORDEAUX.

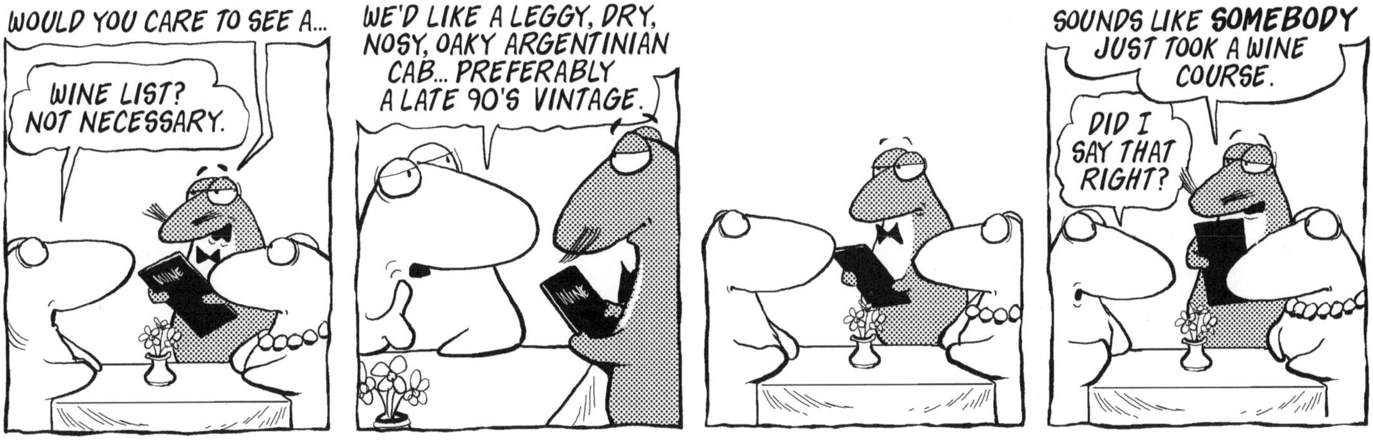
WOULD YOU CARE TO SEE A...
WINE LIST? NOT NECESSARY.
WE'D LIKE A LEGGY, DRY, NOSY, OAKY ARGENTINIAN CAB... PREFERABLY A LATE 90'S VINTAGE.
SOUNDS LIKE **SOMEBODY** JUST TOOK A WINE COURSE.
DID I SAY THAT RIGHT?

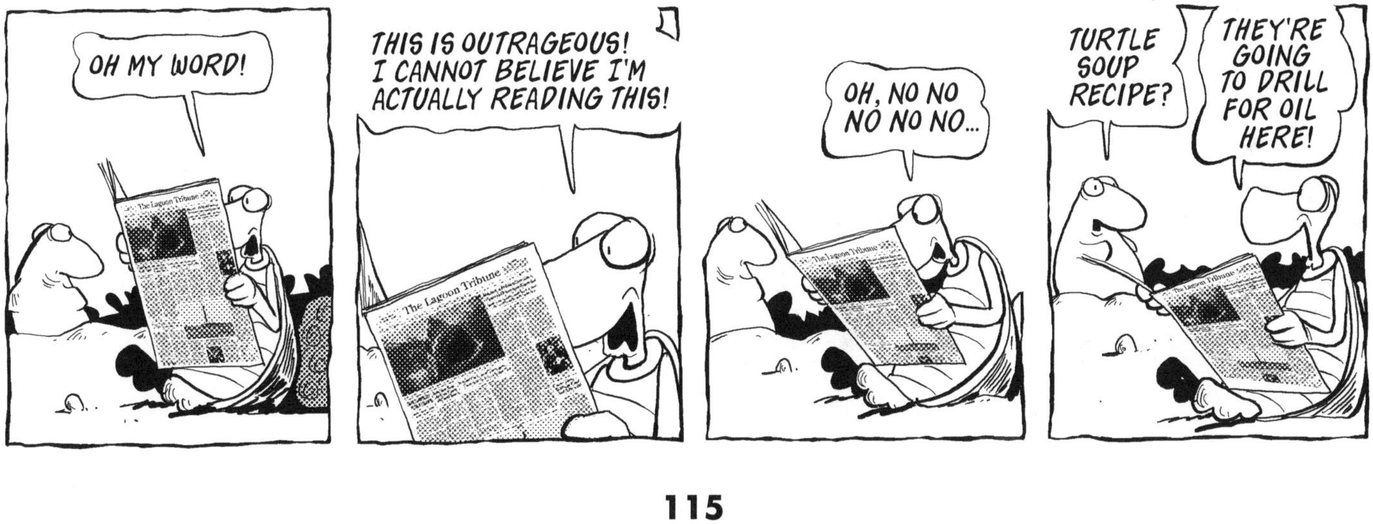
OH MY WORD!
The Lagoon Tribune
THIS IS OUTRAGEOUS! I CANNOT BELIEVE I'M ACTUALLY READING THIS!
OH, NO NO NO NO NO...
TURTLE SOUP RECIPE?
THEY'RE GOING TO DRILL FOR OIL HERE!

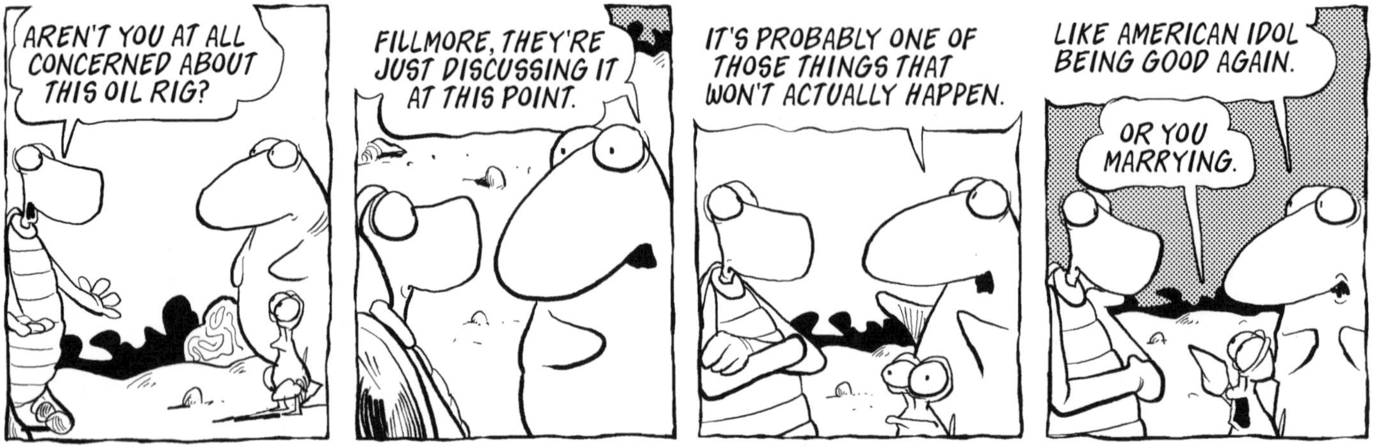
AREN'T YOU AT ALL CONCERNED ABOUT THIS OIL RIG?
FILLMORE, THEY'RE JUST DISCUSSING IT AT THIS POINT.
IT'S PROBABLY ONE OF THOSE THINGS THAT WON'T ACTUALLY HAPPEN.
LIKE AMERICAN IDOL BEING GOOD AGAIN.
OR YOU MARRYING.

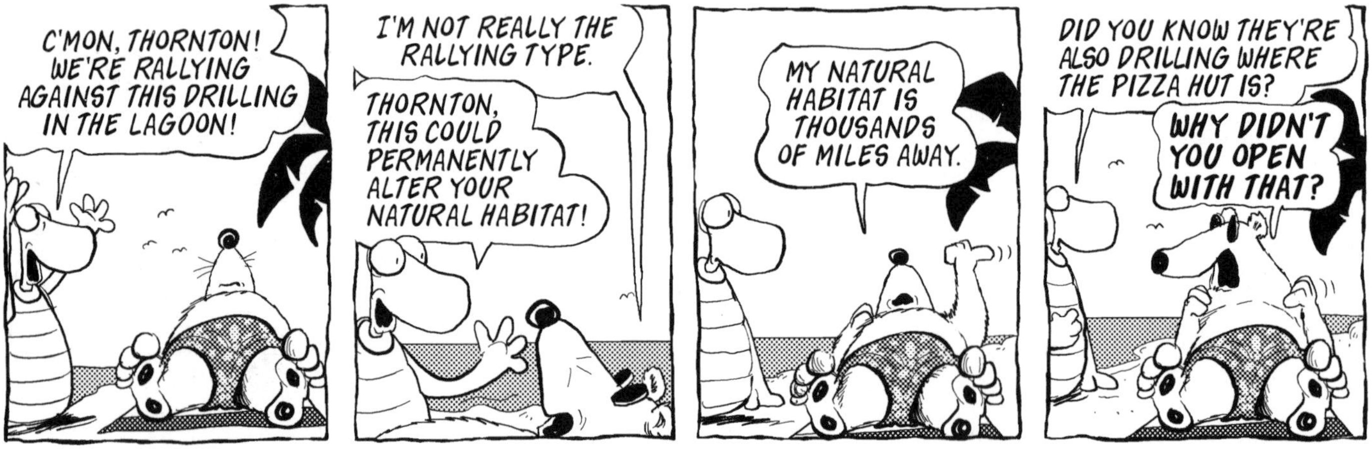
C'MON, THORNTON! WE'RE RALLYING AGAINST THIS DRILLING IN THE LAGOON!
I'M NOT REALLY THE RALLYING TYPE.
THORNTON, THIS COULD PERMANENTLY ALTER YOUR NATURAL HABITAT!
MY NATURAL HABITAT IS THOUSANDS OF MILES AWAY.
DID YOU KNOW THEY'RE ALSO DRILLING WHERE THE PIZZA HUT IS?
WHY DIDN'T YOU OPEN WITH THAT?

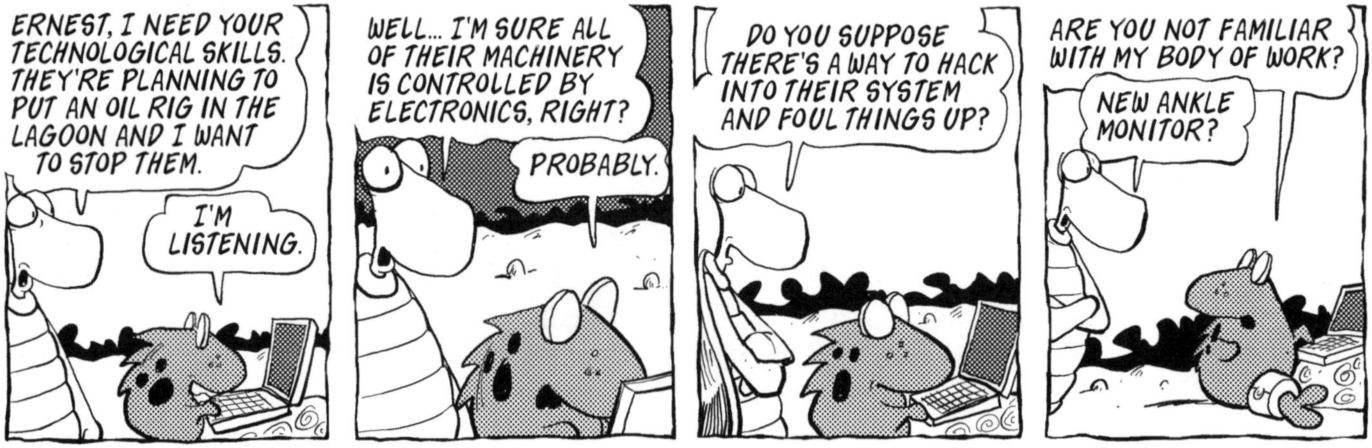
ERNEST, I NEED YOUR TECHNOLOGICAL SKILLS. THEY'RE PLANNING TO PUT AN OIL RIG IN THE LAGOON AND I WANT TO STOP THEM.
I'M LISTENING.
WELL... I'M SURE ALL OF THEIR MACHINERY IS CONTROLLED BY ELECTRONICS, RIGHT?
PROBABLY.
DO YOU SUPPOSE THERE'S A WAY TO HACK INTO THEIR SYSTEM AND FOUL THINGS UP?
ARE YOU NOT FAMILIAR WITH MY BODY OF WORK?
NEW ANKLE MONITOR?

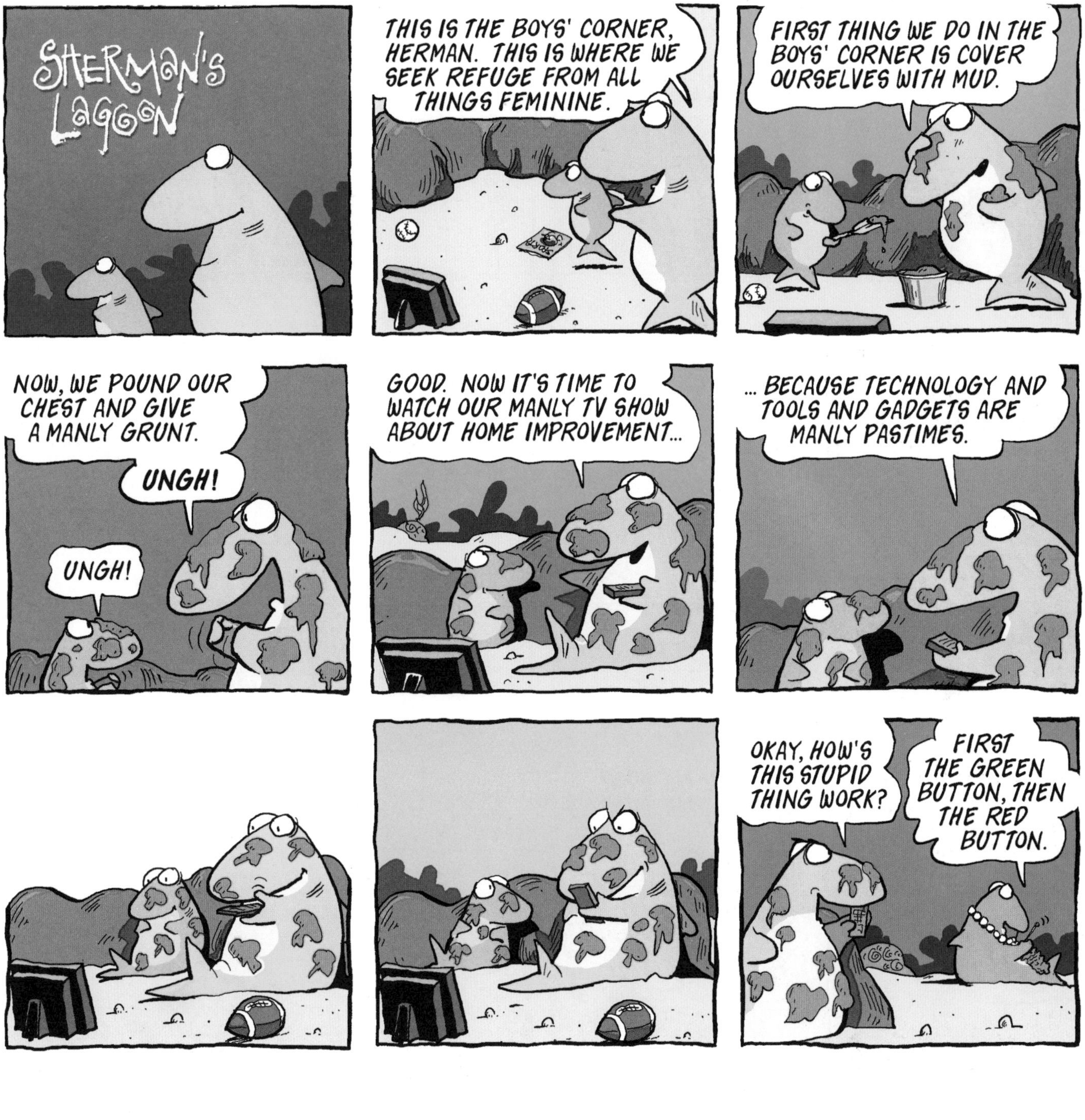
SHERMAN'S LAGOON
THIS IS THE BOYS' CORNER, HERMAN. THIS IS WHERE WE SEEK REFUGE FROM ALL THINGS FEMININE.
FIRST THING WE DO IN THE BOYS' CORNER IS COVER OURSELVES WITH MUD.
NOW, WE POUND OUR CHEST AND GIVE A MANLY GRUNT.
UNGH!
UNGH!
GOOD. NOW IT'S TIME TO WATCH OUR MANLY TV SHOW ABOUT HOME IMPROVEMENT...
... BECAUSE TECHNOLOGY AND TOOLS AND GADGETS ARE MANLY PASTIMES.
OKAY, HOW'S THIS STUPID THING WORK?
FIRST THE GREEN BUTTON, THEN THE RED BUTTON.

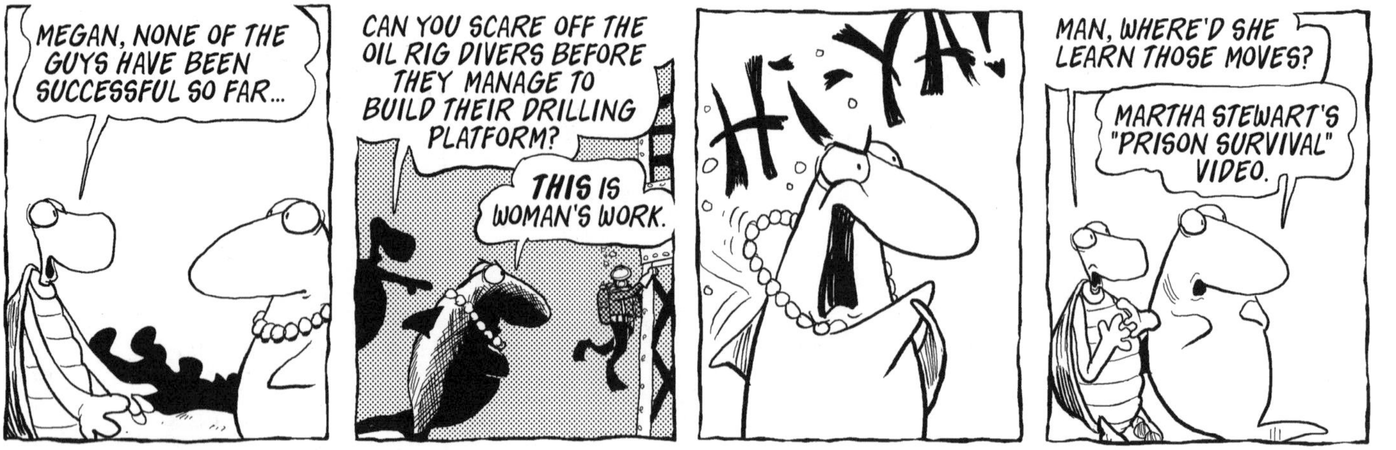
MEGAN, NONE OF THE GUYS HAVE BEEN SUCCESSFUL SO FAR...
CAN YOU SCARE OFF THE OIL RIG DIVERS BEFORE THEY MANAGE TO BUILD THEIR DRILLING PLATFORM?
THIS IS WOMAN'S WORK.
HI-YA!
MAN, WHERE'D SHE LEARN THOSE MOVES?
MARTHA STEWART'S "PRISON SURVIVAL" VIDEO.

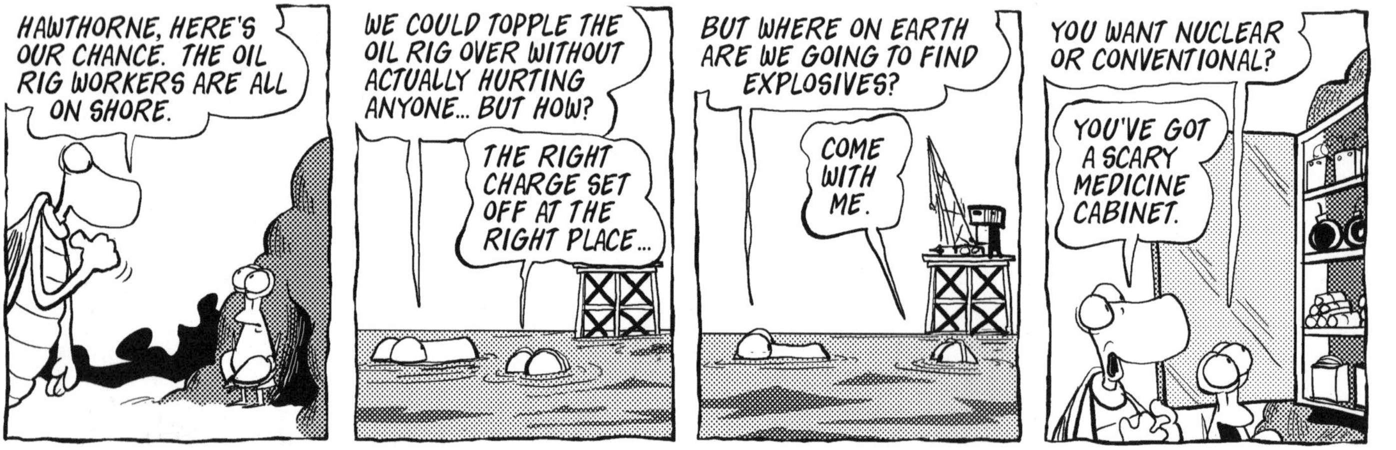
HAWTHORNE, HERE'S OUR CHANCE. THE OIL RIG WORKERS ARE ALL ON SHORE.
WE COULD TOPPLE THE OIL RIG OVER WITHOUT ACTUALLY HURTING ANYONE... BUT HOW?
THE RIGHT CHARGE SET OFF AT THE RIGHT PLACE...
BUT WHERE ON EARTH ARE WE GOING TO FIND EXPLOSIVES?
COME WITH ME.
YOU WANT NUCLEAR OR CONVENTIONAL?
YOU'VE GOT A SCARY MEDICINE CABINET.

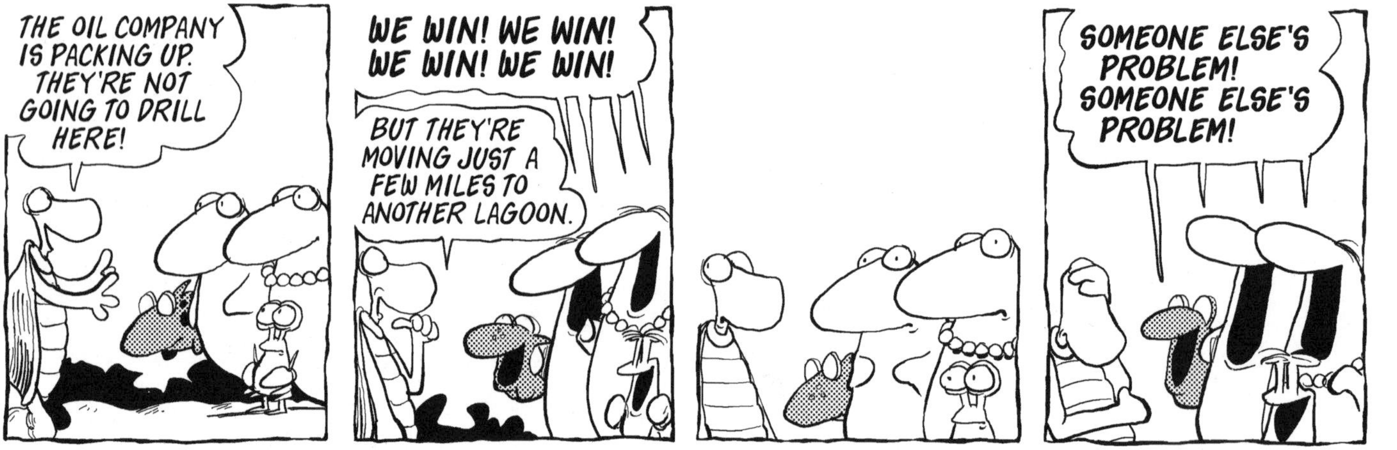
THE OIL COMPANY IS PACKING UP. THEY'RE NOT GOING TO DRILL HERE!
WE WIN! WE WIN! WE WIN! WE WIN!
BUT THEY'RE MOVING JUST A FEW MILES TO ANOTHER LAGOON.
SOMEONE ELSE'S PROBLEM! SOMEONE ELSE'S PROBLEM!

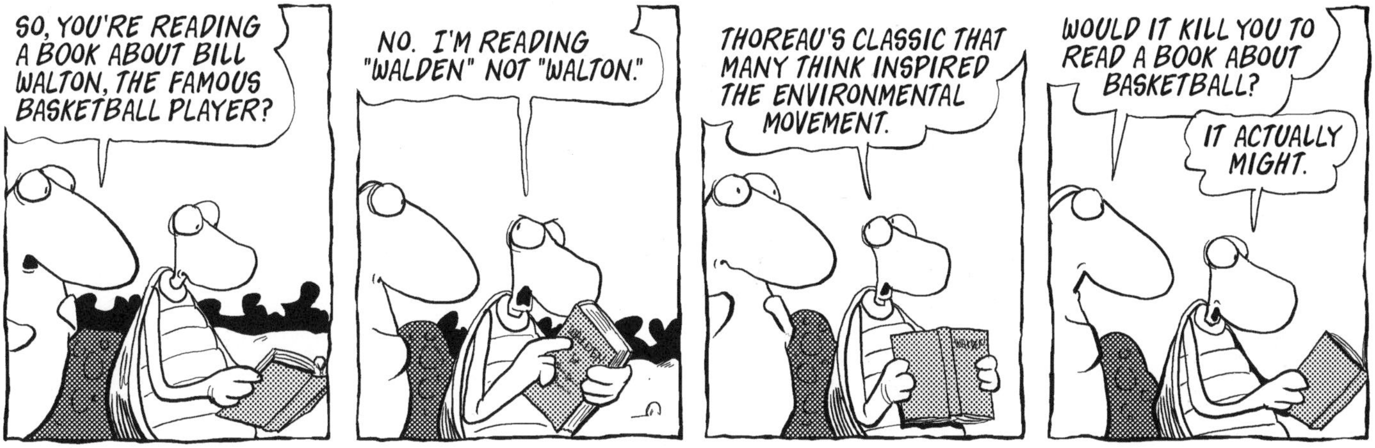
SO, YOU'RE READING A BOOK ABOUT BILL WALTON, THE FAMOUS BASKETBALL PLAYER?
NO. I'M READING "WALDEN" NOT "WALTON."
THOREAU'S CLASSIC THAT MANY THINK INSPIRED THE ENVIRONMENTAL MOVEMENT.
WOULD IT KILL YOU TO READ A BOOK ABOUT BASKETBALL?
IT ACTUALLY MIGHT.

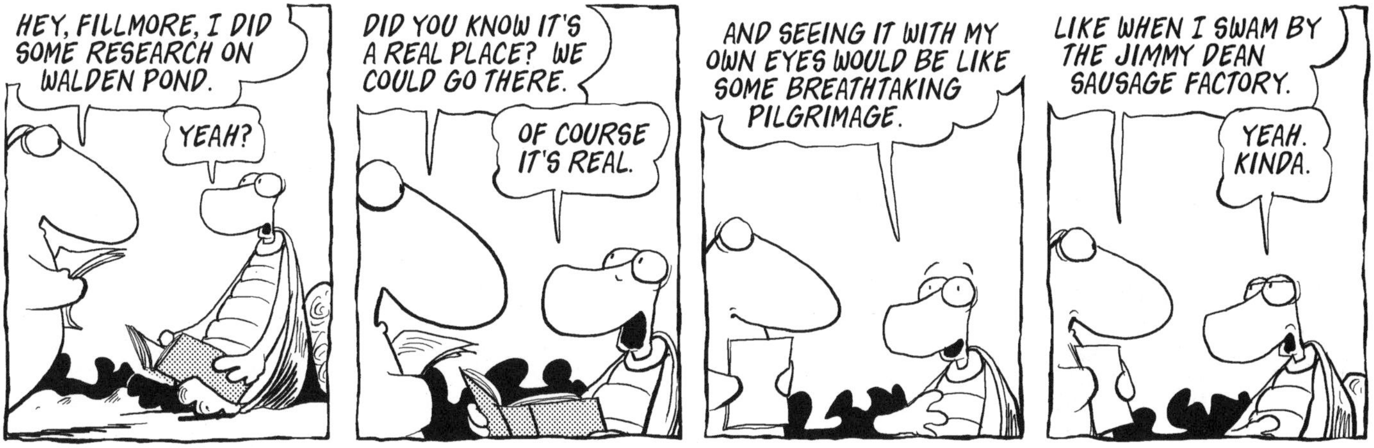
HEY, FILLMORE, I DID SOME RESEARCH ON WALDEN POND.
YEAH?
DID YOU KNOW IT'S A REAL PLACE? WE COULD GO THERE.
OF COURSE IT'S REAL.
AND SEEING IT WITH MY OWN EYES WOULD BE LIKE SOME BREATHTAKING PILGRIMAGE.
LIKE WHEN I SWAM BY THE JIMMY DEAN SAUSAGE FACTORY.
YEAH. KINDA.

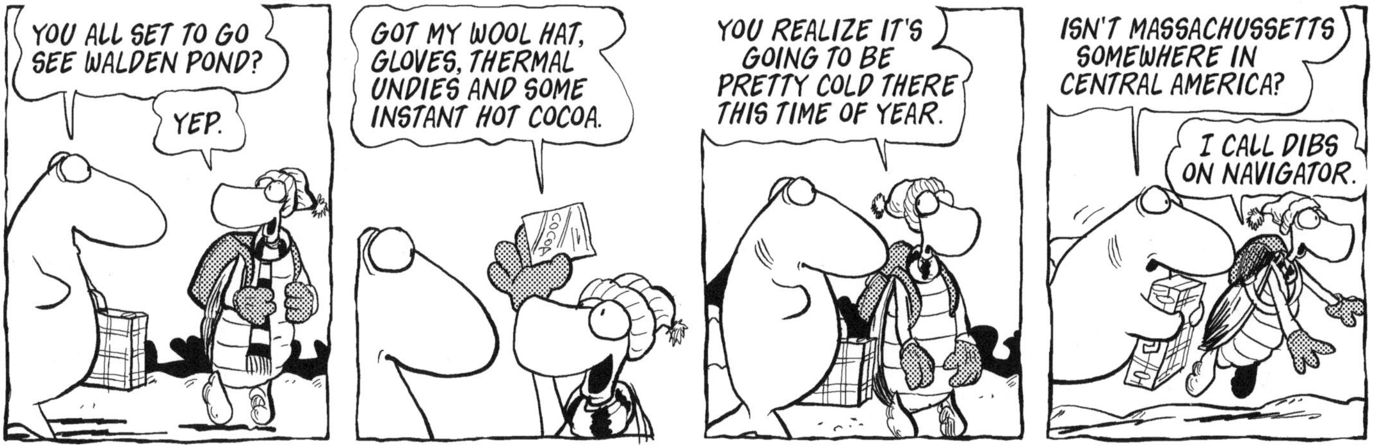
YOU ALL SET TO GO SEE WALDEN POND?
YEP.
GOT MY WOOL HAT, GLOVES, THERMAL UNDIES AND SOME INSTANT HOT COCOA.
COCOA
YOU REALIZE IT'S GOING TO BE PRETTY COLD THERE THIS TIME OF YEAR.
ISN'T MASSACHUSSETTS SOMEWHERE IN CENTRAL AMERICA?
I CALL DIBS ON NAVIGATOR.

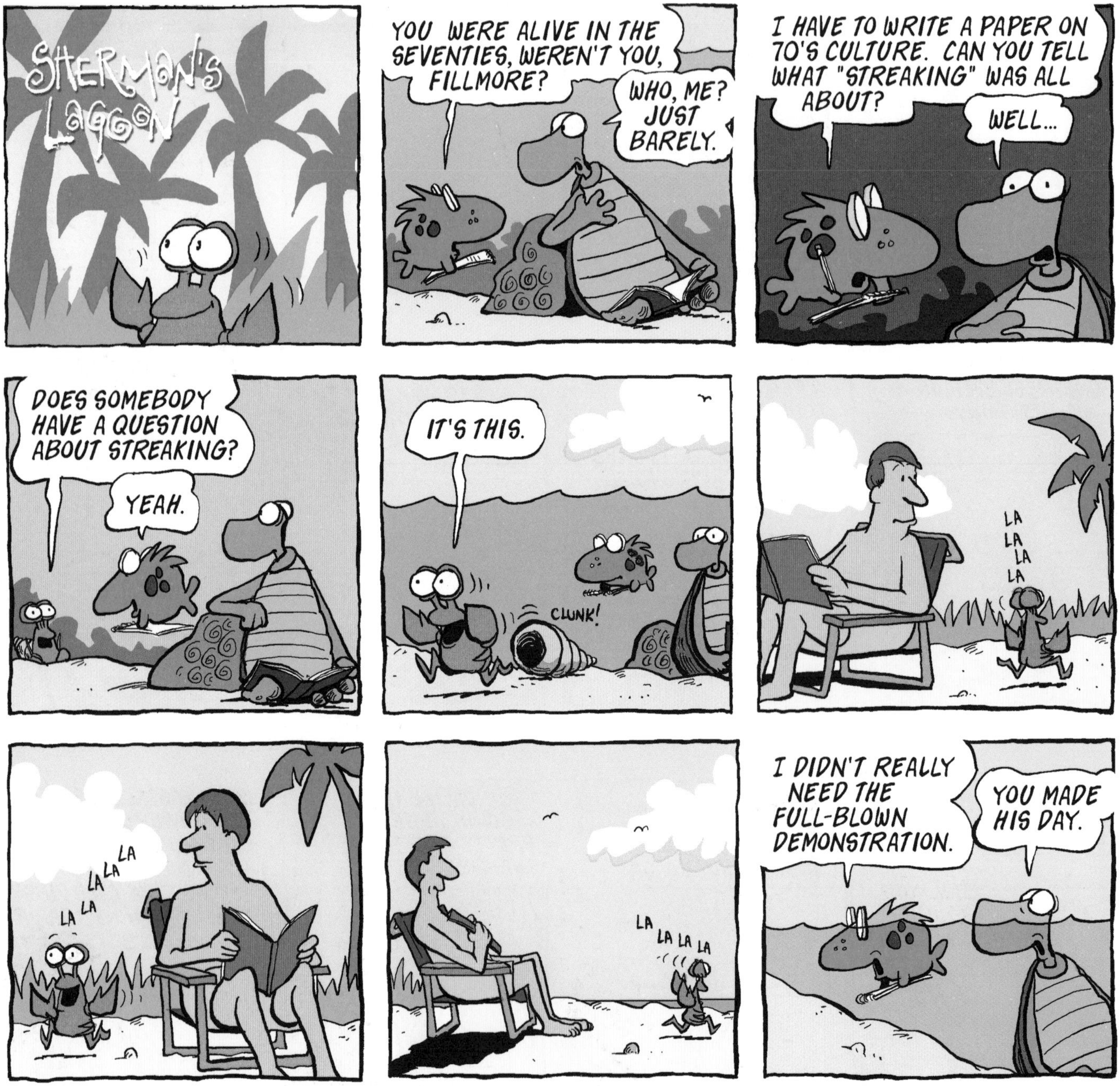
Sherman's Lagoon
YOU WERE ALIVE IN THE SEVENTIES, WEREN'T YOU, FILLMORE?
WHO, ME? JUST BARELY.
I HAVE TO WRITE A PAPER ON 70'S CULTURE. CAN YOU TELL WHAT "STREAKING" WAS ALL ABOUT?
WELL...
DOES SOMEBODY HAVE A QUESTION ABOUT STREAKING?
YEAH.
IT'S THIS.
CLUNK!
LA LA LA LA
LA LA LA LA LA
LA LA LA LA
I DIDN'T REALLY NEED THE FULL-BLOWN DEMONSTRATION.
YOU MADE HIS DAY.

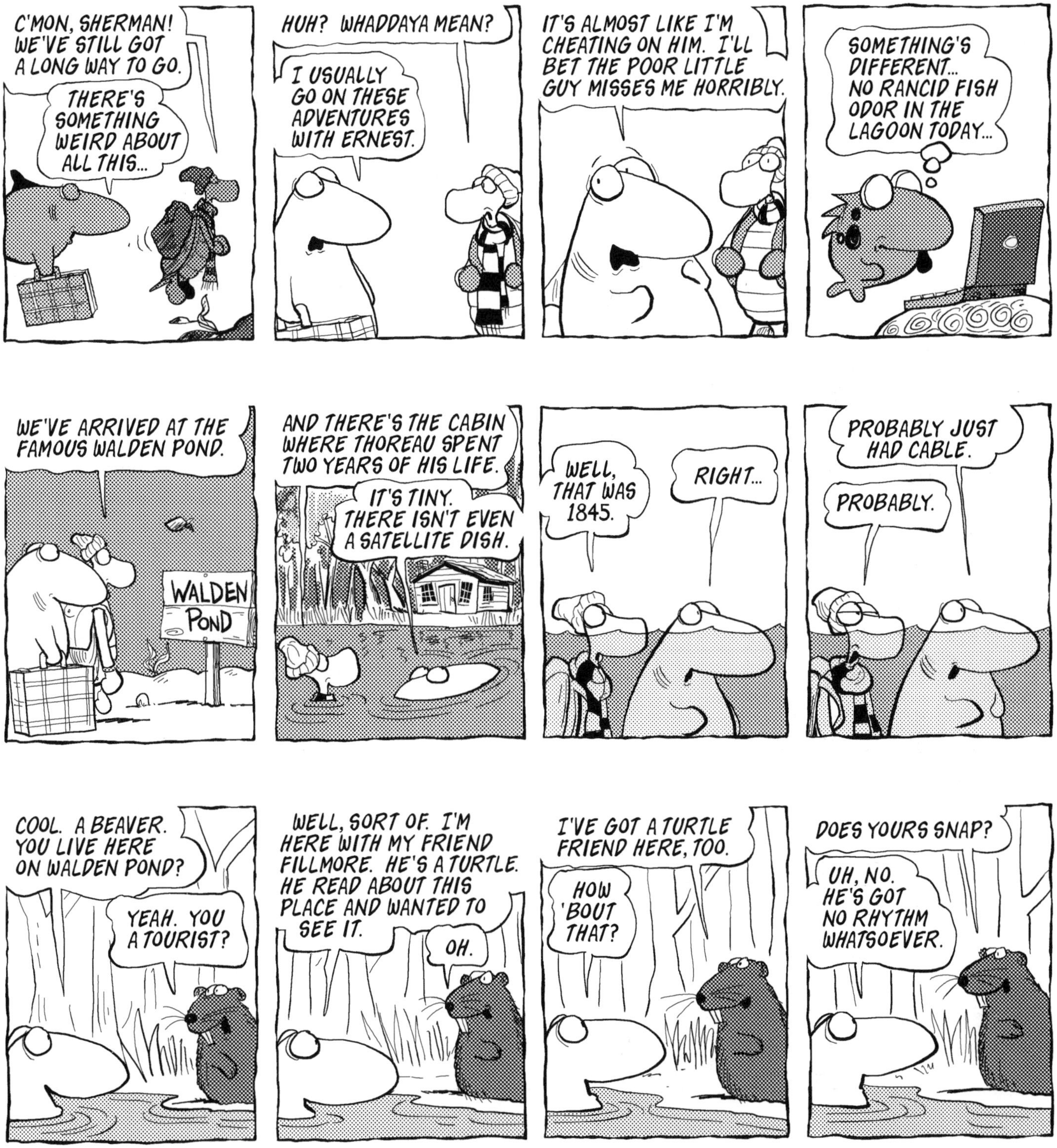
C'MON, SHERMAN! WE'VE STILL GOT A LONG WAY TO GO.
THERE'S SOMETHING WEIRD ABOUT ALL THIS...
HUH? WHADDAYA MEAN?
I USUALLY GO ON THESE ADVENTURES WITH ERNEST.
IT'S ALMOST LIKE I'M CHEATING ON HIM. I'LL BET THE POOR LITTLE GUY MISSES ME HORRIBLY.
SOMETHING'S DIFFERENT... NO RANCID FISH ODOR IN THE LAGOON TODAY...
WE'VE ARRIVED AT THE FAMOUS WALDEN POND.
WALDEN POND
AND THERE'S THE CABIN WHERE THOREAU SPENT TWO YEARS OF HIS LIFE.
IT'S TINY. THERE ISN'T EVEN A SATELLITE DISH.
WELL, THAT WAS 1845.
RIGHT...
PROBABLY JUST HAD CABLE.
PROBABLY.
COOL. A BEAVER. YOU LIVE HERE ON WALDEN POND?
YEAH. YOU A TOURIST?
WELL, SORT OF. I'M HERE WITH MY FRIEND FILLMORE. HE'S A TURTLE. HE READ ABOUT THIS PLACE AND WANTED TO SEE IT.
OH.
I'VE GOT A TURTLE FRIEND HERE, TOO.
HOW 'BOUT THAT?
DOES YOURS SNAP?
UH, NO. HE'S GOT NO RHYTHM WHATSOEVER.

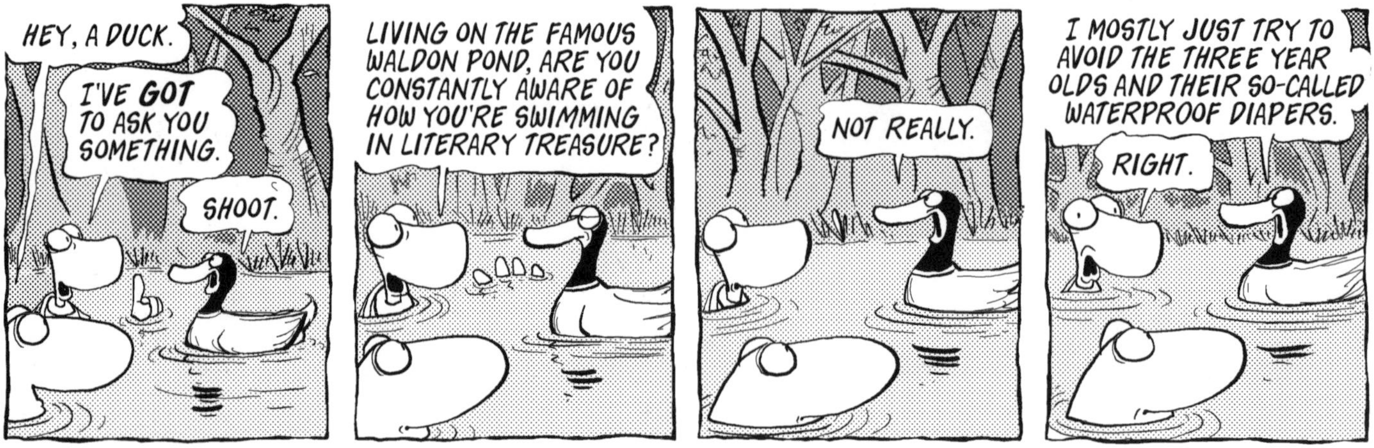
HEY, A DUCK.
I'VE **GOT** TO ASK YOU SOMETHING.
SHOOT.
LIVING ON THE FAMOUS WALDON POND, ARE YOU CONSTANTLY AWARE OF HOW YOU'RE SWIMMING IN LITERARY TREASURE?
NOT REALLY.
I MOSTLY JUST TRY TO AVOID THE THREE YEAR OLDS AND THEIR SO-CALLED WATERPROOF DIAPERS.
RIGHT.

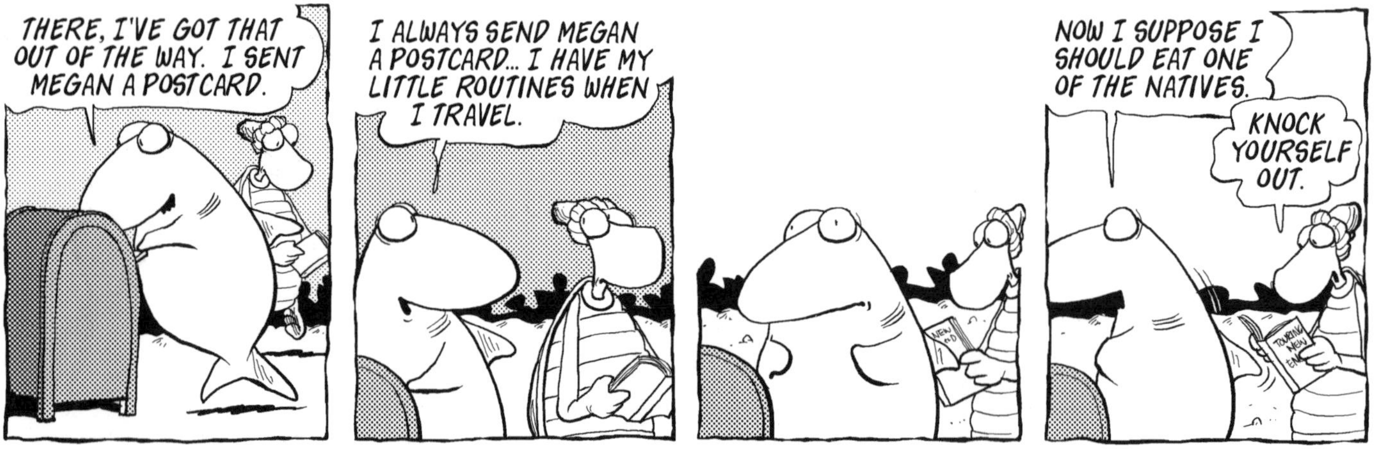
THERE, I'VE GOT THAT OUT OF THE WAY. I SENT MEGAN A POSTCARD.
I ALWAYS SEND MEGAN A POSTCARD... I HAVE MY LITTLE ROUTINES WHEN I TRAVEL.
NOW I SUPPOSE I SHOULD EAT ONE OF THE NATIVES.
KNOCK YOURSELF OUT.

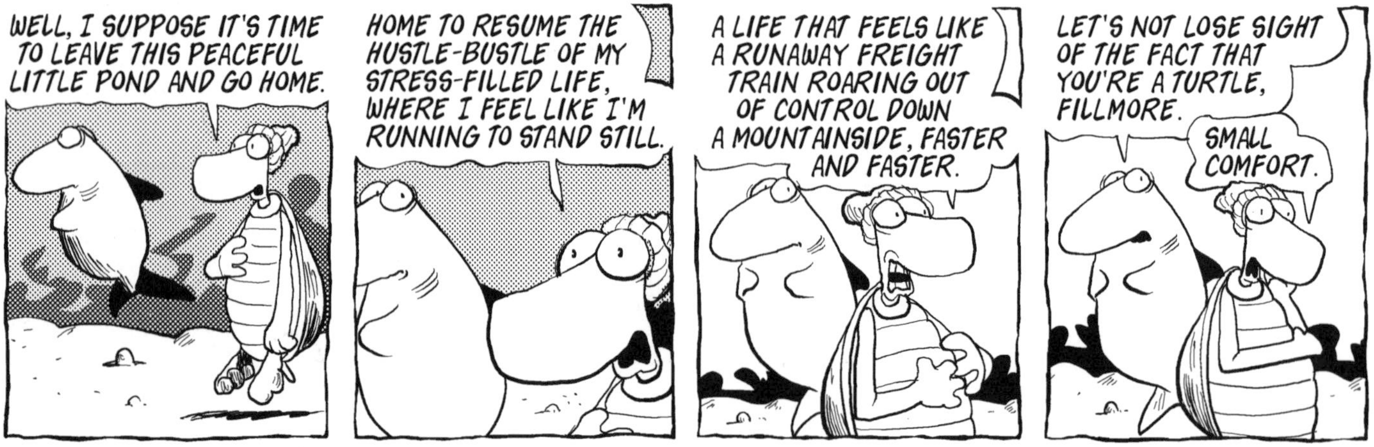
WELL, I SUPPOSE IT'S TIME TO LEAVE THIS PEACEFUL LITTLE POND AND GO HOME.
HOME TO RESUME THE HUSTLE-BUSTLE OF MY STRESS-FILLED LIFE, WHERE I FEEL LIKE I'M RUNNING TO STAND STILL.
A LIFE THAT FEELS LIKE A RUNAWAY FREIGHT TRAIN ROARING OUT OF CONTROL DOWN A MOUNTAINSIDE, FASTER AND FASTER.
LET'S NOT LOSE SIGHT OF THE FACT THAT YOU'RE A TURTLE, FILLMORE.
SMALL COMFORT.

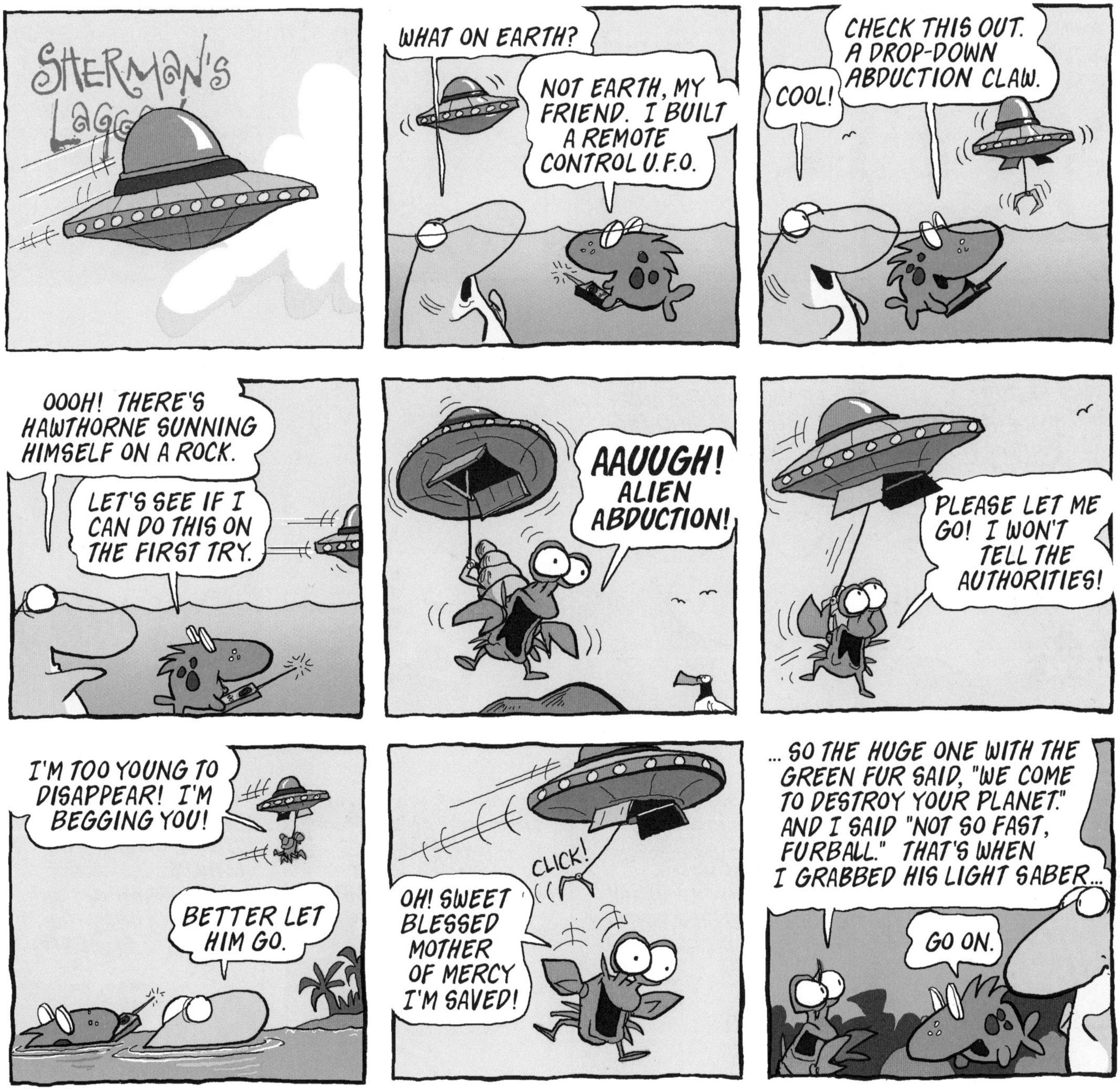
SHERMAN'S LAGOON
WHAT ON EARTH?
NOT EARTH, MY FRIEND. I BUILT A REMOTE CONTROL U.F.O.
CHECK THIS OUT. A DROP-DOWN ABDUCTION CLAW.
COOL!
OOOH! THERE'S HAWTHORNE SUNNING HIMSELF ON A ROCK.
LET'S SEE IF I CAN DO THIS ON THE FIRST TRY.
AAUUGH! ALIEN ABDUCTION!
PLEASE LET ME GO! I WON'T TELL THE AUTHORITIES!
I'M TOO YOUNG TO DISAPPEAR! I'M BEGGING YOU!
BETTER LET HIM GO.
CLICK!
OH! SWEET BLESSED MOTHER OF MERCY I'M SAVED!
... SO THE HUGE ONE WITH THE GREEN FUR SAID, "WE COME TO DESTROY YOUR PLANET." AND I SAID "NOT SO FAST, FURBALL." THAT'S WHEN I GRABBED HIS LIGHT SABER...
GO ON.

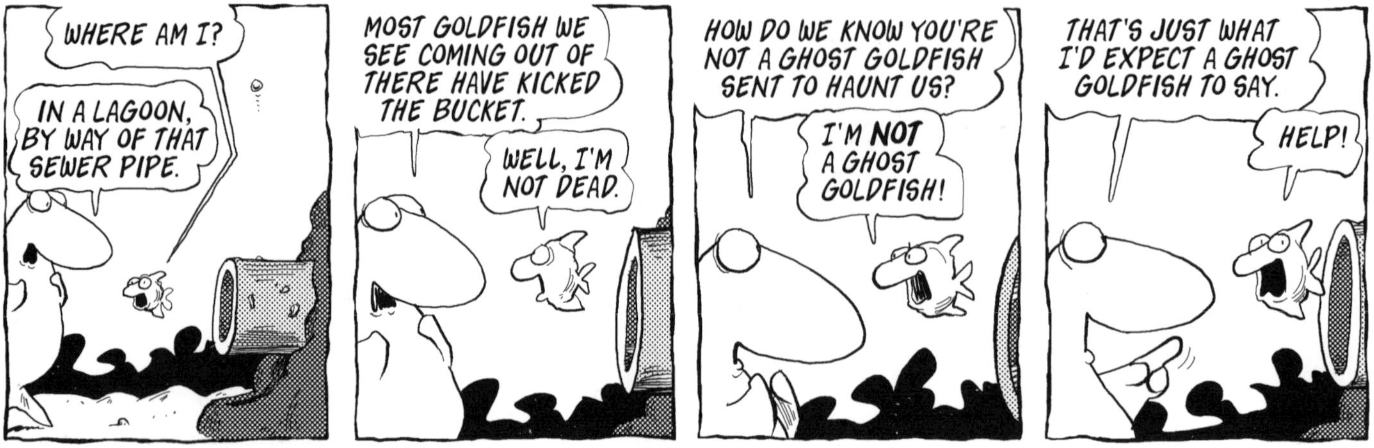
WHERE AM I?
IN A LAGOON, BY WAY OF THAT SEWER PIPE.
MOST GOLDFISH WE SEE COMING OUT OF THERE HAVE KICKED THE BUCKET.
WELL, I'M NOT DEAD.
HOW DO WE KNOW YOU'RE NOT A GHOST GOLDFISH SENT TO HAUNT US?
I'M **NOT** A GHOST GOLDFISH!
THAT'S JUST WHAT I'D EXPECT A GHOST GOLDFISH TO SAY.
HELP!

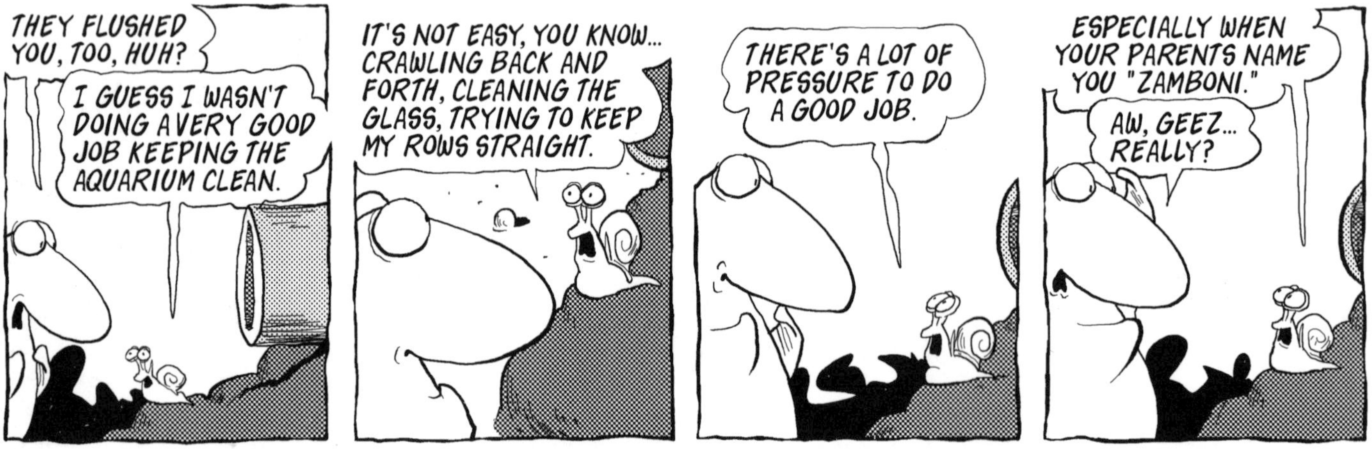
THEY FLUSHED YOU, TOO, HUH?
I GUESS I WASN'T DOING A VERY GOOD JOB KEEPING THE AQUARIUM CLEAN.
IT'S NOT EASY, YOU KNOW... CRAWLING BACK AND FORTH, CLEANING THE GLASS, TRYING TO KEEP MY ROWS STRAIGHT.
THERE'S A LOT OF PRESSURE TO DO A GOOD JOB.
ESPECIALLY WHEN YOUR PARENTS NAME YOU "ZAMBONI."
AW, GEEZ... REALLY?

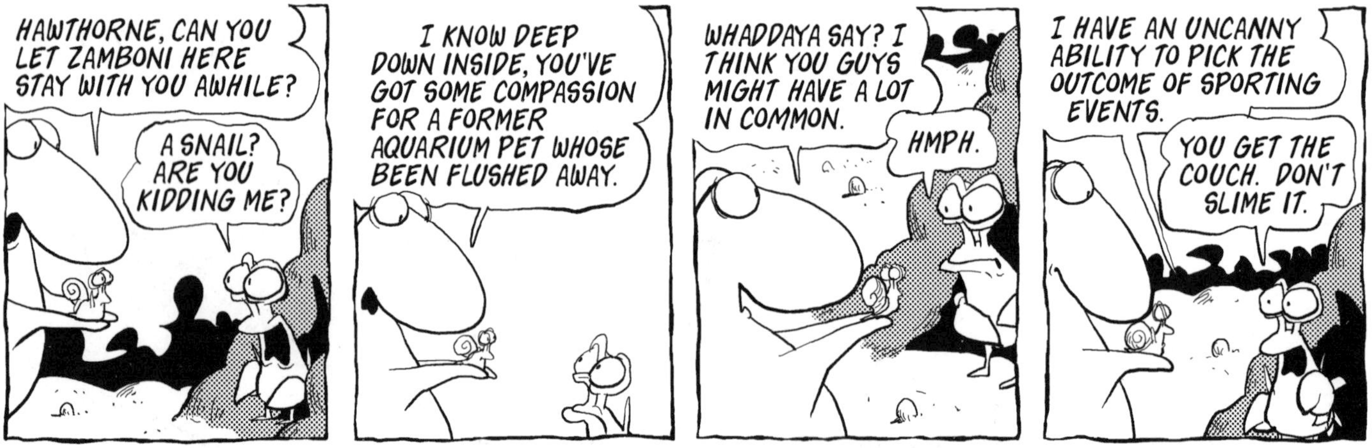
HAWTHORNE, CAN YOU LET ZAMBONI HERE STAY WITH YOU AWHILE?
A SNAIL? ARE YOU KIDDING ME?
I KNOW DEEP DOWN INSIDE, YOU'VE GOT SOME COMPASSION FOR A FORMER AQUARIUM PET WHOSE BEEN FLUSHED AWAY.
WHADDAYA SAY? I THINK YOU GUYS MIGHT HAVE A LOT IN COMMON.
HMPH.
I HAVE AN UNCANNY ABILITY TO PICK THE OUTCOME OF SPORTING EVENTS.
YOU GET THE COUCH. DON'T SLIME IT.

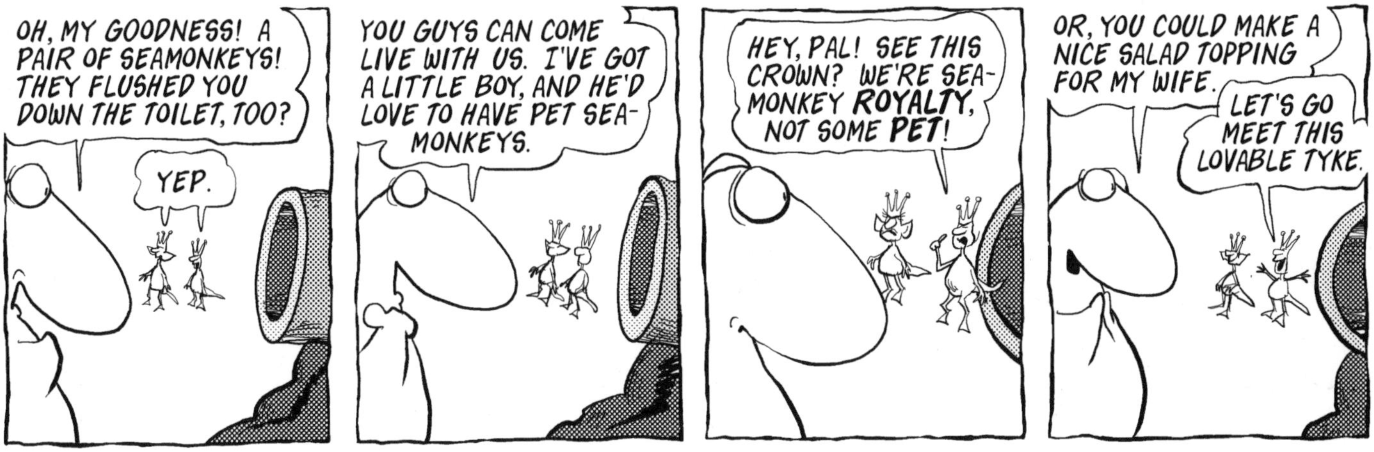
OH, MY GOODNESS! A PAIR OF SEAMONKEYS! THEY FLUSHED YOU DOWN THE TOILET, TOO?
YEP.
YOU GUYS CAN COME LIVE WITH US. I'VE GOT A LITTLE BOY, AND HE'D LOVE TO HAVE PET SEA-MONKEYS.
HEY, PAL! SEE THIS CROWN? WE'RE SEA-MONKEY **ROYALTY**, NOT SOME **PET**!
OR, YOU COULD MAKE A NICE SALAD TOPPING FOR MY WIFE.
LET'S GO MEET THIS LOVABLE TYKE.

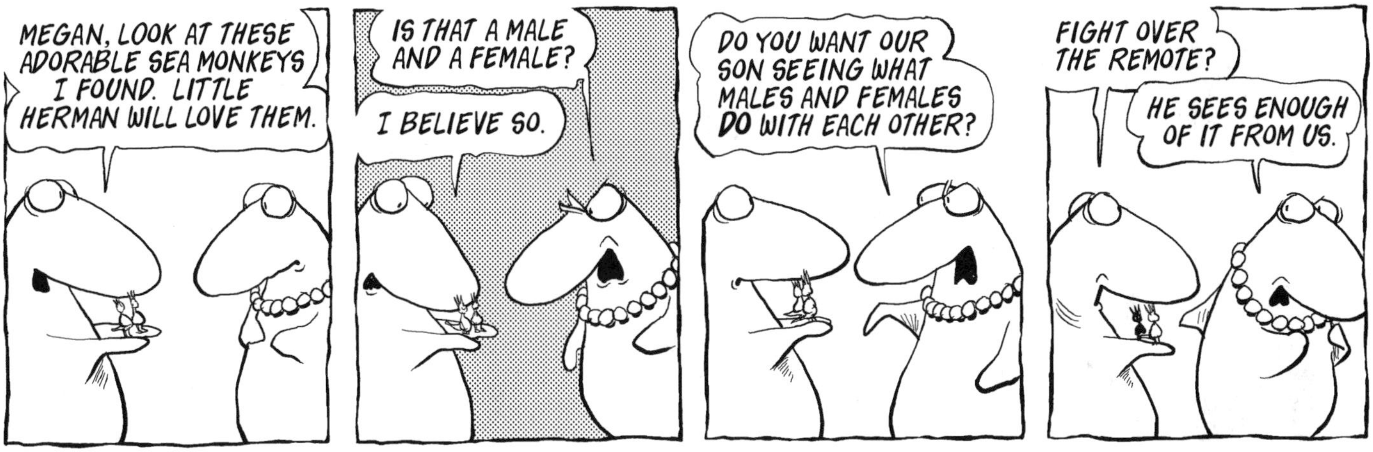
MEGAN, LOOK AT THESE ADORABLE SEA MONKEYS I FOUND. LITTLE HERMAN WILL LOVE THEM.
IS THAT A MALE AND A FEMALE?
I BELIEVE SO.
DO YOU WANT OUR SON SEEING WHAT MALES AND FEMALES **DO** WITH EACH OTHER?
FIGHT OVER THE REMOTE?
HE SEES ENOUGH OF IT FROM US.

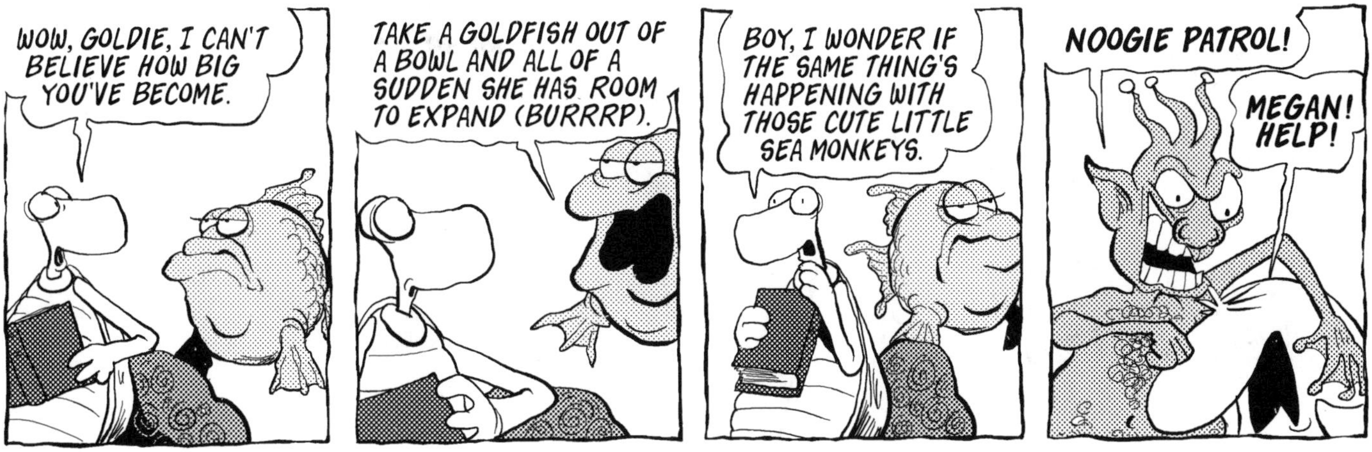
WOW, GOLDIE, I CAN'T BELIEVE HOW BIG YOU'VE BECOME.
TAKE A GOLDFISH OUT OF A BOWL AND ALL OF A SUDDEN SHE HAS ROOM TO EXPAND (BURRRP).
BOY, I WONDER IF THE SAME THING'S HAPPENING WITH THOSE CUTE LITTLE SEA MONKEYS.
NOOGIE PATROL!
MEGAN! HELP!

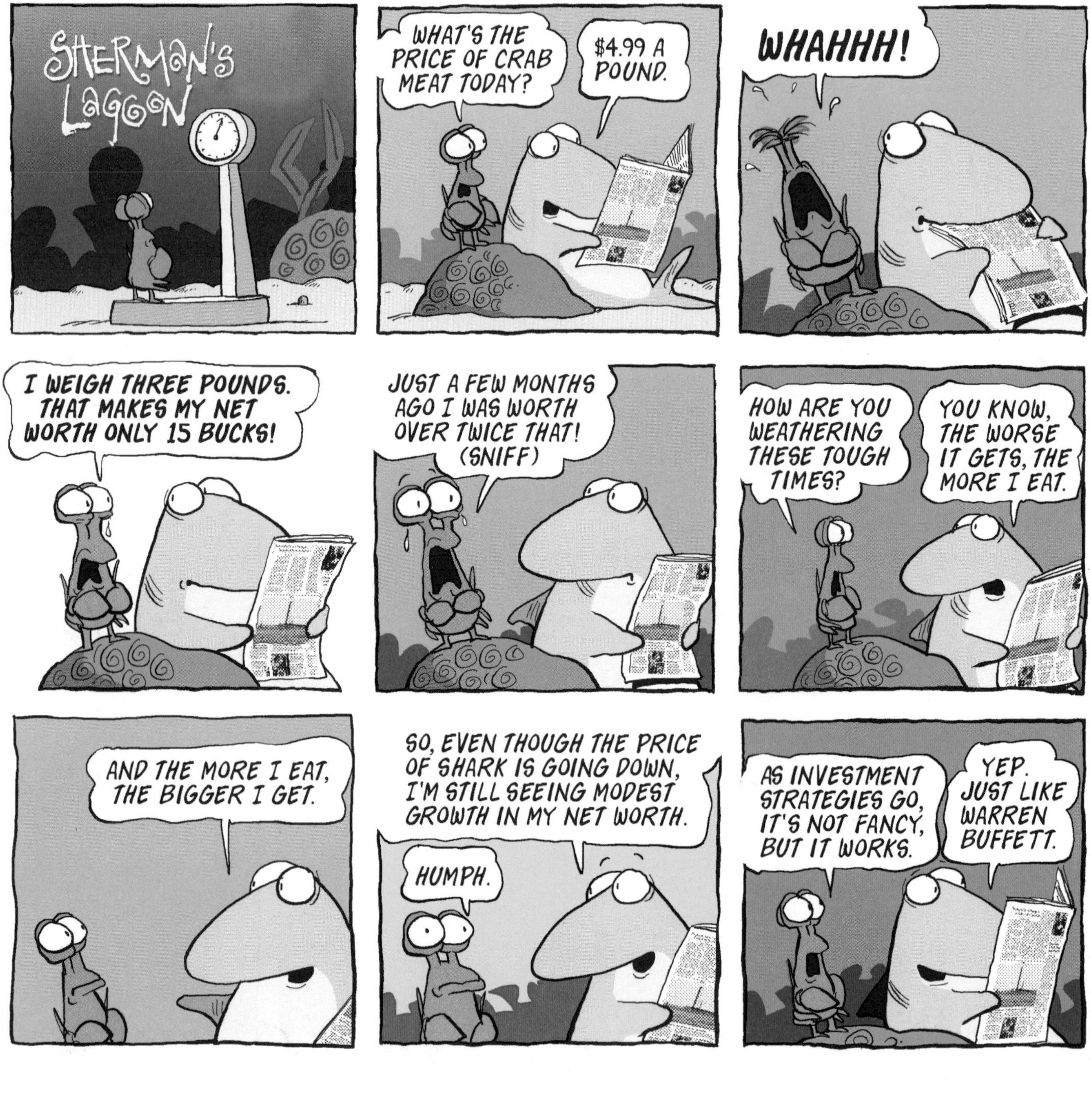
SHERMAN'S LAGOON
WHAT'S THE PRICE OF CRAB MEAT TODAY?
$4.99 A POUND.
WHAHHH!
I WEIGH THREE POUNDS. THAT MAKES MY NET WORTH ONLY 15 BUCKS!
JUST A FEW MONTHS AGO I WAS WORTH OVER TWICE THAT! (SNIFF)
HOW ARE YOU WEATHERING THESE TOUGH TIMES?
YOU KNOW, THE WORSE IT GETS, THE MORE I EAT.
AND THE MORE I EAT, THE BIGGER I GET.
SO, EVEN THOUGH THE PRICE OF SHARK IS GOING DOWN, I'M STILL SEEING MODEST GROWTH IN MY NET WORTH.
HUMPH.
AS INVESTMENT STRATEGIES GO, IT'S NOT FANCY, BUT IT WORKS.
YEP. JUST LIKE WARREN BUFFETT.

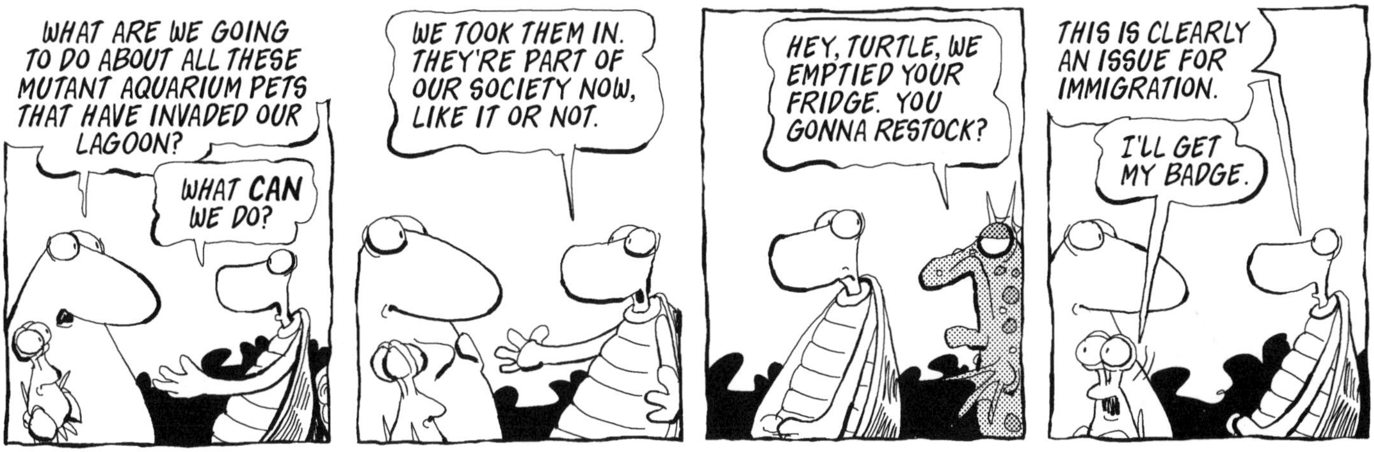
WHAT ARE WE GOING TO DO ABOUT ALL THESE MUTANT AQUARIUM PETS THAT HAVE INVADED OUR LAGOON?
WHAT **CAN** WE DO?
WE TOOK THEM IN. THEY'RE PART OF OUR SOCIETY NOW, LIKE IT OR NOT.
HEY, TURTLE, WE EMPTIED YOUR FRIDGE. YOU GONNA RESTOCK?
THIS IS CLEARLY AN **ISSUE** FOR IMMIGRATION.
I'LL GET MY BADGE.

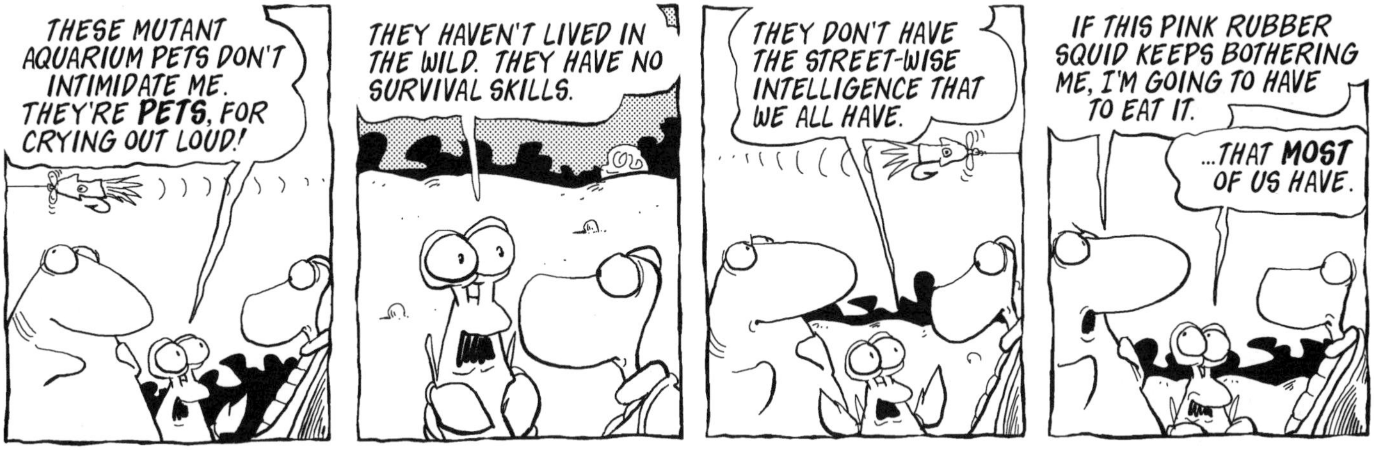
THESE MUTANT AQUARIUM PETS DON'T INTIMIDATE ME. THEY'RE **PETS**, FOR CRYING OUT LOUD!
THEY HAVEN'T LIVED IN THE WILD. THEY HAVE NO SURVIVAL SKILLS.
THEY DON'T HAVE THE STREET-WISE INTELLIGENCE THAT WE ALL HAVE.
IF THIS PINK RUBBER SQUID KEEPS BOTHERING ME, I'M GOING TO HAVE TO EAT IT.
...THAT **MOST** OF US HAVE.

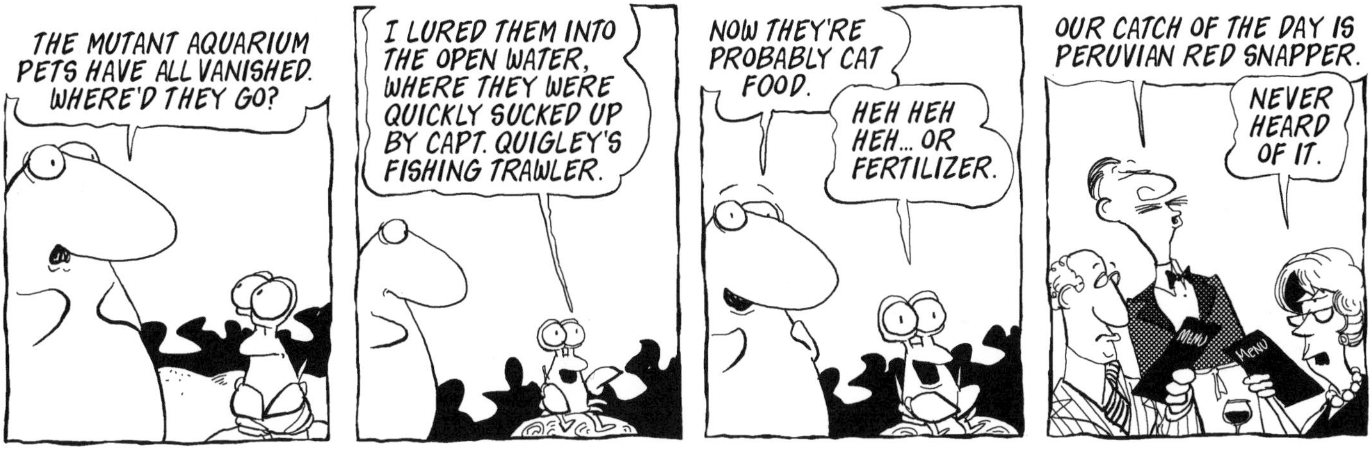
THE MUTANT AQUARIUM PETS HAVE ALL VANISHED. WHERE'D THEY GO?
I LURED THEM INTO THE OPEN WATER, WHERE THEY WERE QUICKLY SUCKED UP BY CAPT. QUIGLEY'S FISHING TRAWLER.
NOW THEY'RE PROBABLY CAT FOOD.
HEH HEH HEH... OR FERTILIZER.
OUR CATCH OF THE DAY IS PERUVIAN RED SNAPPER.
NEVER HEARD OF IT.
MENU
MENU